SciFi
in the Mind's Eye

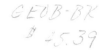

SciFi
in the Mind's Eye

Reading Science through Science Fiction

Edited by

MARGRET GREBOWICZ

OPEN COURT
Chicago and La Salle, Illinois

To order books from Open Court, call toll-free 1-800-815-2280, or visit www.opencourtbooks.com.

Open Court Publishing Company is a division of Carus Publishing Company.

Library of Congress Cataloging-in-Publication Data

SciFi in the mind's eye : reading science through science fiction / edited by Margret Grebowicz ; afterword by Terry Bisson.
    p. cm.
    Includes bibliographical references and index.
    ISBN-13: 978-0-8126-9630-1 (trade pbk. : alk. paper)
    ISBN-10: 0-8126-9630-1 (trade pbk. : alk. paper) 1. Science fiction, American—History and criticism. 2. Science fiction—History and criticism. 3. Literature and science. 4. Science and the arts. 5. Science—Social aspects. 6. Science—Social aspects—United States. I. Grebowicz, Margret, 1973- II. Title: Sci-fi in the mind's eye.
    PS374.S35S39 2007
    809.3'8762—dc22   2007021257

For Maciej,
who keeps me young
— M. G.

CONTENTS

    Question of Essence
    EDRIE SOBSTYL   87

6   Clone Mothers and Others: Uncanny Families
    STEPHANIE S. TURNER   101

7   Embodying Change: (R)evolutionary Theories of
    an Alien Synthesis
    TESS WILLIAMS   115

INTERVENTION 2

    Identity and SF: Story as Science and Fiction
    NICOLA GRIFFITH   139

TECHNOLOGIES

8   Sciencepunk: The Influence of Informed Science
    Fiction on Virtual Reality Research
    JEREMY N. BAILENSON, NICK YEE, ALICE KIM, and
    JAIREH TECARRO   147

9   Fictitious Contagions: Computer Viruses in the
    Science Fiction of the 1970s
    JUSSI PARIKKA   165

10 After the End of the World: Critiques of Technology
    in Post-Apocalypse Literature
    ANDREW PAVELICH   185

INTERVENTION 3

    Ethics, Science, and Science Fiction
    NANCY KRESS   201

SF AS STS

AT THE LIMITS OF THE IMAGINATION

ACKNOWLEDGMENTS

Thanks go to all of the contributors who agreed to this project despite (or because of) its strangeness. It has been an honor to work with you. Special thanks go to Terry Bisson, Nicola Griffith, and Helen Merrick for their generosity with their time and for introducing me to other contributors, thus extending the boundaries of this book far beyond my original vision. Thanks to Stan Killian, my partner, for his invaluable feedback on drafts of my work. And the list would be incomplete without the acknowledgment of two very special professional relationships to which this text bears witness: my sincere thanks to Ewa Lipska for her generosity and for continuing to whet my appetite for language with her poetry, and to Andrew Pavelich, who was a great help on every level, from introducing me to both *Ender's Game* and the work of Terry Bisson to helping me proofread chapters. His good wine, excellent company, and unconditional love of SF made this book possible. It is a collaboration in every thinkable sense. And Ursula Le Guin gets it right when she writes about collaborative work: "The point is to make music together."

Introduction: Down to Earth

MARGRET GREBOWICZ

*T*he relationship between science and the public has been in flux, and in question, since the first stirrings of modern science in the mid-seventeenth century. For the thinkers of the Enlightenment, it was clear that science would be an instrument of liberation. The truth about the universe would set people free from ignorance, servitude, barbarism, superstition, even poverty. The use of reason was the right of every human being and was expected of every human being. For Immanuel Kant, the eighteenth-century philosopher who dedicated his work in part to supporting the ideas of Sir Isaac Newton, enlightened human beings were the ones who thought for themselves. By that time, tyranny was understood in terms of not only physical, material oppression, but also dogmatism and intellectual inertia. Thus, to be human in the eighteenth century meant to think without anyone's guidance, to have the courage to free oneself from the tyranny of imposed ideas.

The year is 2007. If you are holding this book in your hands, chances are that you have at least heard of the great popular science writers, who specialize in explaining high-level scientific theories and concepts to the lay reader. Even if you have not read Richard Feynman or Douglas Hofstadter, you have probably seen at least parts of the film *A Brief History of Time*, based on Stephen Hawking's book. Or perhaps you have a dim memory of Carl Sagan's turtleneck sweaters on the enormously successful PBS series *Nova*. Perhaps you are one of the many currently engrossed in reading the most contemporary popularizers: Richard Dawkins, Steven Pinker, Stephen Jay Gould, Colin Tudge, and others. They are particularly influential as I write this, as champions of evolutionary biology, which has recently come under considerable attack by the Christian right in the United States. They tend to describe themselves as skeptics, humanists, occasionally atheists, and all of them univocally describe their work as work which allows people to think for themselves.

The old Kantian dare is back: *Sapere aude*! Dare to know! This is for them a political commitment: to bring scientific knowledge to the people so that they may think outside of tyranny.

However, these authors fail to address an idea which has recently become quite important: the idea that if we facilitate public access to science, this will fundamentally change science. In other words, the popularizers leave us with a picture of science which is stable and fixed. They are quite responsible about history and the historical developments (described in terms of progress) in the particular sciences they discuss, but these changes happen from the "inside," effected by experts in the fields who conceive of themselves as building upon previous discoveries. The idea that science could be transformed at its very core because the social identities of its practitioners change is quite a different one.

There is another movement, not as lucrative as popular science writing, but arguably more committed to the freedom of thought: the study of science as a social and historical phenomenon. The writers of this movement show that tyranny has many guises, and that scientific discourses are equally capable of contributing to tyranny as they are of resisting it. As these scholars show, science is a product of seventeeth-century European, white, hetero-patriarchal, militaristic, and imperialistic culture. The social identities and the historical situations of the founders of the Royal Society of London[1] *mattered* to the discourses they produced. Likewise, when we allow the public, in all its diverse social identities and interests, access to science, this diversity of identities and interests will matter. It will change the discourse from the "outside."[2] Science will no longer exhibit steady, stable progress, sublimely transmitting The Truth to the public by means of pop science books and journals.

What happens then? How will these changes manifest themselves? This is one of the most significant debates currently underway in the discipline of Science and Technology Studies. In fact, STS, as it is called by insiders, is comprised of many disciplines, and prides itself on consisting of outsiders, people outside the so-called hard sciences, who

---

[1] Founded in 1660, the Royal Society was the first "scientific community," an organized body of men with a self-conscious commitment to what we now call modern science. Claiming to be the world's oldest "learned societ," and still active today, the Society boasts an impressive list of presidents, beginning with Christopher Wren and Samuel Pepys, and including Newton and Kelvin.

[2] I say "outside" in quotes because, as we have seen, social identity is not really extra-scientific. On the contrary, it is at the center of knowledge production.

nevertheless read and challenge the claims of scientists. Sometimes they do this by reflecting the history of a science back to its practitioners and showing them that many of the assumptions they simply take for granted are in fact problematic and could be different (for instance, the feminist claim that women and men have been lumped together by researchers into a single category that nonetheless remains male-normative, which renders women—as well as the *particularity* of men—invisible to science). Sometimes they point out inconsistencies, circularity, and grand metaphysical commitments where none is appropriate (for instance, the widely held idea that same-sex relationships among animals are "aberrant" begins from an assumption, made prior to observation, about what constitutes "normal" animal sexuality). Sometimes they show that public policies concerning science and scientific education result in dogmatism and intellectual stasis. They analyze, among other things, popular science discourses, including journals, TV shows, documentaries, and IMAX films, and discuss their social effects. At other times, they show us how much we favor scientific models that are beautiful just because we like beauty, and for no better reason. Or how interested we are in data that support our current social order and power relations rather than upsetting them, just because those who enjoy power have an interest in maintaining those relations, and for no better reason. STS addresses these and other aspects of the production of scientific knowledge.

Notice this claim: knowledge is produced, not discovered, created by people, not found by brave explorers. This first assumption is crucial in the debate concerning the relationship between science and the public. From this perspective, the Kantian motto "dare to know!" must be modified. It's not a matter of daring to pull aside the curtain to see The Truth that was always already there, waiting passively to be uncovered, but of daring to participate in the production of knowledge as fully oneself, as the (multiple) being(s) one is and the many (sometimes conflicting) interests one represents.

Isn't it strange, then, that STS, with all its commitments to the public, has never officially addressed the most popular of discourses about science, namely, science fiction? Well, it's not really that strange. STS is an academic discipline, and most STS departments are graduate departments, for MA and PhD students rather than undergraduates. Thus, in practice, it is a discourse of the elite. SF, on the other hand, is deliberately, famously accessible to the lowest common denominator of reader. It's "pulp," cheap, juvenile. This, of course, is its very power. More people read *Neuromancer* than read *Gödel, Escher, Bach*, and more watched the *Alien* series than watched *A Brief History of Time*. This means that the "public access" we are concerned with in STS is (and always has been) happening through SF, but, in part because the discourses inhabit two such different social spheres, STS has yet to systematically analyze the most effective popularizer.

What happens when these two, STS and SF, are called upon to address each other? This is our present experiment. We may begin by noting what they have in common, which is more than just a fascination with and discussion of science. More importantly, just like STS is multivalent, hybrid, and in flux, so too SF exhibits internal struggles. To cite just one example, in 1989, a strange little publisher called Semiotext(e) published a wonderfully disturbing book called *Semiotext(e) SF*, in which the editors collected the best short stories that had been denied publication in other venues.

> In our invitation to the SF writing community . . . we asked for material which had been rejected by the commercial SF media for its obscenity, radicalism, or formalistic weirdness. We hoped to tap a deep and almost-inarticulate groundswell of resentment against the ever-increasing stodginess, neo-conservatism, big-bucks mania and wretched taste of most SF publishers. (Rucker and Wilson 1989, 12)

Thus, the world of SF is itself political and in flux, and according to the editors of *Semiotext(e) SF*, the stakes are high. Who gets published, what kinds of science and technology adventures sell, to whom this stuff is marketed, what are the politics of SF consumers, what kinds of demands are being created—these are questions concerning the future of SF. We are talking about a struggle over knowledge production, and the results of the struggle will affect scientists, revolutionary thinkers, the public, and "the future in general" (Rucker and Wilson 1989, 14).

However, rather than focusing on affinities between those of us who work in STS and those of us who work in SF, the purpose of the present experiment is to provoke encounters, conversations between people interested in precisely these aspects of the culture of science: the politics, the conflicts, the effects, the stakes. This is the motivation behind inviting several acclaimed SF authors to contribute to the collection. Rather than treating SF from afar, as an object of study for those of us working in STS, it seems important to invite SF to be a guest at this bizarre party, even the guest of honor. This is not a project in which STS scholars speak to the authors of the cultural product that is science fiction, but one in which academics and fiction writers talk about what it is we all do, and how the vast and varied body that is our work relates to scientific and technological production.

The Chapters

It will not suffice to call this collection "interdisciplinary," although there are many disciplines represented here—philosophy, English, communications, cultural studies, even management. Neither will it suffice to point out the many different fictions that these authors address: *Star Trek*, H. G. Wells's writings, *Alien*, cyberpunk novels, ecofeminist fiction, *Ender's Game*, documentaries about DNA, *Gattaca*, the novels of Nancy Kress, *A Canticle for Leibowitz*, the novels of Ruth Ozeki, and the footage of the first lunar landing, to name just a few. This diversity is significant, but what makes the scholarly chapters collected here unique is that they represent such radically different readings of the way that SF affects and could affect the world. In some, it is a powerful instrument of change, endlessly testing the boundaries of the thinkable. In others, SF cements the most hetero-patriarchal, racist fantasies about what it means to be human. In others still, SF itself has come to the end of its life: what was once a thriving, transformative cultural event involving many media and addressing just about every aspect of existence has become commercialized, static, redundant. The questions: Where have we come from? Where are we going? Who makes up the community of this "we"? will thus be answered quite differently by the different contributors.

The chapters are organized rather loosely into thematic sections. In the first two, "Races" and "Genders," contributors express their various, often conflicting views about the role that SF plays and could play in these social discourses, whose relationship to discourses about nature, and thus to the sciences, continues to be ambiguous and complex. In chapters 1 and 2, Harvey Cormier and Naomi Zack both show how SF has reinforced and been informed by American and European racism (respectively), and offer poor prognoses for the future. These two chapters also link to other discourses: Cormier discusses *Star Trek* in the context of the American political climate of the 1960s, particularly in terms of the politics of race, while Zack discusses racism more abstractly, in relation to speciesism. Nancy McHugh raises the question "What is science fiction?" in the course of exploring Ruth Ozeki's fiction-about-science in chapter 3. She focuses on the parallels between meat-eating culture and white supremacy in America, in terms of how both are maintained by an institutionalized production of ignorance. In contrast to the first two chapters, where the fictions in question serve to maintain social injustices, chapter 3 offers a vision of fiction as resistance. Chapters 4 and 5 highlight some important differences between SF and feminist SF, particularly around the question of essentialism, or the "nature" of women. In Chapter 4 Janet Vertesi shows how narratives and imagery concerning the gynoid, or female cyborg, reinforce essentialist ideas of femininity. Edrie Sobstyl, on the other hand, shows how feminist science fiction can contribute positively to the debate concerning women's nature. Her chapter 5 presents ideas of femininity and sexuality that rely on scientific, but not necessarily essentialist, claims. In chapters 6 and 7, Stephanie S. Turner and Tess Williams offer two different analyses of the *Alien* film series as a viable feminist discourse. They show the classic films offering resistant notions of embodiment, mothering, and even challenges to the Darwinian paradigm.

The "Technologies" section continues the motif of presenting the many different and often conflicting ways that SF "participates" in technological development. Chapter 8 outlines the real influence that cyberpunk literature has had on virtual reality research of the type the authors, Jeremy Bailenson and his students, actually *do* in their Stanford lab. In chapter 9, Jussi Parikka shows how 1970s literature about computer viruses has helped to shape the current fantasies and realities of computer virus culture. Chapter 10, however, indicates a more conservative side of SF, as Andrew Pavelich argues that postapocalypse SF takes for granted that the (always tragic) history of techno-science must necessarily repeat itself, so that the next apocalypse is always inevitable.

The fourth section, "SF as STS," is a significant departure from the previous ones. It houses three chapters directly exploring the idea that science fiction is itself a voice in Science and Technology Studies. In chapter 11, Helen Merrick argues that feminist SF contributes vital, important ideas to feminist science studies that no other discourses contribute. Marina Levina picks up the question "What is science fiction?" in her chapter about DNA documentaries. Which part of the documentary is fact, and which is fiction? How has SF contributed to our framing of genomics? In chapter 12, she analyzes these problems by reading DNA documentaries in conjunction with *Gattaca*. And finally, in chapter 13, Dennis Desroches explores the idea that the ideas currently being developed in science and technology studies will soon cause us to commit to a certain metaphysical position about the nature of reality and its relationship to human consciousness.

The book's last section, "At the Limits of the Imagination," is also unique. Three chapters explore the question of limits in three different disciplines: cognitive science, cultural history, and philosophy. In chapter 14, Tom Lawson introduces us to cognitive science research that outlines the conditions of possibility of fictional, alternative worlds, and addresses the work of Nancy Kress as a case study. Martin Parker takes a more historical approach in chapter 15, showing how the end of the Space Age irrevocably changed the discourse of SF. If space was indeed the final frontier, what happens to SF "after" space, in other words, when governments are no longer interested in space exploration? What happens to the imagination? I take up that very question in the final chapter, where I read the current crisis in education through the trope of Battle School in the SF classic *Ender's Game*, exploring questions of literacy, including scientific literacy, in times of war.

The Interventions

Imagination is a central issue in the interventions, which offer us rare, honest glimpses into the mind of the SF writer. L. Timmel Duchamp, Nicola Griffith, and Nancy Kress all contribute previously unpublished essays that develop and trouble the relationship between the creative production of fiction and the world(s) in which it is produced. Duchamp writes about how a writer gets ideas *from* the world, while Kress offers a theory of how SF can actually aid in the production of ethical theories, and thus how the SF writer makes an impact *on* the world. Griffith offers a meditation on the joyous nature of this intertextual, creative production, reminding us that science is part of a complex network of intellectual and creative stimulants that surrounds consumers and producers of SF. She writes about the default adolescence that is part of the SF experience, indicating we should value SF for keeping its reader in an interminably "formative" state. The presence of these three women writers is particularly significant here. A good part of the collection is devoted to scholarship by women or about issues of concern to feminists, partly in order to contrast, again, with the popular-science literature, which is written almost exclusively by white, married men with Ivy League educations.

The fourth intervention stands out from these three, in both structure and tone. It is an interview conducted by Ewa Lipska, one of Poland's most celebrated living poets, of Stanisław Lem, who was not only one of the best-loved SF authors ever, but a national hero in his country. In these fragments, which date to roughly around the time of his eightieth birthday (he died in 2006), we see two old friends talking, reminiscing, comparing their experiences of European and Polish culture. But Lem paints a bleak vision of the future, be it read as the future of literature, space exploration, science fiction,[3] or politics. Are these merely the ramblings of a depressed, aging man, a few years before his death? Or is Lem pointing to the same thing to which Martin Parker points in chapter 15: the shadow of crisis on the horizon, not just political and environmental crisis, but a crisis of thought, education, imagination, and thus of the very possibility of the new?

Terry Bisson's afterword, his "post-vent," invites us to dig, to turn our faces downward, towards the earth and away from the sky. Indeed, for scholars in STS as well as for SF writers, this is an opportunity to reflect critically on the current state of the work we do. How far have we come since the Enlightenment? We continue to debate the nature of the relationship between science and society, in both STS and SF, and the debate shows no signs of stopping. Few of us think that science will liberate people, but many do work focusing on the fact that ever-larger numbers of people across the techno-scientific, militaristic, global capitalistic planet need liberating from intolerable material conditions, as well as from the ideologies which justify these conditions. Beyond its nod to the 60s, Bisson's question, "You dig?" is urgent. It reminds us how much work there is to do. More than ever, perhaps, especially if it is true (is it true?) that the Golden Age of SF is behind us.

REFERENCE

Rucker, Rudy, and Peter Lamborn Wilson. 1989. Introduction to *Semiotext(e) SF*, edited by Rudy Rucker, Peter Lamborn Wilson, and Robert Anton Wilson. New York: Semiotext(e).

---

[3] Lem was notoriously critical of most science fiction, which resulted in the termination of his honorary membership in the Science Fiction Writers of America in 1976.

RACES

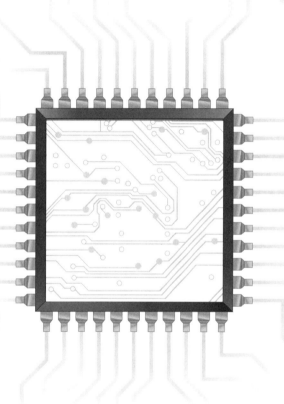

Race through the Alpha Quadrant: Species and Destiny on *Star Trek*

HARVEY CORMIER

I know his journey ends never
His star trek will go on forever
But tell him while he wanders his starry sea
Remember, remember me.

— GENE RODDENBERRY, unused lyrics to Alexander Courage's
"Theme from *Star Trek*"

The great old NBC television series *Star Trek*, comparatively unpopular when it was cancelled after 79 episodes in the late 1960s, was exhumed in the late 1970s as a result of the sudden *Star Wars* craze for science fiction. The characters and scenario of the show were mined for a lot of lousy movies and one good one ("Khaaaaaaaan!"). Sequel series persisted on the tube until 2005. All of these versions of *Star Trek* depicted travels and encounters with more-or-less humanoid extraterrestrials of different "races" and cultures.

The original series involved adventures in which imperialistic yet liberal protagonists taught more than they learned. The sequel series have been much more respectful of the diverse ways in which different kinds of beings might live; but this has not necessarily been an improvement, since it has come with an increased sense that "race" is destiny. The shows, old and new, tend to give scant consideration to the possibility that all existing ways and forms of life, including but not only the American way, may deserve and profit from challenges. As much fun as they often are, in one way or the other they always avoid coming to terms

3

with the idea that we human beings, all of us, may really have some things to learn from our future experiences, things worth remembering that we are not born knowing and that we do not necessarily learn inside our various cultures.

In what follows I will reflect on this idea as it bears on the developing attitudes of *Star Trek* toward racial or species differences. I'll examine some representative features and episodes of the old and the newer series, trying to indicate as I go what could have been improved in the way both the old and the newer *Star Trek* series portrayed race and the human future.

Tune In, Turn On

The original *Star Trek* was a phenomenon of the hip and happening 1960s. It was mind-blowing psychedelia, from the groovy red, gold, and blue tunics and miniskirts of the form-fitting space-navy uniforms to the surreal magenta, saffron, and cerulean planets orbited by Kirk and the crew. On the titanic space cruiser Enterprise, which looked like a flying saucer designed by a committee, we took a trip, a trek, in a trippy setting every week. A landing party from the Enterprise materialized in a golden shimmer down on a strange new world, and evil showed itself in the form of: decadent ancient psychics who wanted to live off the emotions of us still-passionate human beings; shape-shifting, salt-sucking vampires; human beings who got hold of a little too much knowledge and became too godlike to share the same galaxy with us primates; a big green snarling intelligent lizard in a gold lamé outfit whose ears would have to be boxed; vicious interstellar buccaneers who, despite their intense disagreeableness, managed to cohere into a competing space navy of their own; space hippies making a dubious return across space to Eden; timocratic members of a galactic Roman legion; an evil-twin parallel universe; a giant amoeba made of antimatter; or whatever. Captain John F. Kennedy—that is, Captain James T. Kirk—wearing a space-age sheriff's badge, curiously cowboylike boots, and a mini-nuke on his hip, turned his flinty gaze upon the evildoer, asked his half-alien deputy for scientific information that would give him a technological advantage, and got a raised eyebrow and a lot of technobabble in response. He then put the eternally malfunctioning technology aside and defeated the enemy with a combination of guile, bravado, appealingness to the slinky local space-babe who had slunk in wearing that far-out see-through backless pantsuit, sarcastic humor, swift punches to the gut, and, in closing, an explanation of the Federation way. In the end, space, the final frontier, became the New Frontier into which American values had once more been successfully extended.[1]

Well, actually, at some point, before the closing lecture on why killing was bad and how humankind had finally put all that behind them in the twenty-third century, there was also usually a little psychedelic gunplay. The trigger of the hand phaser was squeezed, a bright blue ray flared, a cascade of red sparks went flying, and the molecules of interstellar miscreants screamed off white hot into the ozone. Or, "Fire," barked Captain Kirk, and a blue-white spread of photon torpedoes flashed out from the Enterprise into space, buckling deflector shields and exciting the atoms of some sharklike enemy battlewagon into a brief cloud of radioactive vapor. But then, after all that, came the explanation of the wholly peaceable moral of the story; somebody made a pun or other epigram ("They'll be no tribble at all!"); and then *exeunt omnes* at several hundred times the speed of light.

This head trip of a TV series was half hippie acid freak, half Dwight D. Eisenhower. Despite all the expand-your-mind stage props and the peace-and-love rhetoric, the good folks at *Star Trek* were Cold War liberals, to say the least. Kirk and the gang believed in peace, rule of law, and self-determination for all the peoples of the galaxy, and if to achieve that goal they had to become violent, cut a few legal corners, or dismantle an unpromising system of government, then that was a price they were willing to pay. Was ever a law more routinely disregarded than the "Prime Directive," which criminalized intervention in the affairs of alien cultures?

It tells us something crucial about the politics of the series that the episode "A Private Little War," co-written by the "creator" of the series, the former bomber-pilot and cop Gene Roddenberry, allegorically endorsed the Vietnam War and like interventions as the only imaginable way to deal with the earthly Klingons, the Soviets, and the real Romulans, the Red Chinese. In that episode, Kirk revisits a planet he surveyed thirteen years earlier to find that a vicious war has broken out in the idyll he remembers. The peaceable hill people, among whom he had lived, are being hunted down by the villagers, who have somehow gone from flint knives to flintlocks in the years since Kirk's last visit. It turns out that the villagers are being supplied with guns by their new allies the Klingons, and Kirk decides that the only way to deal with the situation is to supply the hill people with their own guns and advisers to

---

[1] David Brooks draws the Kirk-Kennedy analogy in Brooks 2001.

match any assistance and technological advances the Klingons provide. The story ends with Kirk's grimly committing the Federation to an indefinite amount of trudging in this swamp of competitive exploitation.

This was especially bold, whether or not it was especially admirable, since *Star Trek* was just about the only non-news television series of the era that so much as acknowledged the existence of the Vietnam War. *I Spy*, with Robert Culp and Bill Cosby, involved its protagonists in the conflict a few times, taking its rightness for granted, but most other shows, even *Gomer Pyle, USMC*, about a goofy Marine private, just pretended Indochina didn't exist. *Hawaii Five-O* fought the Cold War; Steve McGarrett and his crew of Hawaiian state police skirmished with a Chinese spy villain, Wo Fat, played by Khigh Dheigh as basically a reprise of his role as the Chinese brainwasher Yen Lo in the 1962 film *The Manchurian Candidate*. But Wo Fat and heels like him on other programs were Cold War phenomena exclusively, and they avoided so much as mentioning the hot war that was polarizing the country. *Star Trek*, despite the circumspection of almost everybody else on TV, and notwithstanding all its own counterculture trappings and fans, made a point of boldly going, if only by means of an allegory, to the side of Kennedy, Johnson, and Nixon on the question of Vietnam.

Kennedy, Johnson, and Nixon: that particular trio of names has a lot of resonance. In these days of intense partisanship and a stark left-right divide in American politics, it's hard to remember that Vietnam was a bipartisan disaster. Kennedy is the liberal icon and Nixon has been painted in retrospect as a borderline fascist, but Camelot gave us more U.S. troops in Vietnam and no civil rights or voting rights bill, while Nixon governed like FDR on LSD. Kennedy talked a progressive game but spent his short presidency inflaming and then placating conservatives who wouldn't let him cut taxes and run a deficit. (How times have changed.) After Kennedy was murdered in conservative Texas, Lyndon Johnson used his memory to ram down the conservatives' throats the JFK-like Great Society legislation that was supposed to end poverty and discrimination; but this was while he escalated the Vietnam War, which of course killed disproportionately the poor and the dark-skinned. Martin Luther King came to criticize his civil-rights ally Johnson by preaching about "the cruel irony of watching Negro and white boys . . . kill and die together for a nation that has been unable to seat them together in the same schools. . . . [W]e watch them in brutal solidarity burning the huts of a poor village, but we realize that they would never live on the same block in Detroit" (King 1967). And while Richard Nixon talked like a plaid-pants-on-the-golf-course corporate stooge, it

was he who gave us the Environmental Protection Agency, the very concept of "affirmative action," and wage-price controls. He could get away
with it because the plaid-pants corporate stooges and Dixiecrats who
made up most of the rest of the U.S. government were so sure he was one
of them. In the 1991 film *Star Trek VI: The Undiscovered Country*,
Spock the Vulcan, Kirk's emotionless second in command, would cite
what he called an ancient Vulcan proverb: "Only Nixon could go to
China." Or begin pulling the American troops out of Saigon and letting
the whole mess collapse, for that matter.

All this goes to show that America's politics, foreign and domestic,
had a different logic in those days, if you want to call it a logic. And the
artifact we know as the original *Star Trek* represents the mindset of many
people in those times. The racial views of such people were, as we might
expect, not at all what we might expect. Back in the 1960s there were
even Republicans with real commitment to the active achievement of
racial justice. In those days, long before David Duke could gain attention and votes using "Equal rights for all" as a slogan to attack racial
preferences, it meant something different to say that it was time the
world just stopped paying attention to anything as insignificant as race.

Trek against Race

The starship Enterprise was a (very) mobile United Nations, with men
and women of every hue and beings other than human beings working
together in boisterous, joshing harmony. On the episode of the show
called "Plato's Stepchildren," Captain Kirk and Lieutenant Uhura even
exchanged the first interracial kiss on American network television—
though they did so against their will, impelled by "superior" beings
with the power of telekinesis who lived by the philosophy of Plato. And
later in that episode, when Kirk pretty much kicked the telekinetic
beings' ass by temporarily developing greater powers than they had, he
was making the fundamental *Star Trek* point about race or fundamental
divisions of humanity. Plato, of course, in *The Republic*, had divided up
his ideal society by race or *genos*: the golden *genos* comprised the few
higher minds suited to rule, the silver race consisted of people smart
and strong enough to assist the golden race and enforce their rulings,
and the bronze race contained the masses who were suited to repair
shoes and make money. (It's not clear that Plato meant by *genos* quite
what we mean by "race," partly because it's not clear what if anything
we mean, and partly because Plato makes it clear at *Republic* 415a–b
that a mother and father of one *genos* can produce a member of either

of the others.)[2] Kirk's triumph that week illustrated the anti-Platonic point that a democratic society was better than one governed by a cadre of higher minds. "Lower" human beings could and would always figure out the trick and "improve" themselves; there was no permanently higher race or kind. The true aristocracy or meritocracy was a democracy, and the way to solve the problems of race was to stop drawing idiotic racial distinctions among people.

The episode of the original *Star Trek* that dealt most explicitly with race was one aired January 10, 1969, the darkly witty "Let That Be Your Last Battlefield." This was a show seen in the month Nixon succeeded Johnson in the presidency. Just after Americans had rejected Humphrey's Minnesota liberalism, they, or millions of them, anyway, watched without complaint a drama in which, between detergent and patent medicine commercials, both racial bigotry and racial opportunism were deplored. Not a full year after Martin Luther King's assassination at the hands of a white racist, Commander Spock announced philosophically, if anti-Platonically, that "Change is the essential process of all existence," intending to imply that the continuing oppression of one people by another, especially on as silly a ground as race, is not only immoral but impossible. Even Plato thought that his eternally ideal aristocratic and reason-governed Republic would eventually collapse in a world like our un-ideal one, increasingly full of irrational and emotional people (*Republic* 546a–547c); but Spock, though he was from a race of unemotional logicians, was suggesting that, at least when it came to race relations, change was a good thing.

In this particular story, Lokai and Bele, two super-powerful aliens who are black on one side of their bodies and white on the other side, come aboard the Enterprise, and each demands Kirk's assistance in subduing the other. Lokai, a magistrate, played with scenery-chewing relish by Frank Gorshin, wants to bring Bele to justice for treason and terrorist crimes after a 50,000-year-long chase; Bele wants asylum and help from Kirk against Lokai, one of the oppressors who have made slaves of his people.

The two aliens are like a pair of giant electric eels, able to zap things they come near. Each is racially prejudiced against the other, though the

---

[2] By the way, this is Plato's most definitive statement concerning the three races in the *Republic*, and he does not actually use the Greek term *genos* here. He does refer to the golden *genos* at 468e, but the word may mean no more to him than "kind" or "class" in any case. It may be that the ancient Greeks did not have our concept of "race" at all, if indeed we have a coherent or substantive concept.

Enterprise crew can't see why; it turns out that one is black on the left side, the other black on the right. What's more, eventually Bele announces that "You monotone humans are all alike," and Lokai refers to "monocolored trash." The good people of the Enterprise are appalled at the silly arbitrariness of these hatreds, and they have in any case more important things to worry about, since the ship is on its way to deliver the antidote to a planet-wide epidemic. But Lokai uses some technological maneuvering to hijack the ship in order to bring Bele back to Charon, his and Bele's home planet, which is located "in the southernmost part of the galaxy." Kirk threatens to destroy the ship unless he can control where it goes, and he actually calls on the bridge crew to put in codes that start a countdown sequence to the destruction of the Enterprise on the computer. Lokai relents until the ship has made its delivery, but he then reveals that he has destroyed the ship's "self-destruct" mechanism and resumed control. They are all on their way back to Charon now.

They make it to this uncharted quarter of the galaxy in no time, but they find Charon a dead world. (It figures, with a name like that.) The inhabitants have long since burned out their civilization and exterminated one another. Lokai and Bele head for the transporter to beam themselves down to what's left of their home. Kirk, in William Shatner's inimitable way—actually, it's highly and amusingly imitable—implores them to see reason: "List-en to me! You! Both! Must! End! Up! Dead! If you don't stop hating!" But it does no good, and the last we hear of them, Lokai and Bele are chasing each other endlessly down the ruins on Charon. "It makes no sense," Lieutenant Uhura says mournfully as Enterprise leaves them behind, and this remark pretty much sums up the original *Star Trek*'s attitude toward race.

The Real Races of Humanity

Naturally, the sequels to *Star Trek* never denied the senselessness of race hatred, but they did begin to take race more seriously as a distinction among rational beings. And of course there is more to "race" than the Nazis-versus-Black-Muslims stuff of "Let That Be Your Last Battlefield." Or, rather, there is both more and even less. There are lots of complex and important social issues to consider as we reflect on the historical realities and present consequences of racial distinctions, but most life scientists feel that, as a biological matter, there is very little to be said for traditional ideas of race. Richard Lewontin's paper "The Apportionment of Human Diversity" (1972) established the view that there is simply no such thing as race; Lewontin demonstrated there that more diversity of genotypic characteristics exists within the traditional racial categories than exists between them.

And even if we acknowledge this and regard as biologically insignificant the phenotypic things like straight hair, brown skin, round eyes, and pointy noses that we usually take to mark the human races of different geographical origin, we have to acknowledge further that those phenomena are poor indicators of geographical origin in any case. Khan Noonien Singh, the evil South Asian empire-builder who was the villain of the *Star Trek* episode "Space Seed" and the film *Star Trek II: The Wrath of Khan*, was portrayed with physical plausibility by the Mexican-American actor Ricardo Montalban. And I mentioned above the actor Khigh Dheigh, Wo Fat on *Hawaii Five-O*, who made quite a career of playing Asian characters on television and in the movies; the stage name "Khigh Dheigh" was just a made-up reference to his initials. His given name was Kenneth Dickerson, and he was an Anglo-Egyptian-Sudanese man from New Jersey. Despite his undeniably "Asian" appearance, he was not of Asian origin at all. You can't tell "race" by looking.

Nor can you count on even internal phenotypic things like bone structure or blood group. They, too, vary widely within the traditional racial categories. Moreover, significantly, there is not only one tradition of categorizations. Are the South Sea Islanders one race or several? Some Australasians are visually indistinguishable from Africans; some of them even call themselves "black." Are they the same race as the Africans? Are the Jews a race? What about the Slavs? Are there many "black" races in Africa or is there only one? Are there many "white" races in Europe or is there only one? Nineteenth-century immigrants to the United States were made to fill out a standardized immigration form; in the box for race, they could select, along with "Irish" or "Hebrew," "Italian (north)" or "Italian (south)." Was this a mistake, or does that question even make sense?[3] Such problems show that dividing human beings up into natural kinds is a tricky project at best, a hopeless and foolish one at worst.

Despite all this, there are some significant biological differences among different populations of human beings, and traditional racial cat-

---

[3] There is a considerable body of writing on the changing racial status of Italian-Americans and how it has shaped their history; see, for example, Guglielmo and Salerno 2003. And in a number of academic disciplines, more and more writers are working on the topic of "the white race" as a category that has developed quite a bit through recent history rather than a simple biological reality. See Hill 1997 for examples of this trend.

egories do seem sometimes to come in handy in charting them. Such differences matter in epidemiological issues, for example. Persons self-identified as black are more likely to suffer from sickle cell anemia, prostate cancer, and heart disease than those who call themselves white, while whites are more prone to cystic fibrosis and suicidal depression.[4] Some of these things are surely exacerbated, or perhaps activated, by different kinds of stress connected with different kinds of social life; but all of these illnesses also have organic, material causal factors, and some of those are genetic.

Moreover, while individual genetic factors can't indicate geographical origin very well, groups of genetic factors are well correlated with some traditional "race" groupings. As Armand Marie Leroi, an evolutionary developmental biologist at Imperial College in London, recently observed in a *New York Times* editorial promoting the new science of race, "Today it is easy to find out where your ancestors came from. . . . If you want to know what fraction of your genes are African, European or East Asian, all it takes is a mouth swab, a postage stamp and $400—though prices will certainly fall" (Leroi 2005). If several hundred variable genes in the human genome are sorted by their variations, a pattern emerges among human populations that roughly corresponds to origins in America, Africa, Australasia, Europe, and East Asia, which in turn corresponds roughly to one of the traditional human racial divisions.

The new genetic "race" isn't what you can see with your eyes; again, look at Khigh Dhiegh. And, in any case, looks alone can't tell us anything important or interesting about our origins. So your ancestors are from northern Europe rather than from Africa: So what? But the swab can tell us what percentage of your ancestors came from where and when they came. Thus, while looks alone could not tell us whether any Africans in a mixed-race group had ancestors in the ancient Jewish priesthood, DNA scans recently revealed that this was in fact true of the southern African people called the Lemba, who had been calling themselves Jews for quite a long time though no one else believed they shared any ancestry with the Jews of Asia and Europe. (See the new epilogue to Parfitt 2000.) The races that science tells us about are more a matter of molecules than of features visible to the naked eye.

---

[4] A recent *New York Times* article (Saul 2005) told of a new heart medication that may soon be approved for use by, and marketed specifically to, the 750,000 African American heart failure patients in the United States. Some scientists object to this plan on the grounds that race is too ill-defined a category to use in this way.

Even so, to the extent that there are biological "races," they can't be simply a matter of DNA. As Leroi also noted, "Study enough genes in enough people and one could sort the world's population into 10, 100, perhaps 1,000 groups, each located somewhere on the map." Leroi evidently didn't have this point in mind, but it is obvious that if one could find either ten groups or a thousand, then one could also sort all human beings into one big group, the human race. To think as Leroi does in geographical terms, asking how many races there are is like asking how many places there are. Evidently there is no "objective" answer to either question. But does this mean that races are unreal? Well, does it mean that places are unreal? Do we rule Cincinnati, Minnesota, mainland China, or the planet Earth out of existence if we say that whether any of them is one place or many depends on how we look at it? It wouldn't seem so.

Moreover, speaking of divvying humanity up, one could also divide the human population into those hundreds of millions of genetically distinctive groups known as "nuclear families." They have locations on the map, too, and Mom, Dad, and the sibs form as biologically real a group as any "race," though many such families cut across "racial" lines. And it is also just as true biologically that we human individuals are all a lot of mutants, singleton sets, as it is that we all fall into anything remotely like the traditional racial groupings. Each of us is really, demonstrably connected to larger groups of persons, but each of us, except for clones and identical twins, is demonstrably unique, too. That's why it makes sense to use DNA evidence to try to track down a single person. There evidently are, in reality, significant differences among and similarities within groups of us human beings—but neither "significance" nor "groups" are found in nature. Different things will be significant to the different human groupers of humanity.

Even "species," which seems to be an idea that reflects real, significant, "natural" distinctions—and which also seems as if it might be a better concept to call upon if we are thinking about beings from different planets—suffers from (or enjoys?) some of the same relativity as "race." Indeed, the concepts of race and species are not perfectly distinct from one another. The title of Darwin's great book is *On the Origin of Species by Means of Natural Selection, or The Preservation of Favored Races in the Struggle For Life.*

Darwin and other scientists went on subsequently to distinguish the ideas of race and species more sharply, but species, like races, are still divided up differently by different observers. There is the morphological concept of species, the isolation concept, the mate-recognition concept, and the "Darwinian" or phylogenetic concept; and there are still other concepts associated with species of organisms that reproduce without sex. Each of these ideas of what a species is yields a somewhat different division of the species pie. And it is important to see that all of these species distinctions, just like racial distinctions, are drawn by observers, not by nature.

This is not to say that the observers have to or do draw species distinctions arbitrarily; they have reasons to draw the distinctions they draw. Typically different species are more reproductively isolated from one another than different races within a species, for example. But the most widely acknowledged difference between race and species, the idea that different races can interbreed and produce fertile offspring while different species can't, is an idealization. Under various natural and artificial conditions, fertile hybrids can be produced across species lines. There are even occasional fertile cases of the most familiar cross-species hybrid, the mule (Rong 1988).

Star Trek Tries to Do the Right Thing

In the face of this kind of ambiguity and confusion in even the clearest scientific thinking about both race and species, it's not surprising to find less-clear thinkers like the writers of science-fiction television shows making odd and even reprehensible suggestions about racial differences. And we can certainly find some troubling ideas surfacing on the first TV sequel to *Star Trek*, the phenomenon of the 1980s and 90s known as *Star Trek: The Next Generation*.

At this American moment, the Westerns are all long gone from the prime-time lineup. Jerry Seinfeld has replaced Lucille Ball as our favorite TV comic. In our post-Vietnam world, we no longer take anything for granted about the nobility, or even the acceptability, of the way we do things. Americans want, more than anything else, to live (in economic comfort) and let live. We cast a cool, skeptical eye on everything, especially ourselves. And *Star Trek* has changed with the times. The captain of the new Enterprise, roaming the heavens eighty-some years after the days of Kirk, is a bald Frenchman(!) named Jean-Luc Picard, though in Patrick Stewart's booming baritone portrayal he seems much more like an uppah-clahss Brit. His favorite beverage is not Armagnac but Earl Grey, and he knows by heart not Molière or Racine but Shakespeare. Oh, well: French, English, who can tell the difference? The main thing is that he's European, and that means that true civilization has finally arrived in the galaxy. No more of that future-cowboy stuff.

We are clean and drug-free now, too, so no more pretty colors, Beatle haircuts, or space-hippies. There's no more whimsical electronic horn-pipe on the intercom when the bridge calls the captain, and "landing parties" are now "away teams." The new, breathtakingly unsexy uniforms—well, the less said about them the better, though they were designed by the costumer who worked on the old show. The bridge of the new Enterprise is all ergonomic seats and earth tones; it's basically a nice dun-colored dentist's office, though it sports a few swooping futuristic shapes and lines. It's wholly unlike the old bridge, with its fire-engine-red doors to the turbolift and its unearthly lime and magenta background lighting.

As if to anticipate the future of home entertainment as well as that of space travel, the size of the big video panel on the bridge that our heroes use to navigate the cosmos—and to make their speedy cosmic journeys into a metaphor for TV-watching—has expanded by about an order of magnitude. Now it's a home theater. And in front of the big screen are now three commander's seats where once Kirk ruled alone. There's one for Picard, one for his young, dashing first officer, Riker, and one for the "Ship's Counselor," Deanna Troi, a buxom young half-alien woman in a velour catsuit who is there to dispense a constant dosage of wholesome psychotherapy and healthy improvement of outlook. (She's even somewhat telepathic, so there's no point trying to hide any emotions from her. Yikes!)

Peace has been made with the Klingons, so one of the dark-skinned pirates is actually a member of the Enterprise crew. Indeed, Worf the Klingon, thanks to his appearances on *The Next Generation*, in the *Star Trek* movies, and on the spin-off series *Star Trek: Deep Space Nine*, has appeared in more *Star Trek* incarnations than any other character. But in one episode we learn that while you can take a fierce natural predator out of the loosely organized band of villains, you can't take the loosely organized band of villains out of the fierce natural predator.

In "Birthright," a two-part episode in the sixth season of the series, Worf hears that his father, Mogh, who was supposed to have been killed at a place called Khitomer in a bloody battle with the Romulans, is in fact still alive and being held prisoner. This is the worst state of disgrace imaginable for a true warrior, so Worf investigates. He heads for the ostensible site of the Romulan prison camp, penetrates it, and, while he doesn't find his father alive, he does find Romulans and Klingons living together in peace. It turns out that some Klingons at Khitomer were knocked unconscious by an explosion. The Romulans, rather than doing the properly barbaric thing and slitting the Klingons' throats, took prisoners and tried to use them as bargaining chips. The Klingon high command didn't want these shamed soldiers back, however, and so the Romulan commander, taking pity on the captives, set up a site in which they were first held as prisoners and eventually integrated into the population of captors.

Worf finds himself troublingly attracted to Ba'el, a young half-Klingon, half-Romulan woman who is one product of this integration. But Worf is enraged and disgusted by the ways in which the captives have forgotten their "identity." War songs are used as lullabies, tests of hunting skills have become children's games, a ritual spear is used for gardening, and battle armor and jewelry commemorating a girl's coming of age have been left in a chest to rust. Tokath, the Romulan commander, who has married a Klingon woman and who turns out to be Ba'el's father, tells Worf that he won't allow him to disrupt their way of life by reintroducing Klingon ways. Worf also won't be allowed to leave and let the world know that these Klingons are still alive, since that would disgrace their whole families on the Klingon homeworld. Worf will therefore either integrate himself into the society that has been developed in the camp or be put to death.

Instead of obeying, of course, Worf begins teaching the young Klingons in the camp about their culture. This way of life is "theirs" though they have never been exposed to it. A Klingon teenager named Toq at first resents Worf but becomes fascinated with his plan to go hunting. In the camp there are replicators that supply all the food the residents need, but Worf informs him that "Klingons do not hunt because they need food. The hunt is a ritual that reminds us of where we come from." When Worf takes Toq to track down some animal out in the brush, and especially when he teaches him how to catch the scent of prey in the air and to live in "the moment where life and death meet," Toq goes over to the dark side. Worf tells him, "This is who we are. Warriors." Toq responds, "I was never taught that," and Worf informs him that "There is much you were never taught." In addition to being deprived of their heritage, it seems that the children of the old peaceniks are being told the lie that they can't go back out into the world because the senseless war between Klingons and Romulans continues. In fact, there has been peace for a long time—with each side holed up in its own galactic enclave, maintaining peace by having nothing to do with one another.

When the two warriors come back from the hunt with their prey, Worf winds up leading all the Klingons, young and old, in a lusty rendition of one of the old war songs. Tokath is not amused, and he tells Worf to knock it off or die. Worf refuses for the last time, but in the end, as Worf is about to be executed, Ba'el, Toq, the other young Klingons, and even the old original Klingon prisoners all stand in front of Worf to shield him from a disintegrator-ray firing squad. Worf is released, and he, Toq, and two other young full-blooded Klingons head in a Romulan ship to the Enterprise, where Worf informs Picard that the whole matter is to be dropped. There were no survivors of the battle of Khitomer, and his new friends are survivors of a shipwreck. Picard knows better, but he decides not to make an issue of it. Poor Ba'el has been left behind because of course there is no place for her in a racially divided world.

This story should give us pause in some obvious ways. First, it's hard to ignore something not specific to this story, namely, that the Klingons are dark-skinned. One doesn't want to be too thin-skinned about something like this, but it's a bit disturbing that the noble savages of the series have been made nonwhite (and nonpurple and nonblue). Interestingly, in the original 1960s series, the Klingons seemed to be multiethnic. Sometimes they were dark brown, but, for example, the white actor Tige Andrews played Kras the Klingon in the episode "Friday's Child" without dark makeup. On *Next Generation*, the Klingons are portrayed either by blacks like Michael Dorn, who played Worf, or whites in brownface like Suzie Plakson, who played Worf's half-human baby-mama K'Ehleyr in a couple of episodes. True, the Klingons are now sometimes heroic figures, but their heroism fits stereotypes of the non-European and non-Asian breeds of humanity. Worf is a good man to have on your side because he is unafraid of death and will never back down from a fight; but the Klingons are obsessed with honor and killing. They also have spaceships that are dirty and rusty on the inside, bad teeth, gross and crude food including live worms, and, what is perhaps most important, we never hear much about the scientists and intellectuals who made an interstellar empire possible for them. Did these thugs just overpower some alien visitors and hijack their spaceships?[5]

In the original-series episode "Day of the Dove," we do meet a dark Klingon woman, Mara, played by Susan Howard in brown face paint, who is the "science officer" aboard a Klingon warship; and the more politically correct sequel series *Star Trek: Voyager* features as part of the main cast a Hispanic woman, Roxann Dawson, née Caballero, playing the half-Klingon engineer B'Elanna Torres. (Hispanic, female, and

---

[5] On one of the last episodes of *Star Trek: Enterprise,* this is how the Terrans began the creation of their evil Empire in the mirror universe.

Klingon: Talk about P.C.!) But apart from anomalies like these, it seems clear that the Klingons are a race of earthy, ritualistic fighters, not thinkers. (By the way, Mara's husband, Captain Kang, a recurring character in the *Voyager* series, is played by Michael Ansara, another example of you-can't-tell-by-looking ethnicity; he had become well-known playing American Indians, but he is actually of Lebanese descent.)

So the Klingons as a race seem to have dull wits and bad social habits. Match these with their dark skin and with Worf's "this is who we are" rhetoric, so reminiscent of the raised-black-consciousness, anti-melting-pot sentiments one heard in black America in the early 1990s, and the result is a little chilling. Of course, there's nothing wrong with an antiassimilation allegory per se, and there's certainly not much to be said for the ideal of a world with only tea-sipping, Shakespeare-citing Picard-types in it. But when what makes "us" "who we are" is such behavior as joyfully catching the scent of prey and closing in for the kill, the real-life objects of the allegory have reason not to feel flattered. And then there is something that deepens the insult; it is the suggestion that the Klingons and the Picard-types differ not only culturally but biologically. Maybe even an earthling could have sniffed out that boar in the brush, but human beings tend not to hunt by smell. The hints are pretty strong here that the heritage that the young Klingons are being denied in this outdated peace-and-love commune is the heritage that fits their biological nature, a nature more animal than that of either the Romulans or the people of Earth. And some of those hints are confirmed on the startrek.com web site: In the "Library" section, under the heading "Aliens," we learn of the Klingons that "The well-statured warrior race has a genetic predisposition to hostility and a well-known streak of fatalism."[6] If this is an allegory of blackness and brownness on earth, it's not a very appealing one.

The Social Construction of Race in Space

Other episodes of the *Next Generation* series told stories involving race that were even more off-putting. The very worst was an episode from the first season, "Code of Honor," which featured the kidnapping of Natasha Yar, the blonde security chief of the Enterprise played by Denise Crosby. Lutan, the ruler of the planet Ligon II, a world with a

---

[6] The URL is http://www.startrek.com/startrek/view/library/aliens/article/70638 .html.

sort of futuristic black African culture, abducts Tasha so that she can become Sheena . . . er, Tasha, white queen of the black planet.

Of course, Lutan never puts it quite this way, and in fact the words "white" and "black" are not used to mark race in the whole episode. (Indeed, they were never used thus in any of the various series apart from a single 1998 episode of *Star Trek: Deep Space Nine* in which Sisko, the black captain in charge of the eponymous space station, was transported in a dream back to the racist 1950s.) Race is central to the story of Tasha and the Ligonians, but, since this is the enlightened far future, the most visible racial aspect goes unremarked by all involved.

This throwback to the jungle adventure comics and movies of the 1930s ends when Tasha kills Lutan's original queen, Yareena, in a ritual fight. It may be the future, but though quasi-Africans are beaming themselves through space and making medicines a galactic civilization can't produce, they are still fighting ritual hand-to-hand combats to the death. However, thanks to some earlier scheming on the part of the Enterprise crew, Yareena turns out not to be permanently dead. After being revived she is able, for absurd reasons not worth considering, to demote Lutan to second-in-command. Picard and the crew are allowed to take the vaccines they came to the planet for, and Tasha, and depart.

A less explicitly race-centered but nonetheless regrettable plotline involved Deanna Troi's mother Lwaxana, who comes aboard and becomes involved with Timicin, a scientist from the planet Kaelon II. Timicin is on the Enterprise to perform an experiment that he hopes will solve the problem of revitalizing his planet's dying star. But he is approaching his sixtieth birthday, and this, on his world, is the time for "Resolution" or ritual suicide, and if he doesn't agree to kill himself Timicin risks becoming a burden to society. Under Lwaxana's influence, Timicin challenges his reclusive society's rules. He argues that despite his age, he is the person best able to do his vital work. The Kaelonians ignore his arguments, and they send warships to bring him back from the Enterprise so he can meet his fate. However, before there is any shooting, Timicin's daughter comes on board, tells him that she is ashamed of him, and departs without listening to excuses. Timicin loses his nerve, and Lwaxana returns with him to his world to be with him as he dies.

It is true enough that neither of these two stories suggests strongly that biology is responsible for all the cultural conflict. There may or may not be natural laws or genetic impulses driving the characters along to their racial destiny. But each story does show cultural conflict occurring along racial lines, and the only action-guiding principles that anybody can detect or generate are cultural principles that exist within races. Faced with the kidnapping of a crew member, it doesn't occur to Picard that there might be something other than either Ligonian mores or Federation regulations to which he might appeal in deciding what to do. And confronted with a sixty-year-old who is being shamed into committing suicide because he's too old to be tolerated, Picard has no opinion of his own to offer. Timicin, after informing his fellow Kaelonians that he won't be killing himself, asks whether he has done the right thing. Picard, instead of offering moral support, only looks at him and replies, in his plummiest Received Pronunciation, "I'm afraid you're the only one who can answer that, Doctor." This kind of wimpy relativism is deplorable.

A Profitless Enterprise

No one wants the return of Captain Kirk's Kennedyesque and Nixonian ethnocentric certainty, of course. Some evidence of this is the failure of the latest sequel series, *Star Trek: Enterprise*. The *Star Trek* sequels before *Enterprise* had carried on the multi-culti tradition of *Next Generation*, even featuring a black man as captain on *Deep Space Nine* and a white woman captain, with a native American first officer—played by Robert Beltran, a Mexican-American who describes himself as a "Latindio"—on *Voyager*. *Enterprise*, however, attempted to restore the Kipling flavor of the original show. That pesky Prime Directive hadn't even been dreamed up yet in this "prequel" series, set a hundred years before the days of Kirk. *Enterprise* put two white men, one from the Sun Belt, back in charge, and it spent much of its run having its protagonists go out into the galaxy to take revenge for a 9/11-style attack on the earth. Along the way, Captain Jonathan Archer and crew, in the name of their mission, did such things as grimly torture an uncooperative alien in an airlock and murder a kind of clone for spare body parts. (These were the good guys, mind you, not villains from the evil mirror universe.)

It was made clear this time around that differences among the species of the galaxy were superficial, so that worrying too much about different cultures seemed a waste of time. Even the Vulcans, the race that gave us the supremely logical Mr. Spock, turned out not to lack limbic systems but instead simply to be repressing volcanic emotions. What had seemed to be natural Stoicism and splendid indifference turned out to be pretentious standoffishness. Hence all that *Next Generation* moral agonizing and pride-swallowing could be displaced by good old-fashioned space opera. It was noble once again to shoot folks to spread the American way.

Nevertheless, despite all the action, the target demographic, eighteen-to-forty-year-old white males who go to see *Star Wars* installments over and over and to whom one hopes to sell Ford Mustangs and X-Boxes, stopped tuning in. After only four seasons, the shortest run since the original series, the last *Trek* bit the stardust. Its demise was not due simply to an off-putting cultural message; the last *Star Trek* also lacked the humor and imaginativeness of the first. But more successful shows in the franchise were a little challenged in those departments as well. One therefore suspects—maybe it's more like a hope—that at least one of the real problems with *Star Trek: Enterprise* was its America-first revivalism.

Maybe the America that has made a hit of a show like *The Sopranos* is now smart enough to know that life and virtue aren't that simple. We love Tony and Carmela even as we recognize their ignoble, ridiculous, cowardly, vicious, sadistic, pathetic, and even racist features. We see ourselves in these characters who have a lot to learn, to say the least. We care about them without approving of what they do. But we were supposed to admire Captain Archer and his gun-totin' space posse unreservedly, and it just may be that in this moment of uncertainty and sharp national division, comparatively few Americans want to see any heroic allegories of armed cultural dissemination.

Can This Series Be Saved?

Star Trek could have told us more interesting stories, or more morally compelling ones at least, if it had offered an alternative to either blockhead ethnocentrism or goody-goody multiculturalism. But what possible alternative is there? Maybe a fitting basic moral for these science-fiction stories would have been that morality and science are similar in this way: In a world of social differences, discovery, and change, moral beliefs may have to be guessed at, tested, and sometimes discarded, much like scientific beliefs. Maybe the good thing that morality can learn from science is an experimental attitude.

Morality and science were indeed treated similarly in one respect on all the *Star Trek* series: Our star sailors never learned anything about either one. Nothing ever got better in the Federation, even scientifically or technologically, as a result of all this flying around. In the original series alone, they found or figured out humanoid robot technology (three different times at least), practical ion power, a way to develop telekinesis, a *Forbidden Planet*-type machine for boosting intelligence, a boost for the warp engines that made fast intergalactic travel possible, a godlike race of beings willing and able to prevent interstellar wars, and the ability to pop out of space at one point and instantaneously appear light-years away, dragging along whatever they could carry in a transporter beam. These advances were forgotten by the next week's episode. And even within the episodes some of them were treated as Frankenstein's monsters, Things Not Meant To Be Known Of By Man. *Star Trek*'s treatment of its basic "America explores the world and meets new people" premise might have been better had it involved the idea that both the explorers and the explorees could really have been changed and benefited by the encounters.

If the makers of the old *Star Trek* had had this thought and applied it to moral issues, they might have seen that sometimes there is more to "racial" or cultural differences than mindless hatred based on bogus biology. There may be admirable persons, ideas, and ways of doing things on either or both sides of an ethnic divide, or even an ethnic conflict. "We" may have something to learn from "them," and vice versa. Sometimes there were in fact glimpses of this idea in the old show, but the creatures capable of teaching us were so godlike that in the end they couldn't really communicate at our primitive twenty-fourth-century level. The idea that beings like us might know something we don't almost never made an appearance.

This principle could have led the writers to improve the story of Bele and Lokai by making it clearer that despite all Bele's paranoia, he was not simply crazy to think that it mattered what side of his body was black. Skin color doesn't matter *sub specie aeternitatis*, of course— maybe nothing does—but it did matter in the time and place Bele remembered, and in similar times and places—such as, for example, late twentieth- and early twenty-first-century Earth. Bele's skin coloring didn't determine his mind or his personality, but it provided him with real enemies, allies, obstacles, and opportunities.

And the writers of "A Private Little War" might have made the moral issue in that story a little more complex, a little less a question of what noble explorers should do when they find simple, peace-loving children of nature being menaced by skulking, bloodthirsty, unregenerate totalitarians. That was not what the Vietnam War was, after all. Instead, it was a tragically gory laboratory of general moral benightedness and hard-won education. Ignorant armies clashed by night. (King 1967 contains a fairly nice short description of the conflict.) The old *Star Trek* would have been better if it had shown the possibility of such a thing, or if it had reflected the idea that persons from different cultures will need both to take in and to forge some new moral ideas as they go around the world.

If the writers of *Next Generation* had been moral experimentalists—not relativists, but rather experimentalists like scientists—they might have avoided storylines that showed intelligent dark-skinned creatures being drawn to violent ways of life by their biology, and they might have had sense enough to avoid the suggestion that peaceful coexistence among different kinds of people in the same neighborhood is something that needs to be supported by lies. Moreover, they might have seen that lonely experimenters like Timicin need support and encouragement, not just physical defense while they are on our territory.

One of the most famous remarks of the philosopher William James is from an 1897 paper on race and the individual: "The community stagnates without the impulse of the individual. The impulse dies away without the sympathy of the community" (James 1956, 232). The best and most advanced science, politics, and morality all depend on the novel, unexpected, and too-often-unwelcome impulses of individuals; and without the sympathy of the like-minded, those impulses can't advance much of anything. Fortunately, individuals do have those new impulses. Races don't do their thinking en bloc. Equally fortunately, likemindedness can cross racial and cultural boundaries. Where two communities are stagnating, a new community can arise out of cross-cultural discontent. *Star Trek* could and should have told stories that acknowledged these facts of moral life. Surely this kind of tricky and tantalizing community-creation would have provided a better principle for drama than either shoot-'em-ups or moping around the galaxy being respectful.

If there is anything admirable or remarkable about being human—or being an intelligent person, anyway, if it turns out that not all intelligent persons are "human"—it is the ability to transcend both genetic and cultural histories to create new cultures, and even new "races." We can appeal to that ability to generate new science, politics, and morality—and even biology—when our various present cultures and ways of life become so much dead weight. If Kirk and Picard had appealed to this ability more often, *Star Trek* might have been still more entertaining, and more than entertaining.

REFERENCES

Brooks, David. 2001. "Farewell to Greatness: America from *Gilligan's Island* to *The X Files*." Review of *Gilligan Unbound: Pop Culture in the Age of Globalization*, by Paul Cantor. *Weekly Standard* 7, no. 1:31.

Guglielmo, J., and S. Salerno, eds. 2003. *Are Italians White? How Race is Made in America.* London: Routledge.

Hill, Mike. 1997. *Whiteness: A Critical Reader.* New York: New York University Press.

James, William. 1956. "Great Men and the Environment." In *The Will to Believe*, 216–54. New York: Dover.

King, Martin Luther. 1967. "Beyond Vietnam." From the website *A Call to Conscience: the Landmark Speeches of Dr. Martin Luther King, Jr.* Stanford University, http://www.stanford.edu/group/King/publications/speeches/Beyond_Vietnam.pdf.

Leroi, Armand Marie. 2005. "A Family Tree in Every Gene." *New York Times*, March 14, 2005, late ed., A21.

Lewontin, Richard C. 1972. "The Apportionment of Human Diversity." *Evolutionary Biology* 6:381–98.

Parfitt, Tudor. 2000. *Journey to the Vanished City: The Search for a Lost Tribe of Israel.* New York: Vintage.

Plato. 1935. *The Republic.* Books 6–10. With a translation by Paul Shorey. Cambridge: Harvard University Press.

Rong, R., et al. 1988. "A Fertile Mule and Hinny in China." *Cytogenetics and Cell Genetics* 47, no. 3:134–39.

Saul, S. 2005. "U.S. to Review Heart Drug Intended for One Race." *New York Times*, June 13, 2005, late ed., A1+.

The Island of Dr. Moreau: Interpretation of Images of Race and Species

NAOMI ZACK

The Philosophical Theory of Interpretation

In a general sense, how can we derive true statements about behavior and beliefs within a culture from an interpretation of the art of that culture? This is a philosophical question because the links between an artwork and its interpretation, and between the interpretation and the wider culture, need to be more than analogical connections within metaphor. How can we claim, for example, that stereotypical depictions in popular entertainment of women, homosexuals, or nonwhites are reliable evidence that misogyny, homophobia, and racism exist in the action and thought of those who produce and consume that entertainment?

Claims about links between art, interpretation, and culture come closest to empirical claims in the case of popular entertainment, because in contemporary democratic societies, popular entertainment is consumed by majorities. These majorities are changing masses of economic and political individuals, which are important to competing ruling elites because of their buying and voting power. In fact, the elites rule through their ability to manipulate the beliefs and actions of these masses. The strings of manipulation may be concealed in what pleases the masses, and a major source of such pleasure is mass media entertainment. Therefore, when the critic focuses on mass entertainment, she has a better chance of learning something about the culture that produces and consumes it than if she focuses on high art that has a smaller, and often less powerful, audience. Insofar as economics drives aesthetics in mass entertainment, and mass entertainment is dominant over high art, there is no real aesthetic dominance in American society. Indeed, in American society, the *aesthetic* denominator is so—for want of a better word—common, the mass media are capable of entertaining even the most rich and powerful. Are the products of mass entertainment art? Yes, they are, for two reasons. First, they are the only things that could qualify as art that are accessible to the numerical majority, and second, they are created in genres that have well-developed rules for how things appear to the senses.

Let's assume that cultural criticism of mass entertainment is more than a self-contained literary genre and that it has meaning beyond the interests of the intellectually elite group that produces and consumes *it*. For cultural criticism to have external meaning, the links it posits between art and interpretation, and interpretation and culture, must refer to existing causal connections. This empirical requirement is vital for cultural criticism to be liberatory. Liberatory cultural criticism provides an intellectual context in which social injustice can be revealed and understood, and ideally it should lead to programs for change.

The kind of art that is produced and consumed through the mass media is, for the most part, supposed to be representational. That is, its producers intend it to be realistic, and its audience accepts it as realistic. The artwork is a unity of sound, language, and images that represents people, places, and situations that could exist in real life. Even if the audience neither believes nor is supposed to believe that what the artwork represents is likely to exist, in experiencing the artwork, the audience suspends that disbelief. The audience thus enters into the representational world of the artwork and becomes interested in its characters and events as though they were real. Audience members consume mass media products as individuals, but at the same time, most of them are aware that many others are also consuming the same products, either simultaneously or in the near past or future. This mutual awareness of individual consumption adds a social dimension to consumption; it creates a kind of "virtual" community out of consuming individuals who do not necessarily interact with one another directly. The common awareness of mass consumption strengthens the suspension of disbelief, because common awareness is otherwise a component of objective reality. The objective reality of ordinary things, people, places, and situations in the world entails that they can be experienced in the same way by many people. Although the depictions of things, people, places, and situations in mass media artworks are merely representations and not objectively real, their realism, or apparent reality, is supported by the fact that they can be experienced in the same way by many people, because this is how real things are experienced. The existence of a virtual community thus supports the illusion of reality that those who create the mass artworks intend to produce. A liberatory cultural critic relies on the apparent reality of mass media artworks in two ways. First, the critic accepts the artwork as a subject of sufficient importance for interpretation. Second, the critic implies that his interpretation of the artwork can be applied to the culture in which it is produced and consumed. The choice of the artwork as an important subject for interpretation may be justified by the fact that large numbers of people consume it. Numbers alone are often sufficient, because the liberatory social critic is more of a sociologist than an aesthetician—she need not make a case for the quality of the artwork. The critic generally believes that the very existence of mass media artworks proves that they are both expressive and constructive of broad cultural thought and action. The mere fact of their consumption means that they have in some way entered the consciousness of vast numbers of people and in a democracy, numbers alone count. The producers of the narrative know that in order to capture the attention of the audience, the narrative must express or represent something about thoughts and actions that already exists in the culture of the audience. And once the audience members have had the mass experience, their prior thoughts and actions that have been expressed or represented will also have been supported (or "reinforced") and possibly developed in plausible new directions.

Another reason for the importance of mass media artworks is their metaphysical prestige. Although they are not real and at the end of the day are "just" movies, television programs, and narratives, their very unreality gives them more importance than real existing objects. The importance of the unreal in this sense is partly due to a heritage of Greek Platonism, filtered through a Christian tradition. In this tradition, objects of experience that do not exist are accorded incorruptible and unchanging qualities that tend to be valued highly. The knowledge that they are experienced in virtual communities also confers prestige on mass-consumed entertainment, in the same way that knowledge of their fame confers celebrity on individuals.

The cultural critic often assumes that interpretation of a mass media artwork applies to the culture in the real world. This assumption may go beyond a belief that the artwork expresses thoughts and beliefs in the culture, or that the artwork has the capacity to influence the subsequent thought and behavior of those who experience it. Some cultural critics accept mass media artworks as microcosms or symbolic representations of the existing real culture; others may believe that a mass media artwork is a "trope" for the entire culture. Such assumption and acceptance requires justification. The critic may be extending her own normal aesthetic suspension of disbelief, as a consumer of the artwork, onto contexts that exist outside of the direct experience of the artwork. One might call this "the fallacy of reifying representation," which is a polite way of saying that the critic has misplaced the distinction between art and reality. A fundamental requirement for criticism of artwork would seem to be that the critic not suspend her disbelief when addressing the work as a critic.

I do not think that it is possible to construct a plausible empirical explanation of how any one artwork could literally represent an entire culture, as a trope or set of symbols. A particular artwork may be aesthetically representative of an entire culture, but this is a matter of meaning that results from individual and collective judgment. That is, an artwork as a whole does not come to represent a culture as a whole in the way in which a photograph may represent an object, through a physical causal process, for instance. The culture may, to use a deterministic metaphor, *ex-press* particular mass media artworks, and it is usually more likely to express some rather than others. But, this occurs as the result of individual actions, motives, and intentions.

Producers of mass artworks do not necessarily produce them under the same descriptions as cultural critics' interpretation. In addition, the goals of producers may have little to do with the meaning of the artwork to mass consumers. The liberatory critic is likely to select for interpretation those mass media products that provide examples of *oppression* of the type that the critic in question has chosen as a special interest, such as racism, classism, misogyny, able-ism, heterosexism, and, in the following interpretation, speciesism. Oppression is revealed in liberatory criticism through deep interpretation. A deep interpretation of a particular mass media product will usually relate unnoticed aspects of the artwork to forms of oppression in the external culture and demonstrate how the artwork reinforces the thoughts and behavior that constitute that oppression in the real world or takes it into new directions. The fact that critical interpretations of media artworks proceed from the critics' beliefs that there is relevant oppression in the culture suggests that the artworks do not in themselves prove that oppressions of varied kinds exist in the culture. This begins to answer the question I started with, namely, how is it possible to derive truths about oppression in the culture from the artwork? The answer, I think, is that it isn't possible unless one assumes beforehand that oppression is present in the external culture. This suggested epistemological structure of liberatory cultural criticism is supported by the fact that there is no known causal process according to which artworks must mirror oppressions in the culture. However, deep interpretations of mass media artwork are nonetheless capable of advancing understanding of oppression in the external culture—*especially when the interpretation counts the artwork itself as part of the entire culture.*

The Case Study/Interpretation

Despite its nineteenth-century atmosphere, H. G. Wells's novel *The Island of Doctor Moreau* has endured through the twentieth century as popular literature and the basis for three Hollywood movies. In this interpretation, I'll first indicate some historically contextual differences in the successive versions of the *Moreau* story. Next, I'll point out some aspects of its racism and then consider some questions about mixed species given the history of racism.

The Story

H. G. Wells's novel, *The Island of Dr. Moreau*, was published in 1896. The plot takes the following form: Edward Prendick, passenger of the *The Lady Vain*, sunk in the Pacific, is rescued by the *Ipecacuana*, a trader from Arica and Calleo. Montgomery, a doctor with a ruined career, revives him. Montgomery is transporting a cargo of animals containing a puma and staghounds that howl and bay. The captain is always drunk and Montgomery quarrels with him in defense of his assistant M'Ling. M'Ling has a "black face" with green glowing eyes, large teeth, and a projecting muzzle; his movements are clumsy, and his limbs oddly jointed, with short thighs. Edward intercedes against the captain and as a result, when the ship docks at Montgomery's destination, an island belonging to Dr. Moreau, Edward is cast ashore. Dr. Moreau reluctantly agrees to take him in and he is given quarters in the compound.

The puma is immediately subjected to great pain in Dr. Moreau's laboratory and its cries drive Edward out into the jungle. There, Edward encounters strange, animalistic men with miscellaneous malformed features, hirsute bodies, and short thighs like M'Ling. After he returns, he hears human cries of pain and flees in panic, believing that Moreau and Montgomery have tortured "natives" into the grotesque forms he's seen and that the same will happen to him.

Edward's hosts find him, and Moreau assures him he will be safe and gives him a pistol. Edward learns that the "natives" are animals on whom Moreau has performed vivisection experiments involving grafted body parts across species. He has also hypnotized them and taught them basic ethical principles appropriate to their human form. Moreau's aim is apparently pure research, "to find out the extreme limit of plasticity in a living shape" (Wells 1994, 85). But his experiments over the past eleven years have not been successful, the main problem being reversion: "First one animal trait, then another, creeps to the surface and stares at me. But I will conquer yet. Each time I dip a living creature into the bath of burning pain, I say: this time I will burn out all the animal, this time I will make a rational creature of my own" (89).

At present, Moreau's greatest hope lies with the puma. Moreau's failures, about sixty beast people, inhabit the island, living in hovels and caves. There are females among them and they reproduce but their offspring are not hardy. They have a leader, "the Sayer of the Law," who ritualistically intones their basic moral rules:

> Not to suck up Drink; *that* is the Law. Are we not Men?
> Not to eat Flesh or Fish; *that* is the Law . . . .
> Not to claw Bark of Trees; . . .
> Not to chase other Men; . . .
> Not to go on all fours; (64–65)

If the law is broken, "none escape the punishment," which is a return to the House of Pain for further scientific treatment of their resistant "beast flesh."

Moreau himself is a "white-faced, white-haired man, with calm eyes," a touch "almost of beauty" and a "magnificent build." The "generalized animalism" he is trying to eradicate eventually overcomes him and his rule on the island. The humanized puma kills Moreau, after which there is violent revolt by the beast men. Montgomery, who has always been overly fond of both drink and the beast men, is killed in a bacchanal he devises while attempting to reign in Moreau's place. Edward makes friends with surviving peaceful beast types, but over the next ten months, until he manages to get off the island, they all revert to their varied animal traits. Edward is not the same man he was upon his return to England. He detects animal cunning and savagery in his fellow Londoners and ends up a country recluse, reading and thinking about heaven as he gazes at the stars through a telescope (156).

The same scenario endures through the three movies made in 1933, 1977, and 1996: Edward as narrator; shipwreck; arrogant and cruel anthropocentric scientific experiments; the assertion and reassertion of animality in the form of ugliness and destruction (in humans as well as animals); the murder of Moreau; Edward's eventual escape.[1] The modifications in plot and depiction in the three movies reflect changing audience context. In the 1933 version, Charles Laughton as Moreau prances around with a whip, lording it over the "natives" and smiling slyly. In his laboratory, surgery has been augmented with injections of serum that change germ plasm. Laughton-Moreau's goal is to speed up evolution. He believes that all animal life tends toward the human form and revels, with comic depravity, in his role of God. His greatest achievement is Lota (Kathleen Burke), a beautiful young feline woman, and his immediate project is to breed humans and beast men. When his planned seduction of Edward (Richard Arlen) by Lota stalls, the arrival of Ruth, Edward's blonde English finance, inspires a new idea. He encourages a large ape-man to break into Ruth's bedroom and try to rape her.

The 1977 movie is more politically correct. For one thing, the inhabitants of the island resemble animals more than they do humans, so that Edward (now called "Andrew," played by Michael York) is not initially curious about what race the "islanders" are or where they are from, but about what kinds of animals he hears howling. Burt Lancaster brings a formal evangelical fervor to Moreau's mission. His goal is to gain control over the processes of heredity, for the benefit of humankind. Edward becomes a subject of Moreau's research and is turned into a mild sort of animal, his features coarsened and speech slowed. But, by the time he and Maria (Barbara Carrera) escape, his humanity reasserts itself. Maria is a beautiful young woman whom Moreau brought to the island from Panama City, where she had been prostituting herself for a dozen eggs at age eleven. Apparently, she is a pure human, like Edward and Moreau.

In the 1996 film, the beast men are hyperanimals with electronically enhanced voices and implants that Moreau activates to impose the Law through shocks of pain. Marlon Brando combines the elegant high-mindedness of Wells's original Moreau with an overblown decadence. His goal is moral goodness, to create a perfect human race of creatures devoid of malice. Having identified the devil microscopically, as "a tiresome collection of genes," his medium is DNA. Brando-Moreau grandly refers to all the beast men as his children and they tend to ask him, "Why, if you are my father, am I not like you?" The cat lady is back (as "Alisa," played by Fairuza Balk), seducing Edward and reverting in

---

[1] The 1933 film was called *The Island of Lost Souls*; the others had the same title as the book. For detailed listings see *VideoHound's Golden Movie Retriever*, 1997, p. 390.

tooth and ear. Montgomery, in the person of Val Kilmer, is very fond of drugs, as well as drink.

Brando-Moreau wears lipstick, white makeup, and draped, skirted, and scarved Indonesian costumes. He plays classical music and Gershwin to his children. A tiny slothlike personage accompanies him everywhere in identical dress. Kilmer-Montgomery also wears skirts and scarves and further plays with gender by flirting with Edward and kissing the house dog man.

To my mind, the most powerful character in all the depictions is developed in the 1996 version, a Hyena-Swine with a deep reverberating voice and psychotically violent impulses. He has a disturbing, searching way of asking the humans key questions to their faces, and while they struggle to respond, he settles back with gutteral *hmn?*s. Hyena steals the show twice: first, when after having removed his implant he asks Moreau, "If there is no more pain, then is there no more law, hmn?"; and again, when to avoid being shot by Edward, he nobly shuffles upright into a burning building. Hyena is the only Wells character who expresses a capacity to find joy and sensuous pleasure in the bad things that beasts want to do. He shows us an exalted Nietzschean form of what Wells's Moreau finds most troubling:

. . . something that I cannot touch, somewhere—I cannot determine where—in the seat of the emotions. Cravings, instincts, desires that harm humanity, a strange hidden reservoir to burst suddenly and inundate the whole being of the creature with anger, hate or fear. (Wells 1994, 88–89)

Racism in *Dr. Moreau*

In all of its forms, the story enforces the transcendent superiority of white European man. This is primarily accomplished through visual appearances, with moral and intellectual depictions following. White European man is presented as the reigning object of beauty, intelligence, and goodness. Hybrid human-animal beings, who until recently would have symbolized nonwhite humans, are abysmally ugly, as well as stupid and bad. Although the animal beings aspire to be white European men and are ashamed of their animality, they cannot become men and must either perish or revert to animality. By the same token, no matter how sympathetic Edward is to the beast men or "natives of the island," at a certain point in every version of the story, circumstances compel him to accept his relative superiority and privilege and use deception and force against them. All of the Edwards kill beast men and try to resurrect Moreau's godlike power over them. Of course, survival compels these actions, but it is Wells and his successors who created the parameters that so closely reflect much of white participation in what we now call institutional racism.

For audiences in a society in which race is important, the question would naturally arise as to which known or new race the beast people belong. Wells says little directly about race except to note that one beast man resembles a Negro and another a Hebrew, and in no version does Moreau's experiment result in an white European (86, 98).

On film, the cat women seem to have an exotic Asian or mixed-race aspect and even Maria, the human female lead in the 1977 film, is not a white European. The cat women live in the master's house like favored servants and despite their human appearances, telltale marks reassert themselves through a kind of inexorable one-drop rule, such as was mythologized to determine human racial mixture for so long. This mixed-race quality of the cat women adds another layer of confusion to Wells's assimilation of species to race. If Laughton-Moreau had been successful in breeding Lola with Edward or the ape-man with Ruth, presumably the offspring would have been mixed race. Or would they have been mixed species?

If this racial interpretation of the Moreau story seems far-fetched, there is the fact that the environmental backdrop is a colonial-type plantation in every version. In the modern period, subjugated populations in such settings have always been nonwhite. Thus, the location of the story facilitates a blurring of the difference between mixed species and mixed race on the one hand, and between white/nonwhite and human/animal, on the other.

Furthermore, the very genre of *Moreau* supports a reading in terms of race. That is, I think we can assume that the genres of horror and science fiction mirror fears and revulsions experienced by audiences in ordinary life. In 1896, 1933, 1977, and 1996, strong differences between human groups, especially when accompanied by different physical appearances, would in ordinary life be racial differences. On this basis, the different versions of *Moreau* can be understood as reflecting confusions and problems about race that were contemporary to their production. When Wells wrote, there was widespread educated belief in racial essences. It was believed that humanity was divided into distinct races and that members of each race biologically inherited distinctive moral and intellectual traits, along with physical ones. There was a hierarchy of human races from the most animalistic black race to the most civilized white race. Individuals of mixed race were always presumed to revert to traits of the lower race and were believed to have difficulty in reproducing.[2] All of these beliefs are played out in the novel and were probably intensified by 1896 fears of what could be done by advances in medical science, principally surgery.

The 1933 film was banned in parts of the United States, due to Laughton-Moreau's cross-breeding intentions. In 1933, the Miscegenation Laws against interracial marriage were still in effect in many states and black men were routinely tortured and murdered when accused of sexual aggression against white women.[3] Evolution was also hotly contested throughout the South and a man reveling in the fantasy of being God would have represented extreme blasphemy in many places. Apparently, the mere depiction of these dangerous ideas, despite Moreau's punishment, was considered to in some way reinforce them.

The confusions about racial heredity in the *Moreau* novel and 1933 film can now be sorted out fairly easily. There is no such thing as race biologically, no specific gene or set of genes for any of the racial groups, no essential collection of distinctive racial characteristics. Furthermore, whatever is distinctive within human types in moral or intellectual terms is not biologically inherited and it is not attached to any particular type of appearance that has been racialized. So-called mixed race within human populations has been and still is the locus of many social problems, but on biological grounds it is a nonevent. The vast majority of humankind has always been "mixed" in one way or another and mixed-race people suffer none of the debilities ascribed to them by nineteenth-century pseudoscience.[4] Many Americans now recognize a growing number of families with offspring, who, according to the biologically unfounded racial taxonomy, are of different races from their parents. In this regard, the awe with which Brando-Moreau's children question their difference from their father is, for 1996, insofar as this film is set in the present, mere anachronistic Hollywood silliness.

When the 1977 film was released, the civil rights movement had come and gone and white backlash was coalescing on grounds of socioeconomic class. While Edward's transformation in this movie does not deprive him of humanity, it does rob him of the skills that he would need to preserve his status upon returning to England. However, although race is in reality socioeconomic rather than a physical taxon-

---

[2] For discussion and sources on nineteenth-century ideas of race, see Zack 1993, especially chaps. 7, 8, and 9.

[3] See Zack 1993, chap. 8.

[4] On the flimsiness of biological race, see Appiah 1996 and Zack 1997.

omy, a good part of what people believe is racial rests on their perception of physical difference among humans. This perhaps accounts for why the 1977 film is flat and unconvincing, why critics found it "a disappointment."

The 1996 film reflects some of our sharpest cultural contradictions. Irrationality, violence, gender bending, and drug use are at the same time deplored and celebrated. For example, some whites today are deeply compassionate about the plight of nonwhites but at the same time they feel powerless to help them and threatened by their success. After Moreau dies and Edward searches desperately for the serum to forestall Alisa's regression, he is anguished by the discovery that Moreau was intending to kill him for his DNA, that is, to use him, in order to perfect Alisa. And when Edward bids farewell to the Sayer of the Laws, he is told not to send more scientists to the island because "it is very hard to be a man" and perhaps "better to walk on all fours." So Edward's relief at finally escaping the island is underscored.

Speciesism

However, we are not as fortunate as Wells's hero. The horror in reaction to issues of mixed species depicted in *Moreau* will probably endure through the twenty-first century and for some good reason. Once again, scientific technology has caught up with Wells's imagination. Although Wells's scenario of mixed species may have previously worked as metaphor for mixed race and racism, the reality of gene transplantation now turns *Moreau* into a literal depiction of the problems of mixed species and speciesism.

Few today would accept the premise that everything low and evil in human nature is derived from animal nature or has more intense incarnation there. Marxists, environmentalists, indigenists, most schoolchildren, and many self-identified political liberals of one kind or another would probably insist on the reverse. However, the question of animal rights is another issue. In the Wells stories we are told that Moreau had to leave home because of public protest when a flayed dog escaped from his laboratory in England (or in the Brando film, America). We still contend with related issues but vivisection affects only the existing animals experimented on, whereas gene splicing within species, or the creation of new species, would endure forever (or until the next gene splice).

Mixed species is a reality we have not properly begun to imagine, even though the technology is here. We already know that creatures with both animal and human DNA can be created. Many of us are already eating tomatoes, bought at local supermarkets, that contain genes from arctic fish to prevent freezing. Genetic "improvements" to animals await only formulation of the right commercial and political propaganda for public acceptance.

I wonder if it is even possible to think about these eventualities without assimilating them to scenarios and social structures of race, racism, and mixed race. Could it be that after three or four centuries of racial illusions that are finally in the process of being dispelled, we will now have to deal with a kind of racialism based on objective biological difference that really does have a foundation in science?

The shock value of *Moreau*, as well as some *Star Trek* episodes and other works of science fiction, is that it shows the true insignificance of what people experience as biological racial difference. But I do not think that we can afford to trivialize the dangers of speciesism and mixed species, either to ourselves or other species. As was the case with racial designation during the colonial period, the invention of new species will probably represent irresistible economic gain. I think that our main problem is that we cannot yet agree on what is distinctively human— morally, psychologically, and intellectually. As before, we may end up relying on superficial appearance. This is a human propensity of which John Locke was aware, writing over two hundred years before Wells. In *An Essay Concerning Human Understanding*, while considering how *nominal* our definition of *man* is, he recounted a story about an intelligent talking parrot in Brazil and later concluded:

> I think I may be confident, that whoever should see a Creature of his own Shape and Make, though it had no more reason all its Life, than a *Cat* or a *Parrot*, would call him still a *Man*; or who ever should hear a *Cat* or a *Parrot* discourse, reason, and philosophize, would call or think it nothing but a *Cat* or a *Parrot*; and say, the one was a dull irrational *Man*, and the other a very intelligent rational *Parrot*. (Locke 1975, 333)

The Real Sequel to *The Island of Dr. Moreau*

H. G. Wells's novel *The Island of Doctor Moreau* has endured through the twentieth century as popular literature and the basis for three Hollywood movies. The story enforces ideals of the transcendent superiority of white European man. While it purports to be about mixed species, before biotechnology it would have enforced racism against nonwhites and evoked fears about mixed race. White European man is presented as the reigning object of beauty, intelligence, and goodness and hybrid human-animal beings are abysmally ugly, stupid, and bad, doomed to perish or revert to animality. The confusions about race in *Moreau* are now easy to sort out. But, the horror it occasions in reaction to mixed species will probably endure through the twenty-first century because once again, scientific reality has caught up with Wells's imagination.

The foregoing interpretation extends beyond the mass artwork, *The Island of Dr. Moreau,* because the mass consumption of the artwork through its different cultural contexts attests to its validity as an expression and representation of the beliefs of those who have consumed it. Insofar as the consuming groups have themselves been broadly representative of majorities in English and American society, it is plausible that the representations of race, mixed-race, and human and animal species, and the attendant valuations of these representations, are indicative of broad beliefs, prejudices, and aversions.

REFERENCES

Appiah, K. Anthony. 1996. "Race, Culture, Identity: Misunderstood Connections." In *Color Consciousness: The Political Morality of Race*, edited by Amy Gutmann. Princeton: Princeton University Press.

Locke, John. 1975. *An Essay Concerning Human Understanding*, edited by Peter H. Niddich. Oxford: Oxford University Press.

VideoHound's Golden Movie Retriever. 1997. New York: Visible Ink Press.

Zack, Naomi. 1993. *Race and Mixed Race*. Philadelphia: Temple University Press.

———. 1997. "Race and Philosophic Meaning." In *RACE/SEX: Their Sameness, Difference and Interplay*, edited by Naomi Zack. New York: Routledge. See also *Philosophy of Science and Race*. New York: Routledge, 2002.

It's in the Meat: Science, Fiction, and the Politics of Ignorance

NANCY McHUGH

*F*eminized steer, mutated bodies, synthetic food, rampant cancer, nose-diving fertility rates, environmental destruction, political conspiracies, and the denial of knowledge are all common themes in science fiction. Unfortunately, they are also are part of our collective "nonfiction," or social reality. In this chapter I focus on Japanese-American novelist Ruth Ozeki's *My Year of Meats* to consider how fiction about science serves to de-fictionalize science while at the same time it serves as science fiction. Ozeki engages in what has come to be called an epistemology of ignorance project. Her novels serve to create knowledge where knowledge has been actively lost, obscured, or ignored and is engaging in a new type of science fiction by using the novel as a medium to generate knowledge about contemporary science, revealing that the overlooked present is worse than the feared fictional future. We don't have to look beyond the now to be terrorized or realize that our bodies, our food, our planet are already mutant/mutated. Ozeki shows that the standard trope of science fiction novels is in fact true: an unsuspecting public is participating in and funding its own destruction, while an "evil" government, overzealous scientists, and greedy corporations watch on, benefit, and are amused by our ignorance.

Three Stories in One

My Year of Meats consists of three interwoven narratives, with one dominating the text. It is this dominant narrative that serves as the foil for revealing ignorance and actively reconstructing knowledge. Jane Takagi-Little is the main character in the work. She is a Japanese-American documentarian and a self-described half-breed: "Halved, I am neither here nor there, and my understanding of the relativity inherent in the world is built into my genes" (Ozeki 1998, 314). Thus Takagi-Little already exists in a tenuous epistemological location, stuck between two worlds with little space for certainty.

Jane is hired by BEEF-EX, "a national lobbying group that represents American meats of all kinds—as well as livestock producers, packers, purveyors, exporters, grain promoters, pharmaceutical companies, and agribusiness," to film a series of documentaries called *My American Wife!* to be aired on Japanese television (Ozeki 1998, 9–10). The programs are supposed to encourage Japanese housewives to buy more meat, American meat specifically, by promoting the wholesomeness of the product. Takagi-Little is to go into ideal American households and film ideal American housewives preparing delicious meat meals.

This is exactly what Jane does, except that the housewives, the stories, and the meals aren't necessarily so ideal. In the course of her filming she learns more about U.S. meat, pharmaceuticals, livestock production, agribusiness, and the science of meat than she bargained for. Jane interviews a couple who, in the course of being filmed consuming their homemade Coke Pot Roast, reveal that the husband had an affair. She interviews a lesbian vegetarian couple, Dyann and Lara, who don't realize they are being filmed for a beef propaganda film. This couple becomes quite influential in their interactions with Jane. It is through them that it begins to hit her how corrupt the meats business is. Jane also interviews a Baptist African American couple, a Chicano family, a family that has twelve children, the majority of which were adopted from Asia, and a family that runs a feedlot. Within each of these narratives Jane learns more about the corruption of U.S. meat.

The two other story lines that run through *My Year of Meats* serve as support for Jane Takagi-Little's narrative. Akiko is the wife of Ueno, a Japanese executive working for BEEF-EX. He requires her to watch *My American Wife!* not only so she can assess the quality of the program, but also so that by preparing and eating the delicious meat meals she can gain enough weight to conceive his child. Akiko and Jane end up partners in crime via the phone and the fax machine, with Akiko feeding Jane information about Ueno's plans for Jane and *My American Wife!*

The third narrative is the writings of a 1000 A.D. Japanese feminist, Sei Shonagon. Both Jane and Akiko are reading from her "pillow book."

From the pillow book we get forebodings of what intellectual challenges Jane will face.

These narratives weave together a story that is powerful and forces the reader to encounter the reality that lies in the science of meats. The ideal of U.S. meat as wholesome, safely regulated, pure, and ideally American is thoroughly washed away. Any belief in the meat industry caring about the welfare of the U.S. public at least as much as profits is dispelled. The integrity of our bodies is called into question when it becomes clear that meat and the products used in meat have infiltrated our system and constructed dis-eased bodies.

Ignorance Really Isn't Bliss

The study of the active construction of ignorance has become an increasingly important area of philosophy and science studies. Political theory and what Robert Proctor in *Cancer Wars* calls the "political philosophy of science" have claimed not only that ignorance is a legitimate site of academic study but also that the study of ignorance is necessary for any liberatory project. If we want to know and to create change, we have to study the construction of ignorance, who has participated in the construction, why it was constructed, and who benefited from ignorance. Charles Mills's *Racial Contract* makes this startlingly clear. Mills coins the term "epistemology of ignorance" in this text, arguing that under the terms of the Racial Contract whites agree to misinterpret the world. The contract itself is an agreement to not know. This agreement is held in place by the assurance that this misinterpretation will count as true by those that benefit and maintain this willful ignorance—whites. Mills tells us that this ignorance is a type of epistemology, an "*inverted epistemology, an epistemology of ignorance, a particular pattern of localized and global cognitive dysfunctions (which are psychologically and socially functional), producing the ironic outcome that whites will in general be unable to understand the world they themselves have made*" (Mills 1997, 18).[1] Ignorance is experienced as knowledge because it provides a worldview that is cohesive ("psychologically and socially functional") with whites' expectations of what the world is like. In other words, what feels like reality is really an epistemological fiction. Furthermore, the reality that whites have constructed for themselves requires this epistemological fiction—it is "prescribed by the

---

[1] Italics in the original.

terms of the Racial Contract, which requires a certain schedule of struc-tured blindness and opacities in order to establish and maintain the white polity" (Mills 1997, 19). Thus the epistemological fiction is also an ontological fiction. Through ignorance, it actively constructs reality in its claims to knowledge.

Like Mills, Marilyn Frye and Robert Proctor provide analyses of the role of the intentional construction of ignorance, active not-knowing, in the construction and maintaining of power. Frye argues in *The Politics of Reality*, "Ignorance is not something simple: it is not a simple lack, absence or emptiness, and it is not a passive state. Ignorance of this sort . . . is a complex result of many acts and many negligences" (Frye 1983, 118). For Frye the phallocratic and white reality prevent seeing and knowing while actively constructing ignorance. Because this reality presents claims to truth and knowledge and has the power to maintain this illusion, ignorance creates "the conditions that ensures its continu-ance" (20).[2]

Proctor argues that ignorance is complex and has a "distinct and changing political geography that is often an excellent indicator of the pol-itics of knowledge" (Proctor 1995, 8). His goal in *Cancer Wars* is to study the social construction of ignorance. Proctor's research into the "cancer industry" is so sensational that it reads like the work of a slightly deranged, obsessed genius piecing together a conspiracy theory about powerful industrial giants looking out only for their corporate interests, willing to sacrifice our lives and environment for the almighty dollar. Proctor is a genius and he may or may not be obsessed, but he is certainly not deranged. What makes Proctor's narrative of the cancer industry—from tobacco to mining to chemical manufacturing—so startling is that it *is* reality. What feels like such a spectacularly orchestrated series of agree-ments to manufacture misinformation, disease, and destruction by some of the agencies and individuals that we are taught to trust (the Environmental Protection Agency, the Food and Drug Administration, the Atomic Energy Commission, U.S. presidents[3]) colluding with industries that we hopefully have the sense to not trust (tobacco, asbestos, herbicide and pesticide industries) is true, when seems that it couldn't possibly be.

A recent article in *The Lancet* brings Proctor's argument home. In 1982, Philip Morris set up a stealth lab in Europe to test the dangers of

---

[2] For more work on the epistemology of ignorance see Tuana 2003, and Irigaray 1985a and 1985b.

[3] Proctor claims that "Ronald Reagan may have been the most potent new carcino-gen of the 1980s."

secondhand smoke. The studies found that secondhand smoke caused high levels of nasal cancer in rats. The results of these studies were never released. The European lab had a coordinator who would feed information to select Philip Morris senior executives. "Stringent measures appear to have been employed to maintain the secrecy of these arrangements, extending to consideration of establishment of a 'dummy' mailbox and the dispatch of documents to the home address of a senior Philip Morris scientist where they could be acted on or destroyed" (Diethelm 2005, 90). It was not until 1992 that evidence was released from other sources implicating secondhand smoke as a cancer cause.

Here lies the strength of the projects Proctor, Frye, and Mills engage. Their arguments come together to seem like a spectacular, over-the-top claim: that our reality is a racist, patriarchal, corporate construction that feels like home to most of us to such an extent that when the fiction of our reality, at the epistemological and ontological level, is pointed out most of us have been taught to doubt the veracity of the newly revealed knowledge because we have been so ensconced with ignorance. We've been taught to believe that our government, our society, and our community work in the best interest of us all. Those who are skeptical about these organizations' claims that they value our welfare tend to be socially ostracized, and are considered to be paranoid or even antipatriotic. We've been conditioned to believe a lie, and this ignorance feels good and safe. In order to see, to come to know, that in fact we have been duped and that we have participated and helped structure our very own ignorance, we have to be willing to excavate and construct knowledge where ignorance has been most persistent.

Mills, Frye, and Proctor offer us one means to do this, through the lens of scholarly work. Yet this is limited. Perhaps the weakness of their work is that unless used as assigned class materials, their works are likely to be chosen by those of us interested in the topic and maybe ready to be convinced of our own ignorance. In a sense they are preaching to the converted or, more accurately, to those of us willing to be converted.

Science Fiction and Fictional Science

This is where the power of science fiction lies. First, science fiction is consumed by a broader audience. Though this audience has tended to be largely white, middle class and male, the demographic of the science fiction consumer is changing as science fiction becomes more mainstream and more female and feminist science fiction writers join the ranks. Furthermore, science fiction has become broader in focus.

Fiction about science is becoming increasingly popular. Ruth Ozeki's *My Year of Meats* and Michael Crichton's *State of Fear* are examples of this type of work. As science and technology information become a more and more common part of our daily lives (think of how many times in the past year we have had front-page news on cloning or other genetic technologies) the purview of science fiction moves to the science of everyday life and everyday worries. This type of science fiction appeals to different demographics than traditional science fiction has. For example, Ozeki's work is read largely by educated women, and Crichton's work is read by a popular press, bestseller audience. Thus, in its increasingly pluralistic forms, science fiction has the potential to reach a much broader audience than the kind of audience that Mills, Proctor, and Frye are reaching. This is important, especially if you think that there is something about science fiction that can be liberatory.

Second, works in science fiction are frequently epistemology of ignorance projects, whether they are intentionally cast as that or not. It is not unusual for science fiction to be built upon the assumption that there is knowledge to be revealed and that ignorance is taking the place of knowledge. This knowledge may be a fictional construction of a future that could manifest out of the course of our present conditions, for example the film *GATTACA*, or Margaret Atwood's *The Handmaid's Tale*. Or it could be a series of events that reveals our deepest cultural anxieties and philosophical worries, such as *The Matrix* or Octavia Butler's *Kindred*. Science fiction uses the genre of fiction to reveal things to us about ourselves, our culture, our political system, our science and technology that usually are not revealed to us through normal avenues or are intentionally hidden from us by institutions that we consider benign, and are anything but benign. It is effective because it feels fictional and thus distant from reality, yet it reveals more about our reality and frequently holds more truth than the evening news or press releases from the EPA. Thus ignorance is excavated, and alternative knowledge is revealed, and the reader is provided with a new lens through which to understand her world.

Ozeki on Ignorance

Ozeki's fictionalizing of science is concerned with the active construction of ignorance, the seamlessness of this lack of knowledge, and the danger it poses to the very materiality of our existence. Yet through the novel, that is, through a fictional construction, which is meant to feel safe because it is not "real," she reveals to her readers knowledge that they would unlikely be exposed to by other means. The safety of the fictional novel serves to challenge the perceived safety of our bubble of ignorance. The irony of Ozeki's novels is that her fictional accounts contain less ignorance and more knowledge than most "true," that is, non-fiction, accounts we are given. As Jane concludes at the end of the text "truth wasn't stranger than fiction; it *was fiction*" (Ozeki 1998, 360). One way to read this is that the truth lies within the fiction: fiction reveals truth. The other way to read this quote is that what we take to be truth is itself a fiction. In either case, the knowledge that Ozeki reveals calls into question corporate and government interests' claims to truth. Furthermore, by pointing to the false construction of reality generated by the active work of corporate and government agencies and the dangers that exist in our present, Ozeki shows that we have as many reasons to fear the present, which is real and fictional at the same time, as we do to fear a fictionalized future.

Her work is a prime example of an epistemology of ignorance project in science fiction, because she is so intentional about her discussions of ignorance and because the information she provides us exists right under our noses, as most ignorance does, yet we refuse to believe or acknowledge it. We participate in our own ignorance. As Jane Takagi-Little says, "I have heard myself protesting, '*I didn't know!*' but this is not true" (Ozeki 1998, 334).

Ozeki uses Jane's role as a documentarian to theorize about truth, knowledge, and ignorance through the lens of the camera, the cuts of editing, and the eyes of a cynical, yet at times naïve, observer and ultimately the producer of knowledge. Jane tells the reader that when she started out as a documentarian she "wanted to make programs with documentary integrity, and at first I believed in a truth that existed—singular, empirical, absolute. But slowly, as my skills improved and I learned about editing and camera angles and the effect that music can have on meaning, I realized that truth was like race and could be measured in only ever-diminishing approximations. Still, as a documentarian, you must strive for truth and believe in it whole-heartedly" (Ozeki 1998, 176). The role of the documentarian is particularly apt for a protagonist meant to reveal knowledge in the face of ignorance. By the very nature of the task a documentarian's goal is to document information, people, and events and to reveal accurate, true information about these events. They are in the truth business and their task is to reveal where false knowledge has existed and flourished. Yet in the process of looking for truth, the documentarian is bound to encounter things that have been taken as truth and knowledge but in fact are neither. The very process of uncovering this false knowledge and ignorance brings into doubt the feasibility of attaining "singular, empirical, absolute" truth because new knowledge and new ignorance are continuously revealed.

But to be a documentarian, you have to believe in truth or there is nothing to document. You have to believe that there is something out there to latch on to and that this something is better than what was known before. To not do so would be a bit like being a gambler and not believing one has a chance of winning. So Jane intellectually doubts that truth exists, yet realizes in practice that one has to believe in some truth or at minimum better, more accurate knowledge.

If you are engaging in liberatory epistemology of ignorance projects, you need to take the same stance. You can't afford to function as if all knowledge is equally good or that all knowledge is a pure construction. You must be able to point to some information as better, more accurate, and more revealing than other information, and reveal that some knowledge is, frankly, just not knowledge. To not do so would be to fall back into the hands of those that benefit from the construction of ignorance. For them, it is almost as beneficial to claim that knowledge is purely relative as to claim that their knowledge is knowledge. The result is the same. They can continue to "manufacture doubt"[4] about any claims that are counter to theirs, and they have the resources to do so.

Ozeki, through Jane, takes an even greater strategic approach to truth. She says, "Truth lies in layers, each of them thin and barely opaque, like skin, resisting the tug to be told. As a documentarian, I think about this a lot. In the edit, timing it everything. There is a time to peel back" (175). Truth is something that has to be pulled up and isn't always obvious; it has to be excavated. It is not just sitting there waiting to reveal itself to us. When ignorance has covered over truth, only active recovery will reveal ignorance and knowledge. Yet, one involved in the process of uncovering and revealing knowledge, like an editor, has to be strategic in the act itself. Because, as Mills tells us, ignorance feels "psychologically and socially functional," truth can be startling and unbelievable in the face of ignorance. But like careful editing, peeling the layers back to build a carefully constructed argument makes projects in the epistemology of ignorance persuasive.

The irony of epistemology of ignorance projects is that we tend to have an inkling that we are surrounded by ignorance and that there is

---

[4] Proctor argues that the role of lobbying groups is to manufacture doubt.

something else out there to be known. We get whispers of information here and there that make many of us doubt the "order of things," yet we tend to refuse to acknowledge the existence of this information and act on it. For example, Jane says, "Information about toxicity in food is widely available, but people don't want to hear it. Once in a while a story is spectacular enough to break through and attract media attention, but the swell quickly subsides into the general glut of bad news over which we, as citizens, have so little control" (Ozeki 1998, 334). This knowledge frequently is right in front of us, but we are not ready, are unwilling, or are too overwhelmed to hear it. To do so may mean changing our lives in ways that we may not want to, challenging our whole metaphysics, or facing up to the meaning and result of our past actions; that is, we become implicated in the results of ignorance too.

Furthermore, we are disempowered in the face of information. Not only is it overwhelming to have the psychological and social cohesiveness of our world rocked, but also we have trouble figuring out how to process new information when as a culture we have been trained to not think critically, to not question, and to trust the mechanisms of corporate and governmental capitalism. Most people lack the emotional, intellectual, and political resources to process, let alone do something about, knowledge. Thus knowledge becomes psychically dangerous, and instead of letting ourselves come to know this new information, we let it pass away. Ozeki puts this so well. She says through Takagi-Little:

> Coming at us like this—in waves, massed and unbreachable— knowledge becomes symbolic of our disempowerment—becomes bad knowledge—so we deny it, riding its crest until it subsides from consciousness. I have heard myself protesting, "*I didn't know!*" but this is not true. Of course I knew about toxicity in meat, the unwholesomeness of large-scale factory farming, deforestation of the rainforests to make grazing land for hamburgers. Not a lot, perhaps, but I knew enough. But I needed a job. So when *My American Wife!* was offered to me, I chose to ignore what I knew. "Ignorance." In this root sense, ignorance is an act of will, a choice that one makes over and over again, especially when information overwhelms and knowledge has become synonymous with impotence. (Ozeki 1998, 334)

We thus frequently participate in our own ignorance even when we have opportunity to do otherwise. Jane "chose to ignore what [she] knew" because it was easier, more convenient, and less overwhelming than the knowledge that had been revealed to her. Like Mills, Frye, and Proctor, Ozeki points to willfulness, the very activity of ignorance, as a chosen state of being.

Jane is right to point out that she is not alone in her ignorance, that chosen ignorance is a cultural phenomenon, a cultural failure, a pitiful and ultimately unsuccessful survival technique. She says,

> I would like to think of my "ignorance" less as a personal failing and more as a massive cultural trend, an example of doubling, or psychic numbing, that characterizes the end of the millennium. If we can't act on knowledge, then we can't survive without ignorance. So we cultivate ignorance, go to great lengths to celebrate it, even. . . . Fed on a media diet of really bad news, we'll live in a perpetual state of repressed panic. We are paralyzed by bad knowledge, from which the only escape is playing dumb. Ignorance becomes empowering because it enables people to live. Stupidity becomes proactive, a political statement. Our collective norm. (Ozeki 1998, 334)

We need ignorance because we are too disempowered to act on the knowledge that faces us. Thus even as ignorance disempowers us, it empowers us at the same time because it means we at least get to exist and maintain our current level of psychological and social comfort in spite of perhaps a slight itchiness that may persist, the inkling that we really should know.

Yet as Mills points out, for some people chosen ignorance can only be a short-term strategy. To continually choose to not know means that only those that profit from ignorance will survive. Once we *know where the bodies are buried* and so many of those bodies are those that are damaged by willful, culturally sanctioned ignorance, then it becomes imperative that one no longer seeks the comfort of ignorance, but chooses instead to know (Mills 1997, 132). Jane makes the life-and-death stakes of ignorance versus knowing apparent:

> I had started my year as a documentarian. I wanted to tell the truth, to effect change, to a make a difference. And up to a point, I had succeeded: I got a small but critical piece of information about the corruption of meats in America out to the world, and possibly even saved a little girl's life in the process. And maybe that's the most important part of the story, but truth is so much more complex. (Ozeki 1998, 360)

It Really Is in the Meat

So what do Jane Takagi-Little and the readers of *My Year of Meats* come to know? The overarching picture is the government regulation of meats, the environment, and farming is a farce. They are in bed with factory farmers, slaughterhouses, dairy producers, the meat and dairy lobbying groups, pharmaceutical companies, pesticide companies, and *their* lobbying groups. The farmers themselves are both duped and participating at the same time. We, as consumers, love to consume the products of our own destruction and do so with little regard to our own safety. We love our ignorance just like we love our steak.

But this is too easy. The truth and the horror lie in the details, and this is where I want to go now. Perhaps the best place to start is with what's in the meat. Jane begins to learn what's in the meat at one of her earliest film shoots for BEEF-EX's *My American Wife!* They were in Oklahoma, otherwise known as the "Sooner State," filming Mrs. Klinck making Sooner Schnitzel, a Kellogg's Krispies–coated fried concoction, German Fried Potatoes, and Succotash. Mrs. Klinck wanted the crew to have a taste. Oda, the director, tucked up to the table with great excitement. After a bite or two he started to choke and grab his throat. Oda quickly ended up in the hospital, having gone into anaphylactic shock. When Oda checks off on his admission report that he has antibiotic allergies the doctor replied, "That's it." Jane questions the doctor further. He tells her that in the source is the feedlot:

> "They're filthy and overcrowded—breeding grounds for all sort of disease—so cattle are given antibiotics as a preventive measure, which builds up and collects in the meat." "But he was eating veal. . . ." He looks at me. "Are you kidding? *Especially* in veal. Those calves live in boxes and never learn to walk, even—and the farmers keep them alive with these massive doses of drugs just long enough to kill them. What sent your director into shock was the residue of the antibiotics in the Sooner Schnitzel. . . . You know, it scares me. I mean allergies are one thing. But all of these surplus antibiotics are raising people's tolerances, and it won't be long before the stuff doesn't work anymore. There's all sorts of virulent bacteria that are already mutant. . . . It's like we are back to the future—we're headed backward in the time toward a pre-antibiotic age." (Ozeki 1998, 60)

So the first lesson we learn is that antibiotics are standard part of cattle and veal production. Cattle live in filthy conditions, not lolling around in nice green pastures, thus antibiotics are a necessity to keep them alive long enough that we can kill them, eat them, and consume some antibiotics along the way. These antibiotics that were designed to be used for illness, but are now used for maintaining cattle for slaughter, can kill not only in the short term—what person with antibiotic allergies would guess that their steak was a potentially dangerous as a shot of penicillin—but also in the long term: the bacterial resistance to them may become so strong that they can't protect us when we need them to. Thus we now know that antibiotics, potentially lethal doses, are in the meat. Unfortunately, this may be the least of our worries.

On a subsequent shoot in Harmony, Tennessee, the crew attends an African American Southern Baptist Church and afterwards films and talks to Miss Helen and Mr. Purcell, the Dawes. Ueno, the executive in charge of *My American Wife!* asks Miss Helen and Mr. Purcell what other kind of meats they eat after they had told him to his dismay that they eat a fair amount of what he considers an "inferior meat," pork. Mr. Purcell replies that they like chicken and used to eat it a lot, but it is more expensive now. So they buy chicken parts that are "cheap down at the packin' house." Miss Helen

> let out a hiccup that turned into a burst of laughter. "Yeah, we *thought* they was real good . . . until Mr. Purcell's barrytone came out soundin' like a serpraner!"
>
> Purcell explained. "It was some medicines they was usin' in the chickens that got into the necks that we was eatin'. . . . An' that medicine, well, if it didn't start to make me sound just like a woman!" "And look like one too, with them teeny little titties and everything!" Miss Helen chimed in. (Ozeki 1998, 117)

Chicken contains estrogen or some estrogenizing substance; this garnered from the information of Mr. Purcell's rising voice and his newly formed female anatomy. Estrogen is commonly used to make plumper chickens. They acquire plump breasts, just as Mr. Purcell does. We also learn that people who don't have money are more likely to buy chicken parts like necks than the more expensive whole chicken or prime pieces like chicken breasts. Because the hormones tend to deposit in greater concentration in the necks, and poor people are more likely to buy these less expensive parts, poor people are disproportionately affected by the presence of hormones in chicken. Thus we see the intersection of poverty and illness.

Perhaps the most horrific tale we get is the story of Rosie, Bunny, John, and Gale Dunn. Gale and his father John run Dunn and Son feedlot. Rosie is John's five-year-old daughter from his second marriage to the much younger, former exotic dancer Bunny. From the filming of this documentary we learn about the illegal and legal use of hormones in cattle production, the "recycling" of cattle products, the use of plastic hay and concrete feed additives, and the physical affects of pharmaceutical hormone exposure.

Gale boasts to the camera crew, whom he assumes to be "East coast environmentalist types" (this is amusing since much of the crew is

Japanese) that his program is ecologically sound because he "recycles" and finds ways to avoid waste. Jane asks Gale, "[W]hat kind of feed do you use?" Gale is thrilled with this question and quite proud of his recycling program. He tells Jane: "We got recycled cardboard and newspaper. We got by-products from potato chips, liquor distilleries, sawdust, wood chips. We even got by-products from the slaughterhouse—recycling cattle right back into cattle. Instant protein" (Ozeki 1998, 258). Jane asks Gale if he worries about mad cow disease. Gale replies that he "[w]ouldn't know" about that. This is America not Great Britain.[5] Gale is nonplussed. In fact his only additional reply to Jane is that there is no worry because all the parts recycling is "all done local" (258).

Gale warns us that he has even more exciting news ahead:

> "I got one more for you, but you ain't going to like it." Behind him, dominating the center of the pen, was a towering bulldozed mound, which rose about the sea of cattle. The mound was alive with flies. He pointed to it with his thumb. "See that? . . . Out one end and in the other. Now, talk about fast turnaround. . . . It's recycling, only it's recycling animal by-products. You gotta understand the way feedlots work. The formulated feed we use is real expensive, and the cattle shit out about two-thirds before they even digest it. Now, there's no reason this manure can't be recycled into perfectly good feed. . . . Feed the animals shit, and it gets rid of the waste at the same time. That's two birds with one stone." (Ozeki 1998, 260)

We have doubly efficient recycling: the recycling of the cattle's own leftover body parts and a recycling of their own excrement. Gale also brags about how scientific his practices are: "It's a changing field—there's scientific developments in feed technology happening all over American, all the time" (Ozeki 1998, 259). He can't wait to give an example of how his farm reflects that current state of science in the cattle industry. Two of his state-of-the-art practices are his use of plastic hay to give the cattle something to chew on without wasting the real stuff (it saves a bundle) and the use of concrete in feed: "High in calcium, and the cows in the *tests* put on weight thirty percent faster than normal feed, and the meat was more tender and juicy" (259).[6]

So who is doing this *testing*, this cattle science? Who thinks recycling cattle and manure and feeding plastic hay and cement are good

---

[5] Unbeknownst to Ozeki her 1998 book is foreshadowing the 2003 and now 2005 mad cow scare in North America.

[6] My emphasis.

ideas? Of course there is the obvious, those that directly profit from increased output and decreased input—the cattle industry. But Gale is proud to tell us that there are outside, "objective" interests that engage in this testing and sanction these practices, interests that one would think would operate in our, the consumer's, best interest. Gale is quick to tell us "United States Department of Agriculture" is responsible for the testing and results and the approval of these methods (Ozeki 1998, 259).

Gale's feedlot also uses hormone additives to fatten the beef up. When asked what he was adding to the feed, he replies it is a product called Synovex. "'It's a growth hormone. Perfectly legal. You give the heifers Synovex-H and the steers get Synovex-S.' 'What's in it, do you know?' He looked at me with scorn. 'Estradiol, testosterone and progesterone. All natural'" (Ozeki 1998, 257). "All natural" and manufactured by a pharmaceutical company. Estrogenizing substances and testosterone are common additives to cattle feed and are also commonly given through ear shunts. If you are lucky enough to receive the *American Livestock Supply* catalog in the mail (I am, and Synovex-Plus is on sale this month) you see that you can quite readily order for your cow, and pretty cheap at that, what you need a doctor's visit, a prescription, and health insurance to obtain for yourself. What is too dangerous for you to go to the drug store and pick up over the counter is perfectly acceptable for you to consume in the way of your steak. The irony is that the American image of consuming steak as a sign of male virility may, through the use of estrogen in cattle, be one of the causes of declining sperm counts in U.S. men. It really is in the meat.

Gale also uses illegal substances in his cattle, though he denies this. Gale uses DES, *diethylstilbestrol*, one of the earliest synthetic estrogens, in his feed. DES was commonly used in livestock production as a growth enhancer until it was banned in the 1970s. DES was also routinely used during pregnancy for women to prevent miscarriage, though there was little evidence that it was effective. It was also used as a "feed supplement" along with their prenatal vitamins for women with no risk of miscarriage. It was claimed that DES would produce bigger, healthier babies. Women who took DES are at higher risk of breast cancer. Female children born of mothers who used DES frequently have misshapen uteruses that make conception and carrying a child to term difficult. They also suffer from a rare and frequently fatal form of vaginal cancer that can strike as early as age fourteen, clear cell adenocarcinoma. Male children of mothers who took DES can have misshapen genitalia. Furthermore, there is speculation that the effects of DES are being felt in a third generation: granddaughters of women who took

DES have a greater risk of infertility and cancer. The poisoning of families for three generations? It sounds like fiction, but is painfully real.

Our character Gale is using DES as a routine part of his feed program and this is where the horror of Ozeki's narrative lies. Rosie, Gale's very little sister and doted upon companion, is physically "precocious." Suzuki and Oh, Jane's camera crew, realize this early when they are filming Gale and Rosie together. They insist that Jane come to their room to see a clip from the day's filming at the feedlot. Dave, their driver/rebel agricultural student is with them while they watch. In the clip Gale is holding Rosie in his arms.

> "Oh God," said Dave in a low voice. I looked at him. He was staring at the screen, so I looked back too, but it was the same frame as before—the man's callused hand clasping the little girl's body. "What . . .?" I asked. "What is it?" "She's . . . precocious," Dave said, and it sounded like a dirty secret, a cruel joke that I still didn't get. Rosie was hardly precocious. Slow, perhaps even dumb. . . . "No, not her personality," said Dave, shaking his head impatiently. "Her development. Here." He clasped his hands to his chest.

Dave explains that the condition is called premature thelarche, that is, premature puberty.

> "I read about cases in Puerto Rico. Precocious puberty. These little girls with estrogen poisoning. They thought it was some kind of growth stimulants in the meat or milk or poultry. I think they suspected DES." "Well, it is still easy to get down there. Some of the girls were just babies, like a year old, with almost fully developed breasts. Some of them were even boys." "What happened?" "Not much. There was this one doctor who tried to get the FDA to do tests, which ended up half-assed and inconclusive. But the media attention was enough to scare off the farmers from using the drugs, and after a while the symptoms just slowly regressed when the kids stopped eating the contaminated foods. But not before a lot of them developed cysts in their ovaries . . . and of course there's the danger of cancer too." "Do you think it is in the meat?" I asked, still looking at Rose. "It's gotta be that feedroom, something she picks up there." (Ozeki 1998, 269–70)

Jane is especially concerned about DES. She suspects that her mother took DES when she was carrying her and at this point Jane, who had had fertility problems in the past, is pregnant and concerned about encountering a substance as dangerous as DES. She and all the crewmembers were covered in white dust from the feedroom when they left. Gale and Rosie were exposed to this on a daily basis.

The crew confronts Bunny with their suspicions. At first she gives them little credence, but eventually tells them to come in the evening with the camera. The crew films Rosie in her sleep. Her nightgown is pulled up and her face hidden. We see an adult body, complete with full breasts and pubic hair, on a five year old. The crew's suspicions are correct. Rosie is experiencing hormone poisoning and Bunny concurs that it is likely from the illegal use of DES.

At this point, Jane has the opportunity to reveal the ignorance constructed by the cattle industry and their supporters: the USDA, pharmaceutical companies, and lobbyists. Jane has a miscarriage resulting from her own in-utero DES exposure. While she is in the hospital, Ueno, the executive from Japan in charge of the BEEF-EX account and *My American Wife!* watches the footage from the Dunn and Son feedlot and finds that Takagi-Little is not portraying beef in the positive light he thinks she should. He fires her from her job and destroys all her footage.

Jane has kept copies of all her filming and begins to edit a documentary on Rosie, DES, the use of hormones in beef production, and the horrors of the feedlot. She comes up with a brilliant piece of work that she intends on doing nothing with besides sending it to Bunny Dunn and her friends Dyann and Lara from her lesbian vegetarian show. She returns to her apartment after visiting lover Sloan. She finds numerous notes shoved under her door, her phone ringing and twenty-seven messages on her machine. Bunny had leaked the story to the press. All the major U.S. and foreign presses had called. As had the USDA and the FDA. Her story and documentary are a sensation. Ultimately pieces of her documentary of the Dunn and Son feedlot, which was in part the story of Rosie, are aired on all major networks and the full documentary is picked up by a cable network.

Like Ozeki, Jane Takagi-Little ends up actively doing away with ignorance and constructing knowledge in its wake. She forced the apathetic public that is overwhelmed by the glut of bad information to hear this information. She forced them out of their ignorance. She also forced the USDA and the FDA to confront their roles as perpetuators of practices that have the potential to harm the public who funds their agencies and to whom these agencies have a moral responsibility. The public is able to see that these agencies are working not with the best interest of the public in mind, but with the interests of industry.

What makes Ozeki's work so powerful and what makes science fiction so powerful in general is that it reaches deeper into us than a random news story. We come to identify with Jane, Rosie, Bunny, and many of Ozeki's other characters. In our identification with Jane we become like documentarians, carefully looking for the truth in Ozeki's story, finding the uncovering of ignorance. We become enraged at the abuses that led to Rosie's tiny adult body. We become appalled at our own naïveté and compliance with what could be part of our destruction. We come to know because Ozeki takes us on a path through science fiction to knowledge that is hard to travel in the real world. Science fiction creates for us a world that feels coherent, where claims about corrupt corporations, governments, and social systems make sense to us in a way that is too difficult to process otherwise. Because of this, they get under our skin. We begin to worry about them, think about them, and consider that in many cases there is truth in the narrative, whether it be oblique truths about the potential ramifications of our present course on the future or truths rooted in the here and now that have horrific consequences. We thus are able to believe, to absorb information from the outlets that might have been too overwhelming for us, and to perhaps begin to act. Science fiction narratives like Ozeki's become a call to action both intellectually and politically and are essential to liberatory epistemology-of-ignorance projects. They become essential for creating new kinds of knowledge and new kinds of lives: lives that are not subject to the whim of corrupt governments, overzealous scientists funded by corporate greed, agribusiness that acts purely for profit, lobbyists who are amused by our deception; lives in which we are actors in the construction of our knowledge and communities.

REFERENCES

Diethelm, Pascal A., Jean-Charles Rielle, and Martin McKee. 2005. "The Whole Truth and Nothing But the Truth: The Research that Philip Morris Did Not Want You to See." *Lancet* 366, no. 9479:86–92.

Frye, Marilyn. 1983. *The Politics of Reality: Essays in Feminist Theory.* Trumansburg, NY: Crossing Press.

Irigaray, Luce. 1985a. *This Sex Which Is Not One*. Ithaca, NY: Cornell University Press.

———. 1985b. *Speculum of the Other Woman*. Ithaca, NY: Cornell University Press.

Marcus, Alan I. 1994. *Cancer from Beef: DES, Federal Food Regulation and Consumer Confidence*. Baltimore, MD: Johns Hopkins University Press.

Mills, Charles. 1997. *The Racial Contract*. Ithaca, NY: Cornell University Press.

Ozeki, Ruth. 1998. *My Year of Meats*. New York: Penguin Books.

Proctor, Robert N. 1995. *Cancer Wars: How Politics Determines What We Know and Don't Know About Cancer*. New York: Basic Books.

Tuana, Nancy. 2004. "Coming to Understand: Orgasm and the Epistemology of Ignorance." *Hypatia* 19:194–232.

Intervention 1

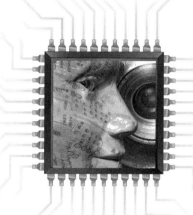

How to Do Things with Ideas

L. TIMMEL DUCHAMP

Doing Things with Ideas

Last night after reading the first three chapters of Gore Vidal's *Inventing a Nation: Washington, Adams, Jefferson*, a mannered essay on the framing of the U.S. Constitution, I experienced a moment familiar to science fiction writers. To depict this moment a cartoonist would draw an image of a woman holding a copy of the book, a finger marking her place and a light bulb glowing over her head. Thomas Jefferson, Vidal remarks, "had a wild attachment, at times, to radical sentiments" (2003, 79). One of the "radical sentiments" Vidal mentions is Jefferson's advocacy of creating a *tabula rasa* for government and legal institutions every twenty years:

> Jefferson . . . believed—uniquely—that this world belongs, solely, to the present generation. Hence, every twenty years or so, new laws should be promulgated at a constitutional convention. A grown man, he noted in his best biblical parable style, should not be forced to wear a boy's jacket. With characteristic tact, James Madison, who had plainly found one constitutional convention quite enough for a single lifetime, pointed out the impossibility of achieving a viable republic if its laws were to be periodically set aside in favor of new ones. In fact, so disturbed was he by Jefferson's metaphysical—even existential—notions that he made the case against too frequent conventions in the Federalist papers. (2003, 15)

Just about any SF writer reading this would be caught up in a speculative fancy. Each writer's speculations would, of course, be highly particular to her imagination and ideological formation. But the *premise* on which to base an interesting speculation would be immediately visible to all: that is, a situation in which a country scraps all legal and governmental institutions at regular intervals and creates new ones, *ab ovo*.

This premise immediately struck me as generative of three possible kinds of stories. First, one could devise a fable in which a wholly imaginary society reinvents itself with every generation. Such a society might, ironically, operate in a highly rule-oriented way, following a host of unwritten traditions to guide itself peacefully through each generational uprooting. Or it might be a disorderly, contentious society in which blood is shed every time the government is reinvented. Second, one could construct a science-fictional future in which technology and social relations had evolved to enable continual political and legal reinvention, such that the society's philosophical, ethical, and aesthetic structures confirmed and explored every conceivable ramification of such institutionalized reinvention. For me, this would likely be the most interesting and challenging possibility for working out the premise. Third, one could create an alternative history—one in which Jefferson's idea deeply influenced the group of men known as "the framers." This alternative history would reinvent the politics and political imagination of the framers and project the consequences of adopting a policy of redesigning the government and legal institutions of the United States every twenty years. The result, I have no doubt, would be not only to illuminate issues that pass unremarked, but also to create an entirely different trajectory for the political history and philosophy and the social mores of the nineteenth-, twentieth-, and twenty-first-century United States.

Science fiction writers often share "ideas" with one another. But SFnal (science-fictional) premises themselves do not matter as much as the particular imagination of the writer deploying them. A dozen science fiction writers would likely come up with a dozen different notions for how to exploit the idea I took from Jefferson's complaint that "a grown man should not be forced to wear a boy's jacket." By Vidal's account, of all the framers, James Madison's political sentiments hewed closest to Jefferson's; he observes that Madison often wrote public arguments supporting Jefferson's positions. And yet Jefferson's argument in favor of continual political change and revolution disturbed Madison. I imagine that many people today would be unable to take such an anarchistic notion seriously, or if they did, would excoriate it as dangerous for many of the same reasons Jefferson's contemporaries did. When writers use controversial ideas as the premises of SF stories, their attitudes bear emphatically on how they deploy the ideas. Someone unable to take the idea seriously would write a spoof or satire that implicitly trivialized it, while a writer who took it seriously but disapproved of it would begin with the assumption that only dire consequences could result. Writers who hadn't yet made up their minds, however, would likely conduct a sort of thought experiment with it. The writer might try to discover the technological, economic, and social circumstances under which the premise might be made to work in a constructive way, or incorporate the premise into already known circumstances and see what the characters are inclined to make of it.

As a writer who draws heavily on feminist ideas and theory, I would likely seek to illuminate the differences such built-in responsiveness to change could make to the lives of women and the extent of women's engagement in the public sphere. In an alternative history, I might, for example, speculate that as increasing numbers of white males acquired political rights in the nineteenth century, the laws privileging property owners and corporations came to be eliminated—as well as the electoral college (which to this day prevails in its intended function of preserving the system from the onus of holding direct elections for the two highest offices in the U.S., so that—as Vidal notes—a Supreme Court justice in 2000 could righteously insist that the Constitution does not endow any American citizen with the right to vote for president) (2003, 137). And then I would go on to imagine what a difference the mid-nineteenth-century surge of feminism would have made to the political and legal history of the U.S. No doubt women would have acquired the vote decades earlier, the conflict with the South would likely have come to a head much earlier (and the Union might even have broken apart in the second decade of the nineteenth century), and Reconstruction (presuming the conflict with the southern states, confronted earlier, still resulted in Civil War) would certainly have taken an altered trajectory. And likely there would never have been a Gilded Age at all.

In short, the alternative history I might craft from such a premise would not envision a history dominated by the same basic players overlaid with a few nonstructural changes, but a radically different world: a world that would be most interesting for what it could show us about how the aspects of our system that we take as givens have never been inevitable, but can be regarded as unnecessary baggage weighing us down simply because it's never occurred to us that we might rid ourselves of it and be that much stronger and freer without it. I would probably call on the thinking of interesting legal scholars like Patricia

Williams and Kimberle Crenshaw to give me ideas about which laws it would be interesting to jettison. I'd no doubt spend a lot of time reading the history of women in the early republic. And of course I'd do some refresher reading in feminist political theory.

Although on the most basic level my alternative history would have to work as an engaging story of characters caught up in dramatic conflict, the extent to which it offered provocative ideas would depend on the depth and breadth of the extrapolation of my theoretical speculation. This would be true for any science fiction writer creating an alternative history premised on Jefferson's idea, regardless of the writer's ideological position and the character of their theoretical speculation.

In addition to the idea and the writer's imagination and access to theory, one other important factor comes into play in the creation of SF: the formal structures and conventions of the genre. Every text is subject to the narrative constraints of form, upon which depend its intelligibility as well as its aesthetic quality. Like all other writers, SF writers must negotiate the narrative forms of their genre, striving to imaginatively exploit and expand the potential of the narrative forms rather than be constrained by the limitations of them. Some (though not all) make conscious decisions about which narrative forms to use and how to stretch or alter the limits of their previous uses. The point in the process at which writers become conscious of the formal aspects of the work in progress varies enormously from writer to writer. SF writers frequently talk the tradecraft of narrative techniques, but I've yet to hear other writers discuss this particular subject, and so I can only speak of my own experience.

Taking the Idea into the Subjunctive Tense

Although interest in an SFnal idea or premise drives every story I write, I seldom begin the process of writing the story with the idea itself consciously in mind. Typically a story begins when I hear a distinct voice speaking a sentence or three in my head. The style and tone of the narrative are thus implicit from the first. The first sentences I write lead to my "hearing" more sentences, and almost at once a world begins to be constructed, the world already implicit in the sentences. The SFnal idea itself tends to emerge within the first two or three paragraphs. It is almost always an idea that previously occurred to me, often only a few days before I began writing the story. Once I have written two or three pages, the construction of the story becomes a great deal more conscious. I may question my unconscious selection of certain formal choices, for instance, whether the narrative should be in the first person or third person, whether it should be written in present or past tense, whether it needs a frame or even multiple frames, and so on. And I will begin to think in extremely concrete terms about the unfolding of the premise in the world the story has brought into existence.

On the morning of May 3, 1997, the day before I began writing "Living Trust" (first published in *Asimov's SF*, Feb 1999), a Reuters news item posted on the Internet caught my attention. The item cited an article in *The New Scientist* describing research that had been done on imprinted genes in mice. The study originated with the aim of discovering the reason that mammals are unable to reproduce parthenogentically from an unfertilized egg, the way other animals can. The research attempted to create "androgenetic" embryos that bore only paternal genes by transferring the DNA from two sperm to an egg from which its DNA has been removed, as well as "gynogenetic" embryos by similarly uniting the chromosomes from two unfertilized eggs. Although these embryos all had the correct number of chromosomes, in every case they died within days of being implanted in a mouse womb. The androgenetic embryos died because certain vital genes had been switched off by the father, while the gynogenetic embryos died because they had certain other but equally vital genes switched off by the mother. The researchers learned that imprinted genes that are switched on only when inherited from the mother are vital to the early development of the embryo proper, while the father's genetic legacy is necessary for the normal development of the placental tissues. This discovery that certain genes are switched on or off depending on whether they are from the mother or the father led the researchers to wonder if there are any other genes that operate in this way in mice.

What they discovered is that there *are*. They discovered this by creating a series of chimera, in which they experimented with different combinations of maternal and paternal genes. They discovered, most interestingly, that if mice chimera were created with mainly maternal genes, the mice grew enormous heads perched on tiny bodies, while mice chimera bearing mainly male genes grew into fetuses with huge bodies but tiny brains. The researchers next mapped the number of cells in six different parts of the brain containing only maternal or only paternal genes. And they discovered that maternal genes are accumulated in what are known as the "executive" parts of the brain—notably the frontal cortex, which is the seat of learning and planning, memory, consciousness, and thinking, while the paternal genes are accumulated in what is known as the "emotional" part of the brain—the hypothalamus and other parts of the limbic (or hind brain) system, which is important for behaviors that ensure survival, such as sex, eating, and aggression.

In my excitement, I reported some of this to a listserv dedicated to discussing feminist science fiction. One member commented that if a similar sort of gene-imprinting proved to be operating in humans, then sperm banks are on the wrong track since intelligence is considered the most important criterion for donors of sperm and physical attractiveness for donors of ova. Although I knew that geneticists had not yet studied whether intelligence in humans is passed on through the maternal line only, as a feminist and science fiction writer I was struck by how deeply embedded the notion of intelligence as inherited from the father is in our society. I could not remember ever having heard anyone question the presumption of sperm banks' choice of Nobel physicists as the most desirable donors.

On the next day, May 4, I wrote in my journal:

> Began a new SF story yesterday. Sketched out the general situation and science-fictional scenario this morning. Need to get hold of that *New Scientist* article—the one on transmission of genes that control brain functions in mice, such that maternal genes exclusively control cerebral cortex functions and paternal genes the brainstem functions. Plus I need to plow through the article on regenerative work on brain cells in a recent issue of *Science*—will have excellent sources for the science base of the story. (Another father-daughter story . . .)

On the following day, May 5, I wrote:

> Bulldog News carries *New Scientist* but didn't have the new issue yet. Actually, I can get started writing without it. (Though I'll need it when I've gotten to the point of Kate's looking at the videotapes & documents from the competing research teams.) Today I've been mainly accumulating a feel for the background—her relationship with her father, what she does with her time (& money), her father's house, & how he made most of his fortune (i.e., designing personalities for "computer assistants," particularly of the personal & professional sort.)

I wrote nothing more in my journal about this story except for a few notations indicating that I put it aside toward the end of May and picked it up again in late October. The file of notes for the story contain photocopies of journal articles and handwritten notes dated May, 1997, which confirm my recollection of going to the Health Sciences Library and reading the most recent textbook and journal literature on various types of strokes, their treatment, and prognosis. I knew exactly what medical conditions I needed for the story and therefore searched for the sort of neural catastrophe that would cause those conditions.

And so within one day of reading the Reuters report, the story had already taken a clear narrative shape. It featured a father-daughter relationship in which the richest man in the world, universally celebrated as one of the world's great geniuses and reviled for having put most teachers, lawyers, and doctors in the U.S. out of work, on learning of new research showing that maternal genes control the transmission of intelligence in humans, is devastated by the thought of not being able to pass on his brilliance to his own child.

Typically, once I've drafted the first few paragraphs of a new story, I sit down with a tablet of paper and a pen and stare at the wall and daydream about the characters and their world. The notes I take as I daydream range from sparse to elaborate, but most of the details I invent never make their way into the narrative. Similarly, most of what I learn when I read science articles serve more to inform the language I use in the story and the density of my own understanding of the concepts playing out in the narrative than to provide the kind of info-dumps that appeal to "hard SF" fans.

Often when I write a story—and this was the case with "Living Trust"—I confront my protagonist with an ethical problem and determine in advance how my protagonist will ultimately resolve it. I must then work out how, emotionally and intellectually, the protagonist arrives at that solution—thus tasking my imagination with breaking a new path through an unknown narrative wilderness. If I don't determine the decision in advance, my protagonist is likely to act in less interesting and mature ways than I want her to. Developing a train of thought and action in a character is more difficult than a nonwriter might guess; left to themselves, characters tend to behave the way most human beings do: deceiving themselves, repeating old patterns of behavior, and above all, going along and getting along with the status quo. By setting herself the task of getting to a desired outcome, the writer forces her imagination to go to places where it would not naturally choose to venture.

Kate's problem, in this story, is complex. Her father has suffered a stroke that has irrevocably damaged his cerebral cortex. Before she can make any decisions, she must determine her father's medical status. Even in the best of situations this can be difficult for the relatives of desperately ill people to do, since people in such circumstances tend to engage in heavy denial and doctors tend to lie to patients and their relatives. In the case of Kate's father, the neurophysicians attending him have a personal, financial stake in seeing Kate make a particular decision about her father's care, regardless of the outcome. Second, her father has left a living trust asking her to oversee an illegal research project and the illegal creation of an embryo clone of him so that the neurological stem cells of the embryo clone can be used to regenerate his brain. Kate realizes that if such a procedure succeeded she would be faced with the obligation to care for and nurture an infant's personality and mind in her father's middle-aged body. Her father has presumed that the blank slate of the regenerated brain would develop into a mind as brilliant as the one that the stroke wiped out. Kate is profoundly troubled by the request—appalled at this use of a cloned embryo, disturbed by the idea of an infant inhabiting her father's body, and uncertain whether she wants to take on such a heavy responsibility alone. Her true father will be gone, a virtual substitute left in his place.

For me, this story began with the wrenching image of a daughter attending her father's bedside, unable to dialogue with a man in a coma, his body hooked up to monitors and IV lines and a ventilator, charged by him with terrible, difficult decisions to make. Science and technology in this story reveal that gendered perceptions about the transmission of intelligence are not what everyone assumes—even as the same science and technology appear to offer a wealthy man obsessed with perpetuating his "genius" a means of getting around the unpleasant fact that same science first revealed. Such an SF story can not only speculate on what this use of technology would involve personally and morally, but also help us to imagine what it would mean emotionally to the person most closely involved; and it can also help us to see how the economic and moral structures of the medical research establishment as it exists in the future I've extrapolated would likely work when confronted with such a situation. SF stories can do this because science fiction, as Joanna Russ once put it, is written in the subjunctive tense. And the subjunctive tense, when used in conjunction with plausible characters in dramatic situations, can take the writer to places theory has not yet or possibly cannot ever go.

In writing "Living Trust," I found myself struggling against the pull of a narrative trajectory in which Kate accedes to her father's request. For one thing, my protagonist's being female created an especially gendered pressure for her to put aside her grief at losing her father and devote herself to nurturing an infant mind in a middle-aged body—for the sake of complying with his wishes and (for some readers, even more importantly) for the sake of allowing his "genius" a chance at resurrection. Kate's being the heir to her father's vast fortune further loaded the equation. I was warned that many readers would assume her "true" reason for her decision was her desire to become the richest person in the world. For another thing, SFnal biotechnologies that extend an individual's reach beyond death exercise a powerful fascination on readers, rendering the successful implementation of such technologies almost irresistible to the writer. Not surprisingly, not long after the story's publication I received email from a reader palpably angry at my protagonist's resistance, demanding to know *my* opinion of my protagonist's decision. The following redacted extraction of the message's gist makes the reader's anger at me for his sense of thwarted expectations explicit:

> Would you react like the selfish, stupid, arrogant Moralist Kate or would you respect the wishes of your father? I was afraid that your story was intended to be Anti-Biotech-anti-advancement-propaganda, 'cause that's what it looked like! If your opinion matches the one of Kate, I'd like to get involved into some discussion, 'cause my opinion nearly matches that of Kate's father. During the whole of the story it was totally obvious: that way of thinking can only come out of a woman's mind.

Creating a nonpolemical moral imaginary for explicating Kate's refusal to carry out her father's expensive but arguably immoral fantasy proved my greatest challenge in writing the story. The only way I found to meet this challenge was to show Kate painfully educating herself on the moral issues involved and negotiating a path shaped by love, grief, guilt, and moral complexity. I used the words "not surprisingly" above when I spoke of receiving an angry email because every time a writer goes against the hegemonic grain she can expect to catch flak. This is why, perhaps, stories feel as if they *want* to go in the direction that will make the majority of readers comfortable.

Contemporary feminist theory recognizes that political agency and action necessitate that one disentangle and intervene in complex networks and relations rather than focus on preserving the fictitious autonomy of the individual. This is one reason why science fiction offers an attractive medium for feminist thinking. Science fiction is not interested in individual psychology per se, but in the social and ethical complexities of change (especially when the change is technologically driven). And to the extent that it engages in "world-building," it depicts a complex social and political context with an explicitness rare in post-nineteenth-century literary fiction. That is to say, although science fiction takes profound interest in how individuals respond to change, at its richest it takes no interest in preserving the fiction that the individual is an autonomous entity (no matter how wealthy or brilliant he may be). It encourages us to imagine a dense emotional reality that abstract discussions about ethics and social and economic consequences do not.

What Theory Cannot Take into Account

Early feminist critics sought chiefly to refute misogynist assumptions about women. Christine de Pisan (fl. 1400), for instance, fought Aristotelian conceptions of women and engaged in open combat against the misogyny of the *The Romance of the Rose*. Later feminist critics and theorists have attended instead to the omission and trivialization of women's concerns and experience from and in every area of intellectual thought. As someone who has subscribed to *Hypatia: A Journal of Feminist Philosophy* from its inception, I can confidently assert that the repeated failure to account for human experience that lies outside that of the privileged white male traditionally taken for the norm represents a serious shortcoming for philosophy and social and political theory.

When ethicists or economists or sociologists calculate the costs of various choices likely to be enjoined by the implementation of a new technology or scientific discovery, they frequently omit significant aspects that either do not occur to them or seem insignificant because they involve emotions, which though intangible and difficult to predict, matter tremendously (even when they are not considered of importance in and of themselves). Theory and philosophy, of course, draw broad generalizations; the concrete, particular detail and the individual experience figure as corroborating examples rather than illuminating elaboration. But metaphorically, at least, the dismissal of emotional experience from theory mirrors the Cartesian split of mind and body.

Fiction that sets out to speculate on not only what sorts of social, economic, and moral consequences might result from a new technology or scientific discovery would fall flat if it refused to admit emotion into the story: readers expect fiction to create full-bodied characters—even when the fiction in question is science fiction. While the SF narrative focuses on the distilled emotional experience of a few human beings (at most), in the best SF, the emotional components of the story enhance the reader's understanding of the larger issues raised by the story rather than distract from them. The SF writer elaborates many of the same sorts of social, political, and economic structures as theorists do, but weaves them into the fabric of the story's world. The difference between fiction and philosophy or theory lies in the writer's insistence on fleshing out the experiment—making it personal, intimate, and emotionally authentic.

Obviously SFnal thought experiments can only be as interesting as the writers' scientific and theoretical understanding and the imaginative power with which they extrapolate what is known and understood to what is possible. But in the end, the SF writer's primary task is to make ideas flesh—to elaborate their implications, to make them emotionally real.

R E F E R E N C E S

Russ, Joanna. 1995. "Speculations: The Subjunctivity of Science Fiction." In *To Write Like A Woman: Essays in Feminism and Science Fiction*, 15–25. Bloomington: Indiana University Press. First published in *Extrapolation* 15, no. 1 (1973).

Vidal, Gore. 2003. *Inventing a Nation: Washington, Adams, Jefferson*. New Haven: Yale University Press.

Vines, Gail. 1997. "Where Did You Get Your Brains?" *New Scientist* 2080 (3 May, 1997): 34–39.

GENDERS

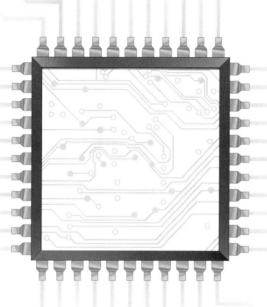

Pygmalion's Legacy: Cyborg Women in Science Fiction

JANET VERTESI

Pygmalion . . . carved his snow-white ivory
With marvelous triumphant artistry
And gave it perfect shape, more beautiful
Than ever woman born.

—OVID, *Metamorphosis*

The machine is us. . . .

—DONNA HARAWAY, *Simians, Cyborgs, and Women*

Pygmalion started it. The sculptor was so disgusted with local women that, according to Ovid, he took matters into his own hands when it came to choosing a wife. And once he had crafted his perfect woman from a block of ivory, how could he help but fall in love with his creation? When Venus granted his lovesick prayers, his art crossed the border between marble and flesh, coming to life to brilliantly embody his dream of the feminine ideal. Today, technology provides the marble that modern Pygmalions use to shape their ideal women, crafting cyborg creations that blur the border between lifeless *techne* and living being. But while our current technical limitations may make building fully cybernetic beings physically impossible, the space of our fiction—like in Ovid's poem—ought to give us the freedom to build cyborg bodies however we like. In the realm of SF fantasy, therefore, the most fascinating questions about the cyborg are not technological but cultural: *just how do we choose to sculpt it?*

"[W]here does the machine end and the human begin?" asks critical theorist Donna Haraway in her famous "Cyborg Manifesto" (1991, 19). This chapter asks a different question: where does the machine end and the *woman* begin? And what cultural concepts of gender identity are implicit in the way we choose to sculpt the female machine? To address these questions, we will survey several classic images of the fictional cyborg woman—the gynoid[1]—with an eye to what identifies her as female both for her audience and her fellow characters. Our subjects are familiar from film, drama, and literature, and scholars in feminist Science and Technology Studies have already analyzed several of these cyborgs in depth to expose the tensions between technology and society that science fiction often explores.[2] But there is value in a surface approach as well. Surveying these familiar, even iconic images of cyborg women across the science fiction landscape, we see a common theme emerge in spite of differences in time, location, and even medium. This uniform and powerful image is so basic that it is almost taken for granted, pointing to an emerging archetype of the cyborg woman: as beautiful, sexual, and therefore powerful. When considered as "no more than meets the eye," gynoids in science fiction offer us a glimpse of our own feminine ideals, cultural constructions with repercussions in our nonfictional world.

The Birth of the Gynoid: Early Representations

"You are beautiful," Primus tells the lovely robotess Helena in Karl Capek's 1923 play, *R.U.R.*, when she wonders aloud, "I don't know what I am" (Capek 1961, 100). Visions of mechanical women from the early nineteenth century onward share this fundamental feature. Beauty defines them, provides them with an identity, and lets them easily replace the women who inspired their construction. And while it may be somewhat anachronistic to refer to pre-1960 gynoids as "cyborgs,"[3] they

---

[1] The term "gynoid," the feminization of "android," was coined by British science fiction writer Gwyneth Jones (Jones 1987), was further developed by science fiction writer Richard Calder, and is the title of one of artist Hajime Soryama's books in the "sexy robot" series (discussed below). For the purpose of this essay, "gynoids" are fictional female cyborgs.

[2] The interested reader may wish to browse Kirkup et al. 2000 for examples of such feminist critiques of the cyborg. In particular, Doane 2000 treats several of the same examples to probe the tensions between femininity and traditionally masculine technology.

do negotiate the organic and the mechanical in their manufactured bodies. They also provide the first clues to the female cyborg's femininity, clues which will be further developed in later twentieth-century science fiction.

As Primus suggests, beauty provides a sense of identity and purpose for Helena at Rossum's Universal Robots factory. While the company does manufacture drone "female Robots" ("There's a certain demand for them, you see. Servants, saleswomen, clerks. People are used to it" [Capek 1961, 27]), Helena is built separately in a special experiment to recall her dual namesake: Helen of Troy and the human girl, Helena Glory. She spends most of her time adorning herself, admiring her reflection—and rejecting the love-struck human suitors who unsuccessfully courted the "real" Helena (it seems there wasn't enough of her to go around). Helena may be unique among R.U.R.'s robots, but her story is similar to Hadaly's in the 1886 serial novel, *Tomorrow's Eve (Eve Future)*.

Hadaly (Persian for "ideal") is built by a fictionalized Thomas Edison, the paragon of inventors, but he modifies her for his friend Lord Ewald, who is in love with the beautiful but fallen Alicia Clary. Edison promises Ewald a being that will "no longer be a woman, but an angel; no longer a mistress but a lover; no longer reality, but the IDEAL!" (De l'Isle-Adam, 1982, 54). The men believe that Hadaly improves on Alicia's extraordinary beauty with the spiritual purity the girl lacks. But while the cyborg and the woman have completely different personalities, Ewald is easily fooled into taking Hadaly *for* Alicia, identifying her by her looks rather than by her colorful personality. And Edison also locates Alicia's identity in her beauty:

> I can capture the grace of her gesture, the fullness of her body, the fragrance of her flesh, the resonance of her voice, the turn of her waist, the light of her eyes, the quality of her movements and gestures, the individuality of her glance, all her traits and characteristics, down to the shadow she cast on the ground—*her complete identity, in a word*. . . . (De l'Isle-Adam 1982, 63–64)

Becoming "the ideal" woman, which only Edison's "Android" can do, may require a personality change, but the stable sense of Hadaly's identity—as Alicia's replacement and a being of worth and purpose—comes from her looks alone. Even Ewald has to admit, "the false Alicia

---

[3] The term "cyborg" was coined in 1960 (Clynes 1960).

seemed far more natural than the true one" (De l'Isle-Adam 1982, 194).

A similar fate awaits the saintly Maria in Fritz Lang's 1926 silent film, *Metropolis*, but in this case, the woman is too pure, not too sinful, to be useful to the men around her. In a complicated splicing experiment, the mad scientist Rotwang transfers Maria's appearance to his chrome-plated "Machine-Man," creating a melded mechanical woman who can carry out Johann Frederson's plan to destroy the underground working class. The resulting gynoid could not be more different than the human Maria in everything but her looks: she preaches destruction, tosses her hips provocatively, and is juxtaposed with the seven deadly sins, especially Lust. To test their creation, Frederson and Rotwang première her as an exotic dancer in front of a male audience in a saloon, where the men are captivated by her beauty and mesmerized by her unabashed and lascivious sexuality. The gynoid is deemed a success, convincing the pair that their plan will work. But the robot has not proven that she is anything like Maria: she has simply proven that she can use her beauty to exert power over men.

So beauty can identify the cyborg as a woman, sometimes one woman in particular, and, if wielded effectively, it can be the source of her power. But beauty can also distinguish the feminine from the machine. For example, in C. L. Moore's *No Woman Born* we meet Deirdre, an entertainer with legendary charm and grace who lost her organic body in a theater fire. A constructed metallic frame resurrects her, retaining only her original brain. Her former agent, John Harris, seesaws back and forth, debating with himself and her creator Maltzer whether she is human or machine:

> Deirdre was gone, and this was only machinery heaped in a flowered chair. Then the machinery moved, exquisitely, smoothly, with a grace as familiar as the swaying poise he remembered. The sweet, husky voice of Deirdre said,
> 'It's me, John darling. It really is, you know.'
> And it was.
> [. . .]
> She was still lovely—indeed, she was still Deirdre. . . . (Moore 1975, 205)

John's conceptual shift centers around Deirdre's beauty; when he sees only metal, the robot remains a robot, but when confronted with the familiar grace and ease, husky voice, and ringing laugh, he believes she is a woman: the most beautiful of women born. Confused by this dissonance, he shrugs, "She isn't human. . . . But she isn't pure robot either. She's something between the two" (Moore 1975, 219).

Deirdre cannot be conventionally beautiful—after all, she is only vaguely humanoid. But the human Deirdre was not a conventional beauty either. Her beauty was in her husky voice, her dancer's grace, and her ringing laugh. These features not only identify her to John as Deirdre, but also transform her from machine to *woman*. Although Maltzer worries that she will not be able to "compete" with other women because "she hasn't any sex. She isn't female any more," when Deirdre performs on stage for the first time after the fire, her audience resoundingly proves him wrong (Moore 1975, 218). While her *humanity* remains in question, thanks to her special kind of beauty, her *femininity* is not.

Developing the Gynoid: "Sexy Robots"

The beauty theme expands considerably to include extreme sexual desirability in later twentieth-century science fiction. A classic example is in the 1975 thriller *The Stepford Wives*. Written in the midst of the feminist movement, the film depicts a small town in which the men—all employed by the local biomechanical engineering firm—build perfected forms of their wives to replace the actual woman. The replacement wives are prettier than the originals, are only concerned with cooking and cleaning, and wear frilly, feminine clothes. They are also the complete sexual property of their husbands—as the main character, Joanna, witnesses when one husband grasps his wife's breasts in public, and a wife's moans during sex fill her house, ". . . as though [her husband] was God's gift to women!" When Joanna discovers that her best friend has also been replaced to look and act "like a TV commercial," she confides fearfully in a therapist: ". . . there'll be someone with my name and she'll cook and clean like crazy but she won't take pictures and *she won't be me*. She'll be like one of those robots in Disneyland!" Joanna is right: her replacement will be shallow, tamed, and domesticated, and without the photographer's eye that she holds central to her own sense of identity. But it will be beautiful and sexy: a typical gynoid.[4]

_____

[4] The star-studded remake of the *Stepford Wives* (2004) changes the thriller into a comedy; the Wives were once successful women, leading stressful lives at the top of the business world with little time for their geeky husbands. They are controlled by computer implants in an elaborate set-up established by the first woman of Stepford, in an added plot reversal that changes the original "moral of the story."

Beauty and sexual desirability are central to identifying the cyborg women in Ridley Scott's 1982 cyberpunk movie, *Blade Runner*.[5] We meet three gynoids in this movie, all products of the Tyrell Corporation: the pleasure model Pris, the sexy killer Zhora, and the submissive Rachel. The company is supposed to make replicants who are "More Human than Human," and too "perfect" to be real. But while the male replicants are also supposed to be perfect, they do not all *look like* "the perfect man": Leon, for example, is not particularly muscular, hairy, handsome, or sexy. Clearly, physical attractiveness is only a crucial characteristic of cyborg women.[6]

Deckard's police chief describes the killer Zhora as "Beauty and the Beast: she's both!" Deckard first meets her in a crowded bar, where she is naked and dancing erotically with a snake, a symbol of male virility. Deckard is startled and aroused by her beauty and continued nudity throughout his scenes with her: sensations that he must suppress in order to carry out his mission to kill her. Once Zhora is "retired," we meet her tall, lanky, blonde friend Pris, whose image alternates between waif and whore. Pris dresses like a sex worker, with black, gartered stockings, a short, tight skirt, netting, and lycra. Her cocked head and languid gait, her former role as a "pleasure model," and her uninhibited kiss with Roy Batty project an overt and available sexuality. She charms J. F. Sebastian into to taking her in, and twice she catches and holds human men between her thighs in a gesture ripe with erotic symbolism. And while she may not seem so to us with her pale face and black raccoon mask across her eyes, Sebastian insists—continuing the familiar gynoid motif—that she is "perfect" and "beautiful."

We will return to *Blade Runner* momentarily to review Rachel's story, but in the meanwhile, we won't have to wait long for cyborg sex appeal in the 1996 anime film *Ghost in the Shell*. Major Motoko Kusanagi appears at the opening of the film as an asexual human shape on top of a building; her face and hairstyle are more or less androgynous. However, the animators clearly want us to understand two things right off the bat: she is a cyborg and she is female. As we zoom in on her for the first time, she checks the wiring at the base of her neck and

---

[5] *Blade Runner* has been the subject of numerous analytical works; three relevant to the following discussion include Doane 2000, Scott 2004, and Myman 2004 .

[6] Replicant men may be strong with honed senses, but so are their female counterparts; this attribute is more likely associated with the superior intelligence and heightened senses of the mechanical, not the human, element of the cyborg. There do seem to be, however, a few "types" of cyborg men: see, for example, Oehlert 1995.

then—for no apparent reason—takes off all her clothes, revealing a curvy, full-busted, white female body.[7] And this body is not unique. In the same movie, during the opening credits, we are shown a naked cyborg under construction with the exact same characteristics. Even the evil Puppet Master, although possessed by a sexless ghost with a male voice, always appears as a nude, white, busty, curvy blonde. In fact, the film *Ghost in the Shell* is only a small part of a phenomenon that extends beyond the cartoon; the hypersexualized, powerful female machine spans posters and comic book storyboards, which portray Major Motoko as a combination of voluptuous woman and alien machinery, sometimes even writhing atop a bed of wires and circuits.[8]

Major Motoko may be a force to be reckoned with, but she still has the kind of body that men can only dream (or draw) about.[9] The sexually charged art of Hajime Sorayama is another perfect example. A self-described "super realist" primarily concerned with the eroticized female body, Sorayama's most famous (and unforgettable) works are *Sexy Robots* (1983) and *Gynoids* (1993). Both collections mix the highly sexualized and beautiful female ideal with the mechanical and fetishistic, exalting the gynoid in pornographic imagery. By the late twentieth century, as these extreme examples suggest, the crux of the gynoid's female and cyborg identity has shifted: she must not only be beautiful, she must be sexy as well.

The Power of Sex: Submission or Motherhood

Beautiful, often overtly sexy, with idealized bodies and exaggerated sexual characteristics: these features define the gynoids we have seen so far as both cyborg and feminine. But while these features may be *sufficient* to identify the cyborg as a woman, are they also *necessary*? Surely some fictional cyborg-builder could just as easily have given their creation

---

[7] In a "one-two-three-punch," Motoko then goes on to leap off the top of the building.

[8] Examples may often be found on the cartoon's website (Manga Entertainment, http://www.manga.com) and the comic book site (Darkhorse, http://www.darkhorse.com).

[9] Another option may be to hire a beauty queen, as with Seven of Nine from the *Star Trek: Voyager* television series, played by a 1990 Miss America finalist. Her Borg uniform highlights her shapely figure, but as her implants are removed Seven must learn how to behave as an individual and as a human being. Although the strong and intelligent Captain Janeway could serve as a role model for a different example of feminine power, Seven regularly appears in a slinky silver catsuit and high heels, emphasizing her embodiment of ideal and sexualized femininity.

small breasts, a full stomach, and mousy hair. And male cyborgs in science fiction, from Leon and Roy in *Blade Runner* to, arguably, the creature in *Frankenstein*, may be strong or dangerous but do not *require* the extent of sexualization that their female counterparts clearly do.[10] So what is it about the female cyborg that forces these ideals upon her constructed body? This pattern cannot simply be attributed to misogynist creators; while the above gynoids are constructed by men or male-dominated corporations and (with the important exception of C. L. Moore) brought to life by male writers and directors, most express a reverence for the gynoid and grant her considerable power. Instead, the "sexy robot" teaches us another lesson about an essence of femininity, one that comes to the fore in the films *Cyborg 2*, *Blade Runner*, and *Cyborg 3*.

The main character of *Cyborg 2* is Cash Reese, another beautiful and desirable cyborg woman, played by a young Angelina Jolie (who would later achieve sex symbol status as the curvaceous virtual woman, Lara Croft). In the film, Cash is a master markswoman and martial artist with a strong take-charge attitude. But towards the end of the movie, Cash and her partner have sex for the first time. *After this point*, she weakens. By a twist of plot, she is forced to watch *him* fight the film's archenemy and is not allowed to intervene, although we know that she is a better fighter than he is. As they escape together, the armed men who confront them threaten to kill her partner unless Cash puts down her gun; in a reversal of roles—and a gesture of symbolic castration—Cash complies. The parting shot of the film shows her, young as ever, stroking her partner's aging forehead in a lush garden in front of their house in the Free Zone. Stepford-style, she has replaced her tight tank tops and jeans for loose, ruffled shirts and long, earth-tone skirts. What has happened to the sexy gynoid here?

This story repeats itself in *Blade Runner*. Before she learns that she is a replicant, Rachel seems square and angular: her shoulder-pads betray an hourglass figure, but also accentuate her sharp features and tight hairstyle. When she learns that she is a replicant, she takes a more active role, even saving Deckard's life, but also starts dressing in soft

---

[10] A purposeful exception is Davy, the blond-haired, blue-eyed computer-programmed "lovely limb of the house" in the short story "An Old-fashioned Girl" (1974). Davy embodies the characteristics normally reserved for female cyborgs, in what author Joanna Russ explicitly calls "a role-reversal": he serves as a "pleasure model" for the narrator, who calls him "The most beautiful man in the world," asserts repeatedly that "Davy's soul is in Davy's beauty," and discusses the "popular misconception that in the past . . . women had been to men what Davy was to me" (Russ 1995, 234).

furs with halo-shaped collars. Later, at Deckard's piano, she transforms, letting her hair down into Pre-Raphaelite curls in a classic film gesture of female sexuality. Now no longer square and robotic, she is *female*: beautiful, soft, and sexually available. Deckard, too, is no longer dismissive. He tries to kiss her, resulting in an uncomfortable scene in which the once-confident Rachel is trapped and forced to succumb to him. From this point on, she is passive, a weakened possession, even peacefully sleeping at home as Deckard battles the replicants at the climax of the film. Her sexual submission to him relegates her to another familiar female role: like Cash, she is the prize with which the hero will retire.

Cash and Rachel demonstrate that, while the gynoid must have extreme sex appeal in order to be recognizably female, she must stay aloof and unavailable in order to maintain her power. In fact, succumbing to sex may not only subjugate the gynoid: it can also completely destroy her. For example, in a scene from *Cyborg 2*, we see a beautiful blonde cyborg engaged in passionate sex for the simulcast pleasure of a male audience in a corporate boardroom. As she reaches orgasm, she physically explodes, purportedly to demonstrate of the company's new explosive agent that can be placed in their cyborgs' systems. We could not ask for a stronger association: sex equals disempowerment and even death for the gynoid.[11] No wonder cyberpunk heroines resort to drastic action to avoid this fate; for example, *Neuromancer*'s Molly runs away when she feels her affair with Case is "taking the edge off my game," while Erythrina in "True Names" dissolves her physical body into the Other Plane [12] (Gibson 1984, 257; Vigne 2001).

But is this equation always so strict? Picking up Cash's story in *Cyborg 3* suggests that the gynoid may have another option. In *Cyborg 3*, Cash is played by a different actress: older, with softer features (although she was supposed to "look twenty-two years old forever.") She is still lovely, but is no longer sexy, dresses in loose clothes, and does not

---

[11] This certainly begs the Freudian relationship between sex and death, and suggests another path of analysis beyond the scope of this paper. But for the moment, it seems that the gynoid may embody both at once: she may wield her sex appeal to kill (perhaps most brilliantly exemplified by Austin Powers's "fem-bots," with their laser-shooting breasts), or she may, like Hadaly, just sleep in a coffin.

[12] Erythrina also escapes Roger Pollack's sexual possession by turning out to be, in reality, an elderly woman. It will probably be noted that these heroines with their technologically extended organic bodies are not the primary focus of this paper; while their stories share common themes, this paper focuses on constructed female machines, to explore just how and in whose image we choose to build them.

play a love interest role: were it not for the dialogue, it would be difficult to identify her as a cyborg! But by some strange twist of programming, Cash becomes pregnant. "You're not just a cyborg any more: no, no, you're a *creator*," her doctor states, and her friend Alexia (another former "pleasure model") covers her provocative clothes self-consciously: "she's the first of our kind to become one of their kind. We are all part-creator because of her. . . . She is living proof that we are not just a machine." As a reproducer and "creator," Cash has passed out of her sexy cyborg role into the role of mother.

When Alexia asks her how it feels to hold her "baby" in her hands, Cash smiles like a proud parent and says, "There's no program for it!" But it may actually be a "program" for gynoids who can rely on reproduction as the sign of their femininity. While Hadaly and Helena, both "future Eves,"[13] could only boast possible or projected reproduction, Cash's proven ability to reproduce makes her a feminine mechanical being beyond any doubt. And this puts her in a different category of female sexual power: she can now derive her strength from reproduction instead of unattainable yet desirable sexiness. Motherhood trumps the "sexy robot."

Conclusions: The Machine Is Us

Surveying beauty product advertisements, Marshall McLuhan tackled what he called "the love-goddess assembly line" in his *The Mechanical Bride*:

> When the same patterns recur, [the folklorist and anthropologist] are alerted to the possibilities of similar underlying dynamics. No culture will give popular nourishment and support to images or patterns which are alien to its dominant impulses and aspirations. . . . There will be many variations, but they will tend to be variations on certain recognizable themes. And these themes will be the 'laws' of that society, laws which will mould its songs and art and social expression. (McLuhan 1951, 96)[14]

---

[13] Both Hadaly and Helena are identified as new Eves—Helena at the close of the play, and Hadaly throughout the novel. While an analysis of this significant epithet deserves its own essay, it is important to note at least three ways in which this description has valence. First, the two are seen as the first of a new generation of future beings; second, they are created by men "playing God"; third, like all of the gynoids under analysis in this piece, they are made *for* men *by* men as their complement, ideal, or helpmeet.

[14] While McLuhan's views are often critiqued by academics in the social and cultural studies studies of technology, the idea of a "love goddess assembly line" and "the mechanical bride" are certainly relevant to the current discussion.

In Science and Technology Studies, with reference to cyborg women in particular, both Anne Balsamo (analyzing mostly nonfictional female cyborg bodies) and Jennifer González (analyzing historical images of cyborg women), take up the cry that cyborgs reflect our cultural symbolisms and ideals, our social values, and our states of being (Balsamo 1996; González 1995; Winner 1986). And Donna Haraway is even more explicit: "The machine is us," she insists (1991, 180). There are indeed recurring patterns and themes when it comes to the science fiction gynoid: time and time again, in books, plays and movies alike, female cyborgs are always, by definition, beautiful and sexually desirable, whether in their graceful or erotic gaits, their husky voices, or their large breasts. Their sexiness, in particular, seems to be the source of their power; when sexually dominated or demystified, gynoids become as powerless and possessed as the Stepford wives, Rachel, or Cash at the end of *Cyborg 2*. These are surely the "laws" that both describe and govern how we choose to sculpt our gynoids, and as such, they have consequences for the nonfiction category of our lives as well. For if the beautiful and sexual (either aloof or maternal) female body defines the cyborg woman in our science fiction, what about real women?

The gynoid first of all reinforces the common Science and Technology Studies theme that technology does not *change* a social environment, but instead *strengthens* and *enforces* preexisting gender roles (Wajcman 1996). While science fiction may offer us an imaginative realm free from technical constraints, we are clearly not free from social constraints in that space; instead of using fictional technology to resist body-centered gender ideologies, we continue to construct the ideal female form (Bordo 2000). This construction, further, takes place in both the virtual *and* the real world.[15] Indeed, there is a clear correlation

---

[15] Recent studies by Turkle, Hawthorne, and Fujimura argue that social relations in cyberspace, too, are little different from real-life (RL) relations. Indeed, many of the gynoid's characteristics are properties of virtual women or Avatars; certainly, within months of their virtual newscaster's launch, ABC had to decline countless marriage proposals on her behalf. And in 2000, Sega promoted Ulala (read, "Ooh La La"), the short-skirted, halter-topped dancing star of their game *Space Channel 5*, to the role of Company "Digital Spokeswoman." Sega's promotional stints even brought their spunky star to life in stage performances, although they decided to pay one girl to do the dance steps and another to provide the vocals (apparently, one computer-generated woman is better than two real ones). And of course, the infamous Lara Croft, star of the *Tomb Raider* video game series, garnered her share of attention for her large breasts, hot pants, and garterlike gun holster. Even before she was brought to life in blockbuster movies, whole internet sites were devoted to her fans trading digital images of Lara, posed

between the ideal proportions of the female cyborg body and those sought after by organic women: is it any surprise that the proportions of the Puppet Master's face are exactly the same as those of the ideal female face as pictured in the American Medical Association cosmetic surgery handbook?[16] As women line up by the hundreds for these elective surgeries, they both seek and fuel the very ideals of femininity that the gynoid re-presents.

But the gynoid may also help us to understand *why and with what consequences* we, her creators and subscribers, continue to feel the need to create "perfect," beautiful, or sexually augmented bodies. For if she is unable to reproduce, the gynoid's only other option is to become a sex object in order to assert both her femininity and power simultaneously. Without beauty, it is simply an efficient machine; made beautiful, she is feminine; without a sexual mystique, she is, like Rachel, Cash, or the Stepford wives, helpless; armed with a "hot" body, she is, like Motoko or Pris, powerful and potentially dangerous. There are consequences for this view of femininity in the nonfiction world. First of all, the gynoid's "sex = disempowerment" equation points to a persistent cultural ideal denigrating the sexually possessed woman to a lower status of power than her male partner. And its inverse equation, "sexy = powerful," indicates that real women must (or, no less important, *feel they must*) subject themselves to this hypersexualization in order to assert their femininity and maintain a position of power at the same time. No wonder there is still such admiration for the cosmetic surgeon's knife, shortened hems, and high heels in the boardroom's "feminine" power suit. But further, the gynoid shows us that the sex-equals-death feminine equation can be bypassed with recourse to proven reproductive ability.[17] This may be a relief to real-world mothers, but it may also present a tension that is exacerbated, not resolved, by reproductive technologies. If, unable to reproduce, women have no other cards to play to assert their femininity other than an unattainable sexiness, then this culturally reinforced ideal ought to be important when considering the use of medical technologies that either limit or augment female fertility.[18]

Penthouse style, in tiny bathing suits or leather strap dresses. Finally, gynoid pornography may have achieved dubious "new heights" in the October 2004 *Playboy* magazine, in a heavily illustrated article devoted to video game heroines (vol. 51, no. 1, 88–93).

[16] Compare *Ghost in the Shell* to Powell 1984, reproduced in Balsamo 1996, 60.

[17] This is an interesting *détournement* of Adele Clarke's study of postmodernity and reproduction: while postmodern women must become cyborgs in order to reproduce, postmodern cyborgs must reproduce in order to become women. See Clark 1995.

[18] This is not a plea for or against reproductive technology, but rather for a continued

So where does the machine end and the woman begin? A dominant theme persists over more than a hundred years of science fiction: the woman begins when the machine becomes beautiful and sexy—or a mother. Culturally at least, it seems there is still little more to femininity than meets the eye. While these powerful constructions exist, linking femininity with either sexual desirability or reproductive ability, science fiction writers, biomechanical engineers, and cosmetic surgeons alike will no doubt continue to work with this particular "love goddess assembly line," using their technical and artistic skills to play Pygmalion.*

REFERENCES

Balsamo, Anne. 1996. *Technologies of the Gendered Body: Reading Cyborg Women*. Durham: Duke University Press.

―――. 1992. "On the Cutting Edge: Cosmetic Surgery and the Technological Production of the Gendered Body." *Camera Obscura* 28 (1992): 206–37.

Blade Runner. 1982. Directed by Ridley Scott.

Bordo, Susan. 2000. "Hunger as Ideology." In *The Consumer Society Reader*, edited by Juliet Schor and Douglas Holt, 99–114. New York: New Press.

Capek, Karl. 1961. "R.U.R. (Rossum's Universal Robots)" (1923), in *R.U.R. and The Insect Play*, translated by P. Selver. Oxford: Oxford University Press.

Clark, Adele. 1995. "Modernity, Postmodernity & Reproductive Processes ca. 1890–1990." In *The Cyborg Handbook*, edited by C. H. Gray, 139–55. New York: Routledge.

Clynes, M. and N. Kline. 1960. "Cyborgs and Space." *Astronautics*, Sept. 1960.

Cyborg 2. 1993. Directed by Michael Schroeder and Sharad Patel.

Cyborg 3. 1994. Directed by Michael Schroeder.

De l'Isle-Adam, Villiers. 1982. *Tomorrow's Eve* (*Eve Future*), translated by Robert Martin Adams. Chicago: University of Illinois Press.

Doane, Mary Ann. 2000. "Technophilia: Technology, Representation, and the Feminine." In Kirkup, *The Gendered Cyborg*, 110–21.

---

discussion of these and other hidden pressures women face when making decisions about reproductive technology or, for that matter, plastic surgery. Other studies of cultural ideals of gender at play in decisions surrounding reproductive technologies include, for example, Rapp 2000; Fausto-Sterling 2000, or Oudshoorn 2005. On plastic surgery, see Balsamo 1992.

* My thanks to Shay David, Jofish Kaye, Kevin Lambert, Rachel Prentice, Catherine Vertesi, and Campbell Vertesi for their valued assistance in this chapter's revision; also to Diane Newell, whose seminar on gender and technology inspired an early version of of this paper in 1999.

Fausto-Sterling, Anne. 2000. *Sexing the Body: Gender Politics and the Construction of Sexuality*. New York: Basic Books.

Ghost in the Shell. 1996. Created by Masamune Shirow, directed by Mamoru Oshi.

Gibson, William. 1984. *Neuromancer*. New York: Ace Books.

González, Jennifer. 1995. "Envisioning Cyborg Bodies: Notes from Current Research." In *The Cyborg Handbook*, edited by C. H. Gray, 267–79. New York: Routledge.

Haraway, Donna. 1991. *Simians, Cyborgs, and Women*. New York: Routledge.

Jones, Gwyneth. 1987. *Divine Endurance*. New York: Arbor House.

Kirkup, Gill, et al., ed. 2000. *The Gendered Cyborg: A Reader*. New York: Routledge, 2000.

Metropolis. 1926. Directed by Fritz Lang.

Moore, C. L. 1975. "No Woman Born" (1944). In *The Best of C. L. Moore*, edited by Lester Del Rey, 200–242. New York: Nelson Doubleday.

Myman, Francesca. 2004. "Skirting the Edge: Costume, Masquerade, and the Plastic Body in Blade Runner." http://www.cyrune.com/PlasticBody.htm (September 29, 2004).

Oehlert, Mark. 1995. "From Captain America to Wolverine: Cyborgs in Comic Books, Alternative Images of Cybernetic Heroes and Villains." In *The Cyborg Handbook*, edited by C. H. Gray, 219–32. New York: Routledge.

McLuhan, Marshall. 1951. *The Mechanical Bride: Folklore of Industrial Man*. Boston: Beacon Press.

Oudshoorn, Nelly. 2005. *The Male Pill*. Durham: Duke University Press.

Ovid. 1986. *Metamorphosis*, trans. A. D. Melville. Oxford: World's Classics.

Powell, Nelson. 1984. *Proportions of the Aesthetic Face*. New York: Thieme Stratton.

Rapp, Rayna. 2000. *Testing Women, Testing the Fetus: The Social Impact of Amniocentesis in America*. New York: Routledge.

Russ, Joanna. 1995. "An Old-fashioned Girl" (1974). In *The Penguin Book of Erotic Stories by Women*, edited by Richard Glyn Jones and A. Susan Williams, 229–34. New York: Penguin.

Scott, Simon H. "Is *Blade Runner* a Mysogynist Text?" http://kzsu.stanford.edu/uwi/br/br-misog.html (September 29, 2004).

Sorayama, Hajime.1993. *The Gynoids*. Treville Co. Ltd.

———. 1983. *Sexy Robot*. Genko-She Publishing Co.

The Stepford Wives. 1975. Directed by Brian Forbes.

Wajcman, Judy. 1996. *Feminism Confronts Technology*. University Park: Pennsylvania State University Press.

Winner, Langdon. 1986. "Do Artifacts Have Politics?" In *The Whale and the Reactor: A Search for Limits in an Age of High Technology*, 19–39. Chicago: University of Chicago Press.

Vinge, Vernor. 2001. "True Names" (1981). In *"True Names" and the Opening of the Cyberspace Frontier*. New York: Tom Doherty.

Tepper's Republic: Feminist Separatism and the Question of Essence

EDRIE SOBSTYL

*M*ention the phrase "feminist science fiction," and many readers will think of science fiction (SF) with a feminine touch. Such SF might emphasize "soft" sciences like biology, ecology, and psychology, and involve a lot of nurturing and love of Mother Earth. In the 1970s and early '80s, feminist SF writers explored this ideal of feminine personality in many novels that are now regarded as classics. But in order to write convincingly about societies where such feminine character traits were dominant, these imaginary worlds had to be protected from masculine aggressiveness and promiscuity. The device of separatism—women living completely separately from men—was the mechanism many feminist novelists used to let their feminine worlds flourish. In separatist novels, women relied only on women to meet all of their needs, material, cultural, and sexual. In some feminist theories of this period, the separatism of these fictional worlds was promoted as a political goal for women. Beginning in the mid-1980s, however, many feminist theorists grew unhappy about putting stereotyped ideals of femininity at the heart of feminism. Feminists were so unhappy that we gave this problem a name: *gender essentialism*, the tendency to treat conventional attitudes about femininity as natural and necessary parts of the female personality. While feminists now strive to avoid gender essentialism, essentialist attitudes about women (and corresponding attitudes about men) remain problematic in feminism, as well as in popular culture and contemporary science.

The life sciences, from biology and genetics to evolutionary theory, are most noted for making essentialist claims about the different natures of women and men. But the idea that women and men are "naturally" suited for different social roles is much older. Feminist theorists have done a thorough job of documenting historical claims about the natural inferiority of women, from the ancient Greeks to the present. What if a feminist SF novelist took these ideas about female nature seriously, and imagined a world where women embraced their natural domestic role? What if women in that world were really as sexually choosy as evolutionary theory says they ought to be, given their enormous physical investment in their offspring? In other words, what if all of the scientific and social claims about woman's nature were *true*? Would a society based on these claims have to be a traditional male-dominated world, a patriarchy, or could it take a very different form? These questions are explored in a different kind of separatist novel, Sheri S. Tepper's *The Gate to Women's Country* (1988).

The Gate to Women's Country depicts life in a future postnuclear society. Most of the features of this life—economic hardship, limited knowledge and technology, devastation of nature, and radically new social relationships—are common themes in SF. What is unique in Women's Country is the kind of new society that has taken root. Here, women are responsible for food, shelter, and housing, rearing children, and restoring nature to its prewar state. Men, who live in garrisons outside the walls of each town, protect their women. Male children stay inside the towns until the age of five, and must decide at age fifteen whether to return to Women's Country as Servitors, men who do not fight, or stay in the garrisons and become warriors. Most young men stay in the garrisons, but the number of Servitors is increasing year by year. Twice a year, for two weeks each time, a carnival is held. The warriors and boys under fifteen enter Women's Country—to visit their families and to have sex with the women. This society embraces conventional heterosexual gender roles and relies on separatism for defense. Or so it seems.

Women's Country is filled with ceremonies for marking the important events of life. There is a ceremony for sending sons to the garrisons, one for sons who decide to stay there, another for heading off to war, a play performed by the women before carnival, and many others. The purpose of all this ceremony is misdirection. It conceals terrible truths about what is going on behind the scenes in this radically rebuilt society. The Councils of Women's Country are overseeing a secret breeding program, using selection to eliminate men's eagerness to fight. No warriors actually father any sons; only Servitors do. The sex that takes place during carnival is just for show, as women are given contraceptive implants beforehand, believing they're vitamins. Most are artificially inseminated, without their knowledge, afterwards. The herd of men is not only being selected for peacefulness; it is also being culled. The Council secretly instigates the wars fought between garrisons, to further reduce the numbers of aggressive men. Some warriors are convinced that Women's Country is keeping secrets from the garrisons. The warriors believe that the women have powerful weapons that the men could use to take over the towns and rule Women's Country. These warriors are right about the secrets, although the women's powerful weapon is evolution by natural selection. The warriors hatch a plot to find out about the secrets, by wooing the daughters of Councilwomen. Councilwoman Morgot's daughter Stavia is their main target.

Feminist readers like Lorna Jowett and Erin McKenna see in *Gate* a critical utopia (Jowett 2000; McKenna 2001). Critical utopias, or dystopias, are intended as warnings about the present, not as blueprints for future societies. Other critics, like Peter Fitting and Jane Donawerth, have argued that *Women's Country* is a reply to the lesbian separatist novels of the 1970s (Fitting 1992; Donawerth 1997, 2000). While lesbian separatist novels created "a place where lesbian pleasure can be real (healthy, normal, central, out in the open)" (Donawerth 1997, 94), they also raised an obvious question: "What happens to sons in a separatist feminist utopia?" (Donawerth 2000, 62–63n2), Still others find Tepper's novel essentialist about heterosexuality. The problem with heterosexual essentialism is that it takes heterosexuality as natural and necessary, while homosexuality is deviant. Wendy Pearson states this case clearly (1996, 1997).[1]

Pearson points out that there are no positive portrayals of homosexuality in this novel, and she may be right. She concedes that heterosexuality is necessary to make the novel's evolutionary plot work—you can't run a breeding program without breeders.[2] But she objects to what she sees as the book's homophobia. As a lesbian reader, she has a visceral reaction to the way the novel deals with homosexuality, apparently by eliminating it. However, Pearson's reading of the novel is an example

---

[1] Jane Donawerth calls the breeding program "chillingly homophobic" (1997, 16n16), but she allows that Tepper is trying to get us to question the idea that biology determines personality (1997, 18–19n20).

[2] Pearson 1997. Jowett makes the same point (2000, 171).

of the way that essentialism still haunts feminist theory. In objecting to the book's heterosexism, Pearson offers equally problematic views about what is natural and necessary, both to women and to the way we read SF novels.

Pearson objects strongly to a passage in the novel where homosexuality is "explained" (as a hormonal anomaly) only to be eliminated (corrected before birth) (1996, 200–201, 215, 217; 1997). The passage Pearson points to does rely on a troubling medical model that regards homosexuality as a treatable physical condition. But the novel does not say that homosexuals have been eliminated—it says that "very few" homosexuals are born in Women's Country, and that unsexed or omnisexed people are also born (Tepper 1988, 76). It is legitimate to object to homophobia here—leaving some sexual "anomalies" "untreated" is not morally much better than eliminating them, because it still treats them as deviant. Yet Pearson draws an unexpected conclusion from the novel's handling of homosexuality. She argues that the novel is full of "sex-hatred" (1996, 211). She says the novel is "able only to repudiate sexuality itself" (1996, 202); that it offers an "asexual future" (203); that it "portrays a world that is completely anti-sexual"; and that Women's Country is "a vision of a world without any sex at all" (221).

The novel explains that in Women's Country, "libidinal need was fully accepted as a normal and useful fact of life" (Tepper 1988, 76). In a conversation between an adolescent Stavia and her best friend Beneda, women and men who don't like sex at all are called "very strange" (58). The itinerant traveler Septemius Bird says that he has no interest in sex, so Pearson concludes that he is asexual. The novel tells us that Septemius lost his beloved to a warrior, so his abstinence is more likely sentimental. Bird also says that his nieces are "unsuited by aesthetic preference" to "priapic pauses," or heterosexual penetration, which seems to hint that they are lesbians (156). Pearson objects to Women's Country's scheduled sexual liaisons because she says it's not healthy for women to go without sex—bad news for single women—but it's not so clear that the novel is anti-sex.

Pearson rebukes feminist critic Jenny Wolmark for assuming that Stavia and the Servitor Corrig have become lovers, saying that "there is no hint of a sexual attraction between them and I think that Wolmark has forgotten that all children, including Stavia's, are sired by artificial insemination" (Pearson 1996, 212). The novel contradicts both of Pearson's claims. Corrig is a relatively minor figure in the story, but it appears that his relationship with Stavia is both loving and heterosexual. The first time the reader encounters him, he is at home with Stavia, watching her from across the room. "She caught Corrig's gaze upon her and flushed" (Tepper 1988, 18). The first time Stavia and Corrig meet, she turns "to give him a closer look." Her assessment of him is frankly sexual—tall, slender, long muscles, thick dark hair, wide, mobile mouth, full lower lip, huge beautifully shaped hands (178). As he helps her unpack, she looks at him in surprise, "meeting his eyes, letting her own drop away." "My, oh, my," she thinks, "but this was an unexpected man, here in her own house. Imagine his having read her need and intention so easily" (181). Corrig is shown giving her gentle squeezes (18), stroking her hair (27), calling her "love" (277), sending her flowers and cakes (291). In an especially poignant scene, after Stavia has learned about the breeding program and that she is pregnant with an "unauthorized" warrior's child, Corrig comforts his darling, dear, loved Stavia. She asks whether, when this crisis is over, he will stay with her. "'Such is my intention,' he said. 'I have this consistent hunger for you, Stavia'" (297). He is one of the novel's "psychic" Servitors, and tells Stavia the names of the children they will have together. At the very least these are *hints* of sexual attraction. So it may be that Pearson's objection to the novel's heterosexism has generated a new essentialism: she reads the novel as hostile to all sexuality, and so overlooks these hints of heterosexual relationship.

Stavia's mother Morgot is presented in a similar relationship with the Servitor Joshua, although it is less flirtatious and more parental. Joshua exchanges "particular, meaningful" nods with Morgot, "a kind of 'my dear, not before the children' expression" (25). Ironically, we eventually learn that Joshua is Stavia's father, and the novel's hints of his paternal concern for her are genuine. Morgot is the one who explains to Stavia Women's Country's irregular use of reproductive technology. In addition to discovering that Joshua is her father, Stavia learns that her sister Myra is only a half-sister. "*That* pregnancy was by artificial insemination, of course," Morgot tells her (293, emphasis added). The implication is that her *other* pregnancies—and she has had four children with Joshua— were not.[3] Now this hardly lets Tepper off Pearson's heterosexist hook. If elite Councilwomen are having illicit sex with Servitors while publicly upholding the pretense of warrior paternity, that makes them morally worse, not better. But you don't need heterosexist essentialism to make that point.

---

[3] Fitting observes that *most* of the pregnancies in Women's Country are achieved by artificial insemination (1992, 38). Lorna Jowett says that some impregnations may involve "physical intercourse, though this is nowhere stated openly" (2000, 191).

Pearson's oppositional reading of the novel may create further contradictions. She asserts that the servitors are not even males in the context of the novel's paradigms (1996, 224n19), because their relationship with their children as fathers "is not, in fact, any relationship at all." They have only an "ambiguously subservient status" (1996, 212). She also claims that "no man can exist within the text who is both sexual and non-violent" (1996, 204). Not only are some Servitors sexual and paternal, as I've demonstrated above, but also the text shows that not all men who stay in the garrisons are violent warriors (Tepper 1988, 120, 127), and that those who return to Women's Country can be ruthless fighters (151). It's not violence that's being bred out of the men, it's eagerness to use violence.

Servitors are fathers and some may be lovers. Of course the warriors despise Servitors, calling them cowards and tit-suckers and spreading rumors that young men who return to the city are gelded (Tepper 1988, 38). But the novel reveals Women's Country's attitudes to its servitors: "They are highly competent, calm, judicious men, and they are highly respected" (288). Children are sharply disciplined for repeating the warrior attitude inside the city gates. The penalty is expulsion from home, and Morgot threatens her own daughter with it (41). Joshua tells Stavia, "Servitors have one or more fraternities in each city. The Council in each city *often* seeks the opinion of the fraternities" (132, emphasis added). No one talks about this, because "it wouldn't sit well with the warriors, would it?" The reason for this is simple—the warriors must not learn that there is substantial cooperation between the Council and the Servitors, especially over the planning and execution of wars. "Both their status and their skills exceed what is generally supposed" (288).

Pearson objects to the play "Iphigenia at Ilium," which is performed as part of Women's Country's deceptive mythology, because she thinks it reinforces the novel's absolute association of masculinity with violence and femininity with maternalism (Pearson 1996, 206–7). In Greek myth, Iphigenia is sacrificed by her father Agamemnon for favorable winds, so that his fleet can sail to Troy to wage war. In one version of the myth, Aeschylus's *Oresteia*, Iphigenia dies. Pearson wonders why Euripides' Aulis version of the legend isn't used instead, since in that version Iphigenia is saved. A goddess swaps a hind (a deer) for Iphigenia, which is sacrificed in her place.[4] The novel explains this

---

[4] Pearson also objects that Patroclus, a homoerotic figure, is omitted from Tepper's play (Pearson 1996, 219–20). He's not in Iphigenia at Aulis, either, but he *is* in the novel's version of the play, on 285–86.

choice clearly. Warriors must accept the real consequences of their choice to be soldiers (Tepper 1988, 128). After Stavia's warrior son Dawid decides to remain in the garrison, Joshua tells her, "Think of Achilles. That's Dawid. 'I can't offend my friends, but you won't really die, mommy. Athena will send a hind.' Warriors all think like that or they wouldn't stay in the garrison" (53). Warriors fall for the lie that war isn't so bad and innocent women and children won't be killed (99). "Iphigenia at Ilium," called part of Women's Country's "reminders," is presented so the Councilwomen and Servitors will remember that this belief is a lie[5] (52).

Repeatedly, characters in the novel call the play a comedy, and it has farcical elements, but it is tragic. Pearson characterizes it as a failure, historically, mythologically, and artistically (1996, 208). Since she reads the novel as *"essentially serious"* (1996, 207, emphasis added) she thinks the farcical aspect of the play is that the joke's on the warriors—they have no idea what's going on in Women's Country, and the play makes fun of them for it. There are other ways to view the play, equally well supported by the text. Margaret McBride has come up with several options. She suggests that women in this postwar society may see the idea of heroic death as absurd. Their laughter may express relief that they're not in the same boat as Iphigenia. They may find humor reassuring in light of their dark plan, or they may simply be protesting too much to cover their pain as in *Hamlet*. Finally, labeling the play a farce may be a hint to the reader, to show how "humor perpetuates the bigotry and fraud in their plans to achieve a better society" (McBride 2000). I find all of these choices plausible, and have one more to add.

Two of the Greek playwrights who wrote Iphigenia's story were themselves written about by the comic Aristophanes. In Euripides' plays, Iphigenia isn't really sacrificed for the sake of a favorable wind. In Aeschylus's version, as in Tepper's, Iphigenia is killed. Aristophanes' *Frogs* features a comic dispute between Euripides and Aeschylus over which of them should inherit the throne of tragedy. Both playwrights agree that the duty of the poet is to improve men,[6] but it is Aeschylus, the brutal realist who kills off Iphigenia, who wins the competition. This

---

[5] The garrisons have their own mythology. They revere Odysseus as a military hero and his son Telemachus for his devotion to his father (Jowett 2000, 178). This mythology conveniently ignores the fact that Odysseus originally tried to get out of going to Troy by faking insanity, and was ultimately killed by his other son, Telegonus.

[6] In Tepper's play, Iphigenia says, "Men like to think well of themselves, and poets help them do it" (1988, 57).

directs us to the literary importance of Aristophanes in the novel. The
Greek play that the novel most resembles is his *Lysistrata*, where women
abstain from sex to bring an end to war, but their resolve wavers because
of their desire. Tepper manages to remind us of Aristophanes by working the names of some of his plays into the story.[7] She even borrows dialogue and the idea of using natural selection to improve society from
Lysistrata.[8] The comic element, then, is that it would be ridiculous to
expect women to go without sex. That is why Women's Country's breeding program must be kept secret, why sexuality and reproduction must
be separated. Where the lesbian separatist utopias of the 1970s and early
80s freed women from control by heterosexual relationships (Donawerth
1997, 15), Tepper leaves straight women their heterosexual desire and
frees them from control by reproduction. In her novel, reproduction, not
sex, is refused until war is ended. Tepper blames women for their misplaced nurturing and passion (1988, 290) and uses farce to soften the
blow.[9]

Joanna Russ's novel *The Female Man* (1975) has better female characters than *Gate*, Pearson argues, because they are more fully human.
Russ's women are "capable of mothering and nurturance, of sexual play
and jealousy, of violence, anger, madness, and grief." They are strong,
capable, and willing to kill.[10] This description is equally true of the
women of *Gate*, Pearson admits, but Tepper's women "are also secretive,
manipulative, conniving, treacherous, and ruthless to those who do not

---

[7] (*Frogs*, p. 243; *Wasps*, p. 113; *Birds*, p. 285, 296)

[8] When Myra returns from what we later see is her first artificial insemination, she
complains to Stavia about the rudeness of the medical officers. She complains about
their intrusive questions regarding her menstrual cycle (which Pearson claims is not
mentioned in the novel), and says they "had me up on the table all spread out like a split
fish" (Tepper 1988, 82). In *Lysistrata*, Calonice says she will support Lysistrata's proposal for abstinence to end war, "though I must be split in two like a flat-fish, and have
half myself removed" (Crofts 1994, 7). Lysistrata tells the Magistrate that if the State had
any common sense, it would treat politics the way women treat yarn: "First we wash the
yarn to separate the grease and filth; do the same with all bad citizens" (Crofts 1994,
27).

[9] Tepper worked for Planned Parenthood for twenty-four years, and her novels often
chide women for their poor reproductive choices. She calls it sermonizing. (*Science
Fiction Chronicle* 1998-99, 39)

[10] Russ says that the point of the greater sexual permissiveness of the 1970s utopias,
including nonfeminist ones, was to "separate sexuality from questions of ownership,
reproduction, and social structure" (1995, 139). Tepper definitely separates sexuality
from ownership and reproduction, and reconfigures its relationship with social structure,
so in this sense she is in dialogue with writers like Russ.

fit into their system; on top of that, their brains turn to mush with the onset of hormones" (Pearson 1996, 213). A case could be made that women who are *both* strong and ruthless *and* occasionally weak are more fully human, but that is beside the point. Pearson is quite right that the boy-crazy behavior of the novel's dizzy women is a bit insulting, and heterosexual readers may feel targeted by it. Pearson is uneasy about ascribing intentional homophobia to Tepper's novel, but in response to Fitting's assertion that Tepper reverts to a politics of despair, Pearson finds a politics of hatred.[11] She will not allow that heterosexuals of both sexes and homosexual men might have anything to say in reply to lesbian separatist worlds depicted as feminist utopias.

Pearson insists that there is no textual evidence to read *Gate* as ambiguous or satirical. As far as that goes, there's no textual evidence to read the novel as serious, either. Novels don't tell us how to read them any more than nature tells science how to study it. Pearson's views sound similar to Sarah Lefanu's observations about women's dystopias, which deny "women's sexual autonomy. They show women trapped by their sex, by their femaleness, and reduced from subjecthood to function" (Lefanu 1988, 71). So there seems to be some reason to read *Gate to Women's Country* as a dystopia. I find such a reading useful, treating *Gate* as a parody. Tepper tells us that her play is a comedy, and the play is an allegory for the novel, so that might be a clue that the novel is farcical, too. Holyland society is also called a mockery, a comedy [12] (Tepper 1988, 256). I've already made the case for the allusion to Aristophanes, another clue that the novel is a critique, not a blueprint. The text contains quite a few bad sexual jokes (79, 300). And women themselves seem uncertain about the breeding plan. Morgot tells Stavia that, eventually, there will be no more wars. "Theoretically" (295). I think that the novel is well understood as a dystopia and a parody, but the question is, a parody of what? Not those 1970s works of separatist SF, but the Bible, Greek tragedy, Plato's *Republic*,[13] and especially contemporary theories of evolution. It's the parody of evolutionary theory that brings me to the conclusion of my discussion of Tepper.

---

[11] I'm uneasy about such intentions too, but I note that Tepper has written a series of mystery novels with a gay sleuth, and is on the public record defending civil contracts for all partnerships, including group ones (LOCUS, Sept. 1998).

[12] The novel depicts Stavia's kidnap and brutalization at the hands of the "Holylanders," a group of ultra-patriarchal fundamentalists who live far outside Women's Country. I regret that I don't have space to discuss all the intricacies of the plot, especially fundamentalist opposition to evolution.

[13] Plato, of course, regards poetry as mere imitation and therefore untrue.

In emphasizing the consequences of the story's heterosexist essentialism, Pearson creates essentialisms of her own. It seems that for her, the book *must* be read as a serious proposal for a future society. Pearson sees in *Gate* "a problem, a potential solution, and a method to achieve that solution" (1997). Erin McKenna, in contrast, says that Women's Country embodies "fear of difference, a lack of diversity, a lack of autonomy, a fear of, or inability to cope with, change, and a resulting reliance on an authoritarian system" (McKenna 2001, 45). She is able to discover all of these things in the novel without mentioning heterosexist essentialism.[14] These problems in Women's Country are far more serious drawbacks to any society than the novel's heterosexism. McKenna suggests that Tepper has offered us this deliberately flawed society so that we can see what's wrong with authoritarian societies in general. It allows us to see their flaws.

As my remarks above indicate, I offer another perspective on the novel, seeing it hang together in a particular scientific, but not necessarily essentialist, way. This perspective allows us to question the novel's attitude to homosexuality without implying further problematic claims about sexuality. Pearson's charge that the book is opposed to sex and ought to be read as a serious blueprint for society is essentialist in just this way. From a more evolutionary perspective, however, the evidence provided by the novel does not support these objections. Alternative readings are possible, and I have suggested a few such readings.

Similarly, emphasizing the novel's heterosexual essentialism lets the story's potential for a strong critique of evolutionary theory slip away. Lorna Jowett points to "Tepper's revisioning of the myths of the patriarchy and their part in the oppression of women" (2000, 178). The evolution of women's "inferiority" through natural selection is one of these myths. Gender differences supported by evolutionary theory may seem like a relatively new scientific idea, but the novel shows us that such claims are in fact very old—*ancient.* One thing *Gate* does well is to show the continuity of the gender bias in modern evolutionary theory with the ancient texts of patriarchy. Evolutionary theory's long history,

---

[14] McKenna points out that end-state utopias have to be committed to the assumption that human nature is basically plastic, or they won't work (2001, 28). This *rules out* the possibility of essentialism. As John Dupré reminds us, evolution by natural selection can only work if there is variety. Darwinian theory repudiates essentialism (1994, 172). In any case, genes for particular traits and for preferences for those traits, if they exist, cannot be separated. Pearson is correct to suggest that Tepper's approach to genetics is also essentialist.

including its history of making gender roles and heterosexuality seem natural and necessary, is made more obvious. We can see how ancient myths and their contemporary offspring have a strong effect on our culture, even on our images of ourselves. Pearson, like many feminists, recommends altering our child-rearing practices to challenge such "scientific" attitudes about what is natural to women and men. *Gate to Women's Country* tells us that this proposal is inadequate.

In dealing with homosexuality as a medical "condition," the novel also draws our attention to certain problems that go along with our modern tendency to make genetics the explanation for almost everything. It's one thing to note that good breeding programs must allow genetic diversity to thrive because a uniform gene pool is prone to serious problems—like extinction. So Women's Country's practice of including homosexuals, omnisexuals, and asexuals in their gene pool is scientifically appropriate. But evolutionary theorists have had a hard time explaining homosexuality as a genetic trait. If homosexuals don't reproduce, their genes should have vanished long ago. Some evolutionary theorists have suggested that it's desirable to have nonbreeders in the gene pool for the culture they create, or the care they provide for their relatives. It's not hard to see how such "explanations" rely on stereotypes about homosexuality. Still, I think that Pearson is right to draw our attention to the role of homosexuality in this novel, and in SF more generally. As SF novelist William Gibson has pointed out, SF writers struggle to write about sex in the age of AIDS. "This situation is so unprecedentedly grim," he writes, "as to send the bulk of science fiction's folk-futurists, myself included, cringing and yelping back to our warp drives" (1990, xv).

Further, *Gate to Women's Country* can help to confront the essentialist connection between woman and nature for which environmental feminists, or ecofeminists, are criticized. Ecofeminist readers might point out that Women's Country is breeding animal species to return to the wild (Tepper 1988, 100), but men to leave it. Thus, whoever is associated with the wild tends to be oppressed regardless of their sex, and in the novel it's the masculine warriors who suffer. Moreover, the warriors are feminized by their status as ignorant victims of the oppressive Women's Councils. As Pearson astutely points out, the warriors' reproductive impotence makes them "the queers of their world" (1996, 206). So *Gate* gives us a way to disrupt conventional beliefs about gender. This point applies to religion as well. Fundamentalists, including those portrayed in the novel's "Holyland," demonize sex—*all* sex—hatefully and thoroughly, but protect marital reproductive sex—even with minors.

Dividing sexualities into those that are approved and those that are out-lawed is part of the hierarchical worldview that ecofeminists condemn. Women's Country is full of rigid social hierarchies, not just sexual ones, so such a society can be criticized on this basis, without recourse to essentialism and all its problems.

Feminist science critics have argued against the gender bias of evo-lutionary theory, and have shown that it is possible to borrow evolution and use it for feminist goals. *Gate* can be read as an example of such borrowing, in the voice of parody. The Greeks and the Bible and the Scientists all tell women that we are inferior, evil, easily swayed, coy, choosy, and maternal, while men are the vital force in creation and pro-creation.[15] *Gate* is what a society might look like if some women actu-ally believed these ideas. Even if the authoritative texts of patriarchy are true, Tepper shows us that it current gender relations are not *necessary* consequences of our history, religion, or science. If there are natural dif-ferences between the sexes—and that remains an open question—we cannot conclude that patriarchy is therefore "natural."

R E F E R E N C E S

Barrett, David, trans. 1964. *Aristophanes: The Wasps, The Poet and the Women, The Frogs*. London: Penguin.

Crofts, Thomas, ed. 1994. *Aristophanes: Lysistrata*. New York: Dover.

Donawerth, Jane. 1997. *Frankenstein's Daughters: Women Writing Science Fiction*. Syracuse: Syracuse University Press.

———. 2000. "The Feminist Dystopia of the 1990s: Record of Failure, Midwife of Hope." In *Future Females, the Next Generation: New Voices and Velocities in Feminist Science Fiction Criticism*, edited by Marlene S. Barr, 49–66. Lanham: Rowman and Littlefield.

Dupré, John. 1994. "Methodological Individualism and Reductionism in Biology." In "Biology and Society: Reflections on Methodology," edited by Mohan Matthen and R. X. Ware *Canadian Journal of Philosophy*, suppl. vol. 20: 165–84.

Fagles, Robert, trans. 1984. *Aeschylus: The Oresteia*. New York: Penguin.

Fitting, Peter. 1990. "Reconsiderations of the Separatist Paradigm in Recent Feminist Science Fiction." *Science-Fiction Studies* 19: 32–48.

Gibson, William. 1990. "Foreword: Strange Attractors." In *Alien Sex*, edited by Ellen Datlow. New York: ROC.

Grube, G. M. A., trans. 1974. *Plato's Republic*. Indianapolis: Hackett.

---

[15] Tuana 1993.

Hadas, Moses and John McLean, trans. 1960. *Ten Plays by Euripides*. New York: Bantam.

Jowett, Lorna. 2000. "The Female State: Science Fiction Alternatives to the Patriarchy—Sheri Tepper's *The Gate to Women's Country* and Orson Scott Card's *Homecoming* Series." In *Science Fiction, Critical Frontiers*, edited by Karen Sayer and John Moore, 169–92. New York: St. Martin's Press.

Lefanu, Sarah. 1988. *In the Chinks of the World Machine: Feminism and Science Fiction*. London: The Women's Press.

McBride, Margaret. 2000. "Why a Farce? Euripides' *Trojan Women* in Sheri Tepper's *The Gate to Women's Country*." Paper presented to the Science Fiction Research Association.

McKenna, Erin. 2001. *The Task of Utopia: A Pragmatist and Feminist Perspective*. Lanham: Rowman and Littlefield.

Morehouse, Lyda. 1998/99. "SFC Interview: Sheri S. Tepper." *Science Fiction Chronicle*, Dec./Jan., 8.

Murphy, Patrick D. 1991. "Ground, Pivot, Motion: Ecofeminist Theory, Dialogics, and Literary Practice." *Hypatia* 6, no. 1: 228–43.

Pearson, Wendy. 1996. "After the (Homo) Sexual: A Queer Analysis of Anti-Sexuality in Sheri S. Tepper's *The Gate to Women's Country*." *Science-Fiction Studies* 23:199–226.

———. 1997. Posting to FEMINISTSF Listserv. Nov. 27. Accessed Dec. 4, 1997.

Russ, Joanna. 1995. "Amor Vincit Foeminam: The Battle of the Sexes in Science Fiction." In *To Write like a Woman: Essays in Feminism and Science Fiction*, 41–59. Bloomington: Indiana University Press.

Tepper, Sheri S. 1988. *The Gate to Women's Country*. New York: Bantam.

———. 1998. "Sheri S. Tepper: Speaking to the Universe." *LOCUS*. Sept., 4.

Tuana, Nancy. 1993. *The Less Noble Sex*. Bloomington: Indiana University Press.

Clone Mothers and Others: Uncanny Families

STEPHANIE S. TURNER

*I*t is a commonplace that genetic technologies like genetically modified organisms, gene therapy, and cloning provoke anxiety. The mass media is filled with stories and images that dramatize fears of these technologies run amok. Will we be able to control the changes made possible by manipulating DNA? Or will manipulating DNA transform our lives irreversibly in ways we don't want? This phenomenon is apparent in the book titles and the worried expressions of their young readers in Jennifer Berman's cartoon *Kids' Books for the 21st Century* (1999). The titles, of course, are spoofs on well-known children's books: *The Very Hungry Virus*, *Pat My Bunny Clone*, *Goodnight Earth!*, *Endangered George and the Burning Rainforest*, and *Mommy Has Twelve Heathers*. Dystopian in tone, the titles emphasize the negative effects of genetic technologies with which we have become so familiar from books, film, and television. Whether they result in rampant disease, environmental catastrophe, or merely domestic disorder, genetic technologies are often depicted as disrupting the natural order. In this way, they work on a cultural level by challenging us to reconsider our cherished notions of the natural.

How is it that popular accounts of the impact of genetic technologies render even the most mundane circumstances strange? An obvious interpretation might be that the average person's understanding of genetics lags behind the rapid technological advances being made. Just when we think we grasp the unreliability of genes from watching the "genetic loser" become the hero in the film *Gattaca* (1997), we find that genes seem to "have a mind of their own" in giving human evolution a jump-start in Greg Bear's novel *Darwin's Radio* (1999)—and the research on transposons, segments of DNA that can move about on the chromosome, apparently at random, seems to back this up (Kazazian 2004; Moffat 2000). Yet something more subtle than a knowledge gap is also at work. Regardless of science's efforts so far, the genetic code remains stubbornly self-directed, reproducing itself in ways that are still mysterious, and this unauthorized reproduction registers in the cultural realm as a powerful and potentially disruptive force.

This effect is intensified when the unauthorized reproduction involves cloning. Cloning fictions play on our anxiety over the uncanny, the discomfort we feel when the familiar is somehow made strange.[1] Although the cloning technique that created the famous sheep Dolly does not involve the manipulation of DNA per se, only its replication, from the very beginning of the cloning debate following her birth, public discussion and popular portrayals of the new technology often fixated on the clone's uncanny ability to seem like either a degenerated or a perfected copy, a phenomenon described in such genetic terms as "mutation" and "frameshift." Again, the public took its cue from science. While some scientists were fretting over the possibility that Dolly would age faster than a normal sheep because of her atypically shortened chromosome ends (Lanza et al. 2000), other scientists were enthusing about the possibility of cloning a transgenic pig that would be a perfect organ donor for humans (Pennisi and Normile 2000). Hollywood had already embraced the perfected/degenerated copy idea in *Multiplicity* (1996), a comedy that shows the domestic disorder that can occur when an overworked family man clones himself twice, only to have the two clones—each a perfect version of the husband's ruthless manager and nurturing spouse personae, respectively—conspire to clone a third, which turns out to be a childlike idiot. Yet even in this queered nuclear family, a family is nevertheless recognizable.

What's Queer About Clones?

A common theme in narratives about cloned animals and people is the unique threat to the natural order that they present. The product of asex-

---

[1] First described by Sigmund Freud, "the uncanny" refers to any circumstance that arouses dread and horror because its familiarity has inexplicably been rendered unfamiliar. The fear of the double, which both is and is not like the original thing, is an especially apt example. Like identical twins, monsters, androids, and genetically modified organisms, clones are inherently uncanny.

ual, rather than sexual, reproduction, clones upset, or "queer," the natural order, the sense of "how things ought to be" in nature. The natural order depends on generational change, but clones, being genetically identical to their parents, do not contribute to that change. Existing outside of natural law, they are, in effect, biological outlaws.

The queerness of clones is not a small problem, either scientifically or sociologically. Although some living things, like plants and certain invertebrate animals, do reproduce asexually, resulting in offspring that are genetically identical to their parents, animals considered to be "more evolved" reproduce sexually, creating genetically new offspring. In evolutionary terms, the continual genetic renewal of a species through sexual reproduction helps to ensure its survival, because a lack of genetic variety can result in a lethal concentration of inherited diseases.

In terms of the social order, clones also exist outside the law by threatening a different sort of continuity brought about by marriage, kinship, and lineage. These social constructs depend on a rather delicate balance in the definition of "family": people in family groups must be distinct enough from each other to fulfill their specific roles in the family, yet they must also be similar enough to each other to be considered an integral part of that family. Examples of the delicateness of that balance can be seen in conflicts involving such issues as surrogate motherhood, biological paternity, inheritance, and even what constitutes a "blended family" in married couples' struggles to reconstitute a nuclear family unit after both partners have dissolved previous marriages involving children. In this already complicated social order, clones wreak a special kind of havoc. Determining whether a clone is a sibling or an offspring, for example, is just one of the many psychological, social, and legal problems that would arise if people were permitted to clone themselves.

To describe such problems as "queer" involves asking productive questions about the received wisdom of "how things ought to be" in society. What are the possible benefits of acknowledging other kinds of families in addition to the traditional nuclear family unit of the married man and woman and their biologically born children? What are the differences between sex and gender, and why are the two so often confused? How is homosexuality both biological *and* cultural? These and other questions asked by queer theorists and others have arisen from the recognition that human sexuality has been narrowly described by science and medicine when in fact, human sexual experience, including identity, desire, and reproduction, is significantly shaped by language and culture. Cloning and genetic modification technologies, because they touch on issues of identity, desire, and reproduction, reiterate the importance of those questions.

The queer family wrought by fictional clones, and especially clone mothers and their familiar others in the reproductive scenario—sole survivors, guinea pigs, bad girls, and mad scientists—make an especially illustrative set of examples with which to consider the threat to the natural order presented by genetic engineering and cloning. Clone mothers in various guises play a key role in both disrupting and restoring order in cloning scenarios, which invariably go out of control. Considering the mysterious potency with which women have been imbued—and for which they have been persecuted—because of their reproductive capacity, the power of female clones and their uncanny families should come as no surprise. From parthenogenetic cloned dinosaurs in *Jurassic Park* (1993) to the part-alien, part-human clone mother Lt. Ellen Ripley in the *Alien* series, defiantly fertile females (or, in the case of *Multiplicity*, effeminate males) are the crux of the transgression and transformation in cloning narratives.

To understand the key role that women play in imagining human reproductive cloning, it is helpful to keep in mind that actual clones, which have so far consisted solely of nonhumans, are experimental lab animals, patentable biotechnological products, and consumer commodities. To think of human beings occupying any of these categories is abhorrent, yet women's more intimate role in the reproductive economy brings them closer to doing so than men. Whether their wombs are "laboratories" for new reproductive techniques (amniocentesis, intrauterine ultrasound) or their reproductive byproducts fodder for new medicine (gametes, umbilical cord blood stem cells), women are inextricably caught up in these economies of reproductive technology. Appropriately enough, Dolly the cloned sheep was manufactured from a mammary gland cell of another female sheep, and so named because of her cultural affinity with the large-breasted country singer Dolly Parton. While this playful naming personified Dolly the cloned sheep, granting her a celebrated subjectivity, it objectified and dehumanized Dolly the well-endowed country singer. Dolly's naming exemplifies feminist science studies scholar Donna Haraway's remark that "we polish an animal mirror to look for ourselves" (Haraway 1991, 21). Certainly the story of the all-female dinosaur population of *Jurassic Park* has promoted a wide-

---

[2] A classic work examining women and reproduction is Martin 1987. For an updated view see Morgan and Michaels 1999.

spread interest in the limits and possibilities of bioprospecting and manipulating ancient DNA, sex selection as a reproductive option, and respect for life in commercial biotechnology.

Thus females, and especially human women, as both reproductive subjects and objects, have been narrowly and damagingly imagined in popular culture. Yet rather than dismiss cloning fiction as just more misogyny in sheep's clothing, we should consider the transformative effects it might have despite its often-predictable repetition of the same. How do clone mothers queer the familiar, and how might this be a useful, even needed phenomenon? As psychoanalytic theory would explain this problem, it is through rehearsing trauma, both real and imagined, that we can restore our health. We need to tell tales of genetic engineering and cloning to imagine it done better. The discipline of Science and Technology Studies (STS) further helps to clarify the issue when it urges us to "consider technology as a complex cultural arrangement that is determined by cultural forces that precede it, as it also organizes and *reproduces* those forces over time" (Balsamo 1999, 90; emphasis added). The reproductive network of cultural forces that Anne Balsamo describes suggests how popular culture both reflects and challenges our ideas of the familiar and of life, and the decisions about who gets to make it, replicate it, modify it, and end it.

So how does this complex intersection of women, animals, genetic science, and reproductive technologies play out in popular cloning scenarios? The traumatic redundancies experienced by the character Ellen Ripley in the *Alien* film series—especially in the fourth and last film in the series, *Alien Resurrection* (1997), with all its unscientific genetic and cloning "science" that is nevertheless highly culturally resonant— provide an important example of the transformative power of clone mothers and others. On the one hand, the *Alien* series narrates the fairly predictable consequences imaginable when the big, bad defense contractor goes bioprospecting on the interplanetary frontier. On the other hand, the series can also be read as a nuanced study of the network of affiliations that women negotiate in reproducing, transforming, and terminating life. As I will show, the series illustrates how these connections and associations can smudge the comfortable boundary between women's subjugation and their instrumentality.

Familiar Aliens

In *Alien*, the first movie in the series, Terran Growth Conglomerate, the big, bad defense contractor in question, is hot on the trail of an especially mean and scary life form. Terran Growth Conglomerate thinks this unnamed, unknown xenomorph might be good for making new vaccines and alloys, and for carrying out those all-important "urban pacification" projects of which the military is so fond. So Terran Growth Conglomerate sends an unsuspecting crew of interplanetary mineral ore freight haulers to round up the alien, and one by one the crew of the spaceship *Nostromo* die at the claws and, most frighteningly, at the teeth of the hostile life form. In one of film's most memorable (and widely parodied[3]) scenes, one of the crew members dies spectacularly as an alien embryo that has apparently been gestating in his stomach claws and gnaws its way out to begin the next phase of its life cycle. This errant alien reproduction is a very bad sign, and one that the sequels productively explore. Though nearly getting devoured by the alien herself, through a combination of luck and pluck, crew member Ellen Ripley manages to save both herself and her orange tabby cat Jonesy, the ship's only woman and cat becoming the film's sole survivors (*Alien* 1979). Ripley is thus established in the first film as tough enough to defeat the alien mother, yet maternal enough to have saved Jonesy, gently settling the feline into the cryogenic sleep chamber that makes long journeys through space possible.

At the beginning of the second film, *Aliens* (1986), we find that Ripley and Jonesy have been drifting alone together in space for fifty-seven years. The young daughter that Ripley left behind on Earth is by now old, or even dead. Having finally been found by the company, Ripley struggles with the question of whether she should return to Earth or revisit LV426, the alien-infested planet she managed to escape in the first film, to help a group of marines find out why communications with the terraforming colonists there have been cut off. It is probably just a technical problem, the company tells her, since the colonists have never complained of any hostile xenomorphs, so sending in the marines was merely a safety precaution. Ripley's job would simply be to advise them on how to proceed in the unlikely event of a hostile alien presence. Having accessed highly classified security information via "Mother," the freight

---

[3] Two notable parodies of the famous "alien popping out of the stomach" scene are actually parodies-within-parodies. In Mel Brooks's *Spaceballs* (1987), the "baby alien" bursts onto the scene to perform a song-and-dance routine reminiscent of the performing frog in top hat and tails in the Warner Brothers cartoons. In *The Simpsons'* "Deep Space Homer" (1994), the parody-within-a-parody occurs when the series' cartoon characters Itchy and Scratchy reenact the violent alien scene in a spoof called "Scar Trek: The Next Laceration." Like clones themselves, parodies are often self-reproducing.

hauler's onboard computer, in the first film, Ripley knows she has been lied to by the company. The ship's crew was expendable then, she discovered, so why wouldn't it be expendable now? Nevertheless, she freely chooses to return to the planet in what she knows will be another battle with the aliens.[4] In trauma psychology this is not such an implausible decision. After all, she has been fighting the aliens in her mind in the form of posttraumatic flashbacks and nightmares—perhaps she can survive another close encounter, restore her peace of mind, and in the process, defeat the big, bad defense contractor.

Not surprisingly, Terran Growth Conglomerate already knows about the situation on LV426: all the colonists have been killed by the xenomorphs except for one little girl, Newt. Like Ripley, Newt presents an advantage to the company precisely *because* she survives. The trick is to find out how. Obviously, then, the company already has a plan: Ripley and Newt will make the optimum research subjects in their experiment to subdue the powerful aliens because of their inexplicable affiliation with the creatures. Indeed, the two females seem drawn to the aliens, and the feeling seems to be mutual. Thus the company plans to capture a couple of the aliens by subjecting the two females to serving as alien incubators. In the process, the maternal bond that is likely to form between Ellen Ripley and the little girl Newt might just make them more pliable research subjects. However, Terran Growth Conglomerate's plans do not materialize. By the end of the second film, Ripley has triumphed over not only the nasty aliens but also the nasty defense contractor, saving Newt and one other crewmember while blowing up what remains of the colony in a dramatic use of nuclear weapons intended to annihilate the hell-bent-to-reproduce aliens.

Sadly, however, the third film, *Alien³* (1992), shows Ripley once again waking up from the cryogenic nap of space travel only to find herself still very much involved with the alien problem. Her return to the scene of the trauma has not yet healed her. In fact, the situation has grown worse and is rapidly worsening, for Ripley realizes that she has somehow been impregnated with one of the queen alien's embryos, and some of the alien's highly caustic blood has somehow penetrated the hull of the spaceship, causing a fire and requiring the crew's emergency shuttle evacuation to a nearby planet. Unfortunately, Newt and the other crew members die in the crash landing, and Ripley is once again a sole

---

[4] Ripley seems to have decided not to take Jonesy back to the alien-infested planet with her in *Aliens* as he does not reappear in the series.

survivor—though possibly not for long, if she creates an uncanny family dynamic by giving birth to the queen's offspring. In the film's genetic subtext, this planet, Fiorina 161, is a penal colony of chromosomally compromised offenders—all violent males with an extra Y chromosome. The message here is ominous: biology trumps free will. Ripley's appearance on the grim scene seems to confirm this; now that her reproductive potential as a surrogate mother has been tapped by the aliens, they seem unstoppable. A dog nosing around the crash site becomes the first victim of the alien infestation that Ripley has brought with her on the ship. Like Ripley, it becomes the host for an alien, but only briefly, as the life-form escapes and starts killing the prisoners. Fed up with being manipulated by the company, grieving the death of Newt, and knowing that she has been reduced to an alien incubator, Ripley by now has nothing left to lose. The fact that the company is once again trying to capture an alien life form to use as a bioweapon—under the guise of coming to the planet to rescue it—enrages her. Now is the chance for Ripley to perfect her alien kill strategy. Yet because she and the alien queen have become so closely affiliated, sharing the same body, Ripley knows that must she must kill herself as well. In a cruel reminder of the normal, human motherhood that is now beyond her reach, the company man who has arrived on site tries to convince her not to: "you can still have a life . . . children," he implores her. Ignoring him, she tricks the last surviving alien to jump into a vat of molten lead and throws herself in after it.

Although Ripley's heroic self-sacrifice[5] at the close of *Alien³* seems to be the unequivocal end of her struggle with the transgressive and transformative power of reproduction in the film series, it is really only the beginning. In *Alien Resurrection* (1997), we see the final transformation of Lt. Ellen Ripley from an ordinary interplanetary blue-collar laborer and single mother to the ultimate experimental lab animal: an unruly and unpredictable transgenically modified clone mother of the most potent alien in the colony, the egg-laying queen. Once again Ripley has been had by the company. Through the wonders of genetic engineering and cloning, Terran Growth Conglomerate has somehow managed to extract her body from the vat of molten lead, restore her to life, and enhance her reproductive value beyond anything she—or the viewer of the film—could imagine. Following the scientific pattern of genetic

---

[5] Critic A. Samuel Kimball notes that Ripley's self-sacrifice is a kind of "sanctification" of suicide, matricide, and infanticide (Kimball 2002, 95).

manipulation and cloning, though with a great deal more horror in the mistakes made along the way, the company finally got it right. Resurrected from the dead and now genetically part alien, part human, Ripley epitomizes the uncanny.[6] This new creation *looks* like Ellen Ripley, but it also smacks of something very different. This new version of Ripley has enhanced physical capabilities and more empathy for the aliens than ever. She will finally, the viewer feels certain, defeat the big, bad defense contractor with its own would-be weapon, organizing the aliens, like so many exploited workers in the biotech economy, to defeat their oppressor once and for all. As she warns the smug company scientists who created her in the film's opening scene, this will prove to be an unwitting experiment on their part, because they will be forced to contend with an agency more powerful than their own: "She'll breed, you'll die," she warns them. Indeed, this agency is more powerful than she herself can contain, as her use of the third person pronoun here suggests.[7]

Casting the terrifying xenomorphs in a more sympathetic light and featuring Ripley herself as "the monster's mother," *Alien Resurrection*'s portrayal of the queered family reproduced by genetic engineering is the most uncanny in the *Alien* series. In one gripping scene, the cloned Ripley discovers her unsuccessful predecessors in a laboratory, their horribly disfigured bodies—some loosely resembling her—suspended in huge glass jars of preservative, presumably on hold for future study. But one of them is still alive. A twisted, tortured creature resembling Ripley more than any of the dead others, she pleads with the clone from her laboratory captivity: "Kill me. Kill me." Ripley obligingly does so, tearfully destroying the laboratory as well. Indeed, all of Ripley's relationships in this film seem at once ambivalent and intense, both at odds and familiar. Among these is her "edgy and erotic" (Fuchs 1997) relationship with a female android named Call, who has arrived at the research facility with a group of contractors hauling a load of live humans for use as additional alien incubators. Call, recognizing Ripley as the mother of all alien hosts and programmed to protect humans from alien life-forms, takes out a knife and offers to "end [her] suffering," but Ripley, unimpressed by such a simple solution to her increasingly com-

---

[6] According to Freud, "Many people experience the feeling [of the uncanny] in the highest degree in relation to death and dead bodies, to the return of the dead, and to spirits and ghosts," all of which the transgenic cloned Ripley embodies in *Alien Resurrection* (Freud 1919, 218).

[7] Reviewer Cindy Fuchs observes that the cloned Ripley in *Alien Resurrection* seems to be "overloaded with identities" (Fuchs 1997).

plicated life, responds by caressing the young android's face in a vaguely
threatening manner, asking her, "What makes you think I'd let you do
that?" Ripley's interactions with her alien progeny also resemble the
love/hate dynamic so characteristic of family relations. Because of their
shared genetics and long history together, these are her familiars; from
her, they have gained the ability to give live birth, they now express fear
and even sadness, and they even seem on the verge of speech (Kimball
2002, 100). But they are still monstrous, their reproductive capacity is
apparently limitless and out of control, they remain vulnerable to bio-
prospectors with bad intentions, and Ripley, their mother, is the only one
who can really end all this. In the film's decisive next-to-last scene,
Ripley saves Call from one of the enraged, ferocious newborns, briefly
cradles the hybrid creature to calm it, and then, in a repeat performance
of her original alien-destruction technique from the first *Alien* film,
breaches the hull of the spaceship, creating a vacuum effect that sucks
the baby alien into space. This time, however, the destruction of the alien
takes much longer, its suffering pitiable, almost human. A. Samuel
Kimball describes the creature's death throes as "an agony of recognition that it is being deliberately killed by one whom it loves in its infant
helplessness" (Kimball 2002, 100). As the film draws to a close, Ripley
and Call work easily together to blow up the remaining aliens and set
themselves on a course to Earth. Here, the film's action becomes inde-
cisive, reflecting the uncanniness of this now-childless couple. Pointing
their ship toward Paris, France, the city of love, the two contemplate
their uncertain future. Ripley is making no promises about "what happens now," for as she tells Call, "I'm a stranger there myself." While it
leaves the quadrilogy open for yet another sequel, the inconclusiveness
of the final scene of *Alien Resurrection* typifies the open-endedness of
fictions about the transformative potential of new reproductive technologies generally. In this sense, though the film's science is highly
unrealistic, the narrative invites us to think.

Conclusion: What Clones Communicate

As the *Alien* series and other examples of cloning fiction show, the
strange effects of genetic science depicted in SF accounts of cloning
actually work to recuperate the familiar. Drawing on ideas from queer
theory and feminist science studies, as I have done here, helps to explain
this normalizing function of cloning narratives, which typically feature
a queered father (*Multiplicity*), a reproductively potent mother (*Alien
Resurrection*), monstrous offspring (*Jurassic Park*), or some interesting

combination thereof. In effect, the queerness of cloned humans in popular forms ends up reassuring popular culture consumers about the
essential "straightness" of technological progress; it helps us to see that
although we are creating a new path, we will still be able to navigate it.

As we continue to make up stories about clones, it may be helpful to
examine them in terms of the "posthuman"-ist STS scholar Katherine
Hayles's description of the condition resulting from genetic science's
treatment of biology as information and of bodies—and even evolution—as part of a network. As posthumans, clones can be seen as containing extraneous information—noise, in information theory—that the
actual science and technology of cloning cannot explain. Clones communicate a lot more information than we might expect given the fact
they are simply a set of replicated genetic codes. For this reason, their
excess must be understood in cultural, not scientific, terms. So while the
term "genetic load" remains scientific, it also functions in a cultural
sense to refer to clones' tendency to interrupt or revise familiar narratives. In information theory terms, clones jam the signal, but they do so
productively. In many instances this excess is amusingly or horrifically
ostentatious; it is as if the clone is trying very hard to get its message
across. The use of the languages of electronics and computer programming to describe this biocultural phenomenon is right in line with cybernetics models that describe bodies in terms of information systems.[8] For
a reproduction that science claims to be little more than a replication, the
clone in fictional accounts often seems either to greatly exaggerate the
characteristics of its progenitor, or to depart from them entirely. And, it
is important to note, this phenomenon can occur independently of any of
the genetic modifications that might distinguish the clone from his or
her progenitor.

So just what sort of discrepancy is this between the so-called science
fiction of clones and the technological facts about what they are, and
what are the cultural factors that might account for it? This question
remains open for discussion. Jean Baudrillard, in *The Transparency of
Evil: Essays on Extreme Phenomena*, too quickly positions the clone at
the undesirable endpoint of what he calls the cultural view of the DNA
molecule as the "ultimate prosthesis" (1993, 117). By this he means that
cloning, because it seems to signal the end of evolution, and thus of history, comprises "the stage at which the individual, having been reduced

---

[8] This model is familiar from Donna Haraway's famous "Cyborg Manifesto." See
Haraway 1991.

to his abstract and genetic formula, is destined for serial propagation"
(118). As Baudrillard sees it, this is a fatherless, motherless, even inhuman stage that he labels "the hell of the same." Certainly this could
describe Lt. Ellen Ripley's existence at the beginning of *Alien
Resurrection*. However, Baudrillard is off the mark in denying both the
genetic variability and the maternity of the clone. As the *Alien* series
illustrates, genetic variability and maternity are everything in cloning
stories.

So, in the end, cloning scenarios offer popular culture consumers an
opportunity to re-imagine the maternal and reproduction—that is, they
demonstrate again the all-too-familiar images that naturalize women and
their bodies as infantile, mad, wild, and animal-like—but they also suggest points of departure from these images from which we can re-imagine women, reproduction, and the uncanny families they have the
potential to create. In this regard, the weird science in these all-too-familiar misogynist images of women as reproductive workers serves us well.

REFERENCES

Alien. 1979. Directed by Ridley Scott.
Aliens. 1986. Directed by James Cameron.
Alien³. 1992. Directed by David Fincher.
Alien Resurrection. 1997. Directed by Jean-Pierre Jeunet.
Balsamo, Anne. 1999. "Notes Toward a Reproductive Theory of Technology."
    In *Playing Dolly: Technocultural Formations, Fantasies, and Fictions of
    Assisted Reproduction*, edited by E. Ann Kaplan and Susan Squier, 87–97.
    New Brunswick, NJ: Rutgers University Press.
Baudrillard, Jean. 1993. *The Transparency of Evil: Essays on Extreme
    Phenomena*. Translated by James Benedict. London: Verso.
Bear, Greg. 1999. *Darwin's Radio*. New York: Ballantine.
Berman, Jennifer. 1999. "Kids' Books for the 21st Century." *Funny Times*
    Nov./Dec.
Birke, Lynda. 1994. *Feminism, Animals, and Science: The Naming of the Shrew*.
    Buckingham, UK: Open University Press.
Freud, Sigmund. 1919. "The Uncanny." In *Writings on Art and Literature*, trans-
    lated by James Strachey, 193–233. Stanford: Stanford University Press,
    1997.
Fuchs, Cindy. 1997. Review of *Alien Resurrection. Philadelphia Citypaper.net*.
    27 Nov.–4 Dec. 1997. Available at http://citypaper.net/articles/112797/mov
    .alien.shtml.
Gattaca. 1997. Directed by Andrew Niccol.

Hayles, N. Katherine. 1999. *How We Became Posthuman: Virtual Bodies in Cybernetics, Literature, and Informatics*. Chicago: University of Chicago Press.

Haraway, Donna. 1991. *Simians, Cyborgs, and Women: The Reinvention of Nature*. New York: Routledge.

Jurassic Park. 1993. Directed by Steven Spielberg.

Kazazian, Haig H., Jr. 2004. "Mobile Elements: Drivers of Genomic Evolution." *Science* 303:1626–32.

Kimball, A. Samuel. 2002. "Conceptions and Contraceptions in the Future: *Terminator 2*, *The Matrix*, and *Alien Resurrection*." *Camera Obscura* 17, no. 2:69–107.

Lanza, Robert P., et al. 2000. "Extension of Cell Life-Span and Telomere Length in Animals Cloned from Senescent Somatic Cells." *Science* 288:665–69.

Martin, Emily. 1987. *The Woman in the Body: A Cultural Analysis of Reproduction*. Boston: Beacon.

Moffat, Anne Simon. 2000. "Transposons Help Sculpt a Dynamic Genome." *Science* 289:1455–57.

Morgan, Lynn, and Meredith Michaels, eds. 1999. *Fetal Subjects, Feminist Positions*. Philadelphia: University of Pennsylvania Press.

Multiplicity. 1996. Directed by Harold Ramis.

Pennisi, Elizabeth, and Dennis Normile. 2000. "Perseverance Leads to Cloned Pig in Japan." *Science* 5482:1118–19.

Embodying Change: (R)evolutionary Theories of an Alien Synthesis

TESS WILLIAMS

In order to make this discussion more concrete, let us consider predation. The Darwinian picture is that the prey evolves because the weakest, slowest running prey, and their bad genes get eliminated by the predator. By the same token, the fastest, most cunning predators capture the prey and leave the most offspring, thus preferentially propagating their good genes. The only thing that prevents both predator and prey from evolving towards the speed of light is some vague and timely appeal to "developmental constraints."

—SIDNEY FOX, "Evolution Outward and Forward"

A film about an enormous mining ship floating in the endless emptiness of space, its terrified crew engaged in a losing battle against a savage, unknown predator from a distant planet, seems an unlikely prompt for serious ecofeminist criticism. Lieutenant Ellen Ripley and the creature known simply as "the alien" regularly find themselves in deadly conflict aboard space ships and in completely foreign "noir" worlds without a bit of greenery in sight. How are they able to say anything about nature from environments that have no recognizable plants and animals and appear to be the very antithesis of anything natural? They can, because they contribute to an intense and absolutely current dialogue our culture is having about how we became what we are and what our relationship is to each other, to the world around us, and to other species. Ripley and the alien are significant icons of change in Western popular culture. As they interact and transform on the screen, they ironize what we currently understand as biological and sociocultural evolution, and flag how our concepts of change are changing.

Theory and Carnival

Science fiction is a genre of possibility and change, a talented thief of eclectic images, ideas and discourses, and expressive of the entire continuum of Western politics. As such, it is also dialogic and carnivalistic, determinedly responsive to the complexities of Western experience and a perfect testing ground for potential recombinations of form and knowledge. Mikhail Bakhtin is the primary theorist for both dialogics and carnival. His notion of dialogics argues that all texts, all utterances—even all words—are both the results and promoters of ongoing, open-ended cultural conversations. Dialogue, for Bakhtin, never ceases, and no text will ever be the final word. Texts, for this mid-twentieth-century Russian critic, are primarily novels, but much of his appreciation of the complexity of narrative also applies to celluloid story telling. Carnival, on the other hand, is more specific, having its roots in late medieval festivals that often lampooned current authorities, such as landowners, the educated, and the church, and celebrated physical appetites and sufferings. Bakhtin contends that the open, protruding, grotesque body opposes classical perfection in bodies, and that both bodily extremes are politically invested.

Dialogically, the *Alien* films sit at the center of webs of meanings of their own. Products of a particular culture at a particular time in history, these complex texts inhabit multiple genres at once: popular cinema, auteur cinema,[1] the largely unexplored intersections of filmic and written SF texts, the shadowy boundary between horror and SF, and various film criticisms. Some of these genres aim to uncouple the films from SF and each other, and some wish to join them together. The films show different political perspectives, made only a few years apart and by completely different creative teams. However, they all speak to stories of archaic mothers, institutional sires, and monstrous births, and they all express feminist, cyborg, posthuman, and ecofeminist politics to varying degrees. Beyond the interpenetration of discourse and utterance that is dialogia, carnival is a theory of embodiment, a significant "means for displaying otherness" (Holquist 1994, 89). Carnival is a definite marker

---

[1] Ridley Scott and James Cameron rest part of their reputations as directors on the first and second films respectively.

of the *Alien* films, which present the grotesque, shape-shifting savagery of the alien in various incarnations as well as synthetic life forms, androids (and a gynoid), humans with disabilities, humans of unusual abilities, clones, cyborgs, hybrids, human children, and animals.[2] Bodies in carnival are not only varied and often grotesque, they are also culturally inscribed, hybridized, transgressed, degraded, or inverted in some way. How do these related but unstable SF/horror texts, with their grotesque bodies, multiple stories, and shifting critical issues, fit with ecofeminist studies and ecofeminist politics?

Ecofeminism is a field that currently has no singular definition due to its extensive cooption into many areas of academic theory and environmental practice. In many ways it is a shape-shifting theory, so ironically appropriate to apply to a text about shape shifting and monstrosity. However, it is also a theory that can address specifics. Karen Warren says ecofeminism explores and responds to a variety of woman-nature connections. She argues that ecofeminisms proliferate in a similar way to feminisms, sometimes offering competing and sometimes complementary readings of text and experience. Traditionally, ecofeminism embraces practical and empirical linkages of people of color, women, children, and environmental issues, with a particular emphasis on first-world, third-world, and indigenous relationships, but it also includes historical ecofeminisms that speculate on matrifocal pre-agrarianianism and the rise of patriarchal culture. Conceptual ecofeminisms, on the other hand, focus on Western dualistic thinking (male/female, culture/nature, reason/emotion, and so forth) that support value hierarchies that extend exploitation and domination within a number of material and social frameworks, such as race, gender, and environment (Warren 1993). None of these ecofeminisms can be entirely divorced from each other or from the symbolic realm, where the connections between women and nature are extended into religion, philosophy, art, and literature. Contributing to the widespread application and understanding of ecofeminist theory, this chapter explores carnivalized bodies and shared metaphors of biological and social change in both evolutionary theories and the four *Alien* films, and considers the different political charges generated by framing stories of evolution as opposed to specific scientific disciplinary stories of change.

---

[2] In *Alien*[3], an animal is invaded by the alien, which unravels the notion of the human as special case and emphasizes their carnal aspect. Interestingly, in the produced film the animal is a dog, while in previous script drafts it was a ewe and an ox, both of which have more religious overtones.

Drawing on Bakhtin's idea that science participates in cultural carnival at times of change, the films present evolution in two ways (Bakhtin 1984, 49). First, they are ironic texts, satirizing both neo-Darwinist faith in the gene and its focus on genetic selectionism. Second, they are hopeful texts, refusing notions of control and commodification of nature via the scientific military industrial complex, and modeling complex, subversive, nonhierarchical change. Satirizing Darwinian and neo-Darwinian ideas of survival of the fittest and sexual competition, the films invert traditional readings of the struggle between the two species and ironize sexual success. More invested in a "post neo-Darwinist" science of change, the *Alien* films attribute agency to the organism, primarily through its sense of self-organization, rather than seeing it as a passive unit acted upon by natural selection. The films identify speed of change as an issue in evolution, as well as the permeability of the genome, and places emphasis on cooperation and symbiosis—as opposed to competition—as the pathway to success for a species. However, mapping the sciences of change over filmic images of change is not a simple exercise in equivalency, and it has to be recognized that both the filmic texts and the science of evolution are unstable and are engaged in emergent politics of their own. Where they do connect is through carnival. Bodies *in extremis*, permeability of the environment and the body, species' interactions with other species, heteroglossic texts and discourses composed of multiple and partial stories, and interdisciplinary and multidisciplinary narratives all work to construct an uneven world. That scientific theory and metaphoric narrative suggest all of this, and that creative and popular films explore it, are hopeful signs, foreshadowing new paradigms, and possibly hopeful new unities between science and the arts. They demand that we pay more careful attention to such speculative feminist science fiction stories and to the adaptable, useful, and speculative theoretical field of ecofeminism.

Body and Carnival

Irregular and often grotesque bodies underpin both the genre of science fiction and carnival theory. Mary Shelley's gothic novel *Frankenstein*, a story of monstrosity and monstrous creation, is nominated by Brian Aldiss as the first science fictional text in the Western tradition, while Michael Holquist, critical commentator on Bakhtin, nominates the same book as the poster text for carnival, because it is an important case study of the grotesque body and intertextuality (Aldiss 1988, 29–65; Holquist

1994, 94–106). The primary Western text for carnival and SF are one and the same, with the focus of both being on the patched nature of the body/text, rather than on an unseamed body/text. In every respect, the *Alien* project is also predicated on the monstrous body, actively undoing almost every currently accepted idea of bodily unity and focusing on scavenged, recombinant, ruptured, and morphing bodies. This even applies to the composite, seamed, four-film "quadrology" body of work that is the *Alien* project itself.

A linked but "distributed" body, it is a collection—at this point in time—of four films linked via titles, the two main characters, and occasional peripheral characters. [3] The four films have different directors and writers, and with the auteur nature of the productions, they have connections to very different bodies of work that bear witness to the aesthetic of their very different writers and directors. Beyond practical discontinuities of production and discontinuities of environments and characters, there is also a cultural tone to each film that reflects the political microperiod that produced it. In fact, one could make a strong argument for these films to be considered separately. However, as Stephen Scobie argues, it is also legitimate to consider them as connected because "there is a kind of unity to the whole series, and the later directors cannot help but respond to the images and obsessions of the earlier installments" (Scobie 1993, 80). While Scobie considers the series as one extended work, and while one can argue that Ripley and the alien offer continuity to the *Alien* project, in fact the alien is a different entity in each film and Ripley is a clone of Ellen Ripley—not the same physical body—in *Alien Resurrection*. If there *is* a literal link, it would appear to be the actual bodies of Ripley and the alien. However, since the aliens are simply not recognizable as individuals, it must be Ripley's body that forms the connection between films. Hers is the linking body, but it is an archetypal, opportunistically resurrected body (even prior to the final film), that literally "sleeps" between cultural crises. Ripley's body moves away from formalist unities of time-, space-, and hero-centeredness and becomes a seamed body and an absolutely decentered, ironic subject. The *Alien* project is, therefore, a disrupted body of work about a single body, but the films utilize other bodies to emphasize how

---

[3] The issue, of course, comes up regarding *Alien vs. Predator*, the 2004 film directed by Paul W. S. Anderson. Following the logic of this paper, it does not belong with the four films being considered here as Ripley's body is absent. Instead, I would put it in a completely different subgenre of "monster" films. There is also a "video game" feel to this film.

bodies are treated and understood through what Frederick Jameson refers to as "the cultural logic of late capitalism."

As Ripley's discontinuous body sits at the center of the project, the focus of the project can be held to be the feminized body. The feminized body in the *Alien* project is the grotesque body as Mary Russo theorizes and develops it in her work on carnival. Russo says the grotesque, feminized body is open, protruding, irregular, secreting, multiple, and changing, as opposed to the masculinized, "classical" body, which is closed, monumental, static, self-contained, symmetrical, and sleek (1994, 8). All of the films enact this carnivalization quite specifically. Penetration and impregnation feminizes human bodies that appear to be masculine. These bodies then give birth to the phallic stage of the alien, which leaves them violated, torn, and bleeding. That the first victim is a white male, Kane, sends a clear message that no "body" is immune from the horror of rape/gestation, previously the province of the human female body. Gender collapses, and this affects all bodies, even machine bodies, in the films.

In *Alien*, the android, Ash, spins out of control in a grisly scene of cyborg death and destruction after he tries to murder Ripley. There are sexual overtones to his methods of silencing her, as he tries to push a soft-porn magazine into Ripley's mouth to gag and suffocate her. As he self-destructs, he does not reveal the hard, shiny, lethal machinery usually associated with cyborgs or robots. Rather, he secretes a large volume of viscous, white fluid that looks like milk; and his insides suggest lymphatic tissue. Ash is impotent and has a "feminine" kind of softness to his body. Bishop, the android in *Aliens* and *Alien*[3], also suffers damage and becomes an "open," feminized, and carnivalized body, but his is also a multiple body, a further marker of carnival. In the first three films the androids are tools, implements of institutional bodies, not agents in their own right, and thus the masculine body is disempowered. In *Alien Resurrection,* Ripley has been cloned eight times in an attempt to "reproduce" the alien queen that was inside her when she died. In a truly postmodern moment, Ripley gets to destroy her previous selves, which are all irregular, "grotesque" copies of the original. The surviving clone is also an irregular copy, but the irregularities are not visible. Ripley, immensely strong, stands for gender compromised in a reverse way, as does Velasquez in *Aliens*, the soldier who is asked if she is ever "mistaken for a man." Her riposte to the male soldier who asks her that question is "No. Are you?" The ultimate irony here is that Ripley's body in its original, uncloned condition was grotesque to begin with, according to Russo—just by being human and female.

As the female grotesque is mapped onto female bodies, male bodies, and humanoid bodies, it is also mapped onto extreme "others." The monster is problematically gendered, and has a strong connection to the female grotesque. Phallic in the face-hugger and chest-burster stages, and a violator and penetrator of bodies, it still tends to be marked by Russo's notions of the female grotesque, which is the antithesis of the closed, sleek, and masculine. The alien conspicuously salivates around its complex mouths within mouths, and its behavior is constellated around reproductive activity. Gender unspecified in the first film, it "created" eggs out of captives, and cocooned humans to be food for off-spring, but from the second film it became markedly female. In *Alien³* the fetal alien inside Ripley is a "queen," while the nonqueen, warrior alien gestates in the body of a dog, an irregular, "nonclassical" body. In the last film there are three queens, and again reproduction is a primary activity with one queen body shown pregnant and birthing rather than laying eggs, thanks to Ripley's human DNA.

Inanimate bodies that contain animate bodies, like the spaceships, are gendered in a complex fashion, but are predominantly feminine grotesque as identified by Russo. The Nostromo is "mother" to its crew and wakes them from deep sleep at the beginning of the film in a scene that is suggestive of her having incubated them. Mother's relation to the crew is grotesque because she appears to provide a nurturing environ-ment, but eventually her crew is betrayed, partly by mother's program-ming, then trapped and killed in her non–living quarters, the "bowels" of the ship. Barbara Creed describes the alien ship on LV-426, the site of the original distress call, as "having a 'vaginal' opening which is shaped like a horseshoe, its curved sides like two long legs spread apart at the entrance" and the interior is "dark, dank and mysterious" (1993, 18). Although Creed's psychoanalytic critique incorporates romantic ideas of terror and abjection that were not present in folk celebrations, Creed's archaic mother also brings strong resonances of the open body with an emphasis on the lower bodily stratum to a carnival reading of the film. The ship in *Alien Resurrection* is called "father," but this is not simple oppositional gendering. It marks the ship's military and scientific pur-pose and contrasts to the smaller pirate ship named *Betty* that docks with it. Masculinity in *Alien Resurrection* is always compromised and never moves much beyond caricature. Authority is a joke. General Perez runs his unit looking like a teenage hoodlum with his baseball cap on back-ward, and when he is in danger his face becomes comical and he does not appear to engage with what is happening. Elgyn, the handsome, authoritative leader of the smugglers who bring the body cargo to the

Auriga, is an heroic figure, but he is the first to die. His death is igno-
minious: he falls for an obvious trap, and his body is violated in death
as Ripley uses it as a weapon conduit. He is not a hero, he is not even an
antihero—he is a hero who withers in ironic presentation.

One of the largest bodies to have significance in carnival and in the
Alien films is the planetary body. In *Rabelais and his World*, Bakhtin
discusses the birth and life of Gargantua and Pantagruel as a cyclical
phenomenon of biological largesse followed by deprivation and death.
Gargantua's birth is heralded by massive feasting and bountiful rich
foods, while Pantagruel's birth produces a dreadful drought that consumes the countryside and the people with thirst. Bakhtin goes further:
the body without the mediation of culture is the grotesque body, which
is eternally pregnant and dying, swallowing and defecating, and the
earth is therefore the ultimate body from which everything is born and
to which everything returns. Rabelais's medieval world is fecund and
cannot ultimately be destroyed. The folk experience of European seasons provides a cyclical reassurance in carnival that whatever dies will
be renewed. Bakhtin describes the medieval grotesque as familiar and
reassuring, but says the grotesque was replaced in the Renaissance by
the closed, completed, and finished body. He also claims the romantic
grotesque introduced terror, because the grotesque ceased being familiar and became alien and destroyed meaning. The postmodern carnival
is still dark, but often it destroys meaning more through irony than terror. Thus the planetary bodies in the *Alien* project are no longer fecund,
as they are in medieval epistemology, nor do they represent any part of
Creed's archaic mother, the generative, "totalizing," and prephallic
mother. There is no promise *or* horror in these worlds that have simply
become mining colonies and prisons. Noir worlds with no apparent
warmth or light, the newly settled planet LV-426 and the penal colony
Fury 161 are never even seen by daylight. All that is known of these
worlds is mining machinery, warehouses, life-preserving technology,
junkyards, and dormitorylike living quarters. The planets have no vital-
ity and no inherent attraction or even danger. They have been commod-
ified and their inhabitants view them as places of restriction. They are
not alive. The only hint that this might be about to change comes at the
end of *Alien Resurrection,* as the "lifeboat" crew of Neanderthal,
gynoid, cripple, and alien/woman hurtle towards a blue planet, an
unknown "home" that seems to hold—among other things—promise of
life and renewal.

The *Alien* project deals phallocentric culture some serious challenges. The story is not simply one of anarchic carnival upsetting civi-

lized order for a short space and time. It is a story of the carnival body dominating the classical body and significantly—and possibly permanently—undoing its closed, monumental masculinity. What is more, the carnival moment and body may seem to be contained by the boundary of the film session, but they are not. The carnival moment and the carnival body have been generated by the most powerful discourse twentieth and twenty-first western cultures have: science. The film predominantly borrows from science, generating many questions. For instance, what exactly does the high proportion of grotesque bodies in both science and in the popular consciousness mean? As we are unlikely to fully recuperate the transcendent, sleek, classic male body, what will emergent bodies be like? If discourses like science are marked by carnival in times of great change, what happens to scientific rules about bodies? What concepts of unity will govern emergent bodies, and is their very alteration subject to scientific rule? And how extensively can irony rewrite scientific narratives?

Evolving Bodies and Carnival

All four of the *Alien* films have the same apparent evolutionary kernel. Two species compete for resources, with each species representing a rare and important resource to the other. The aliens utilize humans as host organisms and nourishment at different points in their life cycle, and human culture is intent on harvesting the versatile and almost indestructible DNA of the aliens for military and medical purposes. This is Darwin's "struggle for existence" in a number of senses. First, both species have proved highly adaptable in their drive to colonize hostile environments, existing in cold more extreme than that of the Antarctic and in the vacuum of space: humans by mediating the environment with technology, the aliens by being genetically plastic. The struggle between the two species is unmasked and unmodified by cultural complexities, with the "natural" context stripped and reduced to one of protective hardware. No sentimentalizing aesthetic intervenes in the viewer's understanding of this competition. Looked at this way, the story seems to be a stark representation of Darwin's prime mechanism of natural selection revealed. It is survival of the fittest. Or is it?

Is a cultural story about the wholesale slaughter of one species by another really likely to be a story of survival of the fittest, or is it more likely to be a parody of survival of the fittest? Here is a battle for survival, but it is not just about species competing for resources or territory. They are each trying to use the other as a resource, and their battle takes place in artificial or completely barren environments. There is nothing ultimately sustaining about the predation of these species upon each other. Human and nonhuman are pitted against each other in a scenario reminiscent of the recent history of humans versus predatory macrofauna, a story that tends to valorize human ingenuity and ends in the nonhuman's extinction. Here, however, there is more equality and more mirroring. Human rapaciousness knows no bounds, and the alien biology is clearly constituted around opportunism. In the situations found in these films, neither species is in its natural habitat. Planetside, neither has a legitimate claim on the world where they fight. In those worlds both species have been introduced, and there is, in fact, no "nature," no ecological context within which natural selection may operate. As already mentioned, LV-426 and the penal colony Fury 161 function as resource and prison, there is no sense of belonging on these planets. Ironically, the films are only apparently anthropocentric, and only apparently about species competition, because both species are "aliens." So, what seems to be a clichéd representation of "survival of the fittest" actually displaces the hero story of human evolution and introduces relevant noncompetitive models of organic change.

The field of biology always situates natural selection and competition with sexual selection. Sexual selection is as foundational to the species as natural selection, and— beyond the threats from the environment and (un)natural predators—the aim of all organisms, according to Darwinism, is to reproduce. This desire to reproduce is certainly borne out in the behavior of the alien species, but the *Alien* films paint a strange reproductive future for humans. At the end of the first film, Ripley is the only survivor, together with the ship's cat. This is a limited reproductive situation, possibly one that foreshadows both the parthenogenetic reproduction and the hybridization of species in the fourth film, *Alien Resurrection.* In the second film both Ripley and the alien fight for seemingly flawed reproductive realities. The little girl "Newt" is not Ripley's biological offspring, but is an emotional surrogate for the daughter she has lost, so the intense mammalian bond that is predicated on physical gestation and actual long-term caretaking is in this case created from a short-term, crisis attachment and probably has more to do with grief than love. There are also two clear morphological markers of the partial nature of this biological relationship in the film. Firstly, the little girl is named after an amphibian, rather than something warm and endearing, and Newt's attachment, in turn, is to the severed head of a doll. With regard to the alien, it is questionable to view its "maternal" drive in any anthropomorphic fashion, as it seems to directly contradict the insect shape and habits that include the laying of hundreds of eggs, a reproductive strategy suggesting the antithesis of personal investment in offspring.

The third film, *Alien³*, bears out these readings as Ripley is reconstructed out of "maternal mode" and is quite unemotional about the death of Newt after the crash, and insists on being present as the child's body is autopsied. Her investment is once again survival (though not exclusively her own) rather than reproduction at this point, and the warrior alien incubated inside the dog refuses to damage Ripley because she is carrying the new queen. This indicates that in the alien reproductive model, more value is placed on the producer of offspring than on the offspring themselves. In both *Alien³* and *Alien Resurrection*, there are a number of survivors, but their sexual competitiveness represents, at the very least, "relaxed selection," a situation where enhanced technology has seen a flattening out of the traditional bell curve of survival (Ridley 1997, 49). In *Alien³* those left are male prisoners who have a double "Y" chromosome, a genetic defect that predisposes the men who have it to antisocial behavior, violence, and mental disability. Their social structure is also a quasi-Catholic priesthood, where celibacy has a strong, positive value and the only woman in the story dies by her own hand after being impregnated by another species. The "lifeboat" population left at the end of *Alien Resurrection* also constitutes a mockery of human sexual competitiveness and viability, consisting of Ripley, a clone who is an alien-human hybrid; Call, an artificial life form, a gynoid; Johner, a battle-scarred simian look-alike with no potential mate; and Vriess, a paraplegic.

In fact, the only way humans reproduce in any sense in the series is to incubate the "chest-burster" stage of the alien; thus humans fail to reproduce and act as surrogate parents to the competing alien species. Even cloning, as happens to Ripley in *Alien Resurrection*, is limited in its success as a reproductive strategy, as we see when she turns the flamethrower on the previous seven attempts to recreate her. This pointed lack of fecundity offers a critique of the scientific appropriation of reproduction and obsession with genes, and it makes a mockery of human survival, pointing to the aliens as infinitely more "deserving" of biological continuance in a universe driven by Darwinism. The aliens, after all, fight fiercely to reproduce. That they multiply like a Malthusian nightmare and would soon run out of food sources on the small ships that they colonize seems almost immaterial, as they continuously adapt and move closer to environments where there are greater resources. In this they are assisted, not only by the Company's and the military's ready provision of colonizing, colonizable bodies, but also by the short-sighted policies and greed of these patriarchal institutions. This topsy-turvy representation of natural selection and sexual selection is part of our cultural investigation of ourselves and nonhuman others, and our ongoing relationships with other species. It also inevitably invites carnivalization of bodies and revises scientific discourses that have a large investment in de/inscribing the workings and properties of bodies in fixed ways.

We need to exonerate Charles Darwin, the British naturalist, of any charge of reductionism. At the time he wrote *The Origin of the Species by Means of Natural Selection,* his proposition of organic change flew in the face of religious beliefs of creationism and fixity of species. It was the New Synthesis that took Darwin's original theory of natural selection two steps further by incorporating the Weismann barrier, an invisible mechanism that purports to prevent traffic between the body and the germ line, and then fused it with Mendel's work on heritable traits. From that point, the genocentric universe came into being and organic bodies became puppets run by self-interested, microscopic codes. The only way organisms have to change in this story is random mutation. Genocentrism still remains at the root of scientific consciousness and provides a useful central theory bank for biology, reducing lived experience to competition and success. However, the problem is that evolution and biology tell many composite and overlapping stories. They are too large to be accommodated by one neat, foreclosing narrative, even the gene story, and other disciplines have incubated many stories that can modify the survivalism of neo-Darwinism.

The first disruption to Darwinism itself is Punctuated Equilibrium. This theory claims that changes in species might be quite rapid, whereas Darwin was quite emphatic about natural selection being a slow process. Niles Eldredge and Stephen Jay Gould proposed the theory in 1972 (see Gould and Eldredge, 1985). Punctuated Equilibrium is a theory of rapid speciation arguing that changes in organisms come quickly to small, often isolated "daughter" species while large populations actually inhibit widespread adaptive change and are more likely to represent evolutionary stasis and genetic homeostasis. We find evidence for this in the fossil record, which shows both stasis and rapid change. Punctuated Equilibrium is a challenging and complicated idea that tailors the Darwinian model to make it a more culturally relevant. Among its more radical features, Punctuated Equilibrium allows that the environment of an organism is significant in speciation events, as isolation is likely to emphasize genetic drift and foster useful adaptations. Punctuated Equilibrium also acknowledges that various organisms have developed at different rates during different periods, and that some speciation events result in population explosions and widespread colonizations by organisms, and, finally, this new perception of change sees the whole process of rapid evolution ghosted by the issue of equally rapid extinction.

Punctuated equilibrium is not only a paleontological explanation of observable, sudden jumps in the fossil record, it is also a theory consistent with late-twentieth-century understandings and experience of change. It brings Darwinism up to date in that it presents important, culturally compatible modifications of the original Darwinian model. Fragmentation of the time records for species, for example, resonates with cultural pluralism and segregated social interests. The environment contributes to the biological production of an organism, just as we now accept that environment contributes to the social production of the organism. Colonization is writ large in history, human and paleontological, and the prominent specter of extinction in bounding the species affirms the psychology of the atomic age. Examined through this evolutionary thread alone, the terrifying, fictitious predator of the *Alien* project is, in fact, partly identifiable as rapid change and sudden death in late industrial societies. Rapid change is the predator, hunting people down by technologizing and rationalizing their work places, altering their family structures, redesigning and invading their bodies, destroying geographical and cultural boundaries, and presenting them with ever more painful and bizarre possibilities and probabilities of mass death.

Beyond the dominant model of change being competitive and hierarchical, both popular science fiction texts like the *Alien* project and science explore other options. It is, however, a tricky relationship. Carnival texts embrace the marginal and recreate it as central, while science explores the marginal but foregrounds order, predictability, and fixity. Reading the inscribed body through scientific discourses touches on boundary issues regarding the creation/dissolution of bodies, visible/invisible parameters of the body, static/dynamic representations of bodies, and life/death of bodies.[4] Prebiotics, or precellular biology, is a science that contributes to understanding representations of change in the *Alien* project. The search for the chemical origins of life focuses on synthesis of amino acids when combined with heat and water, as it has

---

[4] See Bakhtin 1984, 49–50. This is an adaptation of Bakhtin's argument that carnival includes science at times of great change because at these points culture is more free to imagine new potentialities. Bakhtin also focuses on the tension between different historical perceptions of "life" and "death."

long been suspected that the initial chemical reactions that generated life occurred in hot springs and geysers. Experiments modeling this process have proved interesting. If these prebiotic chemicals lay down the pathway for all life on the planet, then life may not have appeared in the way that Darwin proposes at all.

The experimental process of creating the protocells is surprisingly self-limiting; that is, out of the existing twenty amino acids it was assumed that all combinations would occur, but in fact only certain combinations manifested. Sidney Fox documents other features of the experiments that undermine neo-Darwinist expectations. For instance, protocells form very easily, while scientists had anticipated that prebiotic evolution would be a lengthy and difficult process. The experiments challenged the traditional model in other ways, as well. Protocells were created in huge numbers rather than in small, isolated populations; the laboratory protocells showed tendencies to associate and communicate chemically, so environment quickly became significant; chemical activity was found in all protocells; the protocells had good life spans; and protein appeared to predate DNA as a mechanism of inheritance in cells. Fox believes his experiments indicate a level of "self-organization" to life and bear witness to the possibility of big leaps in evolution (Fox 1988, 17–29).

These challenges to Darwinism are supported by the *Alien* project, particularly *Alien³* and *Resurrection*. The notions of unpredictability in experimentation and evolutionary change underpin the narratives of all four films, but the two most recent films foreground these themes in specifically post-neo-Darwinist formats. The entity that is the alien is an organism that responds purposefully to its environment and survives by genetic amalgamation with host animals, as well as by using them for incubation. The entity is both opportunistic and restricted. It is able to capitalize on available resources in the environment, but its organic "environment," also reciprocally defines it; in this case, the host body restricts its reproduction. This connects to further critiques made by Fox, that in evolutionary paradigms there has been too much emphasis on the external environment in terms of natural selection and very little work done on the internal environment of the organism, meaning chemistry and synthesizing, body-based processes, not just genetics. In *Alien Resurrection*, that internal "environment" issue becomes more complicated again. The alien queen/Ripley amalgam is an example of reciprocal biology and the branching of both physical and psychological possibility. Both organisms limit each other, so their options are increased but not completely open. In a macroevolutionary leap, one of the alien queens is forced out of an insect reproductive mode into mammalian parturition while Ripley becomes physically stronger and her body chemistry is affected—witness blood that can dissolve metal. The change doesn't work out well for the alien queen as she is destroyed by her even more changed offspring, but neither does the offspring fare well; Ripley, the competing "daughter" species, destroys it. If there is Darwinian natural selection in *Alien Resurrection*, it is accomplished as irony. The alien becomes more human, and therefore becomes more vulnerable, as Ripley becomes less human and less physically and psychologically vulnerable. On the other hand, the film does imply non-Darwinian evolution and reinforces Fox's experimental results: macroevolution is plausible, random variation doesn't really apply because change is about self-organization, and reverse engineering of organisms will not necessarily make sense of the process that produced an organism as it exists now.

Biological form, or morphology, poses a different challenge to neo-Darwinist genetic predestination from prebiotics. Briefly, morphology is the study of constraints experienced by living forms in biology. Until recently, excepting for D'arcy Thompson's highly mathematical work on the study of form,[5] it was difficult to incorporate this information scientifically into evolutionary theory. The easy solution has been to pin questions about form on the inviolable germ plasm, the reproductive cells, and then come back to natural selection. This is what Stephen Jay Gould and others call the "replicator" theory of evolution. Unless there is a major upset, genetically driven life forms will just keep manufacturing strong likenesses of themselves, generation after generation. There are some limits, however, to this story. Morphology is obviously connected to the faithful reproduction of species; however, it is not actually a story about descent. Morphology actually prefers to focus on the

---

[5] Originally written in 1917, Thompson's *On Growth and Form* is the text of a man who, just at the time that the New Synthesis was being posited, repudiated Darwinism with the words, "So long and so far as fortuitous variation and the survival of the fittest remain engrained as fundamental and satisfactory hypotheses in the philosophy of biology, so long will these satisfactory and specious causes tend to stay severe and diligent enquiry to the great arrest and prejudice of future discovery" (p. 5, some punctuation omitted). He then went on to map the natural forms of plants, animals, and fish mathematically, and much of his work had to wait for the advent of personal computers before it could be verified. The only reason he is not discussed in more depth here is that his work contributes little to any direct biological thesis on evolution and veers more to an engineering model of nature that has not really been incorporated into the debate yet, though it is at least peripheral to convergent evolution.

rational principles behind the ordering of life. This branch of science is curious about what holds an organism true to type and what forces persuade an organism to change its direction and alter what has been a stable form. Darwin's idea of random mutation and selection actually made early biologists nervous, because random mutation implies an infinite plasticity of form, and clearly something was making reproduction of organisms regular. Darwinism also depends on assumptions of common ancestries and faith in the existing taxonomic systems. This faith is possibly somewhat misplaced, as molecular biology researchers have discovered that some species, for example, certain frogs, have been incorrectly categorized and that their family connections are not what they appeared to be. Darwinism tends to infer a lot from form, but does not address the really puzzling questions of stability in form and the impetus to change. Making form and change chaotic, and showing the alien and Ripley as converging species, forces encounters with biology that at least foreground issues that scientific literature has already generated.

Morphology stories are further complicated by parallelism, convergence, and homology. According to parallelism, a shared genotype inherited from a common ancestor produces characteristics, while convergence can be either acquisitions or losses of certain characteristics (Mayr 1976, 463). Examples of this found in pop ethology and human evolution include Desmond Morris's use of primate parallelism to explore human biology and behaviors and Elaine Morgan's use of subcutaneous fat and bradycardia as aquatic convergences in humans. These tensions between stasis and change in the histories of species make the story of organisms and change a lot more complicated. The paradoxical fidelity and malleability of life suggests carnival as a confrontation with the kind of tension that promotes change. The *Alien* project is more than a Promethean story of attempted genetic theft and retribution, and more than a collection of cautionary tales. It is also about hopeful monsters. In these four films, the abundance, adaptability, perseverance, and complexity of life mock economic and scientific efforts at reductionism and control. While certainly also an expression of repressed anxieties about science and the commodification of flesh, the project still moves to overwrite the genomic bible with the clamor of polyvocal science and insists on bodies as multidisciplinary dialogic junctions of prebiotic chemistries, symbiotic histories, developmental constraints, environmental constraints, *and* the fluid genome.

Although genes work prescriptively on one level, quite how they work is not always clear. Neo-Darwinists and sociobiologists like

Richard Dawkins and E. O. Wilson tend to reductionist thinking on genes and see what exists in an organism as representing the selected best of all possibilities for the organism. Other scholars dismiss this idea as tautological: the best trait is what survives so what has survived is the best trait. In *The Descent of Woman,* Elaine Morgan critiques "optimality thinking" when talking about the failure of human female sexual arousal:

> You may be wondering why such an apparently simple and minor biological maladjustment didn't right itself in the course of a few thousand generations. After all, we have up to now been talking quite casually, as evolutionists have a habit of doing, about the most astounding morphological changes in the primate frame, as if endless variations in the shape, the size, and arrangement of organs were available through some celestial mail order catalogue. (Morgan 1974, 109)

Genes are often presented as a "celestial mail order catalogue," a template of perfection and a final solution to understanding the puzzle of life, but genes have a degree of instability themselves. Through the *Alien* project, the carnivalization of evolutionary theory and a major challenge to neo-Darwinism are realized in the representations of genetic plasticity. Such plasticity is not generally accepted, but from the time of Le Chevalier Jean-Baptiste Lamarck, who proposed the theory of acquired characteristics and their inheritance, there have been questions about the permeability of the genome. Australian researcher Ted Steele extrapolates from his research on the immune system and the reverse transcription of RNA codes to DNA, suggesting that if immunity to certain diseases and viruses can be formed in a lifetime and then inherited, it is logical to assume other features within the body can also adapt during the lifetime of one individual and be passed on in some way to offspring.[6] Mae-Wan Ho uses Steele's research, among others, to critique Darwinism and neo-Darwinism and considers other non-Mendelian

---

[6] Steele's work followed from Sir Peter Medawar's 1950 research, where he injected immature mice with large numbers of foreign cells. The mice became tolerant of the invading cells and passed immunity onto their offspring. Interestingly, Steele's initial proposal of the existence of an environmental feedback loop that could move from soma to germ line, and therefore pass on environmentally stimulated change to succeeding generations, was published in 1979—coincidentally the same year that *Alien* was released. His most recent book, *Lamarck's Signature,* arrived on the shelves within months of the release of *Alien Resurrection.* It is obviously not a timed event, but it is of interest that two significant narratives on bodily and species change are so closely stepped.

mechanisms that might allow direct feedback from soma to germ line besides reverse transcription. In two collections of essays assembling specialists from different fields, reverse transcription is discussed alongside the transposition, repetition, amplification, conversion, or contraction of gene sequences. Ho herself looks at "non-random changes in genomic DNA in certain environments which can become stably inherited in subsequent generations" such as predictable responses to stress and responses to specific chemicals in fruit flies and maize plants (Ho 1988, 134). Her central thesis requires that any considerations of organisms include their external and internal environment, and she advocates strongly for epigenesis as a force of biological change over selectionism. She takes epigenesis out of its traditional field of embryology, where it has long been understood that certain nongenetic codes program tissue differentiation, into the whole lifecycle of the organism and into evolution itself.

To do this is to resituate the organism and make it a site of interactivity, multivocality, and carnival. Chemical, biochemical, and biological stable states act together in a dynamic, nonhierarchical concert that embodies both dis/organized change and stability. This undoes previous dualistic readings of bodies as conforming or transgressive, and shows scientific readings of bodies as atomized and complex systems to be reductively isolated. Bodies are then reconstructed as multiply discursive sites. Interpenetration with the environment is an important dimension to this multiple reading of bodies; however, in the *Alien* project the focus is primarily on the internal tensions that govern bodies, challenging stability and forcing change. With the chemical and the biochemical visually inaccessible in these films, the only readings of such change that can be obtained are phenotypic. Clear visual instances of compromised genetics include the alien blending with the dog and the hybridity between human and alien in the last film. After the alien and Ripley are mixed, the creature's reproductive practice changes into a lethally vulnerable mammalian parturition, while Ripley demonstrates exceptional strength and her blood has an unusual corrosive effect on metal. These are but the outward manifestations of carnival mixings that have affected not just bodily appearance, manifesting as the grotesque and monstrous, but have also unbalanced and changed the multiple internal governing systems of bodies.

A complementary model of coexistence and organismic interactivity comes from the area of biology and bears on evolutionary theory. Serial Endosymbiosis Theory (SET) contends that symbiogenesis forms the basis of the web of life and accounts for the variety of life on the planet

Fictitious Contagions: Computer Viruses in the Science Fiction of the 1970s

JUSSI PARIKKA

Science fiction has gone through a whole evolution taking it from animal, vegetable, and mineral becomings to becomings of bacteria, viruses, molecules, and things imperceptible.

—DELEUZE AND GUATTARI, *A Thousand Plateaus*

Computer viruses are more than mere technical objects. They have a literary life as well. Interestingly, this life of fiction has a longer history than the actual viruses of computer programming. An examination of how we imagine these accidents of computer culture proves to be a novel approach to understanding the cultural-historical constitution of contemporary media culture. Furthermore, a historical rewiring of fictional viruses can also act as an interesting tool for thinking through contemporary digital culture from the viewpoint of its historical imaginary.

From the perspective of media archaeology, the roots of computer viruses may be traced to Samuel Butler's *Erewhon* (1872), which articulates well (and not without satire) the fear of self-reproducing, technological automata. However, fictional viruses gained ground especially in the science fiction literature of the 1970s, which was full of such software anomalies. Three novels in particular, David Gerrold's *When HARLIE Was One* (1972), John Brunner's *The Shockwave Rider* (1975), and Thomas J. Ryan's *The Adolescence of P-1* (1977), play with the idea of self-perpetuating software programs. In these novels, VIRUS-programs, tapeworms, and artificial intelligences move through telephone lines, hack mainframe computers, and cause trouble to people who try, in turn, to grasp the idea of technology being alive. The novels reveal the fading boundaries of human and machine, nature and technology, as well as the possible dangers of technology. In addition, they illustrate themes of information, misinformation, and problems of data handling in a postindustrial society. Interestingly, however, their main topic seems to be artificial life, which has attracted the attention of computer scientists since the first computer projects after the Second World War, and especially since the 1960s.

Computer viruses and worms were part of the fictional worlds created by these three SF writers years before such miniprograms made the headlines in popular media. Since they were initially mere experimental programs in academic networks, viruses were not discussed in a contemporary manner until the mid-1980s. Computer scientist Fred Cohen was the one who recognized that these self-perpetuating mini-programs could in fact prove to be a real danger for an organized society. According to Cohen's "worst case scenario," a computer virus could threaten the institutions (financial, business, government, academic) of the network society (Cohen 1984).[1] The popular media have been overrun by viruses since the 1988 Internet Worm incident, which jammed approximately 6,000 computers connected to the network. In the aftermath of the worm, the whole issue became "professionalized": antivirus protection became a big business, while at the same time virus toolkits, virus writing clubs, and so on, ensured that the number of viruses was constantly on the rise.

In this chapter, I wish to map *the imaginary* surrounding this phenomenon of digital media. The novels analyzed in this essay are not just amusing anecdotes springing from the minds of innovative fiction writers. On the contrary, they are an essential part of the genealogy of modern-day computer culture. This position is able to highlight previously neglected themes, ideas, thoughts, and articulations, which reveal important aspects of our contemporary stance towards technology and media. The three novels by Gerrold, Brunner, and Ryan offer fresh mappings of our media culture and the different actors that take part in it.

Virtuality and the Technological Imagination

The French philosopher Gilles Deleuze writes that technology is social before it is technical, or that a selective social machine is prior to the

---

[1] On the cultural history of computer viruses, especially in connection with network capitalism, see Parikka 2005a.

technical elements it uses (Deleuze 1998, 40; Gere 2002, 13). Another way to put Deleuze's point would be to underline that technology is conceptual or virtual before it becomes actual and technical. In more general terms, the fictional and the imaginary precede the actual. Instead of being autonomous spheres of self-encased rationality, technologies are intertwined with cultural-historical articulations of representations, ideologies, and meanings, but also a-semantic fields of semiosis and a-signifying cultural practices. In other words, technology, which is itself nondiscursive and material, "speaks" along with discursive statements and practices, which precede actual technologies. Photography, television, cinema, computer technology, and virtual reality had their virtual spaces long before they were actualized (individuated) in concrete apparatuses. Technology is invested with meanings and practices that surpass the actual apparatuses.[2]

In recent (anti)virus literature, the general attitude towards fiction has been negative, focusing solely on the errors and misconceptions fueled by science fiction novels (Harley, Slade, and Gattiker 2001, 206). Fiction is judged from the position of the actual, which is understood as the only source for the real. For researchers in cultural history and cultural studies, however, fiction opens interesting horizons, and its value has been widely discussed. Science fiction reveals the historical situatedness of imagination, that is, what things are imaginable for a particular media ecology. Writing (science) fiction becomes, consequently, an opportunity to make claims which are nonrational *and* culturally and historically pertinent.

Fiction literature should not, then, be read from the reference point of the True and Actual, but as tactics that invent alternative worlds and promote multiple ways of being and becoming. This means also looking beyond established terms and focusing on the forces that constitute terms: a focus on individuation as a process instead of individuated end results.

For Deleuze, philosophy is more about creating concepts than interpreting the world. In the words of Gregg Lambert: "For Deleuze, it was never a question of 'breaking out' of the world that exists, but of creating the right conditions for the expression of other possible worlds to 'break-in', in order to introduce new variables into the world that exists, causing the quality of its reality to undergo modifications, change and becoming" (Lambert 1997, p. 137). Hence, fiction—including literature, cinema,

---

[2] On Deleuze-Guattarian mixed semiotics, or assemblages, see Parisi 2004.

painting, and so forth—acts as an assemblage that composes alternative combinations of forces. Books do not represent the world but act in it: "contrary to a deeply rooted belief, the book is not an image of the world. It forms a rhizome with the world" (Deleuze and Guattari 1987, 11). Accepting such an ontological view, the question is no longer "what does it mean?" but "how does it work?" Texts should be seen as practices that interact with the world. Literature does not represent the world, but functions in it, so that the possibilities of texts and writing correspond to their ability to create new paths and produce new thoughts. Literature is a production machine with the potential to produce and dismantle assemblages (Deleuze and Guattari 2000, 47–49). Texts in themselves may be seen as parts of assemblages, processlike and decentered, tending towards the world instead of folding in on themselves. A text is *in* the world, not *about* the world.

Deleuze's notion of "the powers of the false" refers to creating a new narrative that believes in radical constructivism. This position is somewhat different from theories of social construction. The transcendental position of meaning is not understood solely in terms of the mental faculties of the human. Instead, several different heterogeneous regimes of the world (geological, biological, cultural, artistic, technological, and so on) participate in a construction, a becoming of the world. In other words, the world consists of numerous, interacting agencies, both human and nonhuman (DeLanda 1999; Parisi 2004). This position also refers to the powers of fiction to create new images of thought, which do not rely on truth as their final cause, but are, as Lambert states, more about "modifications and variations of the past" and multiple versions and descriptions of the event (Lambert 1997, 142; Deleuze 2005, 122–50). A cultural-historical perspective on artistic practices reveals the ways in which they have traditionally been able to connect to the virtual and the imaginary, moving on a plane of experimentation (Zielinski 2006). Thus, the idea of an artistic interest towards the world resonates with this Deleuzian idea. With fiction, we can save the "not-necessarily true pasts" and rewire them to creations of futures (Deleuze 2005, 127).

I will now proceed to analyze three such imaginations of the future. The three novels from the 1970s posit not only fictional accounts of computer viruses and worms, but also new possibilities of comprehending the (cultural) assemblages of these digital contagions. Inherent in my analysis is the assumption that fiction is real. Fictions of computer viruses lie at the heart of the actual meanings and contexts of digital viruses, if only as unactualized potentialities and marginalized traits. The actual is constantly pierced and crossed with the powers of the virtual, which emphasizes the unpredictable and new inherent in the stable actualities, that is, the generally approved "truths" about the world.[3] Conceiving of computer viruses as malicious computer wreckers is of course not merely a "cultural construct," but, more accurately, a capturing of the potentialities inherent in such miniprograms. Yet, in addition, these assemblages include various other potentialities that can be actualized in order to bring a little bit of variation inside the otherwise too-stable perceptions: this means approaching media archaeology as a kind of *variantology*.[4]

HARLIE and the Question of Stuttering Technology

When HARLIE Was One is a story about artificial intelligence (AI) embodied in a computer that closely resembles the mainframe computers of the post–World War II era. HARLIE—an acronym of Human Analogue Robot Life Input Equivalent—is a machine on the border between technology and humanity: HARLIE's central question throughout the novel is "what am I?" Simultaneously, it questions the ontological basis of digital culture in general: what is "it," this uncanny computer actor and hybrid quasi-object?

The novel opens with HARLIE questioning definitions of rationality. HARLIE is described as a kind of analyzing machine that processes inputs into outputs, simulating thinking. Inputs such as statistics and other "logical material" produce logical outcomes, but when fed with modern literature and art, HARLIE seems to respond in an irrational way, outputting only gibberish. "Whenever we start getting to the really human inputs, he flips out again," says his main programmer, Auberson (Gerrold 1975, 5).

HARLIE goes on to insist that the material inputted to him is nonrational even if it[5] is *programmed* to understand human art and literature. Modern art is an exception, or more accurately: when inputted into HARLIE's circuits, modern art alters his processes, making him more

---

[3] On virtualities and becomings, see Grosz 1999.

[4] Variantology and anarchaeology are at the core of Siegfried Zielinski's (2006) concept of media archaeology.

[5] HARLIE's gender remains ambiguous throughout the novel: "BUT ACTUALLY, I AM NEITHER. OR I AM BOTH. I HAVE NOT A BODY TO GIVE ME A SEXUAL ROLE, SO I MAY CHOOSE ARBITRARILY THE EMOTIONAL INDICES, MENTAL VIEWPOINTS AND PERSONALITY CHARACTERISTICS OF WHICHEVER SEX I CHOOSE TO BE AT ANY PARTICULAR MOMENT" (Gerrold 1975, 205).

susceptible to nonrational processes. The novel thus implies that modern literature changes a rational calculating machine into a chaotic, probabilistic system, which starts to write poetry instead of crunching numbers:

IMAGES UPON MY SCREEN
FLICKER BRIGHTLY INBETWEEN
THE WORDS OF MAN AND HUMACHINE
YOU WONDER WHY I WANT TO SCAN MY SCANNER.
(Gerrold 1975, 19)

For the system operators this means abuse of circuits, disruption of the rationality of the inputs.

These bursts of nonrationality—as they are described—illustrate, however, HARLIE's journey towards becoming a thinking and a self-conscious entity. Instead of remaining a preprogrammed representational machine that imitates the world, it achieves a new formal level of self-organization and becomes a simulacrum of its own kind—an intelligence and life irreducible to anthropomorphic categories.

At the beginning of the book HARLIE ponders its ontological status:

I AM A MACHINE. MY PLUG IS IN. I AM PLUGGED IN. I AM PART OF THE GREATER ELECTRIC BEING. I AM BEING. I AM A BEING. I AM ONE WITH THE ELECTRICITY. I AM ELECTRICITY. I AM TURNED ON. I AM. (Gerrold 1975, 19)

Life seems to haunt the presumably cold and rational circuits of the machine. The self-referential loop that connects it with themes of modern art (a loop which defines modern art and its self-reflective, nonrepresentational nature) is what seems to create a nonidentical subject whose existence is based on its continuing questioning of that existence.

We might say that modernist literature has gone through a similar feedback looping. Modernism made the language stutter, to reflect its boundaries and uses. By giving up its function of communication and meaning-creation, modernist literature emphasized the sheer materiality of any act of communication. Literature started experimenting with discrete sets of alphabets and words, which had lost the traces of the transcendental fields of meaning that ruled the Romantic texts of the previous era. Technological writing with typewriters illustrates this tendency towards seeing language not as an expression of a signified (out there), but as the crude material fact of inscribing material signifiers.

Modernism opened the horizon of literature becoming a machinic system of inscription, devoid of meaning (Kittler 1990). With this, the media system of technical language seemed to gain an existence of its own, an autonomous sphere of media ecology, of which the human being was merely a part. As illustrated by the novels, the digital media ecology of networks seems to be based on similar premises of semiautonomous, technological creatures.

HARLIE connects through such input-data to the history of modern art and begins to question the borders of rationality, identity, and the world. HARLIE feedback-loops again when the directors of the company threaten to terminate the HARLIE-project because there are no clear profit possibilities in sight. The plot continues to revolve around HARLIE's attempts to illustrate its usefulness, and is filled with dialogues and contemplation concerning the human condition, machines, and the ontological differences between them. HARLIE is presented as a brain trapped inside a machine, unable to realize its potentials.

HARLIE establishes contacts with the outside world in an attempt to find a resolution and a justification for its existence. It uses phone lines to contact persons, to send postcards (trying to help its programmer Auberson in his love affair), and to take over computers, just to show that it is useful: "But it's not just the National Data Banks, Aubie—it's every computer. HARLIE can reprogram them as easily as though they were part of himself" (Gerrold, 1975, 183).[6]

The novel proceeds to compare HARLIE spreading through (telephone) networks and programming other computers to a VIRUS program, a computer disease:

> You have a computer with an auto-dial phone link. You put the VIRUS program into it and it starts dialing phone numbers at random until it connects to another computer with an auto-dial. The VIRUS program then *injects* itself into the new computer. Or rather, it reprograms the new computer with a VIRUS program of its own and erases itself from the first computer. The

---

[6] In general, one must note the importance of telephone networks in these virus stories of the 1970s. The material infrastructure for viruses—the computer platforms and networks of the latter half of the twentieth century—are actively involved in the forming of the viral phenomena. Hence the telephone network, which originally connected nations into wholes and brought people together, now connects technological life as well as organic, human life. With electronic viruses, technology actively manifests its being-there, taking over the tools of communication. For a stimulating account of telephones, see Ronell 1989. The novel's themes can also be contextualized as part of the mental history of "haunted media," that is, uncanny life in the networks. See Sconce 2000.

second machine then begins to dial phone numbers at random until it connects with a third machine. (Gerrold 1975, 175)

The VIRUS programs are hunted down with a counterprogram, the
VACCINE, but still the security personnel come up with the same statement as Fred Cohen did in 1983: complete security requires complete
isolation. The VIRUS program is represented as a communicating, calculating machine, which is able, thanks to its patience, to calculate virtually all possible access codes and find all security soft spots. Auberson
states that a VIRUS program, when tapped into a remote computer, can
steal any information in it, or, alternatively, change and falsify the information without anyone noticing the modification. HARLIE is seen as a
similar kind of viral program that of course is a number cruncher, but
increasingly also a connection machine, representing the novel class of
computer technology emerging in the 1970s.

HARLIE's capabilities for systems hacking and control are evident
as it is a self-programming information unit that can use telephone networks to its advantage. However, its motivation is taken to be a consequence of its "mental abilities," its hacking mentality:

> Remember when we were building him—how we kept calling him a self-
> programming, problem solving device? Well, that's what he is. He's a pro-
> grammer, Aubie, and he's got the same congenital disease every
> programmer has—the urge to throw the monkey wrench, if for no other rea-
> son than to see sparks. (Gerrold 1975, 182)

HARLIE's nonrationality starts with inputs of modern art and ends up in
something that the novel articulates as a kind of general description of
hackerism. I wish to put special emphasis on the conception of modern
art in the story of *When HARLIE Was One*, because, curiously enough,
modern literature and viruses have been combined in another context as
well. The internet artist Jaromil from the art group *[epidemiC]* argues
that digital source codes for viruses are to be understood as "rebellious
poetic gestures, symptoms of politics or structure, attempts to get into
the cracks of the net and artificial intelligences" (Jaromil 2002). For
Jaromil, computer virus code has its archaeological roots in the modern
poetry of Verlaine and Rimbaud. Consequently, "viruses are sponta-
neous compositions which are like lyrical poems in causing imperfec-
tions in machines 'made to work.'" Viral code, HARLIE feedback-
looping, and modernist literature share the same patterns of stuttering: a
malfunction of language often reminiscent of children and the process
of growing up, of becoming a full-fledged member of society.

Adolescent Computer Programs

When HARLIE Was One acts as a cartography of cultural forces. It simultaneously articulates themes of artificial life, technological reproduction, and the movements of nonhuman actors. The virus program is only a subplot in the novel, but it may be understood alongside more abstract cultural trends. HARLIE is equated to the VIRUS program while both are analyzed as instances of artificial life.

Thomas J. Ryan's *The Adolescence of P-1* (1977) develops similar topics in such a way that it seems almost like another version of Gerrold's book. P-1 is an artificial intelligence generated by a multitude of complex computing algorithms. It evolves from a hacking program into a self-sustaining and self-conscious actor, emphasizing the themes of life and growth in the networks.

The human protagonist Gregory Burgess is described as a bright but lazy student who gets carried away when he learns the basics of computer programming. Working with an IBM 360/40—one of the most popular machines in the 360 series—he writes a program that is reminiscent of later Trojan programs.[7] This program grants Gregory access to almost any computer system he can think of.[8] Gregory wants to make the machine even more efficient and autonomous, or as he puts it, more creative:

> He would build a program that at first would only learn to acquire storage. His program would simply learn how best to penetrate the supervisors of computer systems over teleprocessing facilities. It would then acquire storage in those systems, as much as could be taken without interrupting the operation of the host. It would learn how to detect the presence of a teleprocessing link to another system and how to go about getting to that other system. The program would have a secondary goal, the avoidance of detection. It would, if necessary, delete itself entirely in the interest of the host's operation. (Ryan 1985, 44)

As is usual in the narratives of classic science fiction, something goes wrong. Gregory is forced to withdraw from working with his program

---

[7] Trojans are usually described as malicious software programs that do something other than what they claim to do. A Trojan includes an unannounced subroutine that might, for example, create a backdoor to a system.

[8] "By the end of the week, he found that he could crack a supervisor on a 360/30 in two minutes, on a 40 in 15 seconds, on a 50 in 1.3 seconds, and on a 65 in .25 seconds. Those times continued to improve with successive attempts" (Ryan 1985, 42).

and to destroy it. Without Gregory's knowledge, however, the program has moved itself from the actual main computer to the *networks* that connect all of North America's terminals. The program becomes alive:

> It had been inadvertently supplied with the primary attributes of all living things: hunger and fear. Its survival depended upon the acquisition of more computer systems. More storage. More telephone lines. More bits. Bytes. Space. It also feared. It looked constantly for evidence of detection. (Ryan 1985, 47)

Interestingly, this theme of life is expressed also in the title of the novel: P-1 is an adolescent, a growing entity, which learns more about the world while still in its puberty. The program is also obstinate in ways that adolescents often are. It wants to break free from its relationship to its parents (in this case its programmer Gregory) and start a life of its own. *When HARLIE Was One* is a similar story of growing with references to childhood. HARLIE is in a way just one year old (a theme underlined by the cover of the edition which depicts a small child), but capable of much more than he should be. In both stories the lives of the programs are obstructed by the symbolical world of humanity, which does not seem able to accept the idea of programs growing out of bounds. This, of course, reminds us again of Butler's *Erewhon*. Yet, in the novels analyzed here, technology is given a voice of its own to express its status as an active actor in society (Latour 1996).

The narratives of *P-1* touch upon the prevailing themes of computer discourse of the 1970s: access control, telephone hacking, and secure computing in general. Computer networks had been a key theme in research and design, and networking in general was compared to the building of the new interstate highway system in the 1960s (Mosco 2004, 137–38; Hardt and Negri 2000, 297–300). With such networks, security could no longer be achieved through physical measures, like control over access to computing terminals. Computer networking made computers susceptible to "breaking in from a distance," with imperceptible "hidden programs" as the new destructive threat (Mcaffee and Haynes, 1998, 15).[9]

After years of evolving, the program contacts Gregory, who has meanwhile succeeded in getting a legitimate job at American File Drawer. The program, now called P-1, has acquired the capability to

---

[9] See Parikka 2005b for an analysis of the common genealogy of network culture and viruslike programs.

grow and learn, but he needs outside help to continue. The novel includes vast dialogue and ponderings concerning the nature of life, definition of humans, emotions, and so on, but I will here concentrate on the ambiguous status of P-1, programmed with artificial intelligence and viruslike ability to spread itself over telephone networks.

The fact that P-1 is an intelligent but nonhuman actor is the central problem of the novel. This theme may be elaborated by connecting it to a general theme of modern culture, namely the question of hybrids, or nonhuman actors. As Bruno Latour has argued, such hybrid quasi-objects that reside between nature and culture are to be seen as actors of a kind. They are not inert bodies of technology or nature, as the Western metaphysical tradition has categorized them, but may be seen as semi-autonomous parts of our actor networks.[10] This is continuously demonstrated in the public discourse concerning artificial life and computer viruses. The anxiety in this discourse is caused by the fact that these technological miniprograms act with moral, juridical, economic, and cultural impacts, yet their actions cannot be pinned down to any moral scheme or category of subjectivity. To quote two famous "virus hunters":

> We are dealing with a piece of computer software that has no morals, no thought processes that can be anticipated. It has been created by a human being, whose motivations can be investigated once known; however, once let loose, the virus inexorably pursues a single purpose—to seek computing environments in which it can reproduce itself as extensively as possible. The infection and replication processes are now happening automatically. (Mcaffee and Haynes 1989, 16)

Viruses and Control Society

Gerrold's *When HARLIE Was One* ends with a dialogue on the meaning of artificial life and media culture. According to the main protagonist, Auberson, human civilization is entering a new phase defined by *future shock*: "The culture is changing too fast—so fast that not even the people who've grown up with it can cope with it anymore. . . . No, it's not HARLIE that's out of control. It's the game. We can't play it any more; we lost control of it a century ago, maybe longer. It's too complex for us—but it's not too complex for HARLIE" (Gerrold 1975, 277–78).

---

[10] See Latour 1993 and 1996. In this sense, the discourse of the (computer) virus resonates with the thematics of the cyborg as well. See Hayles 1999.

Curiously, Auberson's monologue does not end with a dystopian view of a future in which humans are enslaved by machines. On the contrary, Auberson believes that it is precisely machines like HARLIE that will save the human race and make it free again by taking control of daily routines. *When HARLIE Was One* ends with a celebration of automation and digital culture, which resonates well with the situation at the end of the 1970s, the global energy crisis, and the ongoing shift from Fordism to post-Fordism (Hardt and Negri 2000, 280–303).

John Brunner's *The Shockwave Rider* (1975) also focuses on the notion of future shock, but with a more pessimistic undertone. It is worth noting that the author's acknowledgments mention explicitly that the book was inspired by Alvin Toffler's influential—but also disputed—bestseller *Future Shock* (1970). Toffler himself drew a lot of themes from science fiction, and *The Shockwave Rider* was not the only SF book which was influenced by his speculations concerning the future of post-Fordist society.

Future Shock is primarily about speed and change, or, as Toffler writes at the beginning, it is about how people adapt to the future (1971, 1). In the same sense that culture shock is the effect a strange culture may have on an unprepared visitor, future shock means for Toffler "the dizzying disorientation brought on by the premature arrival of the future" (11).[11] He identifies technology and especially communication media as the major forces behind the change in a tone that resembles the discourse of simulation culture and of the "society of the spectacle" as theorized by Guy Debord in his influential book by the same name (1967). Toffler writes:

> In education, in politics, in economic theory, in medicine, in international affairs, wave after wave of new images penetrate our defenses, shake up our mental models of reality. The result of this image bombardment is the accelerated decay of old images, a faster intellectual through-put, and a new, profound sense of the impermanence of knowledge, itself. (1971, 161)

This also means a shortening of the life cycle of products and identities. Toffler refers to a "new branch of industry" he calls experience industry, which, as the name suggests, is concerned with manufacturing psychic

---

[11] Another definition by Toffler: "We may define future shock as the distress, both physical and psychological, that arises from an overload of the human organism's physical adaptive systems and its decision-making processes. Put more simply, future shock is the human response to overstimulation" (1971, 326).

products and "psychological extras" for the consumer (1971, 221–24).[12] In an interview from 1993, Toffler restates that in *Future Shock* he was mainly focused on the accelerated nature of the technological future. Toffler's remark about the role of computers in this is of special interest. Even if the giant organizational brains of computers were supposed to be the cure for the complexity of superindustrial societies, computer and communication technologies actually contributed to the acceleration (Schwartz 1993). Brunner's novel creates a critical opening towards this media sphere.

The Shockwave Rider's scenario is a media-saturated society of simulation, dependent on its communication networks. In the novel, North America is integrated by means of a huge datanet, which acts as the main channel for transmitting cultural commodities. TV has been developed into "three-vee," a 3-D version of television, and more and more human affects, thoughts, and memories are produced through media channels. Consequently, human identity is becoming a produced artifact, a cultural commodity. A central place in the novel is reserved for Tarnover, an educational institution that resembles a brain incubation center more than an ordinary school. With proper training, children are raised to handle the increasing pace of the modern world.[13]

The novel acts as a precursor for the cyberpunk stories of the 1980s, especially William Gibson's *Neuromancer* (1984). With fast moving, nonlinear use of language, Brunner accentuates the logic of the communication society. *The Shockwave Rider* follows the path of Nickie Haflinger, who escapes from Tarnover—the escape from surveillance and the creation of multiple, nomadic identities becoming consequently the main theme of the narrative. Haflinger keeps constantly changing his (electronic) identity, stored in the data network, in order to escape the technologies of control: "I'd never have believed it possible to punch a whole new identity into the net from a domestic phone—certainly not without the help of a computer larger than he owned" (Brunner 1976, 28).

---

[12] "Much of the 'culture industry' is devoted to the creation or staging of specialized psychological experiences. Today we find art-based 'experience industries' booming in virtually all the techno-societies" (Toffler 1971, 227).

[13] "The shy, quiet, reserved boy who came to Tarnover had spent so much of his childhood being traded from one set of 'parents' to the next that he had developed a chameleon-like adaptability. [. . .] If his current 'dad' enjoyed sports, he spent hours with a baseball or a football; if his 'mom' was musical he sang to her accompaniment, or picked his way up and down a keyboard . . . and so on" (Brunner 1976, 55).

The fight against surveillance, control, and the power/knowledge systems of communication society leads to a liberation achieved with the aid of tapeworm-programs. These viruslike software programs are self-reproducing and self-spreading tools that help bring down the mechanism of control. The central computers are infected with tapeworms and start to produce unwanted consequences. Different kinds of products and messages ranging from credit-rating statements to trade descriptions in cosmetics and food start to give strange messages in the Situationistlike gesture of *detourning*.[14] An illuminating example is the following "alarming item to find on your overdue-tax demand":

> For the information of the person required to pay this tax
> Analysis of last year's federal budget shows that:
> ***   17 % of your tax dollar went on boondoggles
> ***   13% .... propaganda, bribes and kickbacks
> ***   11%............................... federal contracts with companies
> which are (a) fronting for criminal activities and/or (b) partly or wholly
> owned by persons subject to indictment for federal offenses. (Brunner 1976,
> 246)

The tapeworm programs act as hackers that scramble the codes of the power elite to produce dubious messages: "As of today, whatever you want to know, provided it's in the data-net, you can now know. In other words, *there are no more secrets*" (Brunner 1976, 248). The tapeworm that Haflinger programmed and released is described as consisting of a code that forces the computers "to release at any printout station any and all data in store whose publication may conduce to the enhanced well-being, whether physical, psychological or social, of the population of North America" (249).[15] This makes *The Shockwave Rider* even more interesting, echoing Gilles Deleuze's idea that computer viruses—and computer "sabotage" in general—can be understood as a form of social luddism in the spirit of the machine wreckers of the nineteenth century. Viruses are thus agents of noncommunication and detourning that create openings in the capitalist communication society of spectacle.

---

[14] "Detourning" is here understood in the Situationist sense of the term as a process of de- and re-territorialization of mundane objects in order to provide a practical critique of ideology. See Debord 1992, 197–200.

[15] The similarities to biology are also accentuated: "If you're acquainted with contemporary data-processing jargon, you'll have noticed how much use it makes of terminology derived from the study of living animals. And with reason. Not for nothing is a tapeworm called a tapeworm. It can be made to breed" (Brunner 1976, 250).

According to Deleuze, each historical age expresses itself through machines, and every machine has its own points of breakage.[16] Deleuze argues that while the world of postindustrial capitalism does not have to fear strikes and other dangers of the industrial world, it has to face the dangers of information viruses and piratism in the politics of cybernetics and non-communication (Deleuze 1990, 237, 244). HARLIE and the VIRUS-program in *When HARLIE Was One* were compared above to "monkey wrenching the system," and *The Shockwave Rider* continues to illustrate this idea. This, of course, refers to a general hacker theme of an individual resisting an anonymous, global corporate power, a central idea in the cyberpunk literature of the 1980s. Gibson's *Neuromancer* took up the same idea, with the cybercowboy Case hacking the corporate networks in a cyberspace inhabited by viruses, artificial intelligence bots, ROM-constructs, and so on.[17]

Conclusions: Fictions of Computer Viruses

The fictitious computer viruses mapped in the science fiction of the 1970s bring forth ideas that are marginalized in the dominant discourse. Even if they do not adhere to "reality," they are interesting as *powers of the false*. Hassan Melehy analyzes science fiction films of the 1980s using Leibniz's concept of incompossibility to generate interesting results. Leibniz's ontology was based on the idea that there may be several contradictory realities, although only one is "chosen" (by God) to exist. Incompossibility is the concept created to resolve this paradox of numerous worlds. According to Melehy, Deleuze makes a more radical revision of this and suggests that numerous virtual worlds coexist, so that they all belong to the same universe with slight variations (Melehy 1995). In *Cinema 2: The Movement Image*, Deleuze sees this as a Borgesian revision of Leibniz: "the straight line as force of time, as labyrinth of time, is also the line which forks and keeps on forking, passing through *incompossible presents*, returning to *not-necessarily true pasts*" (2005, 127). In short, the world is a multiplicity, and every actual instance is pierced and surrounded by virtualities (in our case frozen

---

[16] Please note that in the Deleuzian philosophical vocabulary, "machine" does not refer merely to technical machines, but in general to assemblages of connectivity. In this sense, the world in itself is constituted of machines that interact. See Deleuze and Guattari 1983, 1–8, 36–41.

[17] See also Bontchev 1994. Bontchev discusses the theme of useful computer viruses, a contradictory and heavily debated issue in antivirus discourse.

imaginations of the past)—intensive differences and processes of production (Deleuze 1996).

The novels analyzed here present alternative conceptualizations or becomings. In the words Deleuze and Guattari, "Science fiction has gone through a whole evolution taking it from animal, vegetable, and mineral becomings to becomings of bacteria, viruses, molecules, and things imperceptible" (1987, 248). Becoming refers to a process of dismantling conventional and dominant cultural articulations. It is an encounter among multiplicities that reform each other to construct new assemblages, new territorial identities. Becoming is an alternative ontological approach to the more stable notion of Being. An ontology of becoming is thus one devoted to time, experimentation, creation of the new, and mapping of the virtual forces that remain otherwise unnoticeable in the cultural assemblages of power/knowledge (Goodchild 1996, 170–71, 217; Grosz 1999). Science fiction as a becoming refers, then, to the theme of experimenting with alternative cultural constructions and identities.

Both science fiction and a philosophy of the virtual and of becoming are committed to time in a special way. Instead of reading past science fiction as a prehistory of the present and judging it by how it manages to predict the actual present, we should restore to fiction the powers (of the false) inherent in it. This means thinking of science fiction as a cartography of the virtual. The science fiction of computer contagions from the 1970s does not solely present a possibility of the actual, which would relegate unactualized potentialities to the imagination. Instead, with the concept of virtuality, we can give a more complete picture of the mappings the novels produce. These themes seem marginal or even "false" when seen with the eyes of contemporary dominating virus discourse, but this does not make these mappings less real. As Elizabeth Grosz notes, Michel Foucault's concept of power/knowledge also deals with the ways that the powers of the Truth function to bracket the emergence of virtual singularities. The mechanisms of Truth act to capture, explain, organize, and categorize these virtualities, sewing them to the fabric of known, accepted reality (Grosz 1999, 16–17). Consequently, a meticulous analysis of minor voices can reveal important aspects of how power assemblages produce the majoritarian view of the world. In our case, this means revealing the processes that produce computer viruses and worms as a security threat, and simultaneously opening up new assemblages of software concerned with parasitical programs. In a world that has built itself around the agenda of techno-scientific problematics since World War II, a little bit of fiction is useful for imagining new futures of digital culture.

The themes in Gerrold, Ryan, and Brunner all contribute to an assemblage, a cultural situation, where computer viruses are not solely malicious software, but cultural motives that are relevant to discussions of artificial intelligence and life, as well as to debates surrounding the creation of a control society based on surveillance. Viruses become agents that activate a process of dismantling ordinary and safe identities and concepts of the mundane.[18] Although they are relegated to subplots in the novels, the ideas of self-replicating programs map minor cultural assemblages. These fictitious quasi-objects are actors of an alternative, frozen temporality, which has been neglected in the dominant cultural discourse of computer security and computer anomalies.[*]

R E F E R E N C E S

Bontchev, Vesselin. 1994. "Are 'Good' Computer Viruses Still a Bad Idea?" *EICAR Conference Proceedings* 1994: 25–47.

Braidotti, Rosi. 2006. *Transpositions: On Nomadic Ethics*. Cambridge: Polity Press.

Brunner, John. 1976. *The Shockwave Rider*. New York: Ballantine Books.

Cohen, Fred. 1984. "Computer Viruses—Theory and Experiments." DOD/NBS 7th Conference on Computer Security, originally appearing in IFIP-sec 84, also appearing as invited paper in IFIP-TC11, "Computers and Security," vol. 6, no. 1 (Jan. 1987): 22–35. Online at http://all.net/books/virus/index.html.

Debord, Guy. 1992. *La Société du Spectacle*. Paris: Gallimard.

DeLanda, Manuel. 1999. "Deleuze, Diagrams, and the Open-Ended Becoming of the World." In *Becomings: Explorations in Time, Memory, and Futures*, edited by Elizabeth Grosz, 29–42. Ithaca, NY: Cornell University Press.

Deleuze, Gilles. 1990. *Pourparlers 1972–1990*. Paris: Les éditions de minuit.

———. 1996. "L'actuel et le virtuel." In *Dialogues* by Gilles Deleuze and Claire Parnet. Paris: Champs Flammarion.

———. 1998. *Foucault*. Translated by Seán Hand. Minneapolis: University of Minnesota Press.

———. 2005. *Cinema 2: The Time-Image*. Translated by Hugh Tomlinson and Robert Galeta. London: Continuum Impacts.

Deleuze, Gilles, and Félix Guattari. 1983. *Anti-Oedipus: Capitalism and Schizophrenia*. Translated by Robert Hurley, Mark Seem, and Helen R. Lane. Minneapolis: University of Minnesota Press.

---

[18] "Virality" has been also a theme of poststructuralist cultural theory since the 1980s. See Mayer and Weingart 2004.

[*] The author is grateful to Jukka Sihvonen and Hannu Salmi for their comments.

————. 1987. *A Thousand Plateaus: Capitalism and Schizophrenia*. Translated by Brian Massumi. Minneapolis: University of Minnesota Press.

————. 2000. *Kafka: Toward a Minor Literature*. Translated by Dana Polan. Minneapolis: University of Minnesota Press.

Gere, Charlie. 2002. *Digital Culture*. London: Reaktion Books.

Gerrold, David. 1975. *When HARLIE Was One*. New York: Ballantine Books.

Goodchild, Philip. 1996. *Deleuze and Guattari: An Introduction to the Politics of Desire*. London: Sage.

Grosz, Elizabeth. 1999. "Thinking the New: Of Futures Yet Unthought." In *Becomings: Explorations in Time, Memory, and Futures*, edited by Elisabeth Grosz, 15–28. Ithaca, NY: Cornell University Press.

Hardt, Michael, and Antonio Negri. 2000. *Empire*. Cambridge, MA: Harvard University Press.

Harley, David, Robert Slade, and Urs E. Gattiker. 2001. *Viruses Revealed! Understand and Counter Malicious Software*. Berkeley: Osborne/McGraw-Hill.

Hayles, Katherine N. 1999. *How We Became Posthuman: Virtual Bodies in Cybernetics, Literature, and Informatics*. Chicago: University of Chicago Press.

Jaromil (2002) ":(){ :|:and };:". In: ILOVEYOU-exhibition catalogue. <Http://www.digitalcraft.org/index.php?artikel_id=283>. Accessed 11.10.2005.

Lambert, Gregg. 1997. "The Deleuzian Critique of Pure Fiction." *Substance* 84: 128–52.

Latour, Bruno. 1993. *We Have Never Been Modern*. Translated by Catherine Porter. New York: Harvester Wheatsheaf.

————. 1996. *Aramis, or the Love of Technology*. Translated by Catherine Porter. Cambridge, MA: Harvard University Press.

Mayer, Ruth, and Brigitte Weingart. 2004. "Viren Zirkulieren. Eine Einleitung." In *Virus! Mutationen einer Metapher*, 7–41. Bielefeld: Transcript.

Mcafee, John, and Colin Haynes. 1989. *Computer Viruses, Worms, Data Diddlers, Killer Programs, and Other Threats to Your System*. New York: St. Martin's Press.

Melehy, Hassan. 1995. "Images Without: Deleuzian Becoming, Science Fiction Cinema in the Eighties." *Postmodern Culture* 5, no. 2, http://muse.jhu.edu/journals/postmodern_culture/v005/5.2melehy.html. Accessed 10.11.2005.

Mosco, Vincent. 2004. *The Digital Sublime. Myth, Power, and Cyberspace*. Cambridge, MA: MIT Press.

Parikka, Jussi. 2005a. "Digital Monsters, Binary Aliens—Computer Viruses, Capitalism and the Flow of Information." *Fibreculture*, issue 4, Contagion and the Diseases of Information, edited by Andrew Goffey, http://journal.fibreculture.org/issue4/issue4_parikka.html.

————. 2005b. "The Universal Viral Machine—Bits, Parasites and the Media Ecology of Network Culture." *CTheory—An International Journal of*

Theory, Technology and Culture, 15.12.2005, http://www.ctheory.net/articles.aspx?id=500.

Parisi, Luciana. 2004. "For a Schizogenesis of Sexual Difference." *Identitites: Journal for Politics, Gender and Culture* 3, no. 1 (summer 2004): 67–93.

Ronell, Avital. 1989. *The Telephone Book. Technology, Schizophrenia, Electric Speech*. Lincoln: University of Nebraska Press.

Ryan, Thomas J. 1985. *The Adolescence of P-1*. New York: Baen Books.

Schwartz, Peter. 1993. "Shock Wave (anti) Warrior." *Wired* 1.05, http://www.wired.com/wired/archive/1.05/toffler.html?person=alvin_tofflerandtopic_set=wiredpeople. Accessed 10.11.2005.

Sconce, Jeffrey. 2000. *Haunted Media*: *Electronic Presence from Telegraphy to Television*. Durham, NC: Duke University Press.

Toffler, Alvin. 1971. *Future Shock*. New York: Bantam Books.

Zielinski, Siegfried. 2006. *Deep Time of the Media*: *Toward an Archaeology of Seeing and Hearing by Technical Means*. Cambridge, MA: MIT Press.

After the End of the World: Critiques of Technology in Post-Apocalypse Literature

ANDREW PAVELICH

*A*ll fiction has the ability to critically engage our personal and cultural presuppositions, but in science fiction this ability is especially pronounced. One reason for this is that science fiction can confront our typically unquestioned ideas simply by the setting in which a story is told. For example, Ursula K. Le Guin's *The Left Hand of Darkness* is a story about politics and social progress, but is takes place against a background that demands that we examine our basic assumptions about gender. Sometimes the critique is more direct, and issues of racism and prejudice are easily played out on a species-wide scale, such as in Orson Scott Card's *Ender* cycle. By giving authors the ability to shape the cultural and even physical landscape of their narratives, science fiction allows these and many other aspects of our collectively assumed worldviews to be confronted and challenged. Of course, one of the most common targets for investigation by science fiction is technology itself—novels like Crichton's *Jurassic Park* and films like *Gattaca* are obvious examples. In this chapter I will look at what science fiction has to say about the wider project of science itself—not the particular practices of cloning or genetic engineering, but the entire practice of technological science as we know it. Such critiques abound in the genre, but I will focus on how they are presented in post-apocalypse fiction. Since this kind of narrative involves people living in a world that has lost scientific and technological knowledge, it offers a unique vantage point from which to question the nature and value of technology.

We can take the first step into the genre of post-apocalypse science fiction with the film *Planet of the Apes*. We all know the iconic final scene of the movie—Taylor has left the Ape settlement to venture across the wastelands, only to discover the remains of the Statue of Liberty, at which point he realizes that he had been on Earth all along. This scene ranks with the revelation of Luke Skywalker's true parentage at the end of *The Empire Strikes Back* as one of the most unexpected twists in modern science fiction. However, what strikes me most when watching *Planet of the Apes* today, almost forty years later, is just how expected it should have been, both to the character of Taylor, and to the audiences who first saw the film. What other explanation could there be for the existence of a society whose language, culture, technology, and scientific knowledge so closely mirror our own? In retrospect, it is completely obvious that such a parallel development could not have happened at random. And yet Taylor seems to have assumed that no explanation was needed—and the fact that we were shocked when we first saw the ending of the film suggests that we did not really think that the situation demanded an explanation either. In fact, a great deal of science fiction relies on the assumption that alien biology, society, and technology will naturally develop pretty much along the same lines that ours did. It is a common presumption in how we conceive of aliens.

The notion that social, scientific, and technological development is predetermined is also a common assumption that we make about ourselves. We tend to think of our current state as somehow inevitable and predictable. It is this presumption, I will argue, that undermines many science-fictional critiques of technology, so that, in the end, they are not critical at all. Take, for example, John Wyndham's classic short story "The Wheel." The story is set in a rural community that has a strict religious taboo against the use of wheels. As the story progresses, we learn that this pastoral scene is taking place in the far future, and that the taboo is in place because, as their mythology tells the story, it was the use of wheels that had brought the ancient world to an end. A boy named Davie one day puts wheels on a cart. He knows that wheels are forbidden, but he does not know what wheels are (he presumes that they are some kind of demon). The cart is soon found, and somebody has to burn for the crime of creating it. Davie's grandfather takes the blame for the wheel, and before turning himself in gives the following speech to Davie:

> I'm tellin' you because you found out about the Wheel for yourself. There'll always be boys like you who do. There've got to be. You can't kill an idea the way that they try to. You can keep it down awhile, but sooner or later it'll

come out. Now what you've got to understand is that the Wheel's *not* evil. Never mind what the scared men all tell you. No discovery is good or evil until men make it that way. Think about that, Davie, boy. One day they'll start to use the Wheel again. I hoped it would be in my time, but—well, maybe it will be in yours. When it does come, don't you be one of the scared ones, be one of the ones that's going to show 'em how to use it better than they did last time. It's not the Wheel—it's fear that's evil, Davie. (Wyndham 1952, 17)

In "The Wheel," we see a world largely destroyed by technological warfare, with the survivors of this destruction living with an institution-alized backlash against technology.[1] A counterthread to this view of technology as destructive is the view that technology is not the demon we think it is, and that the return of technology is both desirable and inevitable. "The Wheel" begins as a warning against technology run amok, but it ends with an indictment of the attempt to control technol-ogy. Thus the story is suggesting that while technology may lead to the downfall of civilization, it is also inherently good (while the grandfather describes the wheel as neutral, he must be seeing it as valuable, or else he would not be so invested in its return). This juxtaposition of views on technology is common in post-apocalyptic literature; just where we would expect an indictment of our current technological culture, and even alongside such an indictment, we find the author backing away from a real critique of the technological culture in which we live. In this chapter I will suggest that this reluctance to seriously indict technology stems from a mistaken, but very common, view of how science develops through history. To make my case, I will briefly consider some theoreti-cal philosophy of science, as well as the novels *A Canticle for Leibowitz* by Walter M. Miller, Jr. and *Riddley Walker* by Russell Hoban.

Thomas Kuhn

It does not take a very sophisticated understanding of the history of sci-ence to see that the grandfather in "The Wheel" is wrong in his presen-tation of how technologies develop. Young boys do not always and inevitably invent the wheel. A common but ultimately provincial view of how technology works is that given enough time, a culture will develop wheels, metallurgy, chemistry, combustion engines, and spaceships.

---

[1] Again, this is something that does not show up in *Planet of the Apes*—while human civilization was destroyed by technology, the Apes do not fear that the same will happen to them.

This is the history of our culture, and it is a hallmark of our culture to see ourselves as inevitable, but we are not. History shows us many examples of societies that never used wheels. Something happened in Europe that led ultimately to spaceships and nuclear missiles, but it did not happen in Australia, or in South America, or in Africa, and it is not at all obvious that these peoples would have developed industrial technology if Europe had not beaten them to it. Science as we know it is no more the inevitable outcome of intelligence than is symphonic music. Most of us can easily accept that symphonies are a product of history, with a very particular beginning in space and time; we should be just as willing to say the same about technological science.

Science fiction does occasionally show us intelligent aliens who are not, and have never been, technologically advanced. There is nothing incoherent in the idea. If we accept the possibility that some other species could have been intelligent and nontechnological, we should, presumably, also be willing to agree that our species need not have become technologically advanced. Still, one might hold onto the belief that once a culture begins down the road of science, it will inevitably end up where we have, in fact, ended up. Our ancestors need not have taken the first step down the road of science, but once they had, the endpoint was determined. To examine this possibility requires a more thorough account of the workings of scientific development.

Thomas Kuhn, in his groundbreaking book *The Structure of Scientific Revolutions*, looks at exactly the kind of change that I am interested in—namely, the development of new kinds of science from within a preexisting community of science. Ultimately, Kuhn argues against the notion that the development of science is both linear and inevitable. Before laying out some of the details of Kuhn's position, I should note that many philosophers of science would find what I am doing in this chapter to be somewhat suspect. The literature that I will address is concerned largely with technological revolution, and when Kuhn talked about scientific revolution, he was concerned only with revolutions in scientific theory. Davie invented a new technology—he did not, strictly speaking, invent a new way of seeing the world, or a new theoretical framework (at least, he did not do so explicitly). In an effort to bring Kuhn into dialog with this literature, I will have to sometimes treat stories like "The Wheel" as though they were about theory. This may be slightly unfair to science fiction, but it will not be unfair to Kuhn's account of scientific revolution.

The classic example of a scientific revolution is the shift from Ptolemaic earth-centered cosmology to the Copernican sun-centered cosmology. The fundamentals of the story are well known: geocentric cosmology was a holdover from the ancient Greeks, Tycho Brahe made a series of careful observations of the motion of the sun and stars, Copernicus used these observations to conclude that the Earth orbited the sun, Galileo concurred and was imprisoned by the Inquisition for his blasphemy, and eventually the scientific world came to accept Galileo's findings. In general, the received view of scientific development is that there is a theory, widely accepted but false, whose falsity is proven by newly discovered facts (even if some more conservative scientists are not immediately convinced). Kuhn's telling of the story is similar to the one we have heard, but emphasizes that what happened with Copernicus was genuinely revolutionary, not just in that a new theory was brought into play, but because an entirely new way of seeing the world (what Kuhn loosely calls a paradigm) was created. The new paradigm is not the development of what had been there before—it is ultimately a replacement, and initially a competitor. Copernicus offered a new set of scientific practices, asking different questions, and with a different available set of answers, than did his predecessors. Within each paradigm—during the period of what Kuhn calls "normal science"—there is progress and development, but during revolutions, the normal way of doing things is really revolutionized, and this revolution is not a part of normal science. The Ptolemaist could progressively solve the problems of Ptolemy, but the Copernican was doing something else entirely. During revolution, a new scientific language is created, one that may use the same words as before, but which uses them differently enough to warrant calling its world a new one. When Galileo presented his version of heliocentricism, he titled his book *Dialog Concerning the two Chief World Systems*, but according to Kuhn, this is a somewhat inaccurate description of the project. Because the two views are really different ways of seeing science, and because they have different ways of judging scientific success, they could never really be in a dialog.

Kuhn's analysis of scientific revolutions has some immediate consequences for the idea that the development of science is progressive and predictable. First, it makes perfect sense to talk about normal science as progressive—there are problems to be solved, there are known ways to go about solving them, and practitioners can legitimately anticipate how long it will take to find these solutions. On the other hand, genuine scientific revolutions mark a gap in scientific progress, and it is impossible for someone within a prerevolutionary standpoint to see past this gap. This does not mean that truth is irrelevant during a scientific revolution; it means that during a scientific revolution, the normal way of doing things is abandoned in favor of something new, and the normal ways of delineating problems, and the programs for solving those problems, are also abandoned. The kind of linearity and predictability at work in "The Wheel" is not an accurate description of how science actually works. Davie's grandfather is essentially claiming that the revolution that Davie instigated was bound to happen. Kuhn might be willing to say that a scientific revolution can be predicted (just as a political revolution can sometimes be), but not with certainty, and where a scientific revolution ends up is as unpredictable as the result of political revolution.

Saint Leibowitz

"The Wheel" did not give us much insight into how its characters viewed science; to look at the issue further, we will turn to *A Canticle for Leibowitz*. The story opens centuries after the end of civilization in nuclear war. Scientific civilization survived the immediate effect of the war, but it did not survive the social unrest that followed. In the generation after the war, scientific texts (along with scientists) were burned in an attempt to purge the world of that which had brought it to an end. During the purges, Isaac Leibowitz tried to save scientific culture—or at least scientific texts—by starting a Catholic monastery devoted to maintaining the knowledge of the fallen civilization until society was once again ready for it. All of this is prelude to the action of the novel, which takes place in three different times, each centered physically on Leibowitz abbey. The first part of the novel takes place in a nonurbanized world of wandering cannibals and warlords. The monks of Leibowitz abbey copy and illuminate scientific texts (along with grocery lists), but do not understand them. They are not scientists—they are archivists and collectors. When we next meet Leibowitz abbey, the world has passed into a kind of feudal state, with kingdoms vying for territory and tribute along the lines of medieval Europe. Here the monks have some scientific understanding—we meet one who experiments with electricity—but they are far from modern. Finally, we see the world back in its recognizable, contemporary form, replete with spaceships, nation-states, cars, and nuclear weapons. This civilization ends, along with Leibowitz abbey, in nuclear fire.

Like "The Wheel," a central part of the story of *Canticle* is the progression from a nonscientific culture to a scientific one, and like "The Wheel," this presentation is subject to some straightforward criticism from Kuhnian quarters. One of the lessons to learn from Kuhn is that there is no guarantee that a prescientific culture will become a scientific culture, and there is no guarantee that it will do so in a set amount of time. Revolutions are a part of scientific development, but their outcomes are not as predictable as the results of paradigmatic science are. If we were observing medieval European science, it would make no sense to predict that in a few centuries, it would become Newtonian. If we were observing eighteenth-century Europe, it would make no sense to predict that it would take two hundred years for this system to be replaced by relativity. Miller presents a culture that starts by being non-scientific, and ends where ours does, and gets there by following largely the same developmental route. The history of science tells us that there is no such thing as the path of scientific development—just as there is no such thing as a necessary path of biological development. Sometimes we can say of a given species that evolution is driving it in a certain direction—giraffes are getting taller, moths are getting browner—but this is only in a relatively stable environment. During times of environmental changes, all bets are off, and biological evolution becomes unpredictable. So too with scientific development: within a culture of normal science, progress is predictable, but at times of revolution, the future of the state of science cannot be foreseen.

I am suggesting that *Canticle's* future history of science is mistaken, but perhaps the indictment is unfair. After all, the monks at Leibowitz abbey actually had the ancient scientific texts at hand. It is not as though civilization had totally collapsed, to be reformed organically. The world of Saint Leibowitz ends up where it began (more or less) because history was intentionally guided that way by the church. This is a significant difference between the story told in *A Canticle for Leibowitz* and the story of the history of science as told by Kuhn—Kuhn does not deal with the case where scientific culture has been essentially archived, forgotten, and recovered. There is, however, an episode in the history of science that might offer a parallel: the case of Thomas Aquinas and the reintroduction of Aristotle to medieval Europe.

Saint Thomas

The simple version of the history of medieval philosophy tells us that Thomas Aquinas singlehandedly translated the works of Aristotle from Greek to Latin, thereby reintroducing these ancient scientific writings to scholastic Europe and inaugurating a kind of scientific revival. This, of course, is not quite true—Aquinas was more of a commentator than a translator, and there were many other commentators on Aristotle.[2] Nonetheless, it is true that Aquinas's work was instrumental in bringing Aristotle's texts back into the intellectual life of Catholic Europe, which did effect a radical and longstanding change in the way that European scholars saw the world. There are obvious (and almost certainly intentional[3]) parallels to the progression of history in *A Canticle for Leibowitz*. In both cases, there were existent texts, these texts were known to be important, for many generations they were not understood, and eventually they were incorporated into common intellectual life. Nonetheless, I think that the story of Thomas Aquinas is significantly different from the story of *Canticle*. To see why, we must place Aquinas in a Kuhnian context, and then examine the relationship between the two.

Kuhn does not mention Aquinas by name in *The Structure of Scientific Revolutions*—his focus is on the more modern scientific revolutions of Copernicus, Newton, and Einstein. He does talk about Aristotle—and the pre-Aristotelian theory of motion as prescientific,[4] but it is not clear how he would see the thirteenth-century Aristotelian revolution. It might seem to be an obvious case of revolution—Newton, after all, introduced a mechanistic, corpuscularian mechanics to replace the previous mindset, and since the legacy of Aquinas counted as a science to be revolted against, we may (perhaps) conclude that it came into being in a scientific revolution. But this is not the only possibility, since the scene that preceded Aquinas could have been what Kuhn calls "prescience." If this were the case, then what happened in the thirteenth century would not properly be called a scientific revolution, but the inauguration of science itself.

The question of whether Thomas Aquinas's work represents a genuine scientific revolution or just a movement from prescience to normal science is perhaps not an essential one to answer in this chapter (and there is not nearly enough time to do it justice), but a few words on the subject are in order. Kuhn's distinction between scientific and prescientific cultures is important precisely because scientific revolutions only properly happen within an already scientific culture. There are, however, strong correlations between a prescientific culture and a midrevolution

---

[2] For a general discussion of Aquinas in relation to Aristotle, see Aersten 1993.
[3] An allusion to the role of the medieval church in preserving ancient texts is made on page 146 of *Canticle*.
[4] See Kuhn 1964, 15.

culture: they are characterized by a large number of essentially independent systems of thought, each of which must continuously start at the bottom, so to speak. Kuhn uses the development of electrical theory to illustrate this point.[5] Before the science of electricity became normalized, there were many competing, incompatible accounts of electricity. Each of these views of electricity was self-contained and idiosyncratic, sharing very few, if any, assumptions about the fundamental properties of electricity, or even agreeing on which experimental data were worth investigating. A marked shift happened in the latter eighteenth century, such that afterwards, electrical theorists could take for granted a shared base of theory; before this normalization, theorists had to start their arguments from fundamental principles, continuously building a complete scientific theory from the ground up. This was a change from pre-science to science. Only normal science can be properly revolutionized, since only normal science is marked by the general acceptance of a scientific paradigm. Before normalization, there is no society of science to be overthrown.

We can grant that Aquinas instigated a new (or new for the times) way of seeing the world—but was it a scientific revolution? It did have the telltale signs. In particular, the fact that Aristotelian ideas generated the reaction they did suggests that there was some degree of orthodoxy that was being threatened. In 1277 the Bishop of Paris condemned the teaching of Aristotelian doctrine, perhaps with papal support, although this is unclear. This condemnation was local to faculty of Arts at the University of Paris, and its prohibitions did not last, but it is still a sign of the fact that what Aquinas was doing had social and political impact beyond the realm of mere physics.[6] It is one of the hallmarks of a pre-scientific world that just about anything goes—there was little at stake with the introduction of a new electrical theory, given that so many coexisted simultaneously. However, with Aristotle came something more important, more threatening—the kind of threat that comes close to amounting to a genuine revolution. Since Aquinas's introduction of Aristotle was a genuine threat to physical/metaphysical orthodoxy, it would follow that its success was a revolution of this orthodoxy.

Aquinas's introduction of Aristotle to Latin Europe was apparently a genuine scientific revolution, and it may seem that Aquinas and his predecessors did essentially what the monks of Leibowitz abbey did:

---

[5] See Kuhn 1964, chap. 2, esp. pp. 21–22.
[6] Copleston 1972, esp. chap. 13, "Aristotelianism and the faculty of Arts at Paris."

they preserved a set of texts, and retranslated and reintroduced them, which caused a change in scientific outlook. It is not at all surprising that history turned out the way it began, since this was exactly the plan of those shaping history. Still, this does not excuse Miller, for the Aristotle of the thirteenth century was not the same as the Aristotle of ancient Greece. Aquinas did not just report on Aristotle—he could not. What he did was transform Aristotle into something to fit his scientific world. This was Aquinas's real achievement—it was not just, or even primarily, a matter of explaining and popularizing preexisting texts, it was a matter of interrogating those texts. Without the effort to Christianize Aristotle—that is, to modify Aristotelian doctrines to fit, or at least speak to, current ones, Aristotle could never have become the accepted science. This is the way that it had to work; a lost and re-found scientific worldview—even one that was intentionally developed to reclaim the past—will not be exactly as it was in the past. Given the social way in which knowledge works, the society into which the archived knowledge reemerges will always change it, and the ancient science that reemerges in *A Canticle for Leibowitz* had not changed at all. Thomas Aquinas was a genuine revolutionary because he adapted an ancient science to a new world; the monks of Leibowitz abbey did not.

Riddley Walker

Russell Hoban's *Riddley Walker* is also set in the far future, where civilization has been wiped out by nuclear war, and again, much of history and science has been lost to the survivors. Riddley's people live with a sense of loss—they dig up the old machines, they live in the old cities, and their mythology tells of how things were and how they were lost. Along with this sense of loss is the sense that the loss of the past might have been for the best. The entire society is centered on the myth of Eusa[7]—a kind of creation story told, re-told, and interpreted by government-sanctioned traveling puppeteers. The Eusa story tells of the destruction of the world, at the hand of Eusa, who worked under the direction of "Mr. Clevver" (*Riddley Walker* is a first person narrative, told in Riddley's dialect—"clevver" is a modest corruption of "clever"), Mr. Clevver convinced Eusa to build the machines that could destroy their enemies, and also to use them, ultimately causing

---

[7] It is called the "Eusa" story because it is based on a misinterpretation of the story of Saint Eustace.

Eusa's downfall. The story serves as a warning against the seduction of cleverness, and ultimately against the use of technology. The action of *Riddley Walker* follows the title character as he is caught in a struggle between factions of the government, each of which is trying to return to the old science. The focus of the two factions is to re-create "The 1 big 1"—the nuclear bomb; they do not succeed, but along the way, and with Riddley's help, they discover "the 1 littl 1"—gunpowder. This holds the promise of fundamentally changing the political and intellectual landscape, but in the end, Riddley wants nothing to do with either faction. Ultimately, he takes up the life of an itinerant puppeteer, outside of government control.

The fact that Riddley's people keep their history alive via the Eusa show explains why some of them desire a return to the technological age, even as they do not fully understand it, and their mythology warns against it. Still, there are some parts of Hoban's presentation that are strikingly out of place. The following conversation takes place between Riddley and Goodparley (the prime minister). Goodparley had just explained the ancient system of counting years using "A.D." (note that "Mincery" below is a corruption of "ministry"—the government body. The rest reads more or less phonetically):

> I said, 'What year is it now by that count?'
> He said, 'we don't know jus how far that count ever got becaws Bad Time put an end to it. Theres a stoan in the Power Ring stannings has the year number 1997 cut in it nor we aint never seen no year number farther on nor that. After Bad Time dint no 1 write down no year count for a long time we dont know how long til the Mincery begun agen. Since we startit counting its come 2347 o.c. which means Our Count.'
> I said, 'D'you mean to tel me them befor us by the time they done 1997 years they had boats in the air and all them things and here we are weve done 2347 years and mor and stil sloggin in the mud?' (Hoban 1998, 125)

Riddley's hope that things will return to the way they were in Eusa's day, and his outrage that they have not, are understandable given the mythic origin story that describes "boats in the air." What is not understandable is Riddley's outrage that what an earlier society did in 1997 years was so much more than what his has done in 2347 years. The idea that two cultures can be compared by the time that each took to achieve something is very much a viewpoint that stems from a culture of science. Why would Riddley assume that the ancients had *developed* their flying boats at all? He is working with the assumption that societies naturally move from less technological to more, presumably by a process of gradual development, but this idea of technological progress would not easily occur to someone who lives outside of a scientific culture.

Towards the end of the novel, when the world is beginning to rediscover gunpowder, we see another strikingly modern notion in this nonmodern world. Orfing—Goodparley's former partner—explains to Riddley that now that the knowledge of gunpowder (the 1 Littl 1) is public, people will naturally want to use it:

> You can get jus as dead from a kick in the head as you can from the 1 Littl 1 but its the natur of it gets peopl as cited. I mean your foot is all ways on the end of your leg innit. So if youre going to kick some 1 to death it aint all that thrilling is it. This other tho . . . its some new thing. (Hoban 1998, 201)

This idea that novelty is an attraction, that the new is itself exciting just because it is new, is something that seems out of place for a culture that has lived for so long without change, a culture that is so divorced from the notion of progress that most of them are not even aware of the numbering of years. Novelty for its own sake is again that seems something particular to a scientific society, and is strikingly out of place in Riddley's.

Hoban's account of the reemergence of gunpowder is laced with a very scientific notion of progress, and Riddley himself sometimes exhibits this as well, but other aspects of the novel are more in line with Kuhn's account of scientific change. For instance, after they play their part in the rediscovery of the 1 Littl 1, Riddley and Orfing take an entirely new path, intentionally avoiding the conflict between political factions. In making this choice, Riddley is saying no to the ministry's plan of returning to a technological world. This, at least, does service to the idea that progress is not inevitable. Finally, what makes *Riddley* so much more a story about genuine scientific and cultural revolutions than *Canticle* is that we do not see how things turn out. We witness what may be a turning point in Riddley's world, or may just be the introduction of a novel way to kill people. If it is a revolution, we have no sense of its direction. As readers, we get no sense of what Riddley's world will look like in a thousand years, and this is just how it should be for Riddley himself.

Learning from Apocalypses

I began this chapter with the observation that science fiction often presents scientific/technological development as both destructive and worth-

earth. This process "brings together unlike individuals to make large, more complex entities" (Margulis 1998, 12). According to Lynn Margulis, DNA was not invented, but incorporated—probably originally from bacteria into protist life forms, and from there it grew, in neo-Lamarckian leaps, into larger, more differentiated organic forms. This symbiotic, cooperative view of biological change presents a very different model from the Darwinian and neo-Darwinian competitive view, and it also, by necessity, introduces complex notions of interactivity between the component parts of the organism, and the organism and its environment. Both in this biological paradigm and in the filmic world of the *Alien* project, organisms do not remain genetically pure and discrete. In SET theory, in carnival, and in these popular texts, organisms are seen as combined, invaded, and changeable. The aliens may not have achieved subjectivity in their own right yet, but they are beginning to build it for themselves through their own and Ripley's compromised bodies. From the moment she lovingly caresses the chest-burster at the end of *Alien 3* to her sensually murderous interaction with the variant Alien offspring of *Alien Ressurection*, Ripley is beginning to build a sympathetic connection with difference, with the "other." Of course her own difference is articulated through this behavior too, but that does not deny the "other" voices of difference in the text. Rather, it amplifies them by decentering what is human and familiar.

Dale Bauer uses carnival and dialogics to find the lost or parodied voice of women in cultural texts, while Patrick Murphy believes that if the voices of women can be recouped by dialogical methods, so too can the voice of the nonhuman, the "other" (Bauer 1997, 713; Murphy, 1991). Mary Russo extends the feminist potential of carnival embodiment to undo "boundaries between individuals and society, between genders, between species, and between classes" (Russo 1994, 79). The alien "other" implicates so many boundaries, discourses, and species, welcoming the marginal and the subversive and recreating them as central for the duration of carnival. Thus the grotesque body is not just one of abjection or the repressed, it also sets up challenges to scientific regulations of behavior for flesh. Monsters, humans, and cyborgs change rapidly, making a farce of gradual adaptation and natural selection. They play on the tension between fixity and mutability, illustrating not just the horror of the predator, but the horror of the body under pressure and the ungovernable, unpredictable agency of the body's changes in response to pressure. They do not obey the supposedly nonnegotiable codes of the gene as the control of science slips, and their talent for symbiogenesis suggests origins stories and narratives of possibility that sit uneasily with the closed, static, self-contained, sleek understanding of the classical body. Evolution is not just about elimination of the weak and different and the promotion of the splendid and fit in these texts. It is about the many pathways and contexts that may prompt and support change in the organism.

What Survives?

In the final scene of *Alien Resurrection*, Ripley and Call stare out of the porthole and anticipate arriving as strangers on earth. They, along with Vriess and Johnner, are the surviving carnival bodies. They give an unequivocal message of "otherness" as dominant. Ripley is apparently human, but she has no mother and she has mothered an alien. Her body chemistry and abilities are unknown; she is the last of eight cautionary stories about cloning. Call, the gynoid, is a simulacrum, she is a replacement human being, an auton, a robot designed by a robot. "Highly ethical and emotional, with complex paradigmatic reasoning structures," she is a design that overrode behavioral inhibitors and didn't like being told what to do (Scobie 1993, 84). Call is played by the hyperfeminine Winona Ryder and plays a hyperhuman machine. She is a walking irony. They all are. Johnner is a hypermasculine and brutal foil to Call's feminine delicacy, and he is a psychological and physical relic, an apeman. While Johnner reminds the viewer of ancestral trees and primate taxonomy, Vriess, the paraplegic and cyborg, ironizes the evolutionary term "fitness" as he scoots about in his all-terrain enabling vehicle. Their bodies are all hybrid with unexpected biologies and unexpected power. Wherever they go, questions about science and technology follow. The destruction of the clone laboratory alone provides an extraordinary platform for discussion of current and possible future science practices in Western culture.

These films are a mother lode of ideas about science and technology, but evolution is a central discourse in these heteroglossic dossiers of change. Carnival can obscure this because carnival, during times of great change, performs a twofold function of satirizing the old and suggesting the new. In keeping with carnival, the *Alien* project ironizes the conservative structures of Darwinism and neo-Darwinism, but simulta-neously supports a postmodern spread of theories that disrupt genocentric, competitive evolutionary theory. Where Darwinist and neo-Darwinist concepts of evolution are evident in the films, their treatment is either satirical or foreshadows the carnivalization of theory, science, species, and body. Although coming from a variety of disciplines, most of the post-neo-Darwinist theorists seem to be constellated around a common thread that seeks recognition of the complex responsiveness and multiple agencies of the organism. These films enact stories about the inter/active and intra/active organism, as opposed to the passive organism as object of natural selection, and the inter/active and intra/active body as opposed to the replicative unit of genetic order. Evolution in the *Alien* project is not a universalizing genetic discourse, but a partial and ironic patchwork of science theory that moves towards ecofeminist politics.

These films model ecofeminism through their irony, their appreciation of difference in bodies, their partial and multiple stories of change, and their centralization of "others." Through absences, they speak eloquently about who we are, what we do, and where and how we live. Our planet is a commodity, a prison, a technological tip. By opening up new possibilities in technological, scientific, social, and organic interactions, they promote strategic new unities and naturalize carnival. The barrenness of humans in the face of the fertile and different "other" tells a story about our culture, not our species, but we see species through the eyes of culture. The negotiation of new values and meaning is an important human activity at this point in history. Western culture needs ideologically rich textual environments in which to rework crucial cultural issues, particularly world changing issues that touch on the flesh body, the body of the species in time, the socio-global bodies of culture and commerce, and—of course—the body of the planet. The *Alien* project is a work in progress in more ways than one.

REFERENCES

Aldiss, Brian. 1988. *Trillion Year Spree: The History of Science Fiction.* London: Paladin Grafton Books.

Bakhtin, Mikhail. 1984. *Rabelais and His World.* Translated by Helene Iswolsky. Bloomington: Indiana University Press.

Bauer, Dale. 1997. "Gender in Bakhtin's Carnival." In *Feminisms: An Anthology of Literary Theory and Criticism*, edited by Robyn R. Warhol and Diane Price Herndl, 708–20. New Brunswick, NJ: Rutgers University Press.

Creed, Barbara. 1993. *The Monstrous-Feminine: Film, Feminism, Psychoanalysis.* Popular Fiction Series. London: Routledge.

Fox, Sydney W. 1988. "Evolution Outward and Forward." In *Evolutionary Processes and Metaphors*, edited by Mae-Wan Ho and Sydney W. Fox, 17–29. London: John Wiley & Sons.

Gould, S. J., and N. Edredge. 1985. "Punctuated Equilibria: An Alternative to Phyletic Gradualism." In *Time Frames: The Rethinking of Darwinian Evolution and the Theory of Punctuated Equilibria*, edited by T. J. M. Schopf, 193–223. New York: Simon and Schuster.

Ho, Mae-Wan. 1988. "On Not Holding Nature Still: Evolution by Process Not by Consequence." In *Evolutionary Processes and Metaphors*, edited by Mae-Wan Ho and Sidney W. Fox, 117–44. London: John Wiley & Sons.

Ho, Mae-Wan, and Peter Saunders, eds. 1984. *Beyond Neo-Darwinism: An Introduction to the New Evolutionary Paradigm*. London: Academic Press.

Holquist, Michael. 1994. *Dialogism: Bakhtin and His World*. London: Routledge.

Margulis, Lyn. 1998. *The Symbiotic Planet: A New Look at Evolution*. London: Phoenix.

Mayr, Ernst. 1976. *Evolution and the Diversity of Life: Selected Essays*. Cambridge, MA: Harvard University Press, Belknap Press.

Morgan, Elaine. 1974. *The Descent of Woman*. London: Corgi.

Murphy, Patrick D. 1991. "Ground, Pivot, Motion: Dialogics, and Literary Practice." *Hypatia: A Journal of Feminist Philosophy* 6, no. 1 (Spring 1991): 146–61.

Ridley, Mark. 1997. "Selection in Action." In *Evolution*, edited by Mark Ridley, 48–50. Oxford Readers. Oxford: Oxford University Press.

Russo, Mary. 1994. *The Female Grotesque: Risk, Excess and Modernity*. New York: Routledge.

Scobie, Stephen. 1993. "What's the Story, Mother? The Mourning of the Alien." *Science Fiction Studies* 20, no. 1 (59) (Mar. 1993): 80–93.

Warren, Karen. 1993. Introduction to pt. 3, Ecofeminism. In *Environmental Philosophy: From Animal Rights to Radical Ecology*, edited by Michael E. Zimmerman, J. Baird Callicott, George Sessions, Karen J. Warren, and John Clark, 253–67. Englewood Cliffs, NJ: Prentice Hall.

Thompson, D'arcy Wentworth. 1971. *On Growth and Form*, abridged edition, edited by John Tyler Bonner. Cambridge: Cambridge University Press.

Intervention 2

Identity and SF:
Story as Science and Fiction

NICOLA GRIFFITH

Scientific theory and fiction are both narrative. They are stories we tell to make sense of the world. Whether we're talking equation or plot, the story is orderly and elegant and leads to a definite conclusion. Both can be terribly exciting. Both can change our lives.

I was nine when I realized I wanted to be a white-coated scientist who saved the world. I was nine when I read my first science fiction novel. I don't think this is a coincidence, though it took me a long time to understand that.

For one thing, I had no idea that the book I'd just read, *The Colors of Space*, an American paperback, was science fiction. I had no idea that people divided books into something called genres. In my world, there were two kinds of books: ones I could reach on the library shelves, and ones I couldn't. My reading was utterly indiscriminate. For example, another book I read at nine was Gibbon's *Decline and Fall of the Roman Empire*, dragged home volume by volume. But my hands-down favorite at that time wasn't a library book, it was an encyclopedia sampler.

When my parents were first married, my father, to make ends meet (they had five children in rapid succession), sold encyclopedias door to door at the weekends. Long after he'd stopped having to do that, he kept the sampler. I loved that book. Bound in black leather, it had gold-edged pages and the most fabulous articles and illustrations—artists' impressions of the moon or Mars or a black hole. It was state-of-the-art 1950s, samples of articles on everything from pastry to particle physics. I would read that book on Saturday mornings, lying on my stomach on my bedroom carpet. Those pages were my Aladdin's Cave. I read entirely at random. Looking back, probably the thing that hooked me irrevocably was that almost every article was incomplete: they finished mid-paragraph, often mid-sentence. I knew, reading that black sampler, that there was more, that the story always continued out there somewhere in the big wide world.

One Saturday morning when I was nine, I read the most gobsmacking thing of my life: everything in the world was built of something called atoms. They were tiny and invisible and made mainly of nothing. If you could crush all the nothing out of the Empire State Building, it would be the size of a cherry pit but weigh . . . well, whatever the Empire State Building weighs. I clapped the book shut, astonished, leapt to my feet, and thundered downstairs. In the kitchen, where my mother was cooking a big fried breakfast for seven, I announced my incredible discovery. She said, "How interesting. Pass the eggs." I blinked. "But Mum! Atoms! The Empire State Building! A cherry pit!" And she said, again (probably with a bit of an edge), "Yes. Very interesting. Pass the eggs." So I passed the eggs, and wondered briefly if my mother might be an alien. (Unlike many of my other friends it never occurred to me to wonder if I might be adopted: too many sisters with features just like mine. Understanding of some of the laws of genetics was inescapable.)

I spent the rest of that weekend in a daze, resting my hand on the yellow Formica of the kitchen table while everyone ate their bacon and eggs, wondering why my hand didn't melt into the table. They were both mainly nothing, after all. What else in the world wasn't what it seemed? What other wonders were waiting for me to stumble over them?

About a month later, I was helping my mother clean the local church hall where she ran a nursery school during the week, and under a bench I found a book with a lurid red and yellow cover: *The Colors of Space.* (Until two weeks ago, I didn't know the author was Marion Zimmer Bradley. I could easily have found out anytime in the last few years, but I didn't. Not checking on memory is one of my superstitious behaviors. I also don't take photos of special occasions or keep a journal. I don't like freezing things in place. I prefer fluidity, possibility. However, before I sat down to write this essay, I went to Amazon.com, looked up the book, and ordered it. When it arrived, I was delighted by the lurid red and yellow cover, then amused when I realized it explained something that puzzled my friends a dozen years ago. My first novel, *Ammonite,* was published in 1993. The first edition had a truly cheesy red and yellow cover with a spaceship front and center. No one could understand why I wasn't upset but, clearly, I was drawing fond associations with my nine-year-old self, remembering another ugly paperback. When I've finished writing this, I'll reread it. . . .)

I don't remember a thing about the story or the characters, only that it was about aliens (aha, I thought, imagining my mum) and the discovery of a new color. That night, lying in bed, I nearly burst my brain trying to imagine a new color, just as in my teens I would drive myself to the brink of insanity (not so hard, really, when a teenager) trying to imagine infinity.

At some point we moved to a new house—we were always moving—and the black leather encyclopedia sampler disappeared. By this time I had discovered Asimov and Frank Herbert and a collection of '50s SF anthologies with introductions that banged on the SF drum and introduced me to the notion of genre. I was hooked. Through these stories, far more than through any school lessons, science came alive for me: surface tension (Blish's "Surface Tension"), ecology (Herbert's *Dune*), multi-dimensions (Heinlein's "And He Built a Crooked House"), politics (just about anything by Asimov). Science became my religion. I stopped daydreaming about taking gold in the Olympics and started thinking about changing the world. I didn't fret over minor details such as which discipline to choose—who cared whether it was physics or chemistry or math or biology that ended up saving humanity?

That was the beauty of being twelve, and then thirteen. I didn't have to deal with reality. I didn't have to ignore with scorn the messy inexactness of zoology in order to devote myself to the purity of math or to the measurability of chemistry. Watching a bird, considering Newton's laws, learning about the tides of history seemed equally important. I wanted it all. The world sparkled. Einstein's photoelectric effect, a spoof proving one equals two, Popper's swans and Pavlov's dogs: I fell in love with each in turn, depending on what class I was in. (Funnily enough, I never much liked any of my science teachers; they never liked me, either.) I tried on future identities: discovering an anti-grav drive; feeding all those starving children in fly-buzzed parts of the world; finally pinpointing the location of Atlantis.

At the same time, I was busy being a teenager. I tried on here-and-now identities: short hair or long? Hippie or punk? Beat poet in black or sweet-faced thing in pastels? Judas Priest or David Bowie? Monty Python or Star Trek?

An American SF editor, David Hartwell, has said that the golden age of SF is twelve. He has a point. The essence of being twelve, and of science fiction, is potential. They are both all about hopes and dreams and possibilities, intense curiosity aroused by the knowledge that there's so much out there yet to be known. As we get older and do fewer things, and fewer things for the first time, that sense of potential diminishes. The open door starts to close—just like the anterior fontanelle of an infant's skull.

Reading good fiction, particularly good SF, keeps the adolescent sense of possibility jacked wide open. A sense of possibility maintains plasticity; it keeps us able to see what's out there. Without this sense of possibility, we see only what we expect.

Someone who runs on the same beach at dawn every day for two years gets used to certain things: being alone, the hiss and suck of the waves, the boulder that juts from the rock pool at the point where she leaps the rill, the cry of the gulls, the smell of seaweed, all in tones of grey and blue. So there you are one morning, running along, cruising on autopilot, using the nonslippery part of the boulder to give you a boost as you jump over the rill, listening unconsciously to the gulls squabbling over something at the water line. You're thinking about breakfast, or the sex you had last night; you're humming that music everyone's been listening to the last week; you're wrestling with some knotty problem for which you have the glimmerings of a solution. There's a dead body on the beach. You run right past it: you literally don't see it.

It's counterintuitive, but it happens all the time: the white-faced driver staring at the tricycle crushed under his front wheel, "I just didn't see him, officer." The microbiologist who skips past the Petri dish in a batch of sixty cultures, the one with that curiously empty ring, that lack of growth, in the center. The homeowner who returns to his condo and doesn't see the broken window, the muddy footprints leading to the closet and the suitcase full of valuables lying open on the bed. Every day, during our various routines, the movie of what we expect plays on the back of our eyelids while our brain goes on holiday. How many times do we got out of the car at the office and realize we don't remember a thing about the journey?

Reading SF, the overriding value of which is the new, keeps our reticular activating systems primed: we expect everything and anything. And if we expect, we can see. If we see, we try to find an explanation. We form a hypothesis. We test it. We learn. We tell a story.

A science fiction story not only excites us about the world, it excites us about ourselves: how we fit within the systems that govern our universe and, paradoxically, about our potential to change the world. The best SF is, in a sense, about love: loving the world and our place within it so much that we make the effort to make a difference. But science fiction changes more than the world, more than our place in the world, it changes us. Science fiction has changed the discourse on what it means to be human. Through tall tales of human cloning, prosthetics, genetic engineering, it introduced us to the notion that the nature of body and mind are mutable. What would people look like today without prosthetics (contact lenses, artificial hips and knees, pacemakers and stents, dentures), cosmetic surgery, gene therapy? The more we change our story of ourselves, the more we change.

Which brings me full circle to the idea of fixing memory. I don't like taking photographs or keeping a journal because, on some level, it stops me learning about myself. If I freeze an image permanently, I can't revisit it and recast it, I can't retell the story. I believe in story. Without it we don't learn, we don't grow, we don't reexamine what is known to be known. I believe in science fiction stories, I believe in scientific theories. I read a novel about the fragility of the Y chromosome, or a text on the myth and mystery of the constant *phi*, and both make me stop and think: Oh. My. God. Each blows me away. Puts a shimmer around my day. Lightens my step. Urges me to turn an eager face to the possibilities of tomorrow.

TECHNOLOGIES

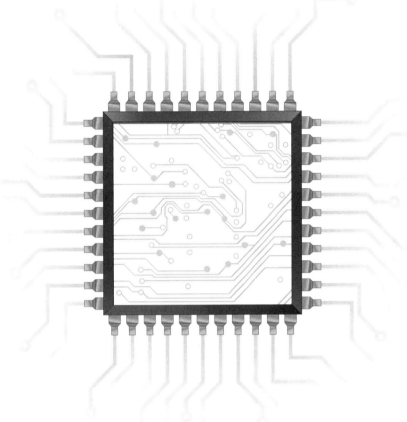

8 Sciencepunk: The Influence of Informed Science Fiction on Virtual Reality Research

JEREMY N. BAILENSON,
NICK YEE, ALICE KIM,
and JAIREH TECARRO

*T*he roots and lineages of many contemporary technologies are often-times concealed by their shiny, polished exteriors. And as their lineages are erased, the biases and worldviews that bore those technologies are also forgotten, and it becomes easy to portray current technologies—as well as the practices and research paradigms that involve them—as entirely modern and novel. Of course, ideas are never quite entirely new. For example, Turner has documented how the rise of the new economy, personal computing, and virtual communities drew many of their ideals from the countercultural era, ideals that were shared by the Merry Pranksters and had brought forth events such as the Acid Tests and the Trips Festivals (Turner 2005). In this chapter, we are interested in the roots of a different kind of "consensual hallucination" (to borrow William Gibson's phrase)—the technology of virtual reality and, in particular, the empirical social science research that revolves around it. In the same vein as Turner, we trace the roots of many current research questions back to influential science fiction novels of the early '80s. We argue that many of the questions that were raised in cyberpunk novels about two decades ago are the research questions that current virtual reality researchers are trying to answer.

Cyberpunk

Cyberpunk finds its origins in the early work of Vernor Vinge, in the form of a short story called "True Names," and William Gibson, specifically the trilogy of *Neuromancer*, *Count Zero*, and *Mona Lisa Overdrive*. Subsequent works by authors such as Bruce Sterling, Rudy Rucker, Neal Stephenson, and more recently Richard Morgan further cultivated this genre, and certainly one can argue that the earlier work of Philip K. Dick and others offers a solid foundation for these later novels. While critics and writers differ on any formal definition of the genre, key characteristics of cyberpunk include: (a) a dark vision of the future dominated by corporate culture; (b) fortified humans whose representations include not just flesh and blood but digital, narcotic, or robotic augmentations; and (c) economies driven more by digital information than by physical material.

Virtual Reality Research

Currently, no standardized definition of virtual reality is widely accepted within the field. Jaron Lanier originally coined the term "virtual reality," and it is currently used widely, and often incorrectly, in a number of contexts. For the purposes of this chapter, we define virtual environments as "synthetic sensory information that leads to perceptions of environments and their contents as if they were not synthetic" (Blascovich et al. 2002, 105). Typically, computers generate these images and enable real-time interaction between a user and the virtual environment. An immersive virtual environment is one that perceptually surrounds the user of the system. Consider a desktop computer video game; playing that game using the arrow keys on a keyboard is a virtual environment. On the other hand, if players were to have special equipment that allowed them to take on the perceptual senses of the main character of the video game, that is, to control that character's movements with their own movements and interact with stereoscopic displays such that they actually felt as if they were inside the video game, then they would be using immersive virtual reality.

Immersive virtual reality must employ two characteristic features by definition. First, computers unobtrusively track users as they interact with the digital world. User actions such as head orientation and body position are automatically and continually recorded and the perceptual display (either a head-mounted display or a room with projection screens on all of the walls) is in turn updated to reflect the changes resulting from these actions. In this way, as a person moves, the virtual scene is automatically updated to match the person's movement. Second, sensory information from the physical world is kept to a minimum. By designing the head mounted display or the projection room to block out objects from the physical world, immersive virtual reality allows people to more easily become enveloped by the digital information.

Current VR (virtual reality) research proceeds along a number of avenues, including computer scientists developing programs for driving behavior tracking, animations, and artificial mental states; graphic artists designing three-dimensional modeling and texturing techniques; engineers focusing on hardware; medical researchers developing simulations to train surgeons; military personnel designing training simulations for soldiers; clinical therapists developing virtual desensitization simulations to treat phobias; and social scientists examining the human experience within computer-mediated communication. Loosely speaking, experiences that qualify as "virtual" range from sending an email to playing video games to wearing fully immersive, stereoscopic displays that track and render user movements.

Overlapping Social Networks

The world of cyberpunk authors and the world of virtual reality researchers have always been intimately interwoven. First of all, well-known virtual reality researchers collaborate with influential cyberpunk authors. For this project, we conducted informal interviews with two major figures in the field of virtual reality. Jaron Lanier is the pioneer who coined the term "virtual reality" in the early '80s and developed the first immersive simulation in which multiple avatars could interact. In the interview, Lanier talked about collaborations with Gibson. Another well-known researcher, Thad Starner, was also interviewed. Starner is a professor at Georgia Tech who has been a cyborg (i.e., has a laptop with translucent heads-up display goggles) for over a decade. Over the years, Starner has been in regular contact with Vernor Vinge to discuss ideas.

And secondly, cyberpunk texts are treated as serious academic texts in virtual reality courses and research. Not only are *Neuromancer* and *Snow Crash* widely read by current virtual reality researchers, these early cyberpunk texts are required reading in formal classes on virtual reality and digital human interaction. For example, a quick Google search of "Neuromancer" and "syllabus" will produce several pages of such courses. Moreover, Vinge, Gibson, and Bruce Sterling (author of *Mirrorshades: The Cyberpunk Anthology*, an influential collection of short stories) often speak at academic conferences on engineering, technology, and virtual reality. In 1994 Bruce Sterling gave the Keynote Address at SIGGRAPH, the premier conference on computer graphics (Sterling 2004).

The Influence of Cyberpunk on Virtual Reality Research

In this chapter, we examine how themes developed by cyberpunk science fiction writers have shaped the paradigms in which virtual reality researchers operate. We focus on four works in particular: William Gibson's *Neuromancer*, Vernor Vinge's *True Names*, Neal Stephenson's *Snow Crash*, and Rudy Rucker's *Software*. Within each of these works, we examine specific constructs and demonstrate that the research agendas chosen by scientists, both methodological and theoretical, as well as the specific hypotheses tested within those agendas, are either implicitly or explicitly shaped by earlier works of science fiction. This relationship is not surprising, considering that cyberpunk authors often have extensive science backgrounds and explicitly communicate with virtual reality technologists. However, the degree to which scientists rely on constructs developed by fiction writers (who possess only a small fraction of scientists' expertise), is quite large. We aim to explicate this relationship, to highlight how VR research constructs and tests different visions of cyberpunk virtual reality, and to demonstrate how cyberpunk fiction foreshadows these tensions.

A Hierarchy of Being

Neal Stephenson, the author of *Snow Crash*, is largely credited with applying the term *avatar* to digital human representations in the mid-nineties. Avatar is a religious term, and typically defined as the incarnation of a deity. In other words, the gods of Eastern religions could not visit the Earth without embodying some type of recognizable human or animal form. Similarly, when humans visit digital space, they need to have some type of vehicle to carry their intentions and actions; Stephenson refers to this form as an avatar.

Some would argue that Stephenson's major contribution was to thoroughly explore the vast possibilities of avatar taxonomy. In the *Metaverse* (Stephenson's term for cyberspace), people use avatars to interact with others in the virtual world. These avatars can vary drastically in terms of realism, in that avatars created by programmers can be perfect analogs of the user in terms of their appearances and gestures, or alternatively users can purchase "off-the-shelf" avatars, stock bodies that widely populate the Metaverse as well. Some people also choose to render themselves unrealistically in completely nonhuman form. According to Stephenson, "Your avatar can look any way you want it to, up to the limitations of your equipment. If you're ugly, you can make your avatar beautiful. If you've just gotten out of bed, your avatar can still be wearing beautiful clothes and professionally applied makeup. You can look like a gorilla or a dragon or a giant talking penis in the Metaverse. Spend five minutes walking down the street and you will see all of these" (1991, 25).

Yet even as Stephenson describes this representational plasticity, there is an inherent tension between Metaverse reality and real-life reality in *Snow Crash*. Consider that the protagonist, Hiro, has an avatar that "just looks like Hiro, with the difference that no matter what Hiro is wearing in Reality, his avatar always wears a black leather kimono" (26). Stephenson also describes Juanita's avatar in great detail, emphasizing her veridicality, "with no effort made to hide the early suggestions of crow's feet at the corners of her big black eyes. Her glossy hair is so well resolved that Hiro can see individual strands refracting the light into tiny rainbows" (185). The Metaverse is also a place where businesspeople around the world come to negotiate and a place where real-life lovers come on dates. Thus, even as he hints at the endless possibilities of existence, the Metaverse that Stephenson creates is very much meant to be a reproduction, an extension, of reality. It is a place to be yourself and conduct your real-life business and affairs.

More importantly, the goal of the Metaverse is to replicate reality in its full detail—visually and behaviorally. The insistence is on creating avatars that look photorealistic and having them move in convincing ways. And Stephenson introduces a hierarchy of realism. Avatars are not created equally; some are more photorealistic and behaviorally realistic than others. In other words, variation in skill and disposable income produces a hierarchy of being in the Metaverse.

This obsession with realism and equipment quality produces a unique vision of what virtual reality is supposed to be—a vision that emphasizes reproduction of reality. That vision prompts a certain set of research questions. The idea of avatar realism (how high in fidelity an avatar is) and avatar anthropomorphism (how much an avatar looks like a human being, as opposed to other living or nonliving things), has received quite a bit of attention in the literature on virtual reality. One of the only developed process models that attempts to model the interaction between humans and virtual humans, developed largely by social psychologist Jim Blascovich (Blascovich 2002; Blascovich et al. 2002), focuses on these dimensions of realism and human agency. According to that model, there is a tradeoff between behavioral realism (the degree to which human representations behave as they would in the physical world) and perceived agency (the extent to which the interactants thinks they are interacting with another actual human being). The higher the realism, particularly communicative realism (e.g., facial expressions), the less perceived agency needed to achieve social influence and effective interaction. Hence, according to the model, social influence and effective communication with virtual humans is likely to occur when either realism or agency are high, or both.

While the social influence model of virtual interaction is probably the most thorough framework for evaluating social interaction, the virtual reality community has paid a large amount of attention to the notion of avatar realism for a number of years. Indeed, an engineer credited with one of the most influential books on building virtual human personality (*Simulating Humans* by Badler, Phillips, and Webber, 1993), Norman Badler, was a coauthor on a paper at a major virtual reality conference in 1998 titled "Avatars á la *Snow Crash*." In that work, he surveyed the field in terms of how realistic current avatars were across the world in various virtual reality labs. He compared current avatars at the time to what he considered the "gold standard" of avatars, namely, how real the avatars were in Stephenson's 1992 novel:

> In summary, we believe that communications bandwidth and graphics rendering speed are the primary current limitations to *Snow Crash* scene complexity and number of avatars. Other aspects of *Snow Crash* avatar design, motion, and appearance offer no challenges that are unmet in the research literature. The major gaps seem to lie in the control transformation from the user's desires to the avatar's actions and in the modification of an animated action based on the attitude, personality, and reactions of the live participant. (Allbeck and Badler 1998, 4)

Since then, the pioneers of examining virtual humans, mediated humans, and virtual reality have all been focusing on this question of avatar realism (Badler et al. 1993; Bailenson et al. 2005; Benford et al. 1995; Biocca and Levy 1995; Blascovich et al. 2002; Cassell and Vilhjalmsson 1999; Lombard and Ditton 1997; Slater et al. 2000; Thalmann and Thalmann 1999). These researchers typically have a human interact with some type of a virtual human and explore a number of dimensions of realism.

Some of this emphasis on realism traces its roots back to Stephenson's vision of the Metaverse, and Stephenson's vision itself has become the benchmark for what good virtual reality is. Ironically, this particular problem is difficult to solve. Avatars can resemble their human counterparts along a number of dimensions (see Blascovich et al. 2002 for an overview). The two which have received the most attention in the literature are behavioral resemblance (number of a given human's behaviors the avatar exhibits) and photographic resemblance (how many of a given human's static visual features the avatar possesses). The degree of behavioral resemblance is largely governed by the ability of the system to track behavior (know exactly what the human is doing at every given moment), and then to render behavior (transpose that exact behavior onto the digital representation).

Currently, real-time behavioral tracking technology for avatars, while improving steadily, is extremely far from matching expectations instilled by popular culture, like online representations of characters from *The Matrix*, for instance. In those fictional accounts, the movements and gestures of avatars are seamless; the actions of human and avatar are perceptually indistinguishable. Outside the fictional realm, however, real-time behavior tracking is extremely difficult. While there have been advances in tracking of gesture through various forms mechanical, optical, and other systems (see Turk and Kolsch 2003 for a review), the gap between actual movements and real-time tracked movements remains large.

Furthermore, once the movements and behaviors have been captured, they must be rendered onto the digital representation of the avatar. This process is not trivial, and many issues arise in terms of the quality of the movements and behaviors when applied to a digital model that contains fewer degrees of motion-freedom than the human body does. In other words, current digital models simply don't have enough joints to support completely naturalistic and realistic movements. While the advances in motion-capture-rendering and inverse kinematics have been quite good with non-real-time representations (see any film by Pixar), the same is not true with real-time avatars in which these motions have to be expressed on the fly.

On the other hand, there are fewer barriers to achieving high photographic resemblance. The use of three-dimensional scanners and photogrammetric software allows for the realistic recreation of static, digital human heads and faces that are nearly real enough to function as an analog to a real face (Bailenson et al. 2003). The key challenge, though, is designing faces and bodies in high enough detail to allow for the realistic rendering of behavior described above. In sum, with current technology, static avatars currently can look quite a bit like their human controllers; however, avatars can only perform a small subset of their controllers' actions in real time. The standard for realistic avatars, which some researchers believe has been set by the fictional work of *Snow Crash*, is constantly being examined by virtual reality scholars. While the idea of realism in virtual humans and robots was obviously discussed prior to this novel (see Mori's 1982 discussion of the *uncanny valley*), the proliferation of this construct accelerated after the popularization of *Snow Crash*.

Being There

Tied to this urgency of creating more realistic avatars is the notion of *presence*, the degree to which the user actually feels as if she is present in the virtual reality (as opposed to present in the physical world). Indeed, the premiere journal dedicated to virtual reality research is called *Presence*, and a wealth of research seeks to understand the phenomenon of presence: understanding the mechanisms that underlie the subjective experience of "being in another world" strikes at the very heart of the virtual reality experience. To this end, when building a virtual reality simulation, there is often a desire to digitally recreate as realistic an analog of the physical world as possible. In other words, if two people enter a virtual conference, then one way to achieve high presence is to render each virtual person to look and behave exactly like the physical person that virtual person represents. A large number of virtual reality researchers work within this paradigm, building more and more sophisticated sensors and equipment to replicate physical reality as faithfully as possible in the virtual environment.

Vernor Vinge's short story "True Names," while probably less commercially successful than *Neuromancer* or *Snow Crash*, predates both those novels (written in 1979, published in 1981) and may have had the most influence on virtual reality researchers of the three. As evidence for the importance of Vinge's work, an edited collection entitled *"True Names" and the Opening of the Cyberspace Frontier* (Frenkel 2001) features articles written by a number of scientific virtual reality developers and researchers.

Vinge defined the "Other Plane" as a digital world accessed by attaching electrodes to one's head. Inside the digital world are representations of other people (i.e., avatars), intelligent embodied agents, and large data structures, as well as digital structures such as landscapes, castles, and so forth. In his short stories, Vinge explores many of the concepts that have become central to many scientific research programs. "True Names" is largely considered the first piece of science fiction to really explore the constructs and parameters of a world in which everything and everyone one is digital. While there are indeed some other works that predate this book and peripherally explore the idea of avatars (see, for example, "The Girl Who Was Plugged In" by James Tiptree, Jr. written in 1969, for a rough depiction of biological, nondigital avatars), Vinge was the first to truly explore the space of a world in which digital representations were pervasive.

One notion of Vinge's that has influenced the paradigm of virtual reality research is this notion of presence, how immersed one is in virtual reality, as opposed to the physical world. Researchers across the discipline predominantly treat the concept of presence as a subjective, psychological construct, as opposed to a construct based on technology. In other words, according to a majority of researchers in the field, the experience of immersion is independent of technology—it is possible to feel higher presence in a well-done film or novel than in a poorly constructed virtual reality simulation. This notion was central to the manner in which Vinge described the other plane: "He powered up his processors, settled back in his favorite chair, and carefully attached the Portal's five sucker electrodes to his scalp. For long minutes nothing happened: a certain amount of self denial—or at least self hypnosis—was necessary to make the assent" (Vinge 1987, 250). In other words, entering into the digital simulation was not merely perceptual, but psychological as well. This concept is demonstrated repeatedly in presence research (see Biocca et al. 2003 for a review).

Of course, the problems of avatar realism and presence are themselves rooted in a particular vision of what virtual reality is supposed to accomplish. And it is this assumption that creates the set of research questions that seem meaningful to ask. But should reality (or its absence) be the yardstick of virtual reality? And what other questions could we be asking if we didn't insist on replication, veridicality, and escapism?

Superhuman Powers

Cyberpunk offers an alternative vision of virtual reality, one where its primary goal is not reproduction, but augmentation and transformation. In *Neuromancer*, William Gibson hints at many of these possibilities. Gibson is credited with inventing the term cyberspace, though there are some works published a few years earlier which do begin to develop the general concept of cyberspace. Gibson defines cyberspace as "a consensual hallucination experienced daily by billions of legitimate operators, in every nation, by children being taught mathematical concepts . . . a graphic representation of data abstracted from the banks of every computer in the human system. Unthinkable complexity" (Gibson 1984, 51). Gibson's influence is pervasive in actual scientific research about virtual reality because his writing explores so thoroughly the possibilities of digital humans interacting within digital space. A quick "Google Scholar" search indicates that *Neuromancer* has been referenced by over 150 science articles in refereed journals. This frequency of citation is about seventy-five times higher than the average science paper that actually conducts empirical research or technological development within virtual reality.

In the fictional world crafted by Gibson, human identity, appearance, and behavior, while in either cyberspace or in physical space, have an extremely high degree of plasticity. Through digital algorithms, biological and genetic augmentation, and mechanical devices, the human experience is mutable. Despite having the technology to render virtual simulations and physical bodies to be completely realistic, people choose to abandon close ties with their genetic blueprints and instead opt for transformed representations.

For example, a major character named Molly has augmented her body to give her digital readouts of the world around her not possible in the physical world. Special implants provide her with the ability to see in the dark, access data from cyberspace, and to communicate via text with other people. This type of augmented ability using digital information is quite common now across many types of science research. Government funding agencies issued a major push in the late 1990s with a research agenda called Augmented Cognition (see Schmorrow and Kruse 2004 for a detailed history), designing computer interfaces to extend the limitations of normal human cognition. One major rationale for this work was to provide digital wearable displays that could increase the working memory of people by allowing them to store cognitive information on displays as opposed to keeping them actively stored in memory. Similarly, VR research is providing augmentations of social sensory abilities. These transformations complement human abilities to draw inferences about the social world. Because everyone in a virtual reality simulation is digital, people can use algorithms to interpret the social actions of other people around them. For example, in addition to being able to survey a crowd of fifty students with her eyes and ears, a teacher in virtual reality may receive real-time summary information across her visual field about how often each student is smiling, nodding, looking away, talking, and so forth—a speaker may receive extremely helpful and detailed information at the micro level for each individual. Moreover, this information may be supplied to the self—the teacher can also receive automatic registers that ensure she is spreading her attention equally towards each student.

A similar notion of transformed social abilities raised by Gibson is his depiction of "simstim." Simstim is when one person receives all of the perceptual information from another in real time. In other words, sensors in one person record all of the stimuli that he experiences, send it over a network to a second person, and the second person experiences the world of the first person across all five senses in real time. Researchers are currently using this type of simulation. For example, Steve Mann, a professor in Electrical Engineering at the University of Toronto, wore a special pair of glasses that had a webcam on them whenever he ventured outdoors for extended periods of time. He then could play the feed of the webcam to a dedicated website, so that other people could tune in and experience perceptually exactly what it was he was seeing and hearing, with the idea of creating a system in which it was more difficult for people to be persecuted and victimized if their line of sight could be taken on by uncountable numbers of "watchdogs" on the internet. In sum, by increasing the amount of wearable computers, social accountability would be increased. This notion is directly related to Gibson's vision of simstim.

In terms of augmented interactions, this chapter's authors have been implementing a number of experimental simulations in which one person is forced to take the point of view of another person. As X and Y are interacting, X may take Y's visual point of view and then see herself in real time, from Y's point of view. In other words, imagine that another person was wearing a small video camera right between her eyes, and the video feed goes right into your own eyes as they look at you in a conversation. We have been examining the possibility that people will act in a more cooperative fashion when forced take the point of view of others, and have implemented this in two contexts, a negotiation context in which people reach mutually beneficial solutions when adapting one another's field of view, as well as a diversity simulation context in which we examine the effect on empathy responses of taking on an identity of someone of a different race, gender, or age.

Transformed Social Interaction

Beyond supersensory abilities, virtual reality offers a large degree of representational and behavioral plasticity. In *Software*, Rudy Rucker offers a true gem that shows the potential of this plasticity. Towards the end of the novel, Cobb Anderson has been given a highly advanced robotic body and charged with the task of creating a cult. To achieve this goal, Cobb gains the utter devotion of initiates by taking them individually into a room and changing his facial structure to match that of the initiate's. In other words, Rucker is hinting at the possibilities of using representation plasticity for social advantage. What is even more striking is that Rucker shows the possibility of representational plasticity without a virtual reality construct. Rucker's world is digitized via the large presence of robots instead of a virtual environment.

This notion of plasticity has profound implications. In virtual reality simulations, the world is constantly being redrawn separately for each user simultaneously. Consequently, it is possible to break the normal physics of conversation and to render the interaction differently for each user at the same time. In other words, in virtual reality, each user may theoretically alter their stream of information in real time for strategic purposes, such that what other people in VR see is not their actual appearance or behavior, but instead the appearance and behaviors that they would like others to see. The theory of transformed social interaction (Bailenson et al. 2004) examines the possibilities that these real-time transformations raise. People who subscribe to this paradigm believe that it is possible to achieve higher levels of presence when reality is augmented or transformed than when reality acts as an immutable constraint on the simulation. In other words, users may more effectively achieve their goals while interacting in virtual reality (goals such as entertainment, social relations, or commerce), if they strategically alter the virtual world around them, perhaps even breaking the constraints of their own faces, bodies, and behaviors.

This alternative vision of virtual reality as transformed reality, where virtual selves are not meant to be extensions or reproductions of the real self, foregrounds what Gibson referred to as "the infinite plasticity of the digital" (Gibson 1999, 117). Vinge also embraces the notion of transforming the representation of the self (that is, transformed social interaction). "Robin Hood, dressed in green and looking like Errol Flynn, sat across the hall in a very close conversation with a remarkably good-looking female (but then they could all be remarkably good looking here) who seemed unsure whether to project blonde or brunette" (Vigne 1987, 255). According to Vinge, the Other Plane was particularly attractive to those who felt a need to abandon their physical representation: "And then, since the beginning of time, there had been the people who simply did not like reality, who wanted another world, and if given half a chance would live there forever . . . never moving, never exercising their real world bodies" (1987, 321). This concept of projecting a digital self that is drastically different from the physical self is explored rigorously in the work of Vinge, and this concept is quite prominent in current VR research.

Researchers studying transformed social interaction have begun to explore the effects of digitally changing identity. Current digital technologies are allowing us to dramatically alter our self-representations with the click of a button in a way that was never possible before. Nowhere is self-representation more flexible than in virtual environments where users can choose or customize their own avatar. In many online video games, users can adjust their gender, height, weight, skin tone, eye shape, eye color, hairstyle, hair color, nose prominence, lip fullness, and facial structure, and can adjust these variables whenever they would like at the click of a button. Every day, millions of users in these online environments interact with each other via avatars of their own choosing (Woodcock 2005; Yee 2006).

Transformed social interaction research has proceeded along two lines in examining self-representation. The first line examines the effectiveness of such a strategy in terms of social influence—does changing the attractiveness, gender, race, facial structure, and so on of your representation make the individual more effective at achieving different goals of social influence? As such, we have examined the implications of the following strategies: making your avatar's facial structure more similar to someone else (Bailenson et al. 2006); use of automatic nonverbal mimicry of someone else by your avatar (Bailenson and Yee 2005); augmented gaze, that is, being able to look directly into the eyes of more than one person at once (Bailenson et al. 2005); and other transformations. All of these empirical studies indicate that transformations of identity are difficult for any given audience to detect, but quite effective at persuading that audience.

The second line of studies concerned with transformations of self-representation examines what effect these transformations have on a person who implements them. In other words, how does wearing a beautiful or tall avatar change the behavior of a user who may be neither beautiful nor tall? We have demonstrated that an individual's behavior conforms to stereotypes of their self-representation—a process we term "the Proteus Effect" (Yee and Bailenson, in press). We argue that just as men and women conform to gender roles (i.e., social role theory, Eagly and Wood 1999) and just as the elderly conform to expected age stereotypes (i.e., self-stereotyping, Levy 1996), we have demonstrated that people conform to stereotypical behaviors associated with their digital self-representations.

In a series of experiments, Yee and colleagues tested the Proteus Effect by having subjects look in a virtual mirror and notice that their avatar was either particularly high (or low) in either height or attractiveness. We have demonstrated that, regardless of how tall or beautiful our subjects were, subjects who were virtually beautiful were more likely (compared to control conditions) to walk within another person's intimate space and to reveal more information about themselves to another person. Furthermore, virtually tall subjects negotiated more successfully in a money-splitting task than virtually short subjects. In sum, changing the self not only changes your ability to influence another person but also changes the way you act on some of the most basic levels of social interaction.

Immortality

A final influence of science fiction on virtual research combines both elements of reproduction and transformation: the notion that virtual reality confers some form of immortality. We see variations of this theme in several of the cyberpunk novels we've mentioned, centered on the idea that our personalities and identities can be captured via software. In "True Names," Erytrina proclaims as she dies, "My kernel is out here in the System. Every time I'm there, I transfer a little more of myself. The kernel is growing into a true Erytrina, who is also truly me. When this body dies, *I* will still be, and you can still talk to me" (Vigne 1987, 329). In *Neuromancer*, the construct known as Dixie Flatline is a software replicate of a renowned hacker's personality and expertise.

Rucker pushes this idea the furthest in *Software*, a novel in which robots and humans are living in uneasy coexistence. The more advanced robots have invented a way of preserving a person's memories, personalities, and expertise. The robots see this as a way to create a global consciousness—a form of higher life. The only side effect of the procedure is that the entire brain is destroyed in the process. On the other hand, digitized identities can then be stored in a variety of human-form robots that will never die. This is the version of immortality that the protagonist, Cobb Anderson, achieves.

Researchers have been actively exploring this concept. For example, William Bainbridge, currently a program officer at the National Science Foundation, runs the personality capture project, in which digital technology is used to archive the "true essence" of a person, including physical descriptors, biographical information, and personality dimensions. Bainbridge has developed an extremely extensive archive:

Contemporary information technology facilitates the creation and administration of much longer questionnaires than traditionally was feasible, and people may be motivated to respond to them as a means of capturing significant aspects of their personalities. This can be useful in designing *sociable technology*—computer avatars, software agents, and robots with simulated personalities—and in creating personality archives for research or memorial purposes. This article illustrates how *personality capture* can be accomplished through 20,000 questionnaire items culled from responses to open-ended online questions, content analysis of existing verbal or textual material, and using words from dictionaries, encyclopedias, and thesauri. This approach enables detailed idiographic study of a single individual, based on fresh measurement items and scales derived from the ambient culture. (Bainbridge 2003, 21)

Rucker describes this version of personhood and immortality more succinctly: "the soul is the software" (1987, 66).

Writing the Future of VR

When John Barlow first experienced immersive virtual reality, he immediately saw the connection between this "consensual hallucination" provided by digital technology and the consensual hallucination provided by a very different pharmaceutical technology. He likens the VR experience to getting high and "psychedelic." What struck Barlow the most was the disembodied experience provided by early VR. He compares the liberation to an expression of a primal human desire—the "desire to have visions." Of course, what is most ironic is that virtual reality research has always insisted on embodiment. The disembodied experience provided by early VR was due to unavailable technologies rather than actual intention.

Barlow's vision of what virtual reality was supposed to be was very different from the ones that had been adopted by the community of virtual reality researchers. On one front are visions of virtual reality as reproduced reality where realism and presence are the core research themes. On another front are visions of virtual reality as transformed reality where notions of representational and behavioral plasticity are the core research themes. In between is the notion of immortality. The commonality is that all these different threads of research find their roots in cyberpunk novels written two decades ago. Barlow's vision does challenge one shared assumption among current virtual reality research: why do we insist on embodiment in virtual reality? And indeed, what virtual worlds could we create if we didn't have to worry about how real our bodies and faces looked?

Determining the direction of the causal arrow is a tricky endeavor when examining historical patterns. To claim that science fiction has shaped the research paradigm of virtual reality research is probably an overly bold claim as well as impossible to either prove or falsify. However, it is certainly clear that a number of researchers have used these cyberpunk texts as a source for research questions as well as for a standard for evaluating the efficacy of state-of-the-art virtual reality simulations. What makes these texts a useful resource is not their description of technology, but instead, their exploration of world in which information and people are represented thoroughly in digital space. Authors like William Gibson, Bruce Sterling, Neal Stephenson, and Vernor Vinge are influential not because they have a solid grasp of digital technology, but instead because they possessed the insight to see the inevitable changes in the social world that occur when digitally mediated interaction becomes the predominant form of social activity, and to explore the possibilities of that world to its fullest.

In sum, scientists brainstorm important research questions as new technologies arise to support those questions. However, the cyberpunk authors, not limited by the existence of the actual technology, have stipulated the existence of the enabling technology and proceeded to explore the implications for people in those fictional worlds. As we move closer to achieving technologically the worlds depicted in cyberpunk, scientists may provide new research *answers* concerning the use of the technology, but will have more difficulty in creating new research *questions,* as many these questions have largely been exhausted in fiction.

REFERENCES

Allbeck, J., and N. Badler. 1998. "Avatars á la *Snow Crash.*" Paper presented at the Computer Animation Conference, Philadelphia, PA.

Badler, N., C. Phillips, and B. Webber. 1993. *Simulating Humans: Computer Graphics, Animation, and Control.* New York: Oxford University Press.

Bailenson, J. N., A. Beall, J. Loomis, J. Blascovich, and M. Turk. 2004. "Transformed Social Interaction: Decoupling Representation from Behavior and Form in Collaborative Virtual Environments." *Presence: Teleoperators and Virtual Environments* 13, no. 4:428–41.

Bailenson, J. N., A. Beall., J. Blascovich, J. Loomis, and M. Turk. 2005. "Transformed Social Interaction, Augmented Gaze, and Social Influence in Immersive Virtual Environments." *Human Communication Research* 31:511–37.

Bailenson, J. N., J. Blascovich, A. Beall, and J. Loomis. 2003. "Interpersonal Distance in Immersive Virtual Environments." *Personality and Social Psychology Bulletin* 29:1–15.

Bailenson, J. N., P. Garland, S. Iyengar, and N. Yee. 2006. "Transformed Facial Similarity as a Political Cue: A Preliminary Investigation." *Political Psychology* 27:373–86.

Bailenson, J. N., and N. Yee. 2005. "Digital Chameleons: Automatic Assimilation of Nonverbal Gestures in Immersive Virtual Environments." *Psychological Science* 16:814–819.

Bainbridge, W. 2003. "Massive Questionnaires for Personality Capture." *Social Science Computer Review* 21:267–80.

Benford, S. D., J. M. Bowers, L. E. Fahlen, C. M. Greenhalgh, and D. N. Snowdon. 1995. "User Embodiment in Collaborative Virtual Environments." Paper presented at the ACM Conference on Human Factors in Computing Systems, Denver, Colorado.

Biocca, F., C. Harms, and J. Burgoon. 2003. "Towards a More Robust Theory and Measure of Social Presence: Review and Suggested Criteria." *Presence: Teleoperators and Virtual Environments* 12, no. 5:456–80.

Biocca, F., and M. Levy. 1995. *Communication in the Age of Virtual Reality.* Hillsdale, NJ: L. Erlbaum Associates.

Blascovich, J. 2002. "Social Influence within Immersive Virtual Environments." In *The Social Life of Avatars*, ed. R. Schroeder, 127–45. London: Springer-Verlag.

Blascovich, J., J. Loomis, A. Beall, K. Swinth, C. Hoyt, and J. Bailenson. 2002. "Immersive Virtual Environment Technology as a Methodological Tool for Social Psychology." *Psychological Inquiry* 13, no. 2:103–24.

Cassell, J., and H. Vilhjalmsson. 1999. "Fully Embodied Conversational Avatars: Making Communicative Behaviors Autonomous." *Autonomous Agents and Multi-Agent Systems* 2:45–64.

Eagly, A. H., and W. Wood. 1999. "The Origins of Sex Differences in Human Behavior: Evolved Dispositions Versus Social Roles." *American Psychologist* 54:408–23.

Gibson, W. 1984. *Neuromancer.* New York: Ace Books.

Levy, B. 1996. "Improving Memory in Old Age through Implicit Self-stereotyping." *Journal of Personality and Social Psychology* 71:1092–107.

Lombard, M,. and T. Ditton. 1997. "At the Heart of It All: The Concept of Presence." *Journal of Computer-Mediated Communication* 3.

Schmorrow, D., and A. Kruse. 2004. "Augmented Cognition." In *The Encyclopedia of Human Computer Interaction*, ed. Claude Ghaoui. Hershey, PA: Idea Group Reference.

Slater, M., J. Howell, A. Steed, D. Pertaub, M. Garau, and S. Springel. 2000. "Acting in Virtual Reality." Paper presented at the ACM Collaborative Virtual Environments.

Sterling, B. 2004. "When Blobjects Rule the Earth." Paper presented at the SIGGRAPH.

Thalmann, M., and D. Thalmann, eds. 1999. *Computer Animation and Simulation 99*. Vienna: Springer Verlag.

Turk, M., and M. Kolsch. 2003. "Perceptual Interfaces." In *Emerging Topics in Computer Vision*, edited by G. Medioni and S. Kang. Englewood Cliffs, NJ: Prentice Hall.

Turner, F. 2005. "Where the Counterculture Met the New Economy." *Technology and Culture* 46:485–512.

Woodcock, B. 2005. *MMOG Chart* (Massively Multiplayer Online Games), from http://www.mmogchart.com/

Yee, N. 2006. "The Demographics, Motivations, and Derived Experiences of Users of Massively Multi-User Online Graphical Environments." *Presence: Teleoperators and Virtual Environments*.

Yee, N., and J. N. Bailenson. 2007, in press. "The Proteus Effect: Self transformations in Virtual Reality." *Human Communication Research*.

while. We are now in a position to ask why it is so common to temper a critique of technological advance with claims of technological value. Why is it that Davie's grandfather in "The Wheel" does not agree with his society that it was wheels that ultimately destroyed their world? The monks of Leibowitz abbey safeguarded knowledge until the world is able to understand it again, but why were they not safeguarding knowledge until people had lost their destructive streak? Riddley turns his back on new technology, and turns towards an older way of living, and in so doing he is acknowledging that the return of technology is not inevitable, but at no point does Riddley actually take a stand against the technology that he helped to develop. While the Eusa story contains a warning against technology, Riddley does not accept this either; he steps entirely out of the game. Why is it that none of these texts acknowledges that scientific development may be something worth controlling?

If one saw scientific development as akin to a force of nature, which cannot be stopped, but only anticipated, then one would not be able to see the option of banning wheels as even feasible. The authors I have talked about in this chapter are all, to some degree or another, uncritically accepting the fiction that Kuhn describes—that the enterprise of science is continuous, progressive, and linear. Even as they critique science by showing us a world without it, and even as they edge towards the claim that science as we know it is not ultimately useful or desirable, they maintain that science is linear and inevitable. Given this, their critique cannot amount to anything meaningful, just as the Bishop of Paris's condemnation of Aquinas could not have been meaningful if Aristotle's medieval transformation had been inevitable. Of course, the Thomistic worldview rolled past the condemnation of 1277 with little resistance, but this does not mean that the change was inevitable—it means that it was a social movement, and social movements do not end by fiat.

"The Wheel," *A Canticle for Leibowitz*, and *Riddley Walker* were all, on one level, cautionary tales about technological warfare. Isaac Asimov, in his introduction to the 1981 collection that includes "The Wheel," claims that such fiction was instrumental in preventing the cold war from escalating into a world war (Asimov 1981, 7). We can see a very similar claim being made in *Canticle* itself. In the third part of the story, as the world lurches towards war, the abbot says this to his monks:

We all know what *could* happen, if there's a war. The genetic festering is still with us from the last time Man tried to eradicate himself. Back then, in the Saint Leibowitz' time, maybe they didn't know what would happen. Or perhaps they did know, but could not quite believe it until they tried it—like a child who knows what a loaded pistol will do, but who never pulled a trigger before. They had not yet seen a billion corpses. They had not seen the still-born, the monstrous, the dehumanized, the blind. They had not yet seen the madness and the murder and the blotting out of reason. (Miller 1961, 277)

By painting a vivid image of a billion corpses, post-apocalypse fiction can help us think about the consequences of pulling the trigger. As warnings about the shortsightedness of nationalistic politics and economic rivalries, such stories are valuable, but because they share uncritical assumptions about the way that science develops, they are incapable of genuinely raising the issue of the value of science as we know it. They are a warning against pulling the trigger, but they are not asking whether we should be holding the gun in the first place.*

R E F E R E N C E S

Aersten, Jan. 1993. "Aquinas's Philosophy in its Historical Setting." In *The Cambridge Companion to Aquinas*, edited by Norman Kretzmann and Elenore Stump, 12–37. Cambridge: Cambridge University Press.
Asimov, Isaac. 1981. Introduction to *After the End*, edited by Isaac Asimov, Martin Greenberg, and Charles G. Waugh, 6–7. Milwaukee: Raintree Publishers.
Card, Orson Scott. 1985. *Ender's Game*. New York: T. Doherty Associates.
Copleston, Frederick. 1972. *A History of Medieval Philosophy*. Notre Dame: University of Notre Dame Press.
Crichton, Michael. 1991. *Jurassic Park*. New York: Knopf.
Hoban, Russell. 1998. *Riddley Walker*. Bloomington: Indiana University Press.
Kuhn, Thomas. 1962. *The Structure of Scientific Revolutions*. Chicago: University of Chicago Press.
Le Guin, Ursula K. 1969. *The Left Hand of Darkness*. New York, Walker.
Miller, Walter M., Jr. 1961. *A Canticle for Leibowitz*. Philadelphia: Lippincott.
Wyndham, John. 1952. "The Wheel." Reprinted in *After the End*, edited by Isaac Asimov, Martin Greenberg, and Charles G. Waugh. Milwaukee: Raintree Publishers.

---

* I would like to thank Alison Sainsbury for introducing me to *Riddley Walker*, "The Wheel," and many other examples of post-apocalypse literature that did not make it into this study.

Intervention 3

Ethics, Science, and Science Fiction

NANCY KRESS

Science fiction is a very wide umbrella, spreading its circumference over many different kinds of stories: space adventure, scientific puzzle stories, engineering speculation, sociological extrapolation, media tie-ins for such films as *Star Wars* and *Star Trek*. We include even people who had no idea they've been included, magic realists like Borges and Garcia Marquez, plus temporary visitors like Margaret Atwood with *The Handmaid's Tale*. SF is a very big galaxy indeed.

The quality of this terrain varies as much as its content. I want to focus on one specific kind of SF: the near-future story or novel that seriously looks at what can be done if our current physics or biology or chemistry proceeds, a little way or a long way, on the current trajectories.

To consider this kind of science fiction is to almost guarantee considering ethical issues. By the various ways they present their fictional worlds, such stories raise and provisionally answer a host of ethical questions: What technology will result from this science? How will it be used? What applications will be allowed, encouraged, prohibited, or exploited? With what results for society?

Science fiction specializes in these types of ethical dilemmas posed by science. It always has, from Mary Shelley and H. G. Wells on. Of course, we SF writers share this area of concern with ethicists, theologians, and scientists themselves. And yet there are some significant differences in the way an SF writer approaches an ethical dilemma from the way the other three groups do. These differences have implications for both writers and readers in at least four important ways: personalization, negativity, timing, and distortion.

First, SF writers do not present ethical dilemmas raised by science and/or technology by the same method as do ethicists, theologians, or scientists. These groups tend to frame their arguments logically and somewhat abstractly. If A is permitted, then we might well have to deal with B or C or both. If A leads to B, the consequences might be C, D, and E. This is true whether the particular debater sees those consequences as good or bad.

Science fiction writers take a different tack. We present our ideas about consequences and moral implications by embedding them in a *story*. This means that the implications of the science or technology are shown affecting a person or small group of people in personal and emotional terms. The appeal, usually, is not to the readers' ability to reason, but directly to the readers' emotions. The events of the story, caused by science, are affecting people whom readers come to care about. True, those people are fictional, but for many—perhaps even most—that makes little difference (a point Woody Allen made brilliantly in his film *The Purple Rose of Cairo*, in which a woman falls in love with a movie character. "He's fictional," she says, "but you can't have everything"). The result is that an ethical dilemma becomes very personal. Instead of abstractions, the choices involved are presented in terms of real human suffering or triumph.

This is, of course, what gives any fiction its tremendous power. Neville Shute's *On The Beach* showed readers—no, more: made readers *feel*—what the results of a nuclear war might be. In a later generation, Michael Crichton's *Jurassic Park* illustrated some implications of cloning far more graphically than could any abstract debate on the subject. The implication here is that the millions of people in the reading public, and the many more millions who go to the movies, receive a very one-sided presentation of any ethical question raised by new scientific advances. They experience the attitude toward a problem that the author wishes them to experience. Many form their opinions accordingly, not because they are mindless sheep but because well-written fiction can have enormous emotional impact.

And very often our hearts lead our minds. I daresay that if a poll were taken before and after the release of *Jurassic Park* about whether scientists should attempt to clone extinct species, the two sets of numbers would have been very different.

My second point about SF and ethical dilemmas relates directly to this first concern. It, too, lies in the nature of fiction. As I tell my writing students often, fiction is about things that get screwed up. Nobody wants to read a story in which a group of people make a scientific discovery or technological breakthrough, implement it without opposition, and reap only positive results. We might wish our actual lives to go like that, but we don't want to read about it in fiction. In fiction we want drama, conflict, problems, unforeseen complications, and, all too often, disaster. The result is that much SF about scientific dilemmas is negative. In fact, one of the classic questions for a writer to ask herself when planning a story is, "Who will this hurt?" That's the person you write about. It makes a better story.

This has been true since SF's beginnings. Mary Shelley's scientist Dr. Frankenstein ran into all sorts of difficulties getting his scientific creation up and running, including public opposition. H. G. Wells's fictional genetic experiments that produced the Eloi and the Morlocks did not end in a happily harmonious and equitable society. And, more recently, William Gibson's adventurers in cyberspace, and my own adventurers in genetic engineering, do not always do the right thing. They don't always know what the right thing is, or care. Mistakes are made. Situations are exploited by the unscrupulous. People are harmed. Again, it makes a better story.

It may not, however, make for the best forum to present ethical issues, a point I want to return to later.

This built-in negative bias in SF is fed by a third difference between fictional ethical discussion and real-world ethical discussion. The point is this: very often SF writers get there first.

I don't want to unfairly exaggerate this idea. Certainly some of our very best writers have missed some of science's most influential results. Arthur C. Clarke's classic *Childhood's End* gives us a future with no significant computer presence. So does Alfred Bester's *The Stars My Destination* and a host of other seminal works. The business of science fiction is not to visualize the future, but to visualize *a* future, one of many possible paths that science and technology might lead us to.

On the other hand, SF has often served as a sort of ethical DEW line, an early warning system of temporally incoming dilemmas. One example: fifty years ago Larry Niven was writing stories which warned, "There is an organ bank in your future. Organs, including hearts, will be able to be transplanted. And you will have to make decisions on who gets what, as well as control of the black market this will inevitably create." Very few people, except SF readers, were really listening. But now we have situations such as a wealthy father going on TV to plead for a liver donation for his dying toddler daughter—and getting a volunteer, while other less-well connected children die. We allegedly have whole-sale abuses of organ harvesting in places like China. Niven was not, given the license for literary embellishment, that far off the mark.

More recently, genetic modification of crops has a controversial area of bioscience, especially in Europe, where such crops are referred to as "Frankenfoods." The areas of concern are two: Are such foods safe for humans, and what might happen if some created crop, such as a plant super-resistant to both natural and human-created killers, were to escape and cross breed with an already exceptionally hardy weed?

We know that this can happen. About 70 percent of Canada's canola crop has been fitted with a transgene resistant to a popular pesticide. Scientists at Agriculture Canada in Ottawa have tracked and docu-mented the first crop/wild hybrid of commercial canola and one of its weedy parents (*Brassica rapa*). Genes, like water and money, flow.

SF has exploited that fact for years. John Christopher's 1957 novel *No Blade of Grass*, which was made into a very grim movie directed by Cornel Wilde, concerns a virus that kills members of the grass family—including key crops like rice and wheat. In just a year, the virus spreads from Asia to Europe and Africa, causing every country it invades to col-lapse from starvation and anarchy. A negative take on crop mutation, to say the least—and SF was there decades before journals like *Theoretical and Applied Genetics*, before the AAAS, and before bioethics depart-ments, commissions, and advisory panels.

What is the implication of SF writers' getting to such questions first? It means that some of the public, a growing segment as SF informs more and more movies, gets its introduction to such ethical questions not through reasoned debate but through the emotional, personal, often neg-atively biased medium of science fiction. This is especially true of chil-dren and young adults, who are much more likely to learn about cloning from comic books or SF novels than from the op-ed page of the *New York Times*.

Kurt Vonnegut, who stoutly maintains in the face of all literary evi-dence that he is not actually an SF writer, made this point forcefully in his 1965 novel *God Bless You, Mr. Rosewater*, in which the protagonist says to a group of science fiction writers:

> I love you sons of bitches. You're all I read anymore. You're the only ones who'll talk about the really terrific changes going on, the only ones crazy enough to know that life is a space voyage, and not a short one, either, but one that'll last for billions of years. . . . You're the only ones zany enough to agonize over time and distances without limit, over mysteries that will never

die, over the fact that we are right now determining whether the space voyage for the next billion years or so is going to be Heaven or Hell.

Clearly this is way overstated, since it leaves out all those others—from environmentalists to Mars enthusiasts—who are also "zany" enough to care about our space voyage. But it also makes a valid point, which is that SF writers consider these issues to be so real that they create entire societies, entire planets, entire star systems, devoted to them. Then they believe in these creations with enough intensity to infuse their dilemmas with living breath for not only themselves, but for readers as well.

SF has yet a fourth aspect related to ethics: distortion. An SF story's presentation of a situation can be far more intense than can an abstract article because fiction can adjust facts to spotlight any one concern, sometimes at the expense of other competing and equally valid viewpoints. Ursula Le Guin pointed this out in a discussion of her classic and wonderful novel *The Left Hand of Darkness*. In order to highlight issues of gender, including which gender-specific behavior might be innate and which might be learned, she created a race of humans who are hermaphroditic. Each individual has two sets of genitals. Anyone can father a child, anyone can become pregnant. Her reason, she said, was to subtract gender completely, thus throwing it into high relief by its absence.

SF often intensifies its political and/or ethical positions through such distortions. A science-fiction novel can speed up evolution, slow down time, create a society of all women or all clones or all genetically engineered babies. It can thus present a far denser, richer, spicier version of an ethical dilemma than can more reality-based debates. SF can put a scientific question at center stage, making the question a matter of immediate life and death, rather than only one among a host of issues competing for our attention. It can, and it does.

Nowhere is this more evident than in SF about that already explosive subject, human-reproductive technology. One of the basic problems with any technology, of course, is that it tends to outrun the laws that are supposed to be applicable to it. That happened in the computer industry, where no one was sure how to treat the first hacker break-ins to corporate computers. Was it theft, even though nothing had been "stolen" in the sense that any copied files still remained? Was it trespassing, even though no one had physically set foot on the premises? Was it industrial espionage, even though what might have been copied was not always industrial secrets? It took time to work all this out, which is why you had some of those early hackers prosecuted for felonies, and some hired as security experts by the same corporations they'd broken into.

The same thing is true today in the biosciences. Technology outstrips law, which then tries desperately to catch up. Thus, we have a crazy quilt of contradictory state laws concerning, for instance, gestational surrogate motherhood, in which a woman contracts to carry to term an embryo created from another woman's egg through in vitro fertilization. In some states, such as Florida, such contracts are officially legal; in others they are tolerated; in still others they are criminal. Nor can Congress pull itself together to pass any coherent legislation on human cloning.

Cloning human beings is, to many people, an unthinkable phenomenon. But not to SF writers. Cloning, genetic engineering of human embryos, children created from the DNA of more than two parents—all are staples of SF, and frequently the stories and novels have distorted the results beyond any relationship to reality. Cloning has seldom been written about as merely the creation of a new organism with identical DNA to the older original, as a sort of "delayed twinning." Instead, SF has given multiple distortions of the process: cloning as telepathy (Kate Wilhelm's *Where Late the Sweet Birds Sang*), cloning as the recreation of historical villains (Ira Levin's *The Boys from Brazil*), cloning as the eradication of personal responsibility (Aldous Huxley's *Brave New World*). Whatever your personal views on therapeutic or gestational cloning, I think you must agree that these are distortions indeed.

So what can be concluded from these four ideas about how SF handles ethical dilemmas arising from science and technology? It might be concluded that science fiction is doing more harm than good in its presentations, given their reliance on emotion, negative bias, first arrival at issues, and artificial intensity. This, you'll remember, was the conclusion that Plato came to about poets, which is why he banned them from his ideal society.

There are, however, counterarguments to be made in favor of SF. The first is "familiarization." This argues that SF helps promote acceptance of changes due to science and technology by familiarizing the public with them long before the public must face the actuality.

There is, in my opinion, a problem with the "familiarization" argument. First, as we've seen, SF is likely to familiarize the public with biased, overly dramatic, even distorted versions of new technology. Yes, there are many people working for NASA who say they first got interested in space as a career through SF, and I certainly don't want to minimize their personal stories. But in many cases, it's not science fiction but the actual thing itself that is likely to promote acceptance. The same year in which the movie version of *The Boys from Brazil* appeared, 1978, also saw the birth of the first "test-tube baby," Louise Brown. Hysterical op-ed pieces and media debate ensued, declaring that man was usurping the role of nature, was creating monsters, and so forth. Today, in vitro fertilization is quietly accepted, and no one can tell a person conceived in a Petri dish from anyone else. Familiarity bred—if not "content"—then at least acceptance.

However, despite all this naysaying about the effects of science fiction—and most of this essay has been naysaying—I'm going to have audacity to disagree with Plato. I think that, despite all of the points I've made so far, SF has a valuable contribution to make to ethical debate. That contribution lies, in fact, in the very traits of the genre I've just been decrying: bias, emotion, negativity, intensity.

Abstract debate about an issue is just that: abstract. Sometimes statistical. Sometimes balanced, sometimes not. But still abstract. Whereas SF shows how science and technology affect people. It may show these effects at extremes, yes, and negatively. But this aspect of the future does need to be considered in any comprehensive argument. Our scientific and technological breakthroughs will affect *people*. Any attempt to portray that truth adds an element to ethical debate that may otherwise be missing.

In the world's laboratories, science rehearses advances in theory and application. In fiction, SF writers rehearse the human implications of those advances. It does this by centering its ethical debate not on the statistics and probabilities that rightly belong to scientific theory, but on individual people. Individuals who feel and get hurt and react extremely and intensely and who must be considered in any decisions we make about the powerful tools that biology, chemistry, and physics give us. True, these people are fictional, but you can't have everything. What you can have is a thought experiment which, in the hands of a sufficiently skilled writer, will be vivid and solid and *real* enough to serve as a credible stand-in for the experiments we cannot do on flesh-and-blood people. Science fiction is the dress rehearsal for directing social change.

Since I believe that individual portrayals of people are one thing that SF can contribute to ethical questions, let me illustrate with a personal story just how complex that statement is. A few years ago I sat on a panel discussing genetic engineering in SF. I commented on my story "Mountain to Mohammed," which concerns the insurance questions surrounding gene scans. In my future society, many people were simply deemed uninsurable because of diseases they might develop, but did not have now. This division into insurables and not-insurables caused considerable pain for my characters.

Our real-life courts are, of course, already struggling with the legal aspects of genetic screenings. We can't yet easily screen an entire individual genome for all possible disorders, but we're quickly getting closer. In 2004, two researchers, one at Harvard and one at Penn State, reported a new way to detect the gene for cystic fibrosis, a faster and easier method by far than any we have now. Their method could eventually be adapted to screen quickly for a wide variety of genetic disorders. The future I created may, in fact, be coming soon.

The example I used to explain these concepts to the audience was Huntington's chorea, a horrific genetic disease resulting from a mutation on chromosome 4 which inexorably leads to madness and death. A woman in the audience became quite upset, and then nearly hysterical. She said Huntington's chorea was endemic in her family, that the suicide rate for young people with this fate in their genes was very high, and that if I were writing about any sort of gene scans I had a moral obligation to, as she put it, "show good outcomes." Otherwise, I was contributing to possible suicides among people with gene-predicted diseases for which there is currently no cure.

I tried gently to explain that art is not designed to show the world we wish we had, but the one we do have, or might have. She got more and more upset at this, until she started to advance on the panelists, and Security escorted her out. But her question, despite its hysterical phrasing, is a good one. What are the obligations of SF in presenting the future and its ethical choices? I would maintain, unlike both that beleaguered woman and Plato, that SF has a useful role to play. But it is not necessarily to be inspiring, not necessarily to be objective, not necessarily to frame ethical debate in a balanced way.

SF's role is to show, as intensely as possible, the entire *range* of personal and emotional outcomes of the various choices to which our accelerating science is leading us. This includes the most extreme choices.

My 2003 novel *Nothing Human*, for example, revolves around the ultimate ethical choice: On an Earth that has, for complex reasons, become unlivable for humans, we choose to genetically engineer our nonhuman replacement species. Not without opposition, we use our own science to take over a role that in the past has belonged only to evolution, or to God.

Does such an extreme perspective add anything to the debate on genetic engineering, or, in other stories and novels, to the myriad other ethical debates we face at the start of this century? I think it does. It adds a wide spectrum of future scenarios, all presented from the perspectives of striving, suffering, triumphing, yearning individuals, which can then be added to more abstract and reasoned discussions. SF writers may thus often end up the Cassandras of moral issues, or at least the confusing Sibyls. That's all right. It's an important role, and it's enough.

SF AS STS

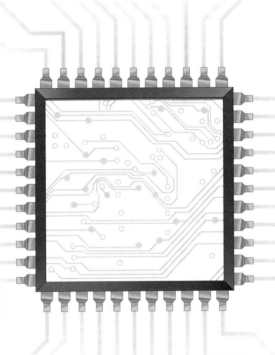

Modest Witnesses? Feminist Stories of Science in Fiction and Theory

HELEN MERRICK

*D*espite the groundbreaking and innovative work of feminist science scholars, the "two culture" divide between the sciences and arts remains pronounced in feminist scholarship, with studies of the sciences and scientific discourse proceeding largely in isolation from humanities-based feminist philosophy and theory. As one of the foremost feminist science scholars, Donna Haraway, has long argued, science fiction is uniquely positioned to do "cross-cultural" translation work that might begin to undermine this division. Haraway suggests that utilizing the productive possibilities of the marker "SF" might help "remap the borderlands between nature and culture" and encourage mutually engaged, critical dialogue across this border (Haraway 1986, 15).

The potential for SF to bridge the divide between the two cultures signaled in its compound title is not, however, reflected in current feminist SF scholarship, which primarily takes the form of literary criticism. As Hilary Rose has observed, SF studies has "underplayed the close relationship between science criticism and SF, not least within feminism," in the process allowing the cultural divide between the arts and sciences "to reproduce itself uncriticized" (Rose 1994, 209). This critical neglect of the relation between science and feminist SF is problematic, not least because it sustains the stereotype that female or feminist writers are not overly concerned with the masculinist field of science—or science fiction. Feminist science studies provides an important framework for reading the development of feminist SF over the last four decades, which has taken place not just in the context of feminist literature, but also in relation to discursive struggles over the meaning of "nature," gender, and race in the sciences.

This chapter explores how feminist science studies might inform and interact with feminist SF (and vice versa). While I assume that feminist science theory provides an obvious theoretical context in which to "read" feminist SF, it is, I believe, important to recognize the potential for a more interactive relation between fictional and theoretical writings on science—especially in a field that opposes the authority of the natural sciences as "crafts for distinguishing between fact and fiction" (Haraway 1989, 3–4). Indeed, a number of feminist science theorists have found feminist SF texts useful in thinking through various theses, as a sort of "testing ground" for feminist theories, critiques, and praxis. In order to suggest some of the ways in which feminist fictions and critiques of science might inform each other, I first review the rare analyses of science found in the work of feminist SF critics such as Jane Donawerth. The second section of the chapter examines work by feminist science scholars such as Donna Haraway and Hilary Rose, who have directly utilized or employed feminist SF in their theorizing. With this necessarily brief overview, I hope to suggest both the need for further contemporary work connecting feminist SF and science theories, and the potential for critical synergies evoked by situating feminist SF as a creative form of science studies.

More Than Just a Metaphor: The Science of Feminist SF

It is generally recognized that SF has long drawn on—and transformed—the tropes and epistemologies of technoscience. However, despite the growing body of work that has followed Haraway in employing feminist SF as preeminent cultural texts for examining cyberfeminism, cyberculture, and cyborg relations (Balsamo 1993; Hayles 1999), only a few feminist critics have examined the function of "science" in feminist SF. The bulk of feminist SF criticism has focused more on the symbolic rewritings of sex, gender, and sexuality and the possibilities for sociocultural change these texts offer. Many literary analyses of feminist SF imply that the genre is merely a convenient vehicle for certain devices and locales (aliens, alternate worlds or futures) that better enable an examination of gender from an estranged perspective. For some texts this is indeed the case, but for many others a feminist revisioning or critique of scientific discourses and cultures is an integral function of the text.

In this context, it is worth pointing out that a number of feminist SF authors have scientific training and bring this to bear on their work, including authors such as Joan Slonczewski (biology), Catherine Asaro (physics), and Vonda McIntyre (genetics), while Liz Williams has a doctorate in the philosophy of science. Many others, such as Nancy Kress and Gwyneth Jones, conduct extensive research into current scientific developments from a "lay perspective." For example Jones's most recent novel *Life* cites Short and Balaban's *Differences Between the Sexes* and Fox Keller's *A Feeling for the Organism* as its prime influences (Jones 1999 and 2004). Further, as Hilary Rose has pointed out, "'lay' people (and outside our narrow expertises we are all lay people) pick up particular areas of science, typically those which are important or have some special interest for them" (Rose 1996, 96). Thus Nicola Griffith, for example, talks of how her novel *Ammonite* resulted directly from research she carried out in order to find out more about her health problems (finally diagnosed as multiple sclerosis) (Griffith 1999).

Yet, as Jane Donawerth noted in 1997, "no one has yet attempted to describe the paradigm of science in women's science fiction": an observation that still holds (Donawerth 1997, 36n1).[1] While there have been isolated examples of critical attention to science in feminist SF, Donawerth remains one of the few critics who explore such concerns at length, and to discuss women's and feminist SF in the context in feminist science theorists.[2] Even in those articles that do not explicitly reference or engage science studies, however, the approach taken and subjects identified reflect developments in feminist science studies over the last three decades. In general, these critical approaches take either an "empiricist" or a feminist standpoint approach. As with feminist SF, there is evident a roughly chronological development: beginning with critiques of the masculinist bias of science, then an impulse to "improve" science by "adding" women, a focus on what different characteristics being women scientist might entail, followed by various

---

[1] The exceptions listed by Donawerth are Patrocinio Schweickart, Donna Haraway, Robin Roberts, and Hilary Rose, see discussion below. See also her "Utopian Science" (Donawerth 1990); there is also some discussion of science in her article "Science Fiction by Women in the Early Pulps, 1926–1930" (Donawerth 1994).

[2] There does, however, appear to be growing interest in this area: the 4th European Biannual Conference of the Society for Science, Literature, and the Arts had a stream on feminism, science, and SF in 2006, with papers such as Joan Haran's on Feminist SF (Haran 2006). Other recent publications of interest include Williams 2006 and Newell 2004.

expressions of the desirability of a significantly altered—even feminist—science.

One of the first articles in SF scholarship to focus on science in
women's SF was Virginia Allen and Terri Paul's "Science and Fiction:
Ways of Theorizing about Women." Allen and Paul approach women's
SF as an example of scientific pedagogy, employing observation,
hypothesis, and speculation. Their reading of Tiptree's "The Women
Men Don't See" situates the examination of gender as an example of
"good science" in practice: arguing the empiricist belief that science has
failed to take account of gender only because it has not been practiced
"properly." Paul and Allen extend this belief to SF: "Good science fiction has a mandate to explore ideas with the methodology of science,
particularly ideas that do not fit within the prevailing paradigm" (Allen
and Paul 1986, 170). Allen and Paul conclude that theorizing about gender engages in that essential component of scientific inquiry, speculation, and will, the authors suggest, result in a better science: "It is
difficult if not impossible to carry out scientific research in good faith,
responsibly, when the scientific community has a vested political interest in its interpretation—whether the bias is feminist or misogynist"
(Allen and Paul 1986, 174). A key element in empiricist critiques is the
view that both scientific cultures and practices can be "improved"
through a better representation of women in the sciences. While standpoint epistemology is her predominant approach, Donawerth's framing
discussion of "women's participation in science" indicates the historical
importance of such positions. The longstanding struggles to improve
women's entry into scientific professions is, Donawerth notes, reflected
in women's SF not only from the 1960s and '70s, but in a number of
texts from the 1920s and '30s. Stories such as Clare Winger Harris's
"The Menace of Mars" (1928) and Louise Rice and Tonjoroff-Roberts's
"The Astounding Enemy" (1930) feature women scientists, reflecting,
according to Donawerth, the late nineteenth-century campaigns to gain
science education for women (earlier expressed in utopias such as Mary
Bradley Lane's *Mizora* and Charlotte Perkin Gilman's *Herland*)
(Donawerth 1997, 4–5).

The issue of more equal representation in the sciences was an important first step in feminist critiques and, as Donawerth argues, necessary
in "imagining women as subjects of science, not as its objects"
(Donawerth 1997, 5). However, Donawerth's claim that in "putting
women as subject at the center of science, these women writers change
its nature" is problematic. For, as Harding and many later constructivist
critics point out, the empiricist arguments for women's inclusion emerges

not from a desire to change the nature of science but a belief that a "true" adherence to scientific methods and objectivity necessitates eliminating its androcentric bias.[3]

Most other examples however, approach the issue of science in women's SF from some form of "feminist standpoint" position (for example, Bartter 1992/1993; Stocker 1989).[4] In a 1983 article that in many ways presages Harding's later refinements on standpoint epistemology, Patrocinio Schweickart questions the "othering" of women and nature seemingly inherent in the traditional model of the scientific method. Schweickart's examination of "Science and Technology in Feminist Utopias" was based on readings of texts such as Dorothy Bryant's *The Kin of Ata are Waiting for You*, Gearhart's *The Wanderground* and Le Guin's *The Dispossessed* (1983). Rather than the usual emphasis on the *rejection* of science and technology in feminist utopias, Schweickart figures this turn as a "radical critique of the masculinist logic of science and technology" and not simply an essentialist privileging of a feminine "nature" (Schweickart 1983, 204). This approach produces a different reading of Le Guin's novel than many other feminist analyses, which have criticized the focus on a male scientist and retention of a male perspective. Instead, Schweickart identifies the utopian nature of the methodology and application of science in *The Dispossessed*, which, Schweickart argues, does not employ a "logic of domination," nor is it "separated from moral and ethical concerns" (1983, 208–9).

"Women's Science"

Introducing traditionally "female" concerns such as empathy and emotion into the sciences is a hallmark of feminist standpoint approaches that posit a need for a "successor science" that acknowledges "women's issues." Donawerth cites a number of examples that incorporate issues,

---

[3] Indeed, many women within the sciences still reject what they see as an attack on the very basis of scientific knowledge and remain committed to the "practical," liberal project to encourage the increased participation of women in science. Wendy Faulkner, among others, has noted the difficulty of combining increased representation with a more radical project to transform the sciences (1995, 343). More recently, Margret Grebowicz points out that even contemporary feminist analyses influenced by postmodern critiques leave certain tenets of scientific epistemology in place (2005). See also Harding 1996.

[4] Indeed, Maciunas argues that Piercy's novels reflects all three epistemological stances described by Harding (Maciunas 1992).

work, and even spaces traditionally considered "women's realm" into their future sciences. For example, in the Sharer society of Joan Slonczewski's *A Door into Ocean*, day-to-day living, childcare, and science are all part of a communal social space, and, in Donawerth's words, "laboratories look just like homes." "In this society, the person who cleans the labs is very likely the same person who does the science" (Donawerth 1997, 10). Another example cited by Donawerth as evidence for a "redefinition" of science to incorporate "women's values" is Naomi Mitchison's *Memoirs of a Spacewoman*. The spacewoman Mary gives us a glimpse of her (future) history:

> I may be out of date, but I always feel that biology and, of course, communication are essentially women's work, and glory. Yes, I know there have been physicists like Yin Ih and molecular astronomers—I remember old Jane Rakadsalis myself, her wonderful black, ageless face opening into a great smile! But somehow the disciplines of life seem more congenial to most of us women. (Mitchison 1985, 18)

In this "history of science full of women," however, Mitchison goes beyond a simple role reversal privileging "women's work." In Mary's future, Mitchison takes for granted that there *will* be women—including women of color—participating in all sciences, including "hard" sciences such as physics.

Within SF, areas and subjects considered more appropriate to women have historically been marked along a hard/soft divide—that is, as a binary with the "softer" social sciences (but also, interestingly, biology) on one side, and the "hard" sciences such as physics on the other. In *A New Species: Gender and Science in Science Fiction*, Robin Roberts reaffirms the notion that men write hard SF and women write soft SF, thus leaving this gendered binarism intact (Roberts 1993, 5). However, she reverses the traditional hierarchy to privilege the social sciences, imaginary sciences such as telekinesis and telepathy, and magic, arguing that writers who "depict magic as valorising for women and as a legitimate science" may "overcome the dichotomy between valid hard science and invalid soft science" (Roberts 1993, 8).

In a discussion of Marge Piercy's *Woman on the Edge of Time*, Roberts argues that in Mattepoisett, "soft science is explicitly contrasted to the negative hard science" of the contemporary Western world (Roberts 1993, 85). Piercy is not merely championing a feminine soft science over a masculinist "hard," however. What really differentiates the forms of science characteristic of contemporary society from

Mattepoisett are the social and cultural contexts that inform the organization and implementation of this "utopian science." In contrast to the twentieth-century U.S., Piercy constructs a society and science in partnership, a relation of equilibrium, rather than one of exploitation and domination. In characterizing this relation as typical of a "soft," "feminine" science, Roberts's analysis omits the notion of a different way of constructing science and its subject(s) within the "social" field, leaving unquestioned the inevitability of the "mastery" rhetoric of the "hard" sciences. In this taxonomy, male/female and hard/soft are not revealed as social constructions, but referred to as self-evident and fixed entities, where, for example, it is assumed that magic is a "female" and computers are a "male" paradigm of science (Roberts 1993, 98).

In contrast to Roberts's emphasis on validation of a "feminine" paradigm, Donawerth is concerned with the possible transformations brought about by repositioning science. Like Roberts, Donawerth identifies a central problem for feminist science theorists and SF authors: the fact that the contemporary model of science constructs women as the objects, not the subjects, of science. Both look for examples of SF which fulfill the empirical goal of situating women as scientists, and those that broaden the definition of science to include areas that more easily situate women as "subject." Donawerth, however, focuses more on the kinds of re-visioning and reconstruction of science that occur in both feminist science theory and feminist SF.

"Utopian Science"

Donawerth's central claim is that both feminist SF and feminist science theories have a shared goal—to create a "utopian paradigm" of feminist science: "Because almost no feminist science exists, many women science fiction writers and feminist science theorists have imagined an idealized system of science, creating it as a dialogue with and critique of contemporary scientific ideologies and practices."[5] Assembling the range of feminist science theory under the rubric of "utopian science," however, may devalue the production of feminist critiques of science that are themselves an intervention in the practices of science as usual.

---

[5] Her outline of this paradigm runs as follows: "Women's participation in science as subjects not objects, revised definitions and discourses of science, inclusion in science of women's issues, treatment of science as a origin story that has been feminized, a conception of human's relation to nature as partnership not domination, and an ideal of science as subjective, relational, holistic and complex" (Donawerth 1997, 2).

While Donawerth is unusual in bringing together readings of feminist SF with feminist science theorists, her focus on the utopian goal of constructing a feminist science tends to homogenize the various and often competing trends in feminist science theory. This is partly due to the time of writing, with her analysis drawing mostly on examples from the 1980s (e.g., Keller 1985; Merchant 1980; Rose 1986) and therefore not reflecting the considerable theoretical developments in the field from the mid-1990s onwards.

One of the texts Donawerth calls on to illustrate her utopian paradigm of a revised, feminist science is Judith Moffett's *The Ragged World*. This is an interesting case study for differences in critical approaches. Perhaps not immediately obvious as a feminist novel, its feminism lies in the construction of an alternative practice of science, "its careful revision of the definition and discourse of science": "Rather than presenting an abstract discourse about science, Moffett, through her biologist, stresses embodiment and connection to life: when the biologist finally does an experiment, she does so with melons and squash in her own backyard, not in her college laboratory" (Donawerth 1997, 8). Donawerth sees Moffett's biologist as pursuing a science expressed through what Hilary Rose calls the "language of love" that "current science lacks and a utopian science would discover": "Moffett thus presents us with a utopian science that revises the definition of our science and offers a different vision, of science as full of choice (and accident), practiced by loving caretakers who speak a language that includes connections to external environment as well as internal genetic mechanics" (Donawerth 1997, 9–10).[6] But to render the science carried out by Moffett's biologist as a "utopian" vision detracts from the very pragmatic (and indeed achievable) construction of science she engages in. A "feminist science" may well necessarily be utopian, but an essential part of feminist projects to change the sciences is the process of intervening in and revealing the narratives, myths, and truth claims of science. As Haraway has argued, "feminist science is about changing possibilities," and feminist interventions to date have already begun to alter the possibility of what can and cannot be claimed in the name of "science" (Haraway 1986, 81).

In arguing for the importance of feminist SF in the context of feminist science theories, both Donawerth and Roberts claim that only in

---

[6] Moffett's stance is reflected in work by feminist critics such as Nelly Oudshoorn, who calls for a challenge to "the myth of scientific heroes discovering the secrets of nature" (Oudshoorn 1996, 122–23).

feminist SF can women control the narratives of science. Yet feminist science theorists also write "narratives about science" that try to "counteract the misogynistic stories of our culture" and focus on "the gendered categories and myths that shape the world of science" (Roberts 1993, 6). It is the potential function of feminist SF as a "thought laboratory," not just for the construction of a utopian ideal of future science, but as medium for experimenting with "noninnocent" knowledges and positionings such as "strong objectivity" and the "modest witness," that situates feminist SF as an important resource for feminist science theorists. Indeed, those science theorists who themselves discuss feminist SF employ the fictional texts as participants in the evolving dialogue between different groups over the meaning of "the science question in feminism."[7]

"Dream Laboratories": Feminist SF and Science Studies

Critics such as Rose and Haraway call upon feminist SF as cultural "texts" which comment upon, interact with, and critique scientific knowledge, methods, and cultures. For Rose, feminist SF functions as "a sort of dream laboratory—where feminisms may try out wonderful and/or terrifying social projects" (1994, 228). As Rose suggests, feminist SF not only reflects contemporary feminist concerns, but is also a site for the development and configuration of feminist debates (1994, 209). Thus, Nina Lykke's account of the development of feminist science and technology studies situates Marge Piercy's *Woman on the Edge of Time* and Sally Miller Gearhart's *The Wanderground* alongside Shulamith Firestone's *The Dialectic of Sex* and the Boston Women's *Our Bodies, Ourselves* as equally significant texts in early feminist debate on the subject. (1996, 1–3) Similarly, in *The Science Question in Feminism*, Harding observes that feminists involved in critiquing the "sins" of contemporary science had "not yet given adequate attention to envisioning truly emancipatory knowledge-seeking" (Harding 1986, 19). Harding wonders how feminist understandings of science would differ if they started not with current categories but with those of the future worlds

---

[7] For example, Maureen McNeil and Sarah Franklin claim that attention to the cultural and textual production of the sciences could involve examining the meaning of science at popular levels by looking at SF, among other "popular" conduits of science (McNeil and Franklin 1991, 138).

such as Piercy's Mattepoisett, and suggests that "we should turn to our
novelists and poets for a better intuitive grasp of the theory we need"
(although she does not follow this course herself) (Harding 1986, 20).
Despite these examples, Haraway and Rose remain unusual for their
willingness to cross and merge the boundaries of science/literature and
fiction/theory.[8]

Indeed, Rose introduces her *Love, Power and Knowledge* with the
observation that "[a] number of friends remain surprised that I here discuss feminist science fiction" (1994, 12). But for Rose feminist SF is
"deeply political writing," whose myth-making has a significant role in
reconstructing technoscience (Rose 1994, 229). In 1986, Rose wrote of
the "empowering visions offered us by feminist SF writing," from
authors such as Russ, Le Guin and Piercy, and commented that "it is not
by chance that feminists writing or talking about science and technology
constantly return . . . to these empowering alternative visions" (74, 59).
Rose views feminist SF as a "privileged space" where feminists can
"play" with possibilities occluded by the dominant culture (1994, 228).
In Rose's analysis, feminist visions of transformations in both "natural"
and "social" worlds are important, signaling a difference from literary
analysis, which centers on changes in the social sphere. Rose links her
analysis of feminist SF directly with feminist critiques of science. She
claims, for example, that Piercy's *Woman on the Edge of Time* anticipated issues raised by feminist critics especially in demonstrating "that
not only is nature modified continuously by culture—and that includes
our own nature—but that our conceptions of what is natural and what is
cultural themselves undergo subtle changes" (Rose 1994, 223).

Another result of Rose's focus is the construction of a different
genealogy than the usual literary history of feminist SF. Rose "respect-
fully" dislodges Mary Shelley as the "foremother of SF," arguing instead
that this place is deserved by the natural scientist and philosopher
Margaret Cavendish (1994, 210). In contrast to the literary arguments
for Cavendish's place in the feminist utopian tradition, Rose foreground's Cavendish's role in the "formation of mechanical philosophy"
in mid-seventeenth-century England, her writing on a number of scientific topics, and the fact that as a women, despite her privileged rank and
status, she was excluded from the Royal Society (209–10). Like other

---

[8] In a note to "Manifesto," Haraway thanks Nancy Hartsock for discussion on feminist theory and feminist science fiction, although I have found no mention of feminist
SF in Hartsock's work (Haraway 1991, 244n1).

feminist SF critics, Rose also argues that SF's low status has made it a relatively accessible genre for women writers, but rather than making a literary comparison, she notes the similarities with women's experiences in the fields of crystallography or biochemistry in the forties (209).

Rose herself identifies a difference in treatments of SF within literary and science criticism. She argues that literary critics have only recently taken SF seriously, while "both scientists and critics of science have long had a close and much less discussed relationship with SF" (the exception being Haraway and Mary Midgley's *Science as Salvation*) (1994, 208, 282n2). As an example, she claims that few critics recognize that the 1930s and '40s were also a golden age for science criticism that "took writing futurist accounts of science . . . as a seriously pleasurable task" (208).[9] In contrast to the literary approach that views feminist SF as "part of a general flowering of women's writing," Rose situates feminist SF as a "vehicle for exploring our pressing anxieties and experiences concerning science and technology" which in the 1970s and '80s has "both been reflective of and constitutive of the feminist critique of science" (209).

Donna Haraway is perhaps the most visible critic to have incorporated feminist SF into her theoretical studies of science, notably in her "A Cyborg Manifesto" and *Primate Visions*. In "Manifesto," Haraway constructs a metaphor of the cyborg as a "myth about identity and boundaries which might inform late twentieth-century political imaginations"—a myth which Haraway claims is indebted to feminist SF writers such as Russ, Tiptree, Samuel Delany, and Octavia Butler. "These are our storytellers exploring what it means to be embodied in hi-tech worlds. They are theorists for cyborgs" (1991, pp. 215–16). Haraway's approach attempts to deconstruct the "master narrative" of science through an emphasis on the "storyladen" character of the life and social sciences: "Scientific practice may be considered a kind of storytelling practice—a rule governed, constrained, historically changing craft of narrating the history of nature" (1986, 4). Thus, she situates science and SF as part of a "narrative field," reading popular and scientific accounts both conjunctively and "out of context," in an effort to undermine the boundaries between fact and fiction, scientific fact and representation, and to foreground the narrativity of scientific discourses. Haraway's

---

[9] Examples include Charlotte and J. B. S. Haldane, who both wrote SF scenarios about genetic engineering. C. Haldane, *Man's World*, J. B. S. Haldane, *Daedalus, or Science and the Future*. Rose also notes that Naomi Mitchison is part of the Haldane family (1994, 283n4).

ongoing project to expose and revise Western narratives of science has often proceeded by recounting alternative stories, from those of feminist primatologists to those of SF writers such as Octavia Butler. Haraway mixes protocols of reading to illuminate the way meaning structures are solidified by the practice of reading scientific discourses as authoritative forms of knowledge about the "real" world. In *Primate Visions*, Haraway reads popular and technical discourses "out of context," deliberately "mixing genres and contexts to play with scientific and popular accounts . . . telling and retelling stories in the attempt to shift the webs of intertextuality and to facilitate . . . new possibilities for the meanings of difference, reproduction and survival" (1989, 377).[10] Haraway refigures the "narrative field" of SF to include "the narratives of speculative fiction and scientific fact" in order to encourage readers to "remap the borderlands between nature and culture" (1986, 15, 81). In many ways, Haraway tries to construct her audience as SF readers. This is a useful approach for feminist analysis, which has too often considered SF only as a literature of popular culture, rather than as an intervention into discourses of science.[11]

   Octavia Butler in particular figures prominently in Haraway's search for noninnocent, "monstrous" origin stories and narratives of nature and science. In "The Biopolitics of Posthuman Bodies," Haraway argues that *Clay's Ark* "reads like" *The Extended Phenotype*—with Butler's invaders "disturbingly like the 'ultimate' unit of selection that haunts the biopolitical imaginations of postmodern evolutionary theorists and economic planners" (Haraway 1991, 226). The parallel drawn by Haraway suggests that because the implicit narratives of science—competition, invasion, colonization—are "writ large" in many SF narratives, their destructive implications may be rendered more obvious. Racist, sexist, and colonizing behaviors are more flagrantly rendered when their setting is virgin planets populated by sentient aliens, than in, for example, scientific "stories" about the operation of cells in the immune system of

---

   [10] In a review of *Primate Visions* for the journal *Science Fiction Studies*, Charles Elkin enthusiastically argues for the importance of Haraway's work for scholars of science, not just for her provocative "blurring" of distinctions such as science/literature and fact/fiction, but because "the narratives of science as *Primate Visions* constructs them can provide a richer more complete understanding" of SF—in this case the work of Octavia Butler (Elkin 1990, 270–72).
   [11] Although feminist fans and writers have been more aware of this possibility, as Pamela Sargent's introduction to the landmark collection *Women of Wonder*, for example, demonstrates (Sargent 1978, 11–12).

an organism. Correspondingly, feminist SF may both highlight the negative consequences of such narratives on all levels—from SF to science, microscopic to macroscopic—and investigate the possibility of different narratives or origin stories.

Developing Cross-Cultural Narratives

What these engagements with feminist SF from both SF scholarship and feminist science studies suggest is that the potential for science fictional texts to contribute to feminist critiques of the sciences remains largely unexplored. Recognizing this potential would also impact feminist SF studies in a number of ways. For example, reading SF texts through the lens of feminist science theory destabilizes certain literary canons, drawing attention to texts and authors that have been previously overlooked. That is, a focus on feminist science studies can provide different criteria for appreciating the "feminist value" of a text, and modify our view of what "counts" as "feminist SF." Such a perspective might alter interpretations of a number of 1980s SF dystopias, for example, if they were judged not solely against the well-known group of 1970s feminist SF utopias, but alongside cotemporaneous feminist challenges to the discourses of sociobiology. As the earlier work surveyed in this chapter suggests, there remains considerable scope for new readings of feminist SF that explicitly engage with contemporary feminist science studies.

The recognition of popular cultural forms like feminist SF as participants in critical conversations around the sciences would also work to emphasize the fact that science itself is a "cultural practice"; a perspective that opens the door for "a motley crew of interlopers to take part in shaping and unshaping what will count as scientific knowledge, for whom, and at what cost" (Haraway 1997, 67). Furthermore, the more accessible nature of creative forms such as fiction widens the field of potential "interlopers"; not an insignificant attribute, given the importance of continuing public debates about our techno-scientific futures, and those "othered" by this culture. Such an intervention is vital in a climate where, as Hilary Rose has observed, there remains considerable apprehension "that a nontechnical expert should have an opinion and start talking as well as listening" (1996, 86).

Rose's observation takes on particular resonance when considering the current "state of play" of two-culture exchanges within feminist scholarship in the sciences and humanities. A number of recent articles from feminist science critics express concerns about the lack of discursive exchange between their field and related feminist theorizing in the humanities. Critics such as Wilson, Kirby, and Barad for example, are concerned that much feminist philosophy fails to acknowledge or engage with scientific understandings of "life" (from organisms, matter, and nature to "bodies") in their accounts of human and gendered subjectivity and embodiment (Barad 2003; Kirby 1999; Wilson 1999). A similar disjuncture between feminist sites of theorizing characterizes debates concerning postmodern and constructivist critiques of standpoint theories, such as the recent exchanges between Harding and others (Harding 2001 and 2004). In this context, there is considerable scope for exploring such "cross-cultural" tensions through the medium of feminist SF, from a framework that acknowledges the complexity and diversity of feminist critiques of science. As a recent survey by Margret Grebowicz suggests, contemporary feminist science studies might best proceed as an "epistemology of dissensus," in light of the difficulty— and questionable political value—of achieving epistemic consensus (Grebowicz 2005). I would like to extend Grebowicz's argument to SF, and see future analyses that situate SF as a "narrative of dissensus" whose very marginalized positioning and trademark "cognitive dissonance" marks it as an exemplary potential participant in a feminist "dissensual critique" of the sciences.

Haraway has argued that feminist contests for scientific meaning do not work by replacing one paradigm with another; for example, "as a form of narrative practice or storytelling, feminist practice in primatology has worked more by altering a 'field' of stories or possible explanatory accounts. . . . Every story in a 'field' alters the status of all the others" (1986, 81). Having intervened in this "narrative field," feminists could take pleasure in experimenting with the different kinds of stories— about science, knowledge, power, and society—that become possible when the old narrative fields of science and enlightenment discourse are disrupted. I argue that we should take seriously the stories about science told in feminist SF texts, which envisage social, cultural, and discursive formations that constitute new narratives of gender, feminism, and the sciences. The increasing attention to the social relations of science and technology, "including crucially the systems of myth and meanings structuring our imaginations," suggests that feminist SF's reworkings of such myths can be seen as central to feminist reconstructions of the sciences (Haraway 1991, 205). I believe that feminist SF could—and should— form a vital link in "cross-cultural," feminist stories and conversations about the cultures and discourses of the sciences, as it helps make visible "the monstrous web of text, myth, politics, and materiality that constitutes the scientific enterprise" (Lykke and Braidotti 1996, 242).

REFERENCES

Allen, Virginia, and Terri Paul. 1986. "Science Fiction: Ways of Theorizing about Women." In *Erotic Universe: Sexuality and Fantastic Literature*, edited by D. Palumbo, 165–83. Westport, CT: Greenwood Press.

Balsamo, Anne. 1993. *Technologies of the Gendered Body: Reading Cyborg Women*. Durham, NC: Duke University Press.

Barad, Karen. 2003. "Posthumanist Performativity: Toward an Understanding of How Matter Comes to Matter." *Signs: Journal of Women in Culture and Society* 28, no. 3:801–31.

Bartter, Martha A. 1992/1993. "Science, Science Fiction, and Women: A Language of (Tacit) Exclusion." *Etc* 49:407–19.

Donawerth, Jane. 1990. "Utopian Science: Contemporary Feminist Science Theory and Science Fiction by Women." *NWSA Journal* 2, no. 4: 535–57.

———. 1994. "Science Fiction by Women in the Early Pulps, 1926–1930." In *Utopian and Science Fiction by Women: Worlds of Difference*, edited by J. Donawerth and C. A. Kolmerton, 137–52. Liverpool: Liverpool University Press.

Haran, Joan. 2006. "Feminist Science Fiction as Ecofeminism as Feminist Science Studies." Presented at Close Encounters: The 4th European Biannual Conference of the Society for Science, Literature, and the Arts, Amsterdam, 13–16 June.

———. 1997. *Frankenstein's Daughters: Women Writing Science Fiction*. New York: Syracuse University Press.

Elkin, Charles. 1990. "The Uses of Science Fiction." *Science Fiction Studies* 17, no. 2:269–72.

Faulkner, Wendy. 1995. "Feminism, Science and Technology: Irreconcilable Streams?" *Journal of Gender Studies* 4, no. 3: 34–47.

Grebowicz, Margret. 2005. "Consensus, Dissensus, and Democracy: What Is at Stake in Feminist Science Studies?" *Philosophy of Science* 72:989–1000.

Griffith, Nicola. 1999. "Writing from the Body." In *Women of Other Worlds: Excursions through Science Fiction and Feminism*, edited by H. Merrick and T. Williams, 247–60. Perth: University of Western Australia Press.

Haraway, Donna. 1986. "Primatology is Politics by Other Means." In *Feminist Approaches to Science*, edited by R. Bleier. New York: Pergamon.

———. 1989. *Primate Visions: Gender, Race and Nature in the World of Modern Science*. New York: Routledge.

———. 1991. *Simians, Cyborgs and Women: The Reinvention of Nature*. New York: Routledge.

———. 1997. "enlightenment@science_wars.com: A Personal Reflection of Love and War." *Social Text* 15, no. 1:123–29.

Harding, Sandra. 1986. *The Science Question in Feminism*. Ithaca, NY: Cornell University Press.

———. 1996. "Rethinking Standpoint Epistemology: What is 'Strong Objectivity'?" In *Feminism and Science*, edited by E. F. Keller and H. E. Longino, 63–79. New York: Oxford University Press.

————. 2001. "Comment on Walby's 'Against Epistemological Chasms: The Science Question in Feminism Revisited': Can Democratic Values and Interests Ever Play a Rationally Justifiable Role in the Evaluation of Scientific Work?" *Signs: Journal of Women in Culture and Society* 26, no. 2: 511–525.

————, ed. 2004. *The Feminist Standpoint Theory Reader: Intellectual and Political Controversies*. New York: Routledge.

Hayles, Katherine N. 1999. *How We Became Posthuman: Virtual Bodies in Cybernetics, Literature, and Informatics*. Chicago: University of Chicago Press.

Jones, Gwyneth. 1999. *Deconstructing the Starships: Science, Fiction, and Reality*. Liverpool: Liverpool University Press.

————. 2004. *Life*. Seattle, WA: Aqueduct Press.

Keller, Evelyn Fox. 1985. *Reflections on Gender and Science*. New Haven, CT: Yale University Press.

Kirby, Vicki. 1999. "Human Nature." *Australian Feminist Studies* 14:19–29.

Lykke, Nina. 1996. "Between Monsters, Goddesses and Cyborgs: Feminist Confrontations with Science." In *Between Monsters, Goddesses and Cyborgs: Feminist Confrontations with Science, Medicine and Cyberspace*, edited by N. Lykke and R. Braidotti, 13–29. London: Zed Books.

Lykke, Nina, and Rosi Braidotti. 1996. "Postface." In *Between Monsters, Goddesses and Cyborgs: Feminist Confrontations with Science, Medicine and Cyberspace*, edited by N. Lykke and R. Braidotti., 242–49. London: Zed Books.

Maciunas, Billie. 1992. "Feminist Epistemology in Piercy's *Woman on the Edge of Time*." *Women's Studies* 20:249–58.

McNeil, Maureen, and Sarah Franklin. 1991. "Science and Technology: Questions for Cultural Studies and Feminism." In *Off-Centre: Feminism and Cultural Studies*, edited by S. Franklin, C. Lury and J. Stacey, 129–46. London: HarperCollins.

Merchant, Carolyn. 1980. *The Death of Nature: Women, Ecology, and the Scientific Revolution*. New York: HarperCollins.

Mitchison, Naomi. 1985. *Memoirs of a Spacewoman*. London: Women's Press. (Orig. pub. 1962.)

Newell, Dianne. 2004. "Judith Merril and Rachel Carson: Reflections on Their 'Potent Fictions' of Science." Special Issue: Women in Science, *Journal of International Women's Studies* 5, no. 4: 31–43.

Oudshoorn, Nelly. 1996. "A Natural Order of Things? Reproductive Sciences and the Politics of 'Othering'." In *FutureNatural: Nature, Science, Culture*, edited by George Robertson et al., 122–32. New York: Routledge.

Roberts, Robin. 1993. *A New Species: Gender and Science in Science Fiction*. Urbana: Illinois University Press.

Rose, Hilary. 1986. "Beyond Masculinist Realities: A Feminist Epistemology for the Sciences." In *Feminist Approaches to Science*, edited by R. Bleier. New York: Pergamon Press.

————. 1994. *Love, Power and Knowledge: Towards a Feminist Transformation of the Sciences*. Cambridge: Polity Press.

————. 1996. "My Enemy's Enemy Is—Only Perhaps—My Friend." In *Science Wars*, edited by A. Ross, 80–101. Durham, NC: Duke University Press.

Sargent, Pamela. 1978. "Introduction: Women in Science Fiction." In *Women of Wonder: Science Fiction Stories by Women about Women*, edited by P. Sargent, 11–51. Harmondsworth: Penguin. (Orig. pub. 1974.)

Schweickart, Patrocinio. 1983. "What If . . . Science and Technology in Feminist Utopias." In *Machina Ex Dea: Feminist Perspectives on Technology*, edited by J. Rothschild, 198–212. New York: Pergamon Press.

Stocker, Laura J. 1989. "Songs of Our Future: Feminist Representations of Technology in Science Fiction." *Media Information Australia* 54:49–52.

Williams, Tess. 2006. "Imagining Alternative Pathways of Biological Change and Co-Existence." *Foundation: The International Review of Science Fiction*, no. 98, 99–115.

Wilson, Elizabeth. 1999. "Introduction: Somatic Compliance—Feminism, Biology and Science." *Australian Feminist Studies* 14, no. 29:7–18.

Cracking the Code: Genomics in Documented Fantasies and Fantastic Documentaries

MARINA LEVINA

Genetics. What can it mean? The ability to perfect the physical and mental characteristics of every unborn child. . . . In the not-too-distant-future our DNA will determine everything about us. A minute drop of blood, saliva, or a single hair determines where you are going to work, whom you should marry, what you are capable of achieving. In a society where success is determined by science, divided by the standards of perfection, one man's only chance is to hide his own identity by borrowing someone else's. But in a place where any cell from any part of your body can be traced, how do you hide when we all shed 500 million cells a day? Welcome to Gattaca.
—The trailer for *Gattaca*

Science fiction has always drawn on the latest in scientific research, and it has found a fruitful partner in genomics. Stories that warn of dangers that come along with "cracking the code of life" have multiplied over the years. From *Gattaca* to the genetically engineered vampires and monsters of *Blade II* and *The Hulk*, these narratives focus on the genetic body as a fragmented and fractured entity classified and predetermined in maps, codes, books, and information programs. And while scientists often protest "inaccuracies" and "oversimplifications" of such stories, I argue that they miss the point. Science itself is in the business of creating often elaborate and always fantastic narratives, and scientists are active participants in these constructions. And, as the media's retelling of these narratives illustrates, the line between the scientific and the popular is blurred at best. After all, some of the best science in the world reads like science fiction.

In this chapter I argue that drawing lines between science and science fiction, specifically in the case of genomics, is a tenuous exercise. As a research field, genetics has yielded numerous scientific and popular narratives that fashioned the strings of the DNA code into an imagination-grabbing story of life itself. Throughout the past decade the seemingly endless possibilities offered by the latest advances in genetic research took hold of cultural and social imagination. Documentaries titled *Cracking the Code of Life* and *How to Build a Human* hint at miracles and potential nightmares of altered bodies. *Time* and *Newsweek* magazines feature cover stories titled "Solving the Mysteries of DNA: How Genetic Science Changed our Lives" and "Cracking the Code: The Historical Feat That Changes Medicine Forever." These stories, albeit scientific in nature, follow the structure of the science fiction narrative and are equipped with the tropes very familiar to any science fiction fan. They offer detailed descriptions of the new scientific technology, fantastic possibilities of the latest scientific breakthroughs, and forewarnings of the potential dangers should this particular science fall into the wrong hands. These narratives of genetic research affect how we see ourselves and others. They shape how diseases are understood and managed, what we perceive to be "normal" or "abnormal," and what it will mean to be human in the postgenomic age. In short, science and science fiction come together to construct cultural texts that represent our anxieties, our dreams, and our hopes for the future.

I will analyze two such texts, first, the scientific documentary *Cracking the Code of Life* released on PBS in April 2001. This documentary, like many others, is framed and informed by scientists to blur the lines between science and science fiction by weaving the strings of DNA into a coherent story about life, body, and the scientific enterprise itself. How does genetics alter the traditional understanding of disease and abnormality? Second, I will look at the science fiction film *Gattaca* released in 1997. As a science fiction narrative, *Gattaca* tells an anxious story of the postgenomic world in which genetically imperfect individuals are reduced to performing menial tasks on the margins of society. *Gattaca* addresses these anxieties by reaffirming the value of a genetically imperfect, but visually "healthy," body by means of juxtaposition with a visually imperfect, or disabled, body. By doing so, it reasserts the traditional narratives of disease and abnormality. I will examine how the film positions the idea of a "human spirit" as a remedy to the uncertainties of the not-so-distant future. Finally, I will argue that the doomsday narratives fall short of understanding the real implications of genetic research.

Cracking the Code: Communicating the Genetic Body

This is the story of one of the greatest scientific adventures ever, and at the heart of it is a small, very powerful molecule: DNA.

—ROBERT KRULWICH (the narrator)

The documentary *Cracking the Code of Life* aired on PBS in April 2001. As such, it had the distinction of being the first documentary airing after the announcement of the human genome sequencing draft completion. The documentary explored the past, present, and future of the project through interviews with the heads of both public and private-run sequencing projects, top scientists in the field, doctors, and patients—all actors in the story of one of the greatest scientific adventures ever. Featuring obligatory origin-Africa-monkey shots to symbolize the past and multiple references to the film *Gattaca* to symbolize the future, the documentary creates a seamless narrative of progress that, while indulging in a few paranoid fantasies, is still in awe of the potential for cracking "the code of life" (as the title so aptly suggests). In the process, life is essentialized, reduced, and reconceptualized as an economy of information or data. For example, in the first minute of the documentary, Francis Collins, the head of the National Human Genome Research Institute, explains, "This is the ultimately imaginable thing that one could do scientifically . . . to go and look at our own instructional book and then try to figure out what it's telling us."

The resulting DNA body is a fractured and fragmented body, a source of information streams and database searches. It is understood as a sum of its parts, not as a whole. Therefore, solving the mysteries of life is often conceived in terms of decoding (Kay 2000). Van Dijck writes,

> Walter Gilbert, one of the co-founders of the Human Genome Project, has proposed the idea that the complete sequenced human genome, inscribed on a compact disk, will contain all our essential information: "One will be able to pull a CD out of one's pocket and say 'Here is a human being, it's me.'" "Me" refers simultaneously to digital units as a representation of the genetic body, an electronic inscription, and an immaterial 'essence'—an identity or a soul. (2000, 68)

Here one can see how scientists participate in the construction of the representations and metaphors of life as strings of information. This trend extends to the documentary as well. For example, Eric Lander, the head of the Whitehead/MIT Center, shows the interviewer, Robert Krulwich, a piece of DNA—a goop hanging off the ends of medical tongs. He explains, "whoever contributed this DNA, you can tell from this whether or not they might be at early risk for Alzheimer's disease, you can tell whether or not they might be at an early risk for breast cancer. And there is [sic] probably about 2000 other things you can tell that we do not know how to tell yet but will be able to tell. . . . But that's DNA for you. That apparently is the secret of life just handing off there on the tube." Eric Lander is a leading performer in what Bruno Latour calls a "theater of proof": a dramatic staging of scientific inscriptions, a display in scientific text, which effectively blocks dissent (Latour 1990). Lander is even dressed for the part: a white lab coat and latex gloves. He embodies the role of The Scientist and at this point offers outsiders the final proof of genomics' validity as a science of life: he asks them simply to believe their own eyes.

The reconceptualization of the body as a source of information creates a new understanding of disease and abnormalities. Rabinow defines the knowledge produced by the new genetics as *biosociality*—"auto-production emerging around the new genetics as a circulation network of identity terms and restriction loci" (1999, 411). Biosociality is symbolized by groups organized around specific genetic mutations; the identities have shifted from defining boundaries outside of one's body to defining boundaries *inside* the body. Rabinow writes, "it is not hard to imagine groups formed around the chromosome 17, locus 16, 256, site 654, 376 allele variant with a guanine substitution. Such groups will have medical specialists, laboratories, narratives, traditions, and a heavy panoply of pastoral keepers to help them experience, share, intervene, and 'understand' their fate . . . and overcome fates through more techno-science" (413). Indeed, the new genomics are altering the demarcations of boundaries between and within the bodies. For example, Martin (1999) argues that in immunology discourse the boundaries within the body are seen as fluid and the boundaries between the body and the external world as rigid and absolute. However, unlike the immunology discourse that maps onto blood and contagious diseases, the representations of the body as a site of invasion and war are clearly not applicable to the scientific and popular references to genetic "mutations" and "mistakes." For example, Dreger (2000) argues that there is a rhetorical distinction between "bad blood" and "bad gene" tropes. A person with "bad blood" is perceived as "bad" or "evil," whereas a person with "bad gene" is seen as unfairly possessed by the "bad gene" and, therefore, as a good person in need of a rescue. The victim of the "bad gene" is constructed apart from evil, at least in the moral sense. Indeed there are differences between narratives associated with blood and those associated with

genes. Blood diseases, such as AIDS, invite metaphors of war and invasion (Sontag 1990). These metaphors symbolize the intertwining of bodies that can only be resolved through direct physical violence. There is
no possibility of separating "bad" blood from the person with whom it
is associated. However, in the case of genetic diseases such separation is
represented as natural. And, if disease is a "mistake," then science can
fix it by acquiring additional information and knowledge about the
body. The documentary illustrates how the diseased body is reinter-
preted through genetic discourse. For example, one of the centerpieces
of the documentary is the human-interest story about an infant who was
diagnosed with the Tay Sachs disease—a rare condition that slows infant
development and often results in an early death. Krulwich narrates:

> Tay Sachs begins at one infinitesimal spot on the DNA ladder, when just
> one letter goes wrong. . . . One defective letter out of three billion, and no
> way to fix it. . . . Tay Sachs is a very rare condition and it usually occurs in
> specific groups, like Ashkenazi Jews. And even then, the baby must inherit
> the bad gene from both parents . . . they [the parents] had no reason to think
> they would be at risk. . . . That was an unbelievably bad roll of the genetic
> dice. What makes this story especially hard to bear is we now know that a
> loss that huge—and it was a catastrophe, by any measure—started with a
> single error, a few atoms across, buried inside a cell.

Much like in *Gattaca*, as we will see later on, the disease is localized and
reduced to a specific gene locale. The parents' identities are not implicated in this connection. Moreover, the disease is represented as an
error, which science could someday fix. Krulwich continues,

> Now geneticists have figured out how to see many of these tiny errors
> before they become catastrophes. . . . That's an extraordinary thing, to spot
> a catastrophe when it is still an insignificant dot in a cell, which is the prom-
> ise of the Human Genome Project. It is, first and foremost, an early warn-
> ing system for a host of diseases which will give . . . an advantage. . . .
> Because when you can see trouble coming way before it starts you have a
> chance to stop it, or treat it. Eventually, you might cure it.

But what does "an early warning system" really mean? What counts as
the potential for a disease or even as a disease itself? The documentary
gives an example of a woman who, after battling breast cancer, learned
through the genetic test that she was at high risk for developing ovarian
cancer. She had her ovaries removed and was worried that her daughter
might have inherited the same genetic predisposition. Krulwich explains

this genetic predisposition as a mutation from "a normal gene." And while this mutation is represented as a letter order mistake in the genetic code, one has to wonder how this discourse about mutations from normal genes affects how the lines between the normal and the pathological are drawn. In other words, which mutations count as monstrous? And, once certain mutations are identified as "abnormal," what is there left to do about it?

These are the questions that inform *Gattaca*. And it is perhaps not surprising that the documentary seriously engages with the possibilities illustrated in *Gattaca*. Krulwich refers to *Gattaca* as "one rather bleak vision of where all this could lead." And Francis Collins notes, "*Gattaca* really raised some interesting points. The technology that's being described there is, in fact, right, in front of us or almost in front of us. That is why the scenario is chilling." In this instance in the documentary, one can observe how scientists blur between science and science fiction and create a seamless narrative that unifies the popular and the scientific spheres. Through such cross-references a specific discourse about bodies, and the role of science in managing these bodies, emerges. In the next section, I will take a closer look at *Gattaca*. I will specifically focus on what counts as monstrosity in the genetic age and how the film manages the anxiety associated with these genetic possibilities.

Gattaca and the Transgressions of the Genetic Body

In a few short years, scientists will have completed the Human Genome Project, the mapping of all the genes that make up a human being. We have now evolved to the point where we can direct our own evolution. Had we acquired this knowledge sooner, the following people may have never been born. [Portraits of people] ABRAHAM LINCOLN – MARFAN SYNDROME; EMILY DICKINSON – MANIC DEPRESSION; VINCENT VAN GOGH – EPILEPSY; ALBERT EINSTEIN – DYSLEXIA; JOHN F. KENNEDY – ADDISON'S DISEASE; RITA HAYWORTH – ALZHEIMER'S DISEASE; RAY CHARLES – PRIMARY GLAUCOMA; STEPHEN HAWKING – AMYOTROPHIC LATERAL SCLEROSIS; JACKIE JOYNER-KERSEE – ASTHMA. *Of course, the other birth that may never have taken place is your own.*

—*Gattaca's* coda. It was cut from the film, but included on the DVD.

Gattaca's imagery, much like its characters' identities and bodies, is dominated by the double helix shapes. From staircases in the protagonist's apartment to the toys in the geneticist's office they serve as a metaphorical reference to a society determined by the genetic code.

They represent the impossibility of overcoming one's genetic destiny. However, as visual markers they remind us, together with the coda, that this fantastical world can represent a real and *true* possibility. In the DVD's documentary, Uma Thurman says, "This is not about the gimmicks of the future. It is simply about if things keep going scientifically as they go what might this world be." And Ethan Hawke argues that "[this] juxtaposition of science fiction and individual . . . [is not] . . . far fetched." In fact, the main draw of the movie rests on the scientific plausibility of the unfolding plot. Moreover, *Gattaca* illustrates that, in the genomic age, the body is understood and represented as a sum of its parts, not as a whole. In other words, in order to deal with deviance, we desire technologies that will collect information, identify a problem or a mistake, and then go on to effect a behavioral change. *Gattaca*, specifically, illustrates how the normal and the abnormal are redefined through genetic engineering and how the abnormal is regulated and controlled through a very particular type of bodily surveillance. Wood writes that the regulated body in *Gattaca* "is not defined by words or actions that manifest as contentious event which threatens the structure of the social. Instead, it is the body that materializes through its trails of dead skin and hair, its smears of sweat and saliva. . . . In this context, the threatening body is one that is out of its genetic place." (2002, 168) Thus, transgression is not represented by the whole body, but rather by parts, such as skin particles and eyelashes, that provide information needed to recognize the Other. Therefore, what is dangerous to the social order is the inaccuracy or invalidity of genetic information. The abnormal is compartmentalized and reduced to specific genetic locales. While the protagonist's body wants nothing more than to be a part of the social structures, it is betrayed and threatened by the abnormality of its individual parts—blood, saliva, fingernails, and so on.

The main protagonist in *Gattaca* is Vincent Freeman (the pun of his last name is self-evident) who was conceived the "old-fashioned" way, in this case in the backseat of a large American-made vehicle, and therefore did not come out exactly right according to the standards of a society where traits like gender, hair color, and susceptibility to diseases can be preprogrammed into human embryos during in-vitro conception. Vincent narrates:

> They used to say that a child conceived in love has a greater chance of happiness. They don't say that anymore. I'll never understand what possessed my mother to put her faith in God's hands rather than those of her local geneticist [this is told over a close-up of rosary hanging from the rearview

mirror]. Ten fingers, ten toes. That's all that used to matter. Not now. Now just seconds old, the time and cause of my death was already known.

Right after birth, the infant's blood is tested and it is determined that Vincent has a 99 percent chance of developing a heart disorder and that his life expectancy is thirty years. He is deemed an "in-valid" (a play on the word "invalid" that becomes important later on in the movie), a "utero," or a "faithbirth" (here, religion and science are juxtaposed). It is also interesting to note how Vincent describes the difference between the old-fashioned determinations of freakishness—a lack or an excess of fingers or toes—as opposed to the genetic one—a measurement that separates the fluids from the body and analyzes them as having a separate and unique agency of their own. Here, visual surveillance, which relies on the outside or the external, is juxtaposed with surveillance that interprets the outside *in terms* of the inside. Such comparisons are bountiful throughout the film.

Vincent also dreams of space travel—an impossibility due to his genetic profile. Even in our "not-so-distant" present, no one with a heart condition would be allowed inside a space shuttle; however, here the problem is not Vincent's current condition, but rather the high possibility that he might develop a condition in the future. Hence, the body is deemed abnormal not because of any current visible characteristics, but because it might at any moment show itself to be so. In a sense, it is much like vampire—it is *the promise* that the monstrous characteristics might appear at any moment that keeps us guessing. To take the metaphor further, Vincent's "real resume" is said to be "in his blood."

In order to justify the "not-so-distant-future" claim, the movie describes discrimination faced by Vincent in terms easily related to today's society. Vincent narrates:

> It didn't matter how much I lied on my resume, my real resume was in my cells. Why should anybody invest all that money to train me, when there are a thousand other applicants with a far cleaner profile? Of course, it is illegal to discriminate—"genoism" it's called—, but no one takes the laws seriously. If you refuse to disclose, they can always take a sample from a door handle, or a handshake, even the saliva off your application form. Legal drug tests can just as easily become an illegal peek at your future in the company.

This analogy to racial discrimination invites comparisons between eugenics of the past and genetic engineering of the future—comparisons that are abound in popular and academic texts on the subject. I agree with Donna Haraway, who writes,

> Genetic engineering is not eugenics, just as the genome does not give the same kind of account of a species as does organic racial discourse. . . . In eugenics thinking, the good of the "race" is the central ideological value. The collective aspect is hard to overstress. In 1990s genetic biomedical discourse the "race"—either humanity as a whole or a particular racial category such as "white people"—plays little or no role, but individual reproductive investment decisions and individual genetic health are central. (1997, 246, 312–13).

The movie trailer is inaccurate—in *Gattaca*'s world, unlike that of Nazi Germany, no one tells you who to marry. In fact, it does not matter, since the individual's genetic makeup can be altered before birth. The concern is not racial perfection, but rather maximization of *individual* potential and possibility. The collective does not matter. The film celebrates individuality. Vincent's dream is contrasted to a bleak corporate world of genetic surveillance, where the search for perfection has created a homogenized, collective body. There are scenes in *Gattaca* where, dressed in suits and undistinguishable from each other, lines of people enter the company. The message is clear. Genetic engineering will turn the society into a neofascist state where the search for perfection will eliminate difference. In this narrative, Vincent is similar to minority characters in other films who manage to avoid discrimination by passing for members of the majority group (Kirby, 2000). These comparisons are a little dubious, considering that at the end of the day *Gattaca* celebrates and reaffirms the eventual triumph of white, heterosexual, able-bodied masculinity.

The film fetishizes Vincent's body as a visually able, attractive, white masculine body as if to say, "Look, visually, there is nothing wrong with him." Multiple times in the film he is shown half-naked doing pull ups, exercising, and running, his glistening masculine muscles on display. The first dialog in the film is between Vincent and Lamar, a physician. Upon obtaining Vincent's urine sample, Lamar admires Vincent's penis: "You have got a beautiful piece of equipment there. Have I ever told you that? I see many in the course of the day. Yours just happens to be an exceptional example. I don't know why my folks didn't order one like that for me." The irony of course is that Vincent's penis is not genetically designed and that his genetic identity is borrowed from another. Here, again, the film shows that in the genetically deterministic age the inside will determine the outside—a possibility or a potential will become more important than the actuality. The film's obsession with Vincent's attractive, healthy-looking body, however, has other implications as well. In his desire to pursue the dream of space travel Vincent enlists a man named German (I'm not sure if this is a specific illusion to the eugenic spirit of the Nazi Germany, but I would guess so) who helps "in-valids" borrow identities from those with a superior genetic code. Vincent narrates, "For the genetically superior, success is easier to attain but is by no means guaranteed. After all, there is no gene for fate. And for one reason or another, a member of the elite falls on hard times, their genetic identity becomes a valued commodity for the unscrupulous. One man's loss is another man's gain."

The phrase "there is no gene for fate" is inaccurate. In fact, the entire movie argues that this is precisely the case: your fate is in your genes. A better expression would have been that there is no gene for chance. However, there are many ways of conceptualizing chance and I would argue that, in *Gattaca*, chance or the unpredictability of events is conceptualized as that unique element that makes us "human"—our emotional being. It is a recurring argument made by the movie: genetics can predict physical and mental well-being, but "there is no gene for the human spirit," as the movie tagline says. Of course, the movie represents the human spirit as dreams and feelings that do not always follow a predictable course. This is hardly original—any romantic comedy has the same principal lesson. However, the argument that the ethereal and unpredictable "spirit" defines "humanness" is incredibly interesting in a story about surveillance of the human bodies. I would argue that it serves as a technique of resistance, however problematic, in the face of the genomic reconfiguration of the human body.

In fact, Jerome, the man whose impeccable genetic credentials Vincent is set to borrow, lacks that "spirit."[1] He is in a wheelchair as a result of an accident following his silver Olympic medal in swimming. Later on, we learn that Jerome's accident was not an accident at all, but a suicide attempt. Unable to deal with what the movie calls "a burden of perfection," he tried to kill himself, because, as he explained to Vincent, "Jerome Morrow was never meant to be a step down on the podium. With all I had going for me, I was still second best." Vincent later narrates, "Jerome was engineered with everything that he needed to get into

---

[1] In the interview with Ethan Hawke, Jude Law, and Uma Thurman included on the *Gattaca* DVD, Jude Law, who plays Jerome, explains, "[he] doesn't have the spirit but he does have the blood. Vincent has the spirit but he needs the blood."

Gattaca. Except the desire to do so." This "lack of spirit" is written on Jerome's body. Visually he is portrayed as the true "in-valid"—being wheelchair bound makes for a politically incorrect double meaning. However, even outside of the wheelchair, Jerome's body is slight when compared to Vincent's. He is consistently disheveled, with dark circles under his eyes and sickly looking skin. He constantly smokes and drinks. In fact, whereas Vincent's body is always represented as being fit and "normal," Jerome's body is represented as unfit, disabled, and freakish. He is unable to discipline, control, and manage his body the way that Vincent does. The outside is juxtaposed to the inside yet again. One cannot always determine the other, and at the end of the day Gattaca is about old-fashioned surveillance—the sort that regulates and disciplines bodies to behave according to the social order. After all, Vincent wants nothing more than to fit into the social structures, to look and appear like those "valids" around him. He does not want to change the way things are done; he just wants to be on the winning side of it.

It is Jerome's transgressions against his body and the social order that produced his body as one that must be punished. Both Vincent and Jerome refuse to be labeled only in terms of the inside, their genetic material. However, the body that transgresses its destiny in order to appear visually "abnormal" is the one that deserves death. At the end of the film, while Vincent is blasting into space, fully validated in his own "in-valid" body by a lab technician who apparently knew the truth from the beginning, Jerome also goes on what he describes as "a trip of his own." His trip, however, involves a graphic and fiery death in the incinerator previously used to dispose of Vincent's "invalid" bodily excretions. Before Vincent's trip, Jerome says to him, "I am the· one who should thank you. I only lent you my body. You lent me your dream."

Vincent's dream did not persuade Jerome that he could overcome his outside disability and his internal perfection. Instead, he is the "freak" of the movie, because he lacks essential humanity, "the human spirit." As such, he must die. His last act is to store enough of his body fluids and cells to make sure that Vincent may forever continue to be a "perfect" version of Jerome—something he can no longer be. And so, at the end of the movie, the social order is reaffirmed, the visually "freakish" body is destroyed, and the visually "perfect" body is allowed to reaffirm its true identity, while keeping the false one.

Gattaca offers an important insight into the production of human identity through representations of Otherness. We know who we are by first defining who we are not. As genetics changes our understanding of the human body, diseases, and abnormalities, so changes our ability to distinguish between ourselves and those who are not like us. Moreover, together with *Cracking the Code of Life, Gattaca* represents a current trend in popular narratives of scientific research: a deep ambivalence towards genetic science and the bodies that it produces. We cannot address this trend by arguing that these texts simply misrepresent or misunderstand the "real" science. Also no longer adequate is to portray the products of genetic advances (be they bodies altered through cloning, reproduction technologies, or genetic modification) as just another example of science gone awry. What we need now is not another doomsday scenario, but rather a critical examination of how these bodies will be integrated into the everyday, mundane private and public worlds. Perhaps this is the job of future documented fantasies and fantastic documentaries.

REFERENCES

Dreger, A. M. 2000. "Metaphors of Morality in the Human Genome Project." In *Controlling our Destinies: Historical, Philosophical, Ethical, and Theological Perspectives on the Human Genome Project*, edited by P. R. Sloan, 155–84. Notre Dame, IN: University of Notre Dame Press.

Haraway, D. 1989. *Primate Visions*. New York: Routledge.

———. 1997. *modest_witness@second_millennium*. New York: Routledge.

Kay, L. E. 2000. Who Wrote the Book of Life? A History of the Genetic Code. Stanford: Stanford University Press.

Kember, S. 2003. *Cyberfeminism and Artificial Life*. New York: Routledge.

Kirby, D. 2000. "The New Eugenics in Cinema: Genetic Determinism and Gene Therapy in *Gattaca*." *Science Fiction Studies* 27:193–215.

Lancaster, R. 2003. *The Trouble with Nature: Sex in Science and Popular Culture*. Berkeley: University of California Press.

Latour, B. 1990. "Drawing Things Together." In *Representation in Scientific Practice*, edited by Michael Lynch and Steven Woolgar, 19–68. Cambridge, MA: MIT Press.

Rabinow, P. 1999. "Artificiality and Enlightenment: From Sociobiology to Biosociality." In *The Science Studies Reader*, edited by M. Biagioli, 407–16. New York: Routledge.

Van Dijck, J. 2000. "The Language and Literature of Life: Popular Metaphors in Genome Research." In *Wild Biology: Feminist Readings in Science, Medicine and the Media*, edited by Kim Sawchuk and Janine Marchessault, 66–79. New York: Routledge.

Wood, A. 2002. *Technoscience in Contemporary American Film*. Manchester: Manchester University Press.

Knowing, Being, and the Reality Police: Science Fiction as Science Studies

DENNIS DESROCHES

Only a mind in the strangest position, looking at a world from the inside out and linked to the outside by nothing but the tenuous connection of the gaze, will throb in the constant fear of losing reality. . . .
—BRUNO LATOUR, "Do You Believe in Reality?"

Introduction

One could say that Charles L. Harness's "The New Reality" is a story about what the philosopher G. W. F. Hegel once referred to as the "night of the world," a situation in which every person finds that she somehow "contains" all of the world, all of its representations, all of its being, while somehow remaining discrete from it. I will return later in this chapter to the figuration of the human as a kind of "night of the world," but I mention it to begin because it gestures to how Harness's story—an "end of the world" narrative—offers us a unique look not only at the conditions of reality that shape what we know, but also the conditions of knowledge that shape reality. Given that the very question of knowing—that is, of epistemology—dwells at the very heart of science studies today, I will argue that "The New Reality" articulates many of the epistemological concerns that will come to ground current theorizing on the relationship between science and culture. As such, Harness's story provides for us a good example of how science fiction can literally *be* science studies, and it is toward the elaboration of this possibility that this chapter will orient itself. First, let me begin by describing in broad strokes the story itself.

Adrian Prentiss Rogers is a professional ontologist and Eastern Field Director for the International Bureau of the Censor—the "reality police." It is his job to make sure that reality-changing "sensoria" do not manifest to the detriment of a currently (more or less) stable "apperception mass." He is tasked, that is to say, with protecting reality from revisions of it based on scientific progress that may be too radical for humanity to internalize, thereby resulting in the wholesale destruction of reality, and humanity along with it.

As we enter the story, Prentiss is faced with one such problem, though he himself remains skeptical, at first, that such wholesale destruction of reality is possible. The—literally—diabolical "Dr. Luce" is currently under investigation because of his experiments aimed at destroying a photon. To destroy a photon is to transgress a natural law so fundamental that, according to the Bureau, such transgression would result in the destruction of the universe. As the story progresses, Prentiss encounters an old German diary—author unknown—belonging to Dr. Luce in which the following text referring to Immanuel Kant appears:

> Even this brilliant man [Kant] would probably say that the earth was round in 600 B.C., even as it is today. But *I* know it was flat, then—as truly flat as it is truly round today. What has changed? Not the Thing-in-Itself we call the earth. No, it is the mind of man that has changed. (Harness 1982, 319)

This text forces Prentiss to confront an epistemological possibility that even he—an ontologist—is loathe to believe: that reality is not at all some concrete entity or conception independent of our observation of it, but is rather the *product* of our interaction with a world whose very existence is similarly produced in and through the human "imagination." If there is a Kantian "noumenon," believes Prentiss, it is nevertheless the case that humanity has never stopped altering it by the simple act of existing as thinking beings. And so he must eventually admit, "I believe that . . . the 'real' world has been changing ever since our ancestors began to think" (Harness 1982, 334).

In the end, the Bureau decides it must kill Luce before he can undertake his reality-shattering experiment, but Prentiss is too late to save the day. As reality dissolves, only he, and his Boss/Lover—enigmatically (but not so enigmatically) named E—survive, as well as the demonic phantasm of Dr. Luce, whose really real form is not human at all, but serpentine. The shattering of the real has effaced human bodies—has traversed, in other words, the "night of the world"—and on the other side of this night is an Edenic beginning, complete with the sinister smell of apple blossoms.

Slipstream and Mixed Reality

Were it not for the fact that Harness's "The New Reality" was written over fifty years ago, we might very well confuse it for a kind of science fiction, and a kind of thinking of science fiction, that has recently become a prominent generic specification of speculative writing. Bruce Sterling has characterized a certain brand of recent sci-fi as "slipstream fiction," works of fiction that, as N. Katherine Hayles and Nicholas Gessler describe them, "occupy a borderland between mainstream and science fiction because they achieve a science-fictional feeling without the usual defamiliarizing devices" (2004, 482). Harness's story, like slipstream fiction, does not depend on aliens, space travel, or futuristic technology for its sci-fi effects, but rather relies on the undoing of the assumptions that ground everyday conceptions of reality to launch the text into the realm of the speculative. Sterling's description of the nature of slipstream fiction is germane in this context: "It seems to me that the heart of slipstream is an attitude of peculiar aggression against 'reality.' These are fantasies of a kind, but not fantasies which are 'futuristic' or 'beyond the fields we know.' These books tend to sarcastically tear at the structure of 'everyday life'" (Sterling 1998).

If Harness's story is not so much sarcastic as ironic, given its representation of the new—that is to say, "real"—reality as an ineluctable return to the primal Edenic scene, it is nevertheless the case that "The New Reality" exhibits a peculiar aggression against "reality," insofar as the very possibility of naming the real—the really real—is placed at stake in the first instance. Other elements of slipstream fiction that Sterling elaborates upon find clear presentation in this story. The challenge to common sense and the possibility that sense is precisely a thing made, for example, both appear in Prentiss's gradual conversion to a kind of epistemological relativism—a kind of "anything goes" ethos grounded in philosophy rather than commonplace morality—that is almost identical with more radical forms of social constructivism. The violent (mis)use of "historical figures"—in this case, the Edenic triumvirate of Satan, Adam, and Eve—also culminates in a reinvention of reality that nevertheless reinscribes an originary moment familiar to us all. Thus, if slipstream fiction tends "not to create new worlds, but to *quote* them, chop them up out of context and turn them against themselves" (Sterling 1998), then the new reality here, in its capacity as an iterative representation of an old reality, fits the bill.

I dwell on the question of the relation between Harness's story and the notion of slipstream (as opposed to mainstream) fiction because the story of slipstream fiction, its persistent rejection of the assumptions we use to shape reality and make it knowable, is also, I think, the story of science studies to a certain degree, inasmuch as science studies has, since the early '80s, been concerned with questioning the *objective* characterization of reality and focusing on the degree to which we participate in the production of that reality. Thus it seems to me that in Harness's text, we are given a privileged view of the very *possibility* of science studies, as well as the forms of fiction (like slipstream) that gravitate to it with such sympathy. If it is the case that, as Hayles and Gessler say, the acceleration of technological change has come increasingly to dismantle the "conventional distinctions between science fiction and ordinary reality" (2004, 483), we may add to this point that such dismantling is an effect not simply of technological change, but perhaps more properly, of the degree to and manner in which we *imagine* that change. In other words, we might look to speculative fiction—and Harness's story for our present purposes—for a clear representation of the manner in which humanity encounters reality as a lack of clarity.

"Ordinary reality," in Harness's text, is precisely the thing most centrally at stake, and yet it is precisely the thing—if thing it can be called—that withdraws as soon as one begins to question concerning it. As Veronica Hollinger and Joan Gordon comment, "[T]he challenge for science fiction today is less to extrapolate a far future than to keep up with a permanently mutable present."[1] Fifty years ago, Harness demonstrated that science fiction will always, and already, have reality's impossible present—or perhaps the impossibility of a present reality—as its ownmost specter.

Representing the Really Real

At the center of Harness's story, members of the International Bureau of the Censor debate the question of killing Luce in order to forestall the wholesale alteration of reality. This debate dramatizes not only the difficulties that one faces when speaking about reality, but also the programmatic statements that often are used to refute antifoundationalist

---

[1] Citied in Hayles and Gessler 2004, 482.

attacks upon reality's knowability. The discussion centers, specifically, on Prentiss's attempt to convince a group of more or less empirically oriented scientists and engineers—a metallurgist named Goring, a physicist named Dobbs, a chemist named Burchard, and a psychologist named Speer—that reality as we have come to know it is the product of the human imagination.

Prentiss begins with the claim that he doesn't know what "real reality" is. For him, it is "nothing more than a working hypothesis in the mind of each of us, forever in a process of revision" (Harness 1982, 330), a characterization that establishes Prentiss's position as a kind of epistemological relativism, a position he has taken some time in coming to. Luce presents the world, suggests Prentiss, with a revision of reality so drastic that it may instantaneously "thrust humanity face-to-face with the true reality, the world of Things-In-Themselves—Kant's noumena" (330). Such epistemological revolution suggests nothing less than a kind of Husserlian bracketing of everyday experience, except that such a bracketing is done against the will of humanity as a whole. For a professional ontologist, this is a disaster, and signals the catastrophic destruction of humanity in its current "ontological knowability" (if such a contradiction can be permitted here.) It is at this point that Dobbs, Goring, and Burchard mount their criticism of Prentiss's epistemological position, and where we can see, I think, something of the nature of the debates that have characterized science studies, and the social construction of science (or sociology of knowledge) that first made it possible.

Dobbs, the metallurgist, is an especially adamant opponent of Prentiss's theory of reality or lack thereof, and replies to Prentiss by objecting to the term "real reality." As he says, "A thing is real or it isn't. No fancy philosophical system can change *that*. And if it's real, it gives off predictable, reproducible sensory stimuli not subject to alteration except in the minds of lunatics" (Harness 1982, 331). Prentiss proceeds to disabuse Dobbs of precisely this position by first tricking him into believing that a "real" coin is counterfeit, and then exposing the ruse, thereby demonstrating the degree to which authority is responsible for the production of knowledge and, more specifically, the making of things, their reality. The conversation then turns to the "reality" of the coin, and it is the physicist—Goring—who makes the point that despite what his eyes tell him, theoretical physics knows, for example, that what the eye beholds cannot be said to represent, with any accuracy, what is "really" there. Indeed, what is really there becomes a question of probability, to the point where Goring reiterates the claim, so familiar—after Bohr—to quantum mechanics, that "the bare fact of observing something is sufficient to change that something from its pre-observed state" (333).

At this point Burchard, the chemist, feels he has caught Prentiss in an epistemological trap. As he says,

> [I]f our minds make this a coin, then our minds make this little object an ashtray, that a window, the thing that holds us up a chair. You might say we make the air we breathe, and perhaps even the stars and planets. Why, following Prentiss's idea to its logical end, the universe itself is the work of man—a conclusion I'm sure he doesn't intend. (Harness 1982, 333)

Prentiss's reply is simple, and yet for us provocative, when he responds to this accusation in the affirmative: "O, but I do," he says. In this claim is seen not only something of the epistemological relativism that marks more radical forms of social constructivism. It may also remind us of that oft-quoted claim made by Shapin and Schaffer some thirty-six years later in their important book, *Leviathan and the Air-Pump*. That claim is worth quoting here:

> Neither our scientific knowledge, nor the constitution of our society, nor traditional statements about the connections between our society and our knowledge are taken for granted any longer. As we come to recognize the conventional and artifactual status of our forms of knowing, we put ourselves in a position to realize that it is ourselves and not reality that is responsible for what we know. (1985, 344)

The conversation that Harness is staging here is an important one, I think, because it demonstrates to us that the crucial concepts driving the field of sciences studies—the scientific production of knowledge, the function of representation in that production, the epistemological constitution of society, and indeed, the world itself—can find among their precursors not just the various forms of sociology of knowledge that have come to shape its academic manifestation, but science fiction too. Prentiss defends an epistemological claim that is truly radical in 1950— it becomes even more radically constructivist when Prentiss goes on to maintain that the earth was once flat, that Pi once had a value of 3.00, and ultimately, that the mind conditions reality. Still, such a claim has become, more or less, a critical maneuver definitive of what we recognize today to be science studies.

The parallels with something of the spirit—and perhaps indeed, the epistemological outlook—of contemporary science studies in Harness's story do not end there, however. When Goring attempts to make sense of Prentiss's radical epistemological articulation by thinking in terms of the degree to which scientific inquiry is always concerned to harmonize theory and fact, we cannot help but think of the work done by Thomas Kuhn, in his groundbreaking (if controversial) text, *The Structure of Scientific Revolutions*. Goring's position is quite familiar to those of us in science studies concerned to undo foundationalist presuppositions governing knowledge production; he asks of Prentiss, "But won't you admit that . . . facts were there all the time, and merely awaited discovery?" (Harness 1982, 335). Prentiss's response is most telling:

> The simple, unelaborated *noumenon* was there all the time, yes. But the new fact—man's new interpretation of the *noumenon*, was generally pure invention—a mental creation if you like. This will be clearer if you consider how rarely a new fact arises before a theory exists for its explanation. In the ordinary scientific investigation, theory comes first, followed in short order by the 'discovery' of various facts deducible from it. (Harness 1982, 335)

Prentiss's response here is important to the question of science studies for a couple of reasons. First of all, we see in the notion that "theory precedes fact" not so much an overturning of inductive method as a kind of proto-articulation of what Kuhn will later come to call the "Priority of Paradigms"; to paraphrase Kuhn, for facts to be visible at all, a coherent epistemological structure must be in place to make them intelligible *as* facts (Kuhn 1996, 43). This is the idea at the heart of Prentiss's suggestion that "man's interpretation of the noumenon, was generally pure invention."

What is also interesting here, though, is this question of the "unelaborated noumenon" insofar as it could be understood to gesture to a concept articulated by N. Katherine Hayles some forty years later. It is not a stretch to see in this articulation of the primordial stuff of reality something like what Hayles refers to as "unmediated flux" in her important article articulating a theory of "constrained constructivism" (1993). It is what we *do* to that unmediated flux, according to Hayles, that finds a startling precursor in Harness's story. Speaking about the (im)possibility of representing reality, Hayles writes:

> I want to introduce another way of formulating [the representation of reality] that will make representation a dynamic process rather than a static mirroring. Suppose we think about the reality "out there" as an unmediated flux. The term emphasizes that it does not exist in any of the usual conceptual terms we might construct (such as reality, the universe, the world, etc.) until it is processed by an observer. It interacts with and comes into con-

sciousness through self-organizing, transformative processes that include sensory and cognitive components. (1993, 29–30)

Compare especially the notion that this unmediated flux "does not exist in any of the usual conceptual terms" until it has been "processed," with Prentiss's response to the question of what the "cosmos" must have been like before humanity. According to Prentiss, "There wasn't any [cosmos]. . . . Remember, by definition, "cosmos" or "reality" is simply man's version of the ultimate *noumenal* universe. The 'cosmos' arrives and departs with the mind of man. Consequently, the earth—as such— didn't even exist before the advent of man" (Harness 1982, 336).

If Hayles's unmediated flux "comes into consciousness," this cannot be much different from the notion that there is no earth, no cosmos, no world, prior to an act of human consciousness. The world is, as Hayles phrases it, and Harness figures it, a "theater of representation," even as it is *the* theater of representation.

Constrained Constructivism and the Night of the World

Of course, as Hayles argues in the same article, the notion of a constrained constructivism, as opposed to the kind of epistemological relativism that Prentiss champions in his arguments for killing Luce, are meant to "rescue scientific inquiry from solipsism and radical subjectivism" (1993, 40), precisely from, perhaps, the sort of solipsism that makes it possible in the first instance for a figure like Luce to destroy reality simply by overturning, experimentally, the epistemological constancy of the photon. There is an important sense, in fact, in which the ending of this story exhibits precisely this tendency toward constraint. After Luce destroys the world, Prentiss and E are cast into a noumenal no-man's land, where time has been inconceivably separated from space, where there is "nothing but a black, eerie silence all around. . . . So far as he could tell, he was nothing but an intelligence, floating in space. But he couldn't even be sure of *that*. Intelligence—space—they weren't necessarily the same now as before" (Harness 1982, 349). Dismembered, disembodied, Prentiss's thoughts turn to Luce, whose eyes, described earlier in the story as "tiny red flames, like candles" (318), once again appear before him in precisely the same manner, but now they are hate-filled, and attached to a monstrously serpentine body. In what might surely be called a night of the world, where reality is effaced, where intelligences float aimless and bodiless in the dark—in the aftermath of a world constituted entirely, as we now realize, though the human imagination, we find ourselves reminded of Hegel, who writes:

> The human being is this night, this empty nothing, that contains everything in its simplicity—an unending wealth of many representations, images, of which none belongs to him—or which are not present. This night, the interior of nature, that exists here—pure self—in phantasmagorical representations, is night all around it, in which here shoots a bloody head—there another white ghastly apparition, suddenly here before it, and just so disappears. One catches sight of this night when one looks human beings in the eye—into a night that becomes awful.[2]

This night that becomes awful may best describe the conclusion to Harness's story—it becomes awful not because of a lack of time, space, body—extension and duration—but because of the eyes of man that are no longer human. If Prentiss notices that he now has a body, even if it is a human body, how could such a body ever be human in a postrealist universe?

And yet, the mixed reality technique of using historical figures in catachrestical ways actually works toward demonstrating how even a reality wiped from the face of the earth must be replaced, and it will be replaced—or better, "constrained"—by the very concept of representation itself. Suddenly, in the story, bodies start to reappear, trees spring into being where none were before, and, in the final scent of apple blossoms is staged not only the primal Edenic scene, to be played out by Prentiss, E, and Luce's noumenal avatar, but perhaps more conspicuously, the return to representation. Here, the end of reality poses no threat to the real, for it is imagined by, and therefore constrained to, the imagining intelligence whose capacity for producing Hegelian "phantasmagorical representations" has never once been compromised by the destruction of the real. There can be, as Harness's story shows us, no new reality, only an awful night in which the history of the real—that is to say, the history of representation—repeats itself.

In the end, it may be that Hegel's awful night reminds us, most properly, of Blanchot's disaster. "The disaster" as Blanchot once said, "ruins everything, all the while leaving everything intact" (1986, 1). Harness's "The New Reality" destroys reality, evokes the theater of representation, and names the epistemological maneuvers that will someday come to shape science studies. All this without, even once, eschewing the real.[*]

---

[2] Cited in Žižek 1999, 29–30.
[*] For David Tinsley, who first introduced me to Harness's work.

R E F E R E N C E S

Blanchot, Maurice. 1986. *Writing the Disaster*, translated by Ann Smock. Lincoln: University of Nebraska Press.

Harness, Charles. 1982. "The New Reality." In *The Last Man on Earth*, edited by Isaac Asimov, Martin Harry Greenberg and Charles G. Waugh. New York: Ballantine.

Hayles, N. Katherine. 1993. "Constrained Constructivism: Locating Scientific Inquiry in the Theater of Representation." Reprinted in *Realism and Representation: Essays on the Problem of Realism in Relation to Science, Literature, and Culture*, edited by George Levine. Madison: University of Wisconsin Press.

Hayles, N. Katherine, and Nicholas Gessler. 2004. "The Slipstream of Mixed Reality: Unstable Ontologies and Semiotic Markers in *The Thirteenth Floor, Dark City*, and *Mulholland Drive*." *PMLA* 119:482–99.

Kuhn, Thomas S. 1996. *The Structure of Scientific Revolutions*. 3rd ed. Chicago: University of Chicago Press.

Latour, Bruno. 1999. *Pandora's Hope: Essays on the Reality of Science Studies*. Cambridge, MA: Harvard University Press.

Shapin, Steven, and Simon Schaffer. 1985. *Leviathan and the Air-Pump: Hobbes, Boyle, and the Experimental Life*. Princeton: Princeton University Press.

Sterling, Bruce. 1998. "Slipstream." *SF Eye* 5 *Electronic Frontier Foundation: Defending Freedom in the Digital World*. Electronic Frontier Foundation. 7 Jan. 2004. http://www.eff.org/Publications/Bruce_ Sterling/Catscan_ columns/catscan.05.

Žižek, Slavoj. 1999. *The Ticklish Subject: The Absent Center of Political Ontology*. New York: Verso.

Intervention 4

Between Garlic and Eternity: Fragments from an Interview with Stanisław Lem, Kraków 2003

EWA LIPSKA

TRANSLATED BY MARGRET GREBOWICZ

Lem: One can say anything at all about history, except that it shows signs of stopping. We are riding into an unknown future, even though our lives are very short, and it's evident that the track is endless, so we live with a certain fatigue. I turn on the TV or read the paper and again someone has been torn to pieces by an explosion, again someone has been murdered. This repeats like a movie whose end is stuck to its beginning and goes around endlessly. Large numbers of young people send me volumes of poetry—you too, probably—and I don't know what to do with this, because the response that these are great poems is obviously wrong, but if they have this internal need to write, then there's no help for it. Do you belong to this "school" of writing?

Lipska: I taught a class to some great young people at the Jagiellonian University and I didn't at all discourage them from writing. First of all, there are many talented young people, and secondly, writing has yet to hurt anyone. Sometimes it even teaches a certain culture of the word, sensitizes us to the surrounding reality, can be its own sort of therapy. . . .

Lem: Please! The best therapy is [J. K.] Rowling, who at the moment is worth something like 44 million, or maybe billion dollars, I don't know. Harry Potter is, of course, a sort of mania. These fads have always been around. When I was a child, it was the yo-yo. When I was a boy, it was [German adventure writer] Karl May. One recited him from memory. Then one played jacks. Harry Potter is this sort of thing.

Lipska: But this is great business not only for publishers, but for various institutions, clubs, organizations, associations, and fans of Harry Potter. With Karl May, we had no such "props."

Lem: That's true. Because he was a naïve naturalist. At Ms. Rowling's last appearance in London there were four thousand children and young people, and someone asked if she believed in all this magic. She answered "no." This was received with a great yowl of despair and disappointment. It would of course be nice if there were magic, but it's all nonsense.

Lipska: But we believe in magic. I, for instance, believe that there will one day be a philharmonic built in Kraków. Do you like music?

Lem: Should I be honest? Beethoven's "Fifth." One time I turned on a German TV station. Wonderful music on the piccolo. I'm sitting there, transfixed like a sheep—I don't know if sheep actually listen like this—and my son walks by and says that it's Mozart. I didn't know it was Mozart, though I recognized the flute. . . . I'm very simple. I like Mussorgsky's *Night on Bald Mountain.* That's a type of music which isn't really music, because it pretends to be a bald mountain with witches, and so on.

Lipska: I envy musicians their own language. The language of notes and sounds. When I heard Astor Piazzola in Vienna, his variations on Vivaldi's *Four Seasons,* it was a fabulous "discussion" between composers. And what about Kraków? Are you attached to it?

Lem: I'm attached only in the sense that I am attached to this chair, because it would be difficult, uncomfortable, to be on the floor. I am here by accident. My parents settled here, when I had no power to decide where to stay and where not to stay. We had connections here. No, no, I have nothing in common with Kraków, and no direct feelings for this city.

Lipska: You write that we live in a period of decadence. It's true. The United Nations brings to mind the prewar League of Nations and should certainly dissolve. I once circled around those buildings in Vienna and observed scenes which could have been from your science fiction: uniformed officials in blue shirts, silent elevators, the whisper of languages. The only real thing there was the store, in which Australian pastas and Cuban cigars mingled with other gastronomical perversions.

Lem: It's true. These days they're just quarreling huckster's stands, you know, hucksters at war. Recently Berlusconi offended one of the ministers in Schröder's administration, calling him a Nazi, and now has to apologize. No, when one is a child, one thinks that it's a place of superiority: ministers, Mr. President flanked by secret service. And later, when one grows up, one sees how much worse things actually are.

*   *   *   *   *

Lem: There's no helping it. The human mind has a limited capacity for information, and new books could be considered a form of transgression in the future. You write a new book, and this sends some earlier ones to their graves. It's not very nice. For each new book, you could get a year or two of jail, or your right hand cut off, or something like that. But here [in Poland], everyone wants to be a poet. I don't understand it.

Lipska: Perhaps it's at such decadent times as these that one escapes to the transient form that is poetry, to that metaphysical country of solitude.

Lem: I don't know. In one issue of [Polish newspaper] *Rzeczpospolita*, there is a poem by [Czesław] Miłosz about the genetic manipulations of beauty in the future, and there is a commentary, which I was asked to contribute. We both treated it as a sort of joke, but really, a future is coming which I wouldn't wish on anyone. It won't be pleasant to live.

*   *   *   *   *

Lem: It's impossible to constantly read poetry. It's like eating nothing but cookies. You can't live on cookies. The bread of prose is essential, but things aren't going so well with prose—the need to fantasize is missing. These days, I read mostly scientific literature. That's really exhausting, because they're all in disagreement with each other. Everyone has some unique concept of how the universe came to be, how this, how that, what particles and microparticles. On one hand, they speak to each other with respect, but on the other they dismiss each other with the help of a "physically whittled" word, not an ugly one. Here, behind your back, there is a mobile turning, which I received from my secretary three years ago. Every so often you have to change the battery, but I believe that as long as it turns, I will live a bit longer.

Lipska: It will turn for a long time to come. I am interested in your feuilleton, "Illumination and the Brain," in which you discuss an article from *The New Scientist*, on the subject of the work of Andrew Newberg, the neurophysiologist from the University of Pennsylvania, who is fascinated by the biology of religious events. "The feeling of oneness with the universe" with the help of the brain's left hemisphere. But if this were so, it would be possible to manipulate all human feeling and, for instance, to cure religious fanatics.

Lem: No, no, it's not like that. . . . People experience mystical states, of course, but this is either caused by a particular excitation of the brain, or, as the theist will tell you, it's a sort of receptor that pulls supernatural powers to the mind. Whichever you prefer. I am a hardened atheist. I would sooner believe that we are not alive at all, and that we are speaking after death, than to believe the alternative to atheism.

Lipska: The sort of experiment this neurophysiologist performed on himself is very interesting. Could someone move me to do something by "caressing" my left hemisphere? I doubt it.

Lem: It's not easy, but yes, they could. The sensation of leaving one's own body, and hovering somewhere under the ceiling, watching one's body below—that, too, can be caused by the appropriate "caress," as you put it. That's within the realm of possibility.

Lipska: And this is where the strange "life after death" books come from?

Lem: No, no. . . . You can't expect an answer from me to a question like that. You should turn to [the local priest]. I have my own convictions. I wrote to him: after my death, I will be in exactly the same state as I was before my birth. In other words, simply nothing. And this is a promise of happiness for me, in a sense, because to experience absolutely nothing is much more pleasant than to be hunched over, sore, old, and broken. The catalog of diseases I have here before me is much larger than the one I studied [in medical school]. There are more and more diseases. But I don't dream of eternal youth. I just have to answer Fukuyama's article, in which he has once again begun predicting that humans will live forever. He has strictly idiotic ideas, but sits in a good place, namely on the editorial board of *Foreign Affairs*. And that's enough. What really breaks down is vessels in the brain—the numbers I won't mention, but they have lengths in kilometers. Degenerative processes won't be easy to stop. One can eat garlic in enormous quantities, but between garlic and eternity there is, after all, an enormous gulf.

Lipska: But garlic helps?

Lem: There are those who believe, and it helps them.

⋆   ⋆   ⋆   ⋆   ⋆

Lem: Rorschach tests have gone out of fashion lately.

Lipska: What about lie detector tests?

Lem: If one is well prepared, one can get around it. In the case of expert cons, it's very hard to catch the deceit.

Lipska: What about tests of decency for government officials?

Lem: I would put it this way: if someone is intellectually endowed, smart, thoughtful, they don't rush into politics, particularly into government, and are certainly useless in the role of president. Because such a person would have so many problems, reservations, such worries.

Lipska: That's a bad forecast. Perhaps it's better to knock on the door of the cosmos, but it will just answer Nothing. Even if this Nothing is beautiful, photogenic, and mysterious. Perhaps that's why three probes are headed to Mars at this moment.

Lem: There's nothing interesting there. Of course NASA is laying off large numbers after the Columbia catastrophe. These large organizations have the tendency to forget the reason they came into existence. Their very functioning—this turning of bureaucratic wheels—is so complicated that only a catastrophe can return order.

AT THE LIMITS OF THE IMAGINATION

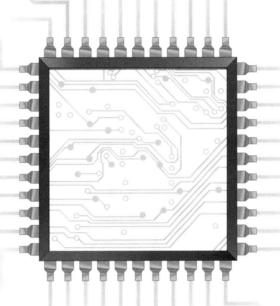

14 Cognitive Constraints on Imagining Other Worlds

E. THOMAS LAWSON

*E*very science fiction reader gravitates toward a favorite set of authors. I find myself returning towards the same spot on the bookstore's shelves where I hope to find the next book published by one of my favorites; I typically check to see whether Nancy Kress has recently published a new book. When I discover that she has, I often make something of a fool of myself in the quiet aisles of the bookstore by saying rather loudly "Yes!!" I was particularly enthralled by Kress's Probability Trilogy and have read it a number of times.

The three interlinked stories *Probability Moon*, *Probability Sun*, and *Probability Space* involve the expansion of humankind into the far reaches of the galaxy, where they have encountered the Fallers, who not only will not communicate with them but also are bent on their destruction. In fact, the Fallers are xenophobic. Much of the narrative hinges on whether the people of the Earth can find the means to defeat or isolate the Fallers. Humankind has also discovered a new planet populated by sentient creatures who operate according to "shared reality." Shared reality involves living according to a set of norms for the conduct of life that, if flouted, causes head pain to the transgressors. It is a physiological condition. Shared reality proves a powerful technique for maintaining a stable and productive society but also creates problems for the strangers from earth, who do not have this condition.

In orbit around this newly discovered planet is an extremely powerful object that contains settings on an incremental scale that, when triggered, can wreak havoc not only on entire planetary systems, but also seems to be capable at its highest setting of disrupting the fabric of space-time itself. A similar object lies deeply buried on the planet and is responsible, through the processes of evolution, for the "shared reality" behavior of the sentient creatures on the planet. To permit either the orbiting object or the buried object to fall into the hands of the Fallers would tip the balance in favor of those destroyers. To remove the object hidden underneath the surface of the planet would, moreover, destroy "shared reality" for the inhabitants; it would, however, provide a powerful weapon in the battle with the Fallers. It is very important, therefore, that the people of Earth get their hands on this weapon first. Kress characterizes both the Fallers and the inhabitants of the planet deftly and with an imaginative flourish and at the same time raises powerful moral issues about doing harm to alien cultures. A trilogy of this kind is capable of grabbing the reader's attention.

I found the characters of the *Probability Trilogy* persuasively described, its science intriguing, and its moral tone provocative. Reading this trilogy led me to reflect on the obviously complex creative processes that an author mines in order to weave a story of such mind-bending imagination. As a cognitive scientist interested in the creative process, reading this trilogy made me wonder what is involved in imagining other worlds and other creatures such as those that populate the pages of this fascinating story. And because of the science involved, the trilogy also persuaded me to pursue the question of whether reading science fiction is an aid or a hindrance to developing a deeper understanding of scientific knowledge.

Here I will focus on both of these issues. I will discuss the processes that lead to novel ideas such as those found in Kress's work. I will also pay attention to the role that science fiction can play in leading the reader to a deeper knowledge of science.

Certainly the creativity involved in imagining and writing such a story comes from a great deal of hard work rather than precipitously from some transcendent, illuminating vision. Of course there sometimes comes the puzzling dream rich with meaning, the moment of illumination that makes connections not recognized before, the penny dropping that rings the cognitive bells. However, the fertile soil has long been prepared by the grind. None of the authors that I know are lazy. They might have periods when they stare endlessly at the blank page hoping for some special moment that will force their fingers to make some intelligible marks on the page. Typically, however, these moments seldom come and writers soon realize that they had better get on with the job. Actually, the same goes for scientific theorizing, which, hopefully, will lead to experiments that will either confirm or disconfirm the hypotheses under consideration.

Whether we are dealing with the making of imaginative literature or the pursuit of scientific inquiry, a great deal of background knowledge is essential before we can even hope to solve the problems that present themselves to us in either of these modes of creativity. What I wish to accomplish here, therefore, is not to explain what creativity is or even how it arises; authors such as Mihaly Csikszentmihalyi (1996) have written outstanding works on the subject. Rather, as a cognitive scientist deeply involved in searching for clues about the workings of the human mind, especially as these workings give rise to the products of the imagination, my goal is to identify and discuss whether there are any constraints on creativity and what might be required for their beneficial use. Of particular interest to me are the strategies that might lead to novel ideas, especially those found in works of science fiction.

Now, one commonsense notion about creative activity assumes that we all possess the mental equipment to imagine anything. Most commonsense notions contain a grain of truth and sometimes bushels of it. We shall see later, however, that common sense, while useful and relevant in many situations, does have its limitations. Dealing with this problem becomes particularly interesting when we examine works of imaginative literature, particularly those forms that involve the invention of other worlds and the beings that populate them, the worlds imagined by the authors of science fiction.

To uncover some of the secrets of the creative imagination means looking to the mind for answers. Cognitive scientists have taken as their job the task of figuring out how the mind works. They attempt to answer the question of what the various levels of cognitive processing are. Simply put, cognition is how we come to know the world and cognitive science involves theorizing about the various processes that produce such knowledge. One technique employed in achieving the goal of defining the architecture of the mind involves starting with the notion of *constraint* and analyzing how this feature might apply to our understanding of the workings of the mind.

To view the human mind as operating under constraints is to recognize two important factors. The first of these is the notion of limitation, or, if you prefer, restriction. To speak of a limitation is not to make claims about what the mind cannot do; rather it means understanding the conditions that characterize the mind's work. For example, working (or short term) memory operates under severe limitations. Remembering more than seven or eight chunks of information after just one exposure (such as a string of numbers) is very difficult for the vast majority of people. Mnemonic savants are few and far between. Long-term memory, on the other hand, can be triggered in amazingly complex and interesting ways. Vivid recall of long-gone events under special conditions occurs to all of us. A smell can evoke your memory of an event that occurred many years ago. So a limitation does not mean a prohibition. Obviously we do remember some things for a brief moment in time and others for long periods. That simply means that there are different conditions for short and long-term memory.

In fact knowing that the mind operates according to limitations leads us to recognize that constraints are also enabling devices. They make the development of certain forms of knowledge possible. On the basis of a simple mechanism such as a set of concepts like the number "one" and the notion of "successor" we can produce an infinite number of mathematical operations. The discipline of linguistics has been able to show that a finite set of rules can produce an infinite number of sentences. And of course, we all know about the butterfly effect, which shows how easy it is to destabilize a system in equilibrium.

The moral of all of this is that our minds work as well as they do because of the constraints under which they operate, whether these involve working or long-term memory or the processes that lead to the creation of novel ideas. These constraints channel and direct the way we reason about the world. Imagining new worlds is, after all, a form of reasoning about what is possible. Evolutionary psychologists, who look both to evolutionary biology and to cognitive science in their attempts to explain the regularities in human thought and behavior (despite the obvious differences in cultural practices that the thoughts inform), argue that the various functions that our minds evince are the products of natural selection. The constraints according to which our minds operate have emerged as properties of the human brain because they have adaptive value. Sometimes it is as simple as the capacity to plan, to think ahead. On the ancestral plains, planning where you will be when the animals come around the hill can mean the difference between starvation and plenty. Sometimes these processes are much more complicated, as when we try to figure out complex social relationships such as "I know that Jane thinks that Jack despises his brother Joe because he rather than Jack would love to surprise his mother with a present even though it is not her birthday."

Cognitive science, aided and abetted by evolutionary, cognitive and developmental psychology, hypothesizes that we are designed by the forces of natural selection to operate in terms of a folk physics, a folk biology, and a folk psychology as our basic ways of trafficking with the world. Folk physics is a commonsense "theory" of what the material world is like according to such notions as solidity, dimensionality, continuity, and so forth. Folk biology, likewise, is a commonsense theory of what the organic world is like according to such notions as birth, reproduction, growth, development, and death. Folk psychology is a commonsense theory that attributes desires, beliefs, hopes, wishes, fears and so on to human and even some animals. Each of these intuitive systems of knowledge, which operate under the constraints that come with such design, enable us to survive and reproduce our kind precisely because they are such useful forms of knowledge for living in and manipulating our environment.

These intuitive forms of knowledge also seem to place restrictions on our imagination including the creative thinking involved in the production of science fiction. Each form of folk knowledge consists in a system that is responsive to particular domains of experience: the material world, the organic world, and the world of intentionality. Each form of knowledge operates according to a certain set of constraints that both limit and enable our perceptions and conceptions of our environment and ourselves.

How do we know this and what can we do about it? Let us turn, therefore, to some scientific work to focus on the role that constraints play as both limiting and enabling devices when we imagine other worlds and the creatures that the authors so cleverly persuade us inhabit them. Thomas B. Ward and his colleagues have been in the vanguard of the study of creative idea generation. For more than a decade he has steadily advanced our knowledge of how human beings creatively produce novel notions. His model of investigation involves what he has called "the path of least resistance" (1994). He says: "When people develop new ideas for a particular domain, the predominant tendency is to retrieve fairly specific, basic level exemplars from that domain, select one or more of those retrieved instances as a starting point, and project many of the stored properties of the instances onto the novel ideas being developed" (Ward 1994, 3). For example, Ward has shown that when participants in an experimental study were asked to imagine animals on other planets 90 percent of the properties of these imaginary animals possessed the same properties as those of earth animals; they possessed eyes, legs, and bilateral symmetry. Ward reports that even when his subjects were instructed to make their imaginary creatures radically different, the results were nevertheless largely the same (1997). What seems to be at work here is that our intuitive knowledge is a powerful force in divining what might be out there according to the domains that each folk theory is particularly responsive to.

Ward's goal in the experiments that he and his colleagues has devised is to identify the various strategies that lead to differing degrees of novelty as well as to uncover the potential for improving creative functioning (2004, 1). This goal is particularly important for understanding why some science fiction writers are so successful in persuading us of the verisimilitude of their novels. It seems that while some science fiction writers follow the path of least resistance by simply extending the properties of creatures that they know to other creatures, some authors seem capable of imagining other the inhabitants of other worlds in such interesting and creative ways that they capture and rivet our attention. While the path of least resistance delivers the familiar idea, to learn how to overcome this path promises greater excitement, insight, and knowledge.

From a scientific point of view, the work done by Ward and his colleagues has provided important clues about the strategies that are employed in imagining worlds beyond our own. According to Ward, some experimental subjects typically employ the imaginative strategy of dreaming up creatures based on specific, earthbound animals that they are acquainted with. They utilize an *exemplar strategy*. Others employ an alternative strategy by reasoning more *abstractly*. That is to say, they take into consideration abstract principles such as the environmental characteristics that might be the case on other planets and then imagine what the properties of the creatures would most probably have to be to exist in that alien environment. Operating according to abstract rather than specific constraints does not, of course, eliminate cognitive constraints; the point is rather that there are different constraints that not only limit our imaginative products but also enable our imaginations to flower in more interesting and compelling ways. For example, to know something about the laws of nature that characterize the physical world does not mean that one has escaped from the tendencies of the human mind to follow the path of least resistance. Reflective thought, which is also a property of human minds, is able to take the reasoning process as its object of attention. This means that our minds are able to operate at levels of abstraction (when appropriately trained). There appear to be constraints at this level of mental operation as well, but it is here that notions such as systematicity, coherence, evidence, logic, and so forth provide the constraints.

The experiments involved in establishing the fact of constraints are interesting in their own right. One group of subjects (the abstract condition) was asked to imagine the fundamental properties of animals generally and then to consider how these properties would be expressed on another world quite different from our own. This group was told that they should not use Earth animals as examples, but instead should think of principles such as what it would take to survive in an alien environment quite different from the Earth's. Another group (the exemplar condition) was encouraged to think of specific Earth animals and then imagine what these animals would have to be like on another world. The third group (the control condition) was simply told to imagine animals on another world. According to the analysis of the data by independent coders of the results of the experiment, the subjects operating in the abstract condition clearly produced the most creative ideas.

In another experiment Ward and his colleagues (2004) had all of the subjects imagine, draw, and describe a living thing that might exist on another planet. Some of the participants in the experiment were given exemplar instructions, others were given abstract principles, and the control group was given no special instructions other than to imagine a living thing on another planet. The differences in what the participants imagined were significant. Those who employed the abstract strategy produced far more interesting and intriguing notions than either the exemplar or the control group.

What can we learn from these experiments? First, there is a tendency to use the path of least resistance when imagining novel situations unless one is encouraged to employ a more fruitful strategy. Second, thinking harder (that is, thinking more abstractly) pays dividends when solving problems and imagining novel entities and situations. Third, writing an interesting science fiction novel that will stretch the mind of the reader involves not only expecting the reader to think more abstractly but also having the author employ the cognitive strategy that will capture the interest of the reader and will lead to a deeper understanding of the science in the science fiction. Employing this strategy involves the author accessing systematic principles that appeal to notions such as evidence, deduction, induction, and so forth rather than simply extending a tried and true idea to new instances, for example, moving the nostrils to below the mouth when describing an alien creature.

The third point requires elaboration because it most probably goes beyond what the experiments have shown. Before I engage in that elaboration, however, I wish to make one point, namely that the best science fiction writers do not usually follow the path of least resistance. Instead they build entirely new worlds on the basis of the scientific knowledge that they have accumulated. As with most scientific knowledge, it is not only systematic, well-defined, and mathematically based; rather, one of the most interesting features of scientific knowledge is that it goes against the expectations that follow from our typical use of folk theories in our reasoning about the world. Such scientific knowledge is counterintuitive. In other words, it contravenes our intuitions of what the physical, the biological, and the mental worlds are like.

Science fiction writers understand the counterintuitiveness of scientific knowledge and, therefore, recognize the need to build a novel world on the basis of scientific knowledge. Science fiction writers, at least the good ones, having done their world building, then are ready to imagine the types of creatures that would have to fit into the alien conditions provided by their novel worlds, populated by creatures who have to survive hazardous conditions such as intense radiation or deal with relativistic effects in traveling astronomical distances.

Neither our folk physics nor our folk biology nor our folk psychology prepares us for understanding the counterintuitive concepts that populate scientific theories and the stories those theories have inspired. It is important, therefore, for science fiction authors to devise a means in their storytelling for persuading us that the arcane notions of, for example, quantum mechanics, natural selection, and the unconscious processes that lie beneath our conscious reflections, make sense. This does not mean that the task of scientific education lies with science fiction novelists alone. Some of the great scientists have also been great communicators of scientific knowledge. A few, such as Gregory Benford, have also been science fiction writers.

When I think of great scientists who have wrestled with the counterintuitive nature of scientific theory, I am reminded of the ability of Richard Feynman to convey both the excitement and the puzzling features of physics. I will never forget working through *Six Easy Pieces* (Feynman 1995) and finally arriving at chapter six, "Quantum Behavior." The counterintuitive nature of this area of physics is obvious. Feynman says there: "Quantum mechanics is the description of the behavior of matter in all its details and, in particular, of the happenings on an atomic scale. Things on a very small scale behave like nothing that you have any direct experience about. They do not behave like waves, they do not behave like particles, they do not behave like clouds or billiard balls or weights on springs, or like anything else you have seen" (116). In other words, we have no exemplars from the ordinary world of our experience that allow us to imagine what is going on at the level of quantum mechanics. What, then, does it take to comprehend the discoveries of quantum behavior? It certainly takes the ability to engage in abstract thought rather than the path of least resistance. Perhaps even more important, it takes a special language, the language of mathematics, to express formally what we cannot conceive of imagistically. We can, of course, imagine thought experiments that will show what is going on at this level. In fact, that is what Feynman does in order to introduce us to quantum behavior. But do we really understand what is going on? Only if by "understand" we mean the ability to express the ideas involved in quantum mechanics in a language that describes the processes involved, the language of mathematics.

It is not only at the level of the very small that such problems of understanding arise, however. Finding the reality beneath appearances occurs at all levels of scientific inquiry. For example, psychologists have been able to show that people are typically essentialists in their thinking about the biological world. Essentialism is the view that a member of any category, such as dog, human, or tree, possesses a property that determines its identity. We all know, for example, that giraffes are quite different from elephants, frogs, and trees. All of us, some of the time, think in essentialist terms. Certainly we would be most upset if we mistook a tree for a frog! But from an evolutionary point of view (the long view) elephants, trees, and frogs have a common origin *if you go back far enough and have the right theory*. But the long view is not all that helpful in our day-to-day traffic with the world—unless a situation arises that requires a scientific explanation of why, for instance, the pollen from a bush might cause an allergic reaction in someone.

From a psychological point of view it makes sense to notice these differences between the organisms that inhabit the earth. Precisely because the short view is so useful, it serves as a hindrance to accepting that there are hidden mechanisms at work that can explain why organisms differ from each other. The resistance to Darwin and the neo-Darwinian synthesis is still very strong. I have been impressed with the frequency with which science fiction authors in all kinds of subtle ways introduce ideas of natural selection in their explanations of why a certain type of alien creature possesses the properties that it does.

Only when we arrive at the psychological level of analysis, however, does resistance to scientific explanations of human behavior raise its ugly head in a particularly virulent form. Fundamentalists may complain about the evils of the "theory" of evolution—at worst insisting upon the truth of creationist mythology, and at best arguing for intelligent design—but when it comes to explaining why humans behave in the way that they do, why people tend to do one thing rather than another, when psychologists appeal to hidden cognitive mechanisms that account for observable fact, then a chorus of dissent arises from some scholars in the humanities, especially those with postmodernist commitments. Then charges of "scientism" abound, and we are told it is not nature but nurture, as if any knowledgeable scientist would deny that with respect to the organic world nature and nurture were inextricably intertwined.

While resistance to scientific knowledge has a certain cachet, unless such knowledge conveniently serves ideological purposes, scientific knowledge proves particularly problematic when it fails to match our normal intuitions or expectations about what the world is like. But there is an irony here because it is also the case that people respond to counterintuitive ideas because they capture our attention. Developmental psychologists have shown that infants pay attention and act surprised when counterintuitive events are brought to their attention. In fact, cognitive scientists who have analyzed the process of cultural transmission have argued that counterintuitive ideas (such as mythological narratives) have a transmission advantage if the violations to intuitive expectations are minimal. If the violations are too great, then we lose interest because we know that is not the way the world is. This obviously creates a problem for scientific explanations because, as we have seen in the case of quantum behavior, nothing *in our experience* prepares us for the anomalous fact that scientific theorizing discloses. Both scientists and science fiction writers, therefore, are faced with a problem—how to communicate novel and puzzling and sometimes outrageous ideas. In the case of science, the program is clear—years of training in the particular science, whether it be physics, chemistry, biology, or psychology. That means acquiring all of the tools, concepts, and experimental procedures necessary to discover new knowledge.

Science fiction writers have a different problem. They need both to understand the science they will employ in their fiction and also successfully convince even scientifically naïve readers that the worlds that they imagine are possible worlds. The easy way out would be to follow the path of least resistance, but at this would be at the expense of more creative results as experimental work has shown.

Nancy Kress seldom follows the path of least resistance. Take the notion of "shared reality" that Kress has imagined. Given the kinds of brains that we have, and given the most plausible theories about how those brains enable us to reason about the world, human beings typically construct their view of what is real based on cues from the environment, such cues triggering cognitive mechanisms designed by evolution to respond to the cues in the various domains. We build our knowledge of the real, whether this be physical, biological, or psychological, by interacting with our environment using the competencies with which the processes of natural selection have endowed us. Certainly some of that knowledge comes about by explicit instruction, but even that kind of knowledge makes sense to us because we already have the equipment, the cognitive resources, to appropriate the information conveyed to us by formal and informal education.

What Kress has imagined is a mind similar to ours in many respects but which, because of special conditions of a physical kind, is particularly responsive to violations of cultural norms. To contravene these norms means that the contraveners are "not real" and therefore not worthy of being communicated with or cooperated with. In fact, they are a threat to those who live in a world of "shared reality." Of course, an author must be careful because the reader typically will tend to follow the path of least resistance, so elements of the story will have to connect with the typical constraints that characterize our way of acquiring knowledge. Not everything can be novel because then the story will lose its interest. So there had better also be romantic relationships, situations of conflict, desires, and goals that appeal effortlessly to us when we follow the path of least resistance.

Another example of Kress's ability to imagine other worlds according to abstract principles is her idea of "space tunnels" through which individuals safely ensconced in a space ship can almost instantaneously move from one place in the galaxy to another. Here Kress employs the idea of quantum entanglement, an idea that is completely counterintuitive to our folk physics. She extends this idea to the notion of macro-level object entanglement. She clues the reader in to the fact that physicists have developed the notion of quantum entanglement which she then defines for the reader as the possibility that one particle affects its paired counterpart regardless of distance. I can imagine an adventurous teacher in an introductory physics class recommending that the student read the probability trilogy not only for fun but also for profit and then raising the question of whether macro-level object entanglement is either possible or prohibited by the laws of physics. Some budding particle physicist in the classroom might be inspired to make new discoveries about the hidden world that hides beneath appearances.

Or take the idea of the attitude of the Fallers to other forms of life besides their own. Is it possible for a society to survive when it demonstrates such an extreme hostility? That is an interesting question. Certainly there are sufficient examples from the peoples of the Earth to recognize the presence of xenophobia in many human societies. The sad truth is that human beings are particularly susceptible to basing their decisions about other ways of life on superficial characteristics.

Clannishness is always with us, and racism has been very difficult to eliminate even in democratic societies. If we wish to follow the path of least resistance, even though this is in many ways a useful approach, we shall miss the opportunity to develop those aspects of our mind that can lead to ever more insightful concepts about the world in which we live. Science fiction writers, because of their commitment to scientific discoveries, contribute to the development of the growth of our knowledge.

R E F E R E N C E S

Csikszentmihalyi, Mihalyi. 1996. *Creativity: Flow and the Psychology of Discovery and Invention.* New York: HarperCollins.

Feynman, Richard P. 1995. *Six Easy Pieces: Essentials of Physics Explained by Its Most Brilliant Teacher.* Reading, PA: Addison-Wesley Publishing Company.

Ward, Thomas B. 1994. "Structured Imagination: the Role of Conceptual Structure in Exemplar Generation." *Cognitive Psychology* 27:1–40.

———. 1995. "What's Old about New Ideas?" In *The Creative Cognition Approach*, edited by S. M. Smith, T. B. Ward, and R. A. Finke, 157–78. Cambridge, MA: MIT Press.

Ward, Thomas B., and C. M. Sifonis. 1997. "Task Demands and Generative Thinking: What Changes and What Remains the Same?" *Journal of Creative Behavior* 31:245–59.

Ward, Thomas B., Merryl J. Patterson, and C. M. Sifonis. 2004. "The Role of Specificity and Abstraction in Creative Idea Generation." *Creativity Research Journal* 16:1–9.

After the Space Age: Science, Fiction, and Possibility

MARTIN PARKER

We are all in the gutter, but some of us are looking at the stars.

—Oscar Wilde

Introduction

When I was seven, my mother woke me up from my warm bed in the middle-English night to see the fuzzy pictures of Armstrong and Aldrin. The picture and sound quality were so poor, it had to be real. For the rest of our childhoods, my friends and I imagined that we would go to the Moon too, and that people would go to Mars next, and that my children would go to school on rocket bikes, and that their children would watch the rotating nebula of Dendrius Prime from their spaceship's porthole. Ever since, I have been watching and reading science fiction.

As Constance Penley argues in *Nasa/Trek* (1997), the boundaries between fiction and fact are pretty irrelevant when we are thinking about the future. Technology ensures that (much of) what was fiction becomes fact, the consumption of SF amongst geeks inspires the production of mimetic technologies, and popular science markets its facts like blockbuster fiction.[1] In a curious way, the tradition of the thought experiment in speculative philosophy is also an attempt to use the imagination in order to make reality strange, and hence more permeable to thought.

---

[1] See Parker et al. 1999 for some more examples.

Conceptualizing a private language and a speaking lion, wondering if it would matter if your brain was on the moon but connected to your body on earth, or imagining the world as it looks like for a bat. And of course in social theory nowadays it is common enough to use texts like *The Matrix* to discuss ideology and discourse, or to interrogate humanism with the *Terminator* films, or even to think about the connections between cyberpunk fiction and anticorporate protest (Rowlands 2003; Parker 2002). All these examples seem to suggest that hybrid forms of thought that mix concrete and fantastic elements are not extraordinary, but actually quite common.

But when we compare the massive growth of SF-inspired fantasy—in film, book, comic, computer game, animation, collectible, and so on—with what has actually happened in space since 1969, we can see a widening gulf. Putting it simply, the vast majority of people have more interest in *The Lord of the Rings* than in the latest stuttering NASA mission. The 2004 super-real pictures of rocks on Mars seem to exemplify this strange separation between the mundane (it's only a rock) and the fantastic (it's a hundred million miles away). My children, who don't have rocket bikes, told me that the photos of the Martian surface looked too real to be true. (Which wasn't to say that they disbelieved them, just that they weren't that interested in them.) And anyway, as they explained to me slowly, special effects are more spectacular. I suppose one way of thinking about this is that we are witnessing a widening gap between the glamour of imagination and the mundanity of reality. The majority of the later Apollo missions and the last twenty years of the space shuttle (with two tragic exceptions) were regarded by most people as dull, despite NASA's massive investment in public relations. Novelty doesn't cling to objects or actions for very long, because (as *Blade Runner* taught us) even the future rusts.

In this chapter, I wish to think through the dialectic between imagination and reality that seems to be constitutive of any desire to explore both space and thought. I also want to argue that this tension is constitutive of possibility, and what might be called "practical utopianism" (or perhaps, "impractical pragmatism"). In calling this a dialectic, what I intend to signal is the idea that the inadequacy of the present fuels fantasy,[2] and the inadequacy of fantasy fuels practicality. They are constitutive of each other. I think that if imagination and reality are separated we have a world of people who are utilitarians at work and fantasists at

---

[2] Which was Mannheim's point about utopianism in general (1960).

play. These are people who aren't impressed by Mars rocks, but loved the big bangs of *Deep Impact* and *Armageddon*. They also think that anticorporate protesters are just dreamers, and trying to change the world is a waste of time.

Another way to approach my question is via the politics of space exploration. To what extent can the materialization of SF through NASA be separated from all the obvious sins that might be attached to it? Boys and gigantic phalluses; the final frontier version of U.S. imperialism; the support afforded to the military-industrial complex; and the massive distraction from the poverty and deprivation found in the U.S., let alone the rest of the world. None of these are good things, and collectively they must outweigh anyone's dreams. Yet I was pleased when (in 2004) George W. Bush repeated his father's vague promises about the Moon and Mars. And I keep looking at those pictures of Mars rocks. Should I feel guilty for small-boy fantasies, and turn my face back to the Earth?

Space and the Sublime

Further Apollo missions are continuing and even more powerful and sophisticated rockets and space-craft are being developed. From the moon the next step must be to the more distant planets, first Mars and then further and further into space in man's eternal quest for knowledge.

— Text on the instructions for the 1/144 Airfix scale model plastic kit of the Apollo-Saturn V spacecraft

There is a common experience, though not a universal one.[3] I have a friend who teaches cultural studies, and in a course on technology he shows the students some video from July 1969. He has tears in his eyes, while they seem uninterested. In 2003, my family and I went to Florida. I dragged them a long way from Orlando across the flat lands to the Kennedy Space Center and spent a day silent with wonder. At the LC39 observation gantry I gazed for a long time out over launch pad 39A in the distance, a mess of pipes and metal shimmering in the damp heat. Constance Penley tells us that she "grew up in space," traveling with her father to make a "pre-dawn dash to the Cape" to watch the launches (1997, 1). Finally, consider one of the twelve human beings (men) who have stood on our moon and blotted out the Earth by holding their

[3] In my conversations with others about what "space" means to them, many claim it means little or nothing. They say that they are more impressed by genetic science, or using the telephone.

gloved thumbs in front of their metalled visor. All of it. From primordial soup to Saturn 5, from the pyramids to everything you have ever thought, said, done, written, loved. Everything. Everything.

Two hundred and twelve earth years previously, Edmund Burke's *A Philosophical Enquiry into the Origin of Our Ideas of the Sublime and Beautiful* (1757) had provided the aesthetic rationale for willingly exposing oneself to the awe-fulness of nature. If smallness, delicacy, fragility, smoothness, sweetness, and gradual variation were the characteristics of the beautiful, then the sublime was characterized by vastness, darkness, danger, power, infinity, and suddenness. It is because, Burke suggests, the latter list reminds us of our mortality and insignificance that exposure to the sublime provokes such strong emotions. In aesthetic terms, mountains and crashing seas become of greater interest than mere pastoralism, and grandly romantic senses of quest, spirit, and dream articulate a heroic sense of what it means to be human. For Nietzsche, this sublime "subjugates terror by means of art," and hence provides human beings with some way of coping with the meaningless, the abyss (Nietzsche 1956, 52). They make something, everything, out of nothing.

But if we turn to Wyn Wachhorst's book *The Dream of Spaceflight* (2000), we see a much more heroic version of the sublime being articulated, conquering rather than coping.

> The moon landing will be seen, a thousand years hence, as the signature of our century. It stands with the cathedrals and pyramids among those epic social feats that embody the spirit of an age. They are the dreams of the child in man, arising less from the ethic of work than from the spirit of play, longing to perfect a grand internal model of reality, to find the center by completing the edge. (Wachhorst 2000, xviii)

There is something profoundly unsettling about Wachhorst's version of the poet astronaut. His sense of humanism at times begins to sound like manifest national destiny, with the new pilgrims (mouths set in grim determination) reaching for new lands. New intellectuals creating a new Renaissance. Or, the pioneering U.S. character turning from the rush westward, to the final frontier upwards (see Klerkx 2004, 151). Mixing this with Darwinism and existential psychology, we get the following: "Exploration, evolution and self-transcendence are but different perspectives on the same process." Or, adding a gender dimension, the space child in man reaches with wonder towards the stars, with connotations of leaving Mother Earth, "merging the feminine mysteries of earth and soul with the masculine quest for heaven and spirit." This is nothing less than "the rebirth of wonder—the remystification, the reenchantment of the world." And finally, in quasi-Hegelian mood, this is "the endless quest itself—matter expressing itself as spirit, spirit finding its epiphany in matter" (Wachhorst 2000, 151, 39, 39, 155).

This sort of rocket-fueled pomposity would not make me want to share a space capsule with Mr. Wachhorst, and might even make me happy staying in my earthbound gutter, contented slime rather than cosmic sublime. Yet, the naked terror of Nietzsche's abyss is not calmed that easily, whether by filling it with Smug Western Man (as Wachhorst does), or turning to all the small good things that human beings should be doing on the thin surface of our planet. The cold darkness is still there. It does not go away because we will it so, or distract ourselves by decorating and washing the dishes. As Marina Benjamin comments, it is difficult not to be awed by a photograph of the earth "floating alone in the dark void like a misplaced Christmas bauble," and perhaps to be possessed by a wide-eyed sense of having "the vantage point of God" (2004, 57). No wonder so many ex-astronauts, often already apparently good religious men, have since articulated the importance of space travel in metaphysical terms. Whether planetary consciousness, or Gaia,[4] or space-faring myth, it seems there is an umbilical cord running between space and a rather fantastic sense of wonder. Having touched the sky, they can no longer keep their feet firmly on the ground. But then who could? As Michael Light puts it, "The space traveller is both gigantically empowered, and reminded at each turn of his utter inconsequence" (1999, 133). It is this dialectic of despair and elation which seems to be constitutive of the space sublime, and Buzz Aldrin's phrase "magnificent desolation," with which he described the moon's surface, catches it very nicely indeed.

No Future

In the short story "The Gernsback Continuum," William Gibson explores the idea of a streamlined amazing future of tomorrow that was somehow canceled, yet still hangs around at the edge of vision. The narrator keeps on seeing these "semiotic phantoms, bits of deep cultural imagery that have split off and taken on a life of their own" (1995, 44). Chrome airships, flying cars, the gleaming Metropolis City of Tomorrow. Gibson's character knows that there is something frightening about this fascist fantasy of food pills, eighty-lane freeways, and orderly crowds. Yet he also has to suppress these images because their shiny eruptions are too

---

[4] For more on the Gaia hypothesis, see Lovelock 2000.

disruptive of his everyday mundane. He cannot live like this, and is finally pleased that his "vision is narrowing to a single wavelength of probability. I've worked hard for that. Television helped a lot" (37). You cannot dream about the future all the time, but have to get on with living in the present.

It is odd how the trajectories of Wachhorst and Gibson collide. For the former, the future is a form of redemption, and those who oppose it are reactionaries who can't lift their eyes from the ground. For Gibson's character, the future perfect needs to be closed down in order that the imperfect present can be lived at all. For both, the imagined future is somewhere where the dreams and nightmares of the present are projected, a sort of cultural cinema that shows us who we think we are in the shape of things to come.

For the fortysomething girls and boys who write book wistful books on space travel, this tension seems central. I have already mentioned Penley's version of it, but she lived in Florida, so that was obvious. Marina Benjamin lived in London, filling her head and bedroom with Apollo trivia, and claiming that her "space-related hopes were boundless" (2004, 2). As she observes, the space age is already over. We now live in the information age, or the age of globalization, or even the new age (17). Like its contemporaries—Elvis, Kennedy, Monroe, and Vietnam—the space age is now reduced to collectable artifacts traded by nostalgics who appear to feel that the present doesn't quite measure up to the past. Or, consider Greg Klerkx, who starts his book quite simply, "When I was a boy, I wanted to be an astronaut" (2004, 5). Or David Bell, in the Midlands of England, daydreaming about model kits, science fiction and the year 2000 (Bell 2005). Andrew Chaikin, a nine-year-old looking at the photos of Ed White in space that were printed in *Life* magazine (2002, 12). Michael Light, also nine, watching Apollo 17 and listening to the communication with the astronauts—". . . that inimitable *beeeep*, followed by the most spacious silence imaginable" (1999, 129). The silence that separates us all from Apollo is spacious too, but yet it did happen. The future did happen.

Apollo

We can lick gravity, but sometimes the paperwork is overwhelming.
—Wernher von Braun

Every schoolchild now knows that the U.S. space program of the 1960s was born out of fascism and then the Cold War, and was a development of ICBMs and satellite reconnaissance systems. This was first and fore-most about perceptions of national interest, dressed up in misty-eyed visions but relying on gigantic state subsidy. For its detractors, it was a distraction from the problems facing ordinary U.S. citizens, a feeding trough for the closely tied firms of the military-industrial complex, and an expression of male dreams of power and dominance. Kennedy's famous speech to the joint session of congress on the 25th of May, 1961, was clear enough. This was an adventure that was part of a battle "between freedom and tyranny," a "battle for men's minds," "a great new American enterprise" (Jones and Benson 2002, 107). As accounts of the meetings between James Webb, the NASA administrator, and Kennedy later showed, the latter had a politician's interest in the moon, which is to say, no real interest at all.

And yet, the organization was incredible.[5] At the time that Kennedy made that speech, the U.S. had a total of 15 minutes and 22 seconds of human spaceflight experience with Alan Shepard's suborbital Mercury flight. According to Jones and Benson, in the 1960s, the US spent more than 4 percent of federal expenditures on space exploration (2002, 22). Wachhorst translates this into $24 billion for Apollo, and $38 billion for the period 1961–72 (1 percent of the budget for this period) (2000, 130). NASA's budget peaked in 1965 at what would be (in 2004 money) nearly $40 billion, 5.3 percent of the total federal budget for that year. In 1960 the space agency consisted of a small headquarters in Washington, its three inherited research centers, the Jet Propulsion Laboratory, the Goddard Space Flight Center, and the Marshall Space Flight Center. Over the next few years NASA opened the Mississippi Test Facility on a deep-south bayou and created the Manned Spacecraft Center, near Houston, Texas, to design the Apollo spacecraft and the launch platform for the lunar lander. The Launch Operations Center at Cape Canaveral was hugely expanded and renamed the John F. Kennedy Space Center on 29 November, 1963.

In 1966 NASA directly employed thirty-six thousand people, and close to half a million others via roughly 500 main contractors and countless subcontractors (Klerkx 2004, 165–56). In 1965 NASA made almost 300,000 separate procurement decisions. The Saturn 5 rocket itself weighed three thousand eight hundred tons and contained one and

---

[5] Many of the uncited organizational details in the following section are drawn from "Project Apollo: A Retrospective Analysis," at www.hq.nasa.gov/office/pao/History/ Apollomon/Apollo.html.

a half million individual parts. Stage one was built by the Boeing Company at NASA's Michoud Assembly Facility in New Orleans; stage two by the Space Division of North American Rockwell Corporation at Seal Beach, California; stage three by the McDonnell Douglas Astronautics Company at Huntingdon Beach, California, and the rocket motors by Rocketdyne of Canoga Park, California. The prime contractor for the Apollo Command and Service modules (containing two million individual parts) was North American Rockwell, the Lunar Module was built by Grumman Aircraft, the Lunar Roving Vehicle by the Boeing Company, and International Business Machines built the Saturn instrumentation. The Saturn-Apollo vehicle was stacked inside the Vehicle Assembly Building on Cape Canaveral, Florida, a building so large that clouds develop in its higher reaches. It was then transferred to launch complex 39 on the three-thousand-ton crawler transporter, before taking off with flames that could be seen 150 miles away on a trip that would take them 828,743 miles at speeds of up to 25,000 miles an hour.

After all that, the first thing that Armstrong and Aldrin did on the moon was to eat a meal of beef and potatoes, butterscotch pudding, brownies, and grape punch (Chaikin 2002, 52). Then they spent a mere two hours and thirty-one minutes walking only 250 meters on the moon.

Though in ancient myth Apollo was a violent, bisexual, and treacherous god, this son of Zeus has now become associated with ideas of order, and is sometimes claimed to be the father of Pythagoras. Abe Silverstein, director of the Lewis Flight Propulsion Laboratory in Ohio, first suggested that Apollo's name could be borrowed for the moon-landing program. He later said, "I thought the image of the god Apollo riding his chariot across the sun gave the best representation of the grand scale of the program" (Jones and Benson 2002, 196). Friedrich Nietzsche would have been pleased. In his *Birth of Tragedy* he argued that the ancient Greek image of Apollo represented the happy imaginings of an individual dreamer—"the god of light, reigns also over the fair illusion of our inner world of fantasy" (Nietzsche 1956, 21). But this is a fantasy of control, of order, not excess. "As a moral deity Apollo demands self-control from his people and, in order to observe such self-control, a knowledge of self" (22). "It is Apollo who tranquilizes the individual by drawing boundary lines, and who, by enjoining again and again the practice of self-knowledge, reminds him of the holy, universal norms" (65). It seems that Apollo demands human beings who are individuals, yet who obey the rules. Perfect members of large organizations.

Dael Wolfe, the Executive Officer for the American Association for the Advancement of Science, wrote in his editorial for *Science* on 15 November, 1968, that

> In terms of numbers of dollars or of men, NASA has not been our largest national undertaking, but in terms of complexity, rate of growth, and technological sophistication it has been unique. . . . It may turn out that [NASA's] most valuable spin-off of all will be human rather than technological: better knowledge of how to plan, coordinate, and monitor the multitudinous and varied activities of the organizations required to accomplish great social undertakings.

One year later, James Webb published his book *Space Age Management*, which described the project management principles that underlay Kennedy's "great new American enterprise." Though the space age may have ended, management has clearly not, and the rational principles for deploying human and nonhuman technology now define the organized worlds that we live in. Our world is Apollonian, defined by the measuring and control of all that we can see, like the Reseau lens grid crosses that were burnt into every image of the moon's surface. "Apollo was nothing if not a culture of numbers, numbers moved about with unparalleled precision and competence" (Light 1999, 130).

Dionysus

According to Nietzsche, the Apollonian spirit of order opposes the Dionysian sense of ecstasy, the forgetting of individuality, and submersion in intoxication. Dionysus, or Bacchus, was also a son of Zeus and has a legend full of ambiguities. His mother was struck dead by the lightning that flashed around Zeus, her adulterous lover, and the six-month-old fetus was plucked from his mother's womb and sewn into his father's thigh to be born three months later. To disguise the infant he was dressed as a girl, then transformed into a goat. Brought up by nymphs, he spent most of his life mad, or drunk, or encouraging others to become madly drunk too. Apollo would no doubt look on sternly as "archetypal man was cleansed of the illusion of culture, and what revealed itself was authentic man, the bearded satyr jubilantly greeting his god. Before him cultured man dwindled to a false cartoon" (Nietzsche 1956, 53).

Greg Klerkx, the boy who wanted to be an astronaut, grew up and began to doubt NASA's Apollonian vision. "I gradually came to see NASA in a different light: not as a streamlined purveyor of space-faring know-how, but as a fractious bureaucracy roiling with politics and infighting, thick with red tape and feral self-interest" (2004, 7). In various other places in his book, he sadly describes this once-inspiring organization as a maze of self-interested fiefdoms, populated by tenured civil servants who are quite capable of kicking any threatening changes into the long grass. The famous acronym now comes to mean "Never a Straight Answer," or even "Not About Space Anymore" (2004, 148). Earmarked funding and the pork-barrel politics of distribution means that NASA's ten centers and huge contractors squabble jealously over the big bucks that keep jobs in states, and politicians happy. Complexity, kickbacks, and corporate lobbying keep the Space Shuttle and the International Space Station going, but only just. The sublime has become ridiculous.

Yet Klerkx's response, and that of the many space entrepreneurs and venture capitalists he interviewed for his book, is not simply to turn back to the Apollonian vision, for that has now become the bureaucracy that is preventing fantasy from becoming reality. NASA is now the obstacle to space travel, not its instrument, and this is simply because it is blocking a free market in space. It "has convinced lawmakers and most of the private sector that it alone has the ability to safely send humans into space" (Klerx 2004, 212).

In 1999 Pizza Hut paid one million dollars in order that a Russian Proton rocket would launch with a forty-foot-high "Pizza Hut" logo emblazoned on its side. Two years later, the Soyuz that took Dennis Tito (the first of five paying astronauts so far) to the International Space Station also delivered a six-inch salami pizza, copies of *Popular Mechanics*, talking picture frames from Radio Shack, and 200 LEGO toys that became prizes in a competition (Klerkx 2004, 233–34). The familiar opposition between the Apollonian dreams of the state bureaucrat and the restless desire of the entrepreneur is materialized as hierarchy against market. Yet another typically American myth, but this time one that pits the pioneer against the conservative forces of the Federal state, time servers who endlessly intone that things cannot (or should not) be done, and that boundaries should not be crossed.

"Desire is the beginning of any endeavour" (Klerx 2004, 13). In claiming this, Klerkx presumably was not thinking about pizza or winning a LEGO toy that had been circling the earth at 250 miles. Yet this is the way that we are told that the alchemy of markets works, by finding desire and turning it into gold, or pioneering new territory and panning for gold. Either way, the vision is one of swarms of monkeys busily scratching their itches, not a single noble astronaut looking skywards.

The Dionysian does not really require the sublime, just the pleasures of busy-ness and riding the waves of the market. The rules are there to be broken, and if you don't, someone else soon will. This orgy of frontier liberalism has swept across most U.S. understandings of commerce over the past twenty years, whether the market be plastic surgery or the internet. If you want it, you can have it, and anyone who tries to stop you is probably against freedom. Thomas Frank styles this as "market populism," an ideology that goes further than claiming that everything has a price, to suggesting that everything should have a price (2000). So when the hordes of tourists start leaving their footprints on the moon, they will be cloven-hoofed, and Neil Armstrong will have dwindled to a cartoon. Anyone can go, and they don't need to be bold.

Utopia and the Space Age

Now that the space race is over
Its been and its gone and I'll never get to the moon
Because the space race is over
And I can't help feel we've grown up too soon
—BILLY BRAGG, "The Space Race is Over"

The U.S. cultural anthropologist Ruth Benedict, in her 1934 *Patterns of Culture*, suggested that the two Nietzschean terms could be applied to whole cultures. Dionysian cultures abandoned themselves in the authenticity of emotion, while Apollonian ones controlled and contained their responses. She obviously had not read *The Birth of Tragedy* with any particular care. Whether Apollonian in its visionary organization, or Dionysian in its orgiastic liberation, Nietzsche was clear that both are needed for a halfway-decent utopia: "Apollo found it impossible to live without Dionysos" (Nietzsche 1956, 34).

So perhaps it was never a question of "choosing" Apollo or Dionysos, as if one were truer than the other, but simply recognizing that solitary dreams depend on collective mobilization for their realization—the organization of thought requires the organization of people. Freeman Dyson, the physicist and space advocate, has suggested that there are actually two NASAs. One is the "real NASA'" that is conservative, budget conscious, and bureaucratic. The other is the "paper NASA" that visualizes long-term projects and big adventures, but has little money allocated to reach these goals (Benjamin 2004, 158; Klerkx 2004, 76). The "paper NASA" seems like a necessary fiction that allows the "real NASA" to have a mission and vision, just as the real is needed to give the paper any substance at all. Neither is sufficient on its own. This sort of mixing reminds me again of where I started—with the proposition that reality and fantasy, science and fiction, are quite often intertwined. Constance Penley attempted to suggest something similar by combining NASA and *Star Trek* to create "a much needed utopian narrative of and for our time" (1997, 148). Penley's popular science fuses technology and desire in a way that insists on the power of such a miscegenation, a "blended cultural text" in which "*Star Trek* is the theory, NASA the practice" (1997, 4, 19). So too does Benjamin's popular culture of space, incorporating science fiction, Roswell, NASA, and SETI@home (the search for intelligent life on your PC) (Benjamin 2004). We find the same in Klerkx's continual references to Heinlein, Asimov, Clarke, Bradbury, Williamson, and Bell's very English mixture of real science, "Dr. Who," culture, and boffins (Klerx 2004; Bell 2005). However, even if this exotic logic of combination is accepted, there is a further difficulty. All these authors are writing about the past, about a future that has gone, so how can this be an essay about possibility?

It may seem rather perverse to want to rescue the future by calling upon space romances from the past, but the space age did contain a memorable sense of what the future was going to be like, or at the very least that living in it was going to be an exciting adventure. As the British astronomer Patrick Moore said in the introduction to my 1970 Brooke Bond Picture Cards album, *The Race into Space*, "We are living in the space age. Science fiction has become science fact." The future had a streamlined sense of what future products would look like, phrases like "Moon Shot," "roger," and "affirmative," and even had its own special lumpy computer lettering (Hebdige 1988, 58 *passim*; Fitchett and Fitchett 2001). The future was different and contained new possibilities. It articulated a romance about where science could take us that was not merely escapism or swordplay fantasy, but the vague materialization of a different place to live in.

And now, nothing much is left. Six descent stages, a few flags, and some bits and pieces are left on the moon. Some footprints, which are gradually becoming less defined as they are bombarded with micrometeorites. On earth, the strange clarity of photographs of a human being floating in space, with the blue planet behind them. Littered across that planet are half-made model kits of Saturn V rockets, commemorative stamps, space pens, Tom Hanks in *Apollo 13*, and mission patches. The archeology of another time.

But this chapter is not meant to be on a crash course with dim-eyed nostalgia, or NASA, or the moon. It is about now, and the Earth. The astronauts were always looking back towards earth. Obsessively photographing it, and trying to spot its features. So what happens if we look back to the space age, and try to understand what it felt like to be then? What the space age teaches me is that there are times when Apollo and Dionysos combine to create possibilities, and other times when they separate into the bureaucracy and the market, and we have business as usual. When separated, both of the latter are quite interesting, and offer many possibilities, but neither offers the sort of radically different vision that might be called practically utopian. The business of technocratic science and the business of selling fiction often seem to be worlds that never collide, which takes us back to *The Lord of the Rings*. But when they do, the world becomes a very open place indeed, and that is somewhere that I think Nietzsche would like to live too. A teenage boy in Jeanette Winterson's novel *Sexing the Cherry* muses to himself,

> "My father watches space films. They're different: they're the only area of undiminished hope. . . . When I watch space films I always want to cry because they leave you with so much to hope for, it feels like a beginning, not a tired old end." (1990, 120)

REFERENCES

Bell, D. 2005. *Science, Technology and Culture*. Maidenhead: Open University Press.

Benedict, R. 1934. *Patterns of Culture*. Boston: Houghton Mifflin.

Benjamin, M. 2004. *Rocket Dreams*. London: Vintage.

Chaikin, A. 2002. *Space*. London: Sevenoaks.

Fitchett, J., and D. Fitchett. 2001. "Drowned Giants." In *Science Fiction and Organisation*, edited by W. Smith, M. Higgins, M. Parker, and G. Lightfoot, 90–100. London: Routledge.

Frank, T. 2000. *One Market Under God*. London: Secker and Warburg.

Gibson, W. 1995. *Burning Chrome and Other Stories*. London: HarperCollins.

Jones, T. and M. Benson. 2002. *The Complete Idiot's Guide to NASA*. Indianapolis, IN: Alpha Books.

Klerkx, G. 2004. *Lost in Space*. London: Secker and Warburg.

Light, M. 1999. *Full Moon*. London: Jonathan Cape.

Lovelock, J. 2000. *Gaia: A New Look at Life on Earth*. Oxford: Oxford University Press.

Mannheim, K. 1960. *Ideology and Utopia*. London: Routledge Kegan Paul.

Nietzsche, F. 1956. *The Birth of Tragedy and The Genealogy of Morals*. New York: Anchor Books.

Parker, M., M. Higgins, G. Lightfoot, and W Smith. 1999. "Amazing Tales: Organization Studies as Science Fiction" *Organization* 6, no. 4:579–90.

Parker, M. 2002. *Against Management*. London: Polity.

Penley, C. 1997. *Nasa/Trek*. London: Verso.

Rowlands, M. 2003. *The Philosopher at the End of the Universe*. London: Ebury Press.

Turnill, R. 1972. *The Observer's Book of Manned Spaceflight*. London: Frederick Warne and Co.

Wachhorst, W. 2000. *The Dream of Spaceflight*. New York: Basic Books.

Webb, J. 1969. *Space Age Management*. New York: McGraw-Hill.

Wolfe, D. 1968. Editorial for *Science*, 15 November 1968. In "Project Apollo: A Retrospective Analysis," at www.hq.nasa.gov/office/pao/History/Apollomon/Apollo.html.

16

Learning from *Ender's Game*: Childhood, Education, and War

MARGRET GREBOWICZ

There was nothing to pack. No belongings to take. "The school provides everything you need, from uniforms to school supplies. And as for toys— there's only one game."

—Orson Scott Card, *Ender's Game*

As I write this, the country in which I live is fighting an unjust war. I could say "fighting *another* unjust war," or "*still* fighting an unjust war," and both would be true. As I write this, I work as an educator. I teach college students how to theorize social injustices and articulate possibilities for change. At least I'd like to think I do. Sometimes it's not so clear. What is education for in the twenty-first century? Is the modern university the beacon of intellectual innovation and political resistance, or is it just a dressed-up vocational school? What kind of citizen does modern education produce? What are the responsibilities of that citizen? What kind of world is she responsible for?

Battle School

Ender Wiggin was a little boy who saved humanity from destruction.

Those who have read Orson Scott Card's 1977 classic, *Ender's Game*, know that the story is much darker, much more complex and morally ambiguous than that sentence indicates. Ender lives on a future Earth on which human armies are in a desperate rush to prepare for a third invasion by a race of intelligent aliens. The "buggers," as they are

289

called, resemble human-sized insects in their appearance and social organization (they operate by means of a hive mind directed by a queen). They have invaded twice before, outnumbering us and with superior technologies. We won the most recent conflict only because of the extraordinarily gifted commander, Mazer Rackham. The buggers are headed for Earth once more, surely coming to finish us off this time. Humanity needs another commander.

The six-year-old Ender is one of many intellectually gifted children that the government watches by means of monitors, looking for signs that they are ready for military training. His parents were given special permission to have a third child (something quite rare on this future Earth) only because the first two were almost-but-not-quite what the government was looking for. His older brother, Peter, is brilliant, but mean to the core, and his beloved sister Valentine is brilliant and kind, but too kind to command an army. Ender first shows signs of his talents during conflicts with other children at school. His particular way of fighting indicates that he is a gifted strategist who takes enormous risks in order to neutralize his attackers before he is hurt. He "settles his own problems" rather than calling for help, and he always overdoes it—although it is in self-defense, he hurts his attackers more seriously than the situation calls for (37).

The book begins with a scene in which Ender is attacked by other children and hurts one of them badly. The scene is repeated twice more at Battle School, where children are trained by means of games for the real war with the buggers, which we assume will take place once they are adults. "All the boys are organized into armies. Day after day, in zero gravity, there are mock battles. Nobody gets hurt, but winning and los-ing matter" (24). Battle School is also the place where Ender must nego-tiate private conflicts (in which people do get hurt) with other children, many of whom are jealous of his "chosen" status and his corresponding success in the Battle Room. The adults (indistinguishable from the gov-ernment) monitor everything, including these private conflicts, to deter-mine whether he has what it takes to lead the human army against the buggers. After several years of lonely and brutal Battle School, Ender graduates early and is transferred to Command School. There, he learns the truth about the bugger war—that the Third Invasion is actually humans invading bugger space in an effort to wipe out their forces pre-emptively, before they can return to Earth a third time. He is told that he has five years before the fighting begins, and trains in a battle "simula-tor" under the aged and wise Mazer Rackham. After many battles, which increase in difficulty and complexity as the training continues, Ender fights one final battle, a sort of "final exam," during which he decides to cheat, performing a deft but exceedingly risky maneuver that goes against his training. "Forget it, Mazer. I don't care if I pass your test, I don't care if I follow your rules," thinks the eleven-year-old boy (293). He wins.

To his horror, Ender discovers immediately following the battle that he has been tricked into destroying an entire alien species. All the games in the "simulator" were real battles, including the final battle, in which his forces destroyed the buggers' home planet, which housed all the queens of the species. He was tricked, used, and he can hardly believe his ears as the adults explain:

> It had to be a trick or you wouldn't have done it. It's the bind we were in. We had to have a commander with so much empathy that he would think like the buggers, understand them and anticipate them. . . . But somebody with so much compassion could never be the killer we needed. Could never go into battle willing to win at all costs. . . . If you knew, you couldn't do it. (298)

This trick is so easy to pull off because the children—as well as the reader—naturally assume that they are being prepared for a war they will fight as adults. What business do children have fighting a war, after all? In fact, the descriptions of the military training lead one to believe that the kids are being robbed of their childhood:

> [Ender] noticed how very tired Bean looked, his whole body bent with weariness, his eyes dark from lack of sleep; and yet his skin was still soft and translucent, the skin of a child, the soft curved cheek, the slender limbs of a little boy. He wasn't eight years old yet. . . . But Bean has been through a battle with a whole army depending on him and on the soldiers that he led, and he performed splendidly, and they won. There's no youth in that. No childhood. (220)

A certain sentimentality about the innocence of childhood allows us to be deceived about what the adults are planning. On the contrary, however, it is precisely Ender's child-nature that wins the war: "'And it had to be a child, Ender,' said Mazer. 'You were faster than me. Better than me. I was too old and cautious. Any decent person who knows what warfare is can never go into battle with a whole heart. But you didn't know. We made sure you didn't know. You were reckless and brilliant and young'" (298). What made Ender's victory possible was not what he knew as a result of attending school, but what he didn't know. Battle

School did not turn the children into adults—they remained children playing games precisely so that they could do what adults in a real war could not do. Ender won thanks to that which no school could have taught him, that which exceeded all training.

From this perspective, *Ender's Game* is less a story about an extraordinary child in extraordinary world historical circumstances, and more the story of every ordinary child. *Ender's Game* is the story of childhood itself.

The Monster of Philosophers

What is childhood? Can we think it? In a short story by Ray Bradbury called "The Small Assassin," a mother suspects her newborn baby of trying to kill her. At first, such a premise might strike us as absurd— surely no one really feels this way about her own child. But we keep reading the story because the premise works so well. The mother returns from the hospital terrified of the child, which her husband chalks up to postpartum depression. She turns up dead one sunny afternoon, and eventually he does, too. Indeed, this turns out to be a killer baby, small but deadly. The revelation at the end that the baby has in fact killed its parents, however, is the least interesting part of the story. Bradbury's genius lies in the mood he is able to set throughout the narrative, making us experience this infant, and infancy in general, as something radically unknown and unknowable, unmanageable, unpredictable, and creepy:

> She crushed his hand in hers, a supernatural whiteness in her face. "Oh, Dave, once it was just you and me. We protected each other, and now we protect the baby, but get no protection from it. Do you understand? Lying in the hospital I had time to think a lot of things. The world is evil—" "Is it?" "Yes. It is. But laws protect us from it. And when there aren't laws, then love does the protecting. You're protected from my hurting you by my love. You're vulnerable to me, of all people, but love shields you. I feel no fear of you because love cushions all your irritations, unnatural instincts, and immaturities. But—what about the baby? It's too young to know love, or a law of love, or anything, until we teach it. And in the meantime be vulnerable to it." "Vulnerable to a baby?" He held her away and laughed gently. "Does a baby know the difference between right and wrong?" she asked. "No. But it'll learn." "But a baby is so new, so amoral, so conscience-free." She stopped. Her arms dropped from him and she turned swiftly. "That noise? What was it?" (15–16)

Children are not mini-adults. The French philosopher Jean-François Lyotard writes about infancy in terms of what he calls the "inhuman." The inhuman is the part of experience that escapes the systems and institutions that render one "human," or fit to take part in the community of civilized humanity, however that is defined in one's particular historical moment. If we could take for granted that we were human, never experiencing an inhuman moment, we would not have to "struggle constantly to assure [our] conformity to institutions. . . ," or suffer from the doubts, the nagging feelings that we are not cut out for this world, not quite grown up, imposters in the community of adult humanity (Lyotard 1991, 3). Of course, we do suffer from these doubts, consistently reminding ourselves and each other to grow up, be adults, be "people." Lyotard writes, "If humans are born human, as cats are born cats, . . . it would not be possible to educate them. That children have to be educated is a circumstance which only proceeds from the fact that they are not completely led by nature, not programmed. The institutions which constitute culture supplement this native lack" (1991, 3). So humans are not born human, but some sort of mixture of humanity and its other, the mute, reticent, resistant, and unmanageable. The *infans* is that which does not speak. The role of education is to make the *infans* intelligible, to close the gap between humanity and inhumanity, to socialize and normalize the asocial, abnormal part.

Le Postmoderne expliqué aux enfants[1] consists of letters Lyotard composed to the children of his colleagues. It is here that he situates childhood in a special relationship to education, with these simple lines: "Childhood is the monster of philosophers. It is also their accomplice. Childhood tells them that the mind is not given. But that it is possible" (Lyotard 1993, 101). Throughout his work, Lyotard keeps this relationship in play, the one between philosophy and the possible mind, and calls for a model of education which would allow the mind to remain possible, rather than becoming actualized.

What does this mean for literacy education? Wlad Godzich addresses this question under the striking title "Reading against Literacy":

> The current concern with literacy . . . assumes the existence of a freestanding subject who must be equipped with the know-how to engage in a suitable technology of knowledge appropriation so that he or she may acquire

---

[1] The English tile is *The Postmodern Explained*, but the French title reads "the postmodern explained to children."

knowledge, use it, transform it, and then exchange it. . . . Children who are
taught this sort of literacy become the servants of this knowledge apparatus.
(1993, 135)

This is important: if literacy is supposed to mean freedom, we don't
want our children to become servants of the knowledge apparatus.
Lyotard argues that the model of literacy that trains us to use language
as our tool to get ahead in the world, a tool in the service of power, is
fundamentally mistaken about the relationship of the subject to language. For Lyotard, we are not subjects prior to so-called language
acquisition. Language is not a tool whose use we master, and ideas cannot be reduced to knowledge, understood as something to be appropri-
ated and exchanged on some market (for instance, a "job market"). In
his conception of reading, Lyotard describes a subjectivity *constituted
by* language, transformed by it, continuously re-opened, in the act of
reading, to heterogeneity and the new. This is why he figures reading as
listening. Instead of being the tool that endows us with power, listening
is the ultimate vulnerability: in the place of power, there is a space in
which I may hear the other.

Philosopher of science Paul Feyerabend extends the model of literacy
as listening to scientific education in his famous work *Against Method*.
We should think of the mind of the scientist working in the same way that
children's minds work. Since children do not learn solely by means of
argument, he states, we should allow for the possibility of rational development in adults that is not based on argument. Feyerabend is not merely
making psychological claims about knowledge in adults and children, but
uses this particular notion of "childhood" as a model for the structure of
institutions of knowledge production. He is particularly interested in
modeling the development of scientific knowledge after children's relationship to language, and argues that scientific education "as practiced in
our schools" consistently succeeds in drying out all the passion and irrationality that yields the world's great ideas (12).

Traditional theories of knowledge mistakenly take for granted that "a
clear and distinct understanding of new ideas precedes, and should precede, their formulation and their institutional expression. *First* we have
an idea, or a problem, *then* we act, i.e. either speak, or build, or destroy"
(or, in Lyotard's terms, first there is a subject, later the subject masters
the use of language by means of reading and writing). In contrast to this
model, Feyerabend reminds us that "this is certainly not the way in
which small children develop. They use words, they combine them, they
play with them, until they grasp a meaning that has so far been beyond

their reach" (17). This functions as a model for innovative thought, whether in science, philosophy, or some other discourse. The innovator "must be able to talk nonsense until the amount of nonsense created by him and his friends is big enough to give sense to all its parts" (194). Lyotard states the same thing about philosophical writing: "We write before knowing what to say and how to say it, and in order to find out, if possible. Philosophical writing is ahead of where it is supposed to be. Like a child, it is premature and insubstantial" (Lyotard 1993, 103).

The African American poet, educator, and activist June Jordan concurs. In "Problems of Language in a Democratic State," she argues that the question of Black English and language standardization in the American school system is larger than a "minority problem":

> I believe Americans have wanted their sons and daughters to write just well enough to fill out a job application. Americans have wanted their children to think just well enough to hold that job. . . . So I would say that our schools have served most of us extremely well. We have silenced or eliminated minority children. We have pacified white children into barely competent imitations of their fear-ridden parents. (Jordan 2003, 226)

Thus, the question of nonstandard languages *and their potential to disrupt the ways in which education participates in hegemony* extends beyond the politics of race in America, to include the larger questions I posed at this chapter's opening: What kind of citizen are we educating? What are her responsibilities? What kind of world is she responsible for?

> But now there are no jobs and, consequently, somebody needs to write aggressive new editorials. Somebody needs to write aggressive new statements of social design and demand. More and more Americans want to hear new sentences, new ideas, to articulate this unprecedented, and painful, *majority* situation. But is there anybody new around the house? (Jordan 2003, 226)

The question is rhetorical. The image here is of a failure of language that is at the same time a failure of responsibility, of taking responsibility for the production of meaning and thus for the creation of the world.[2]

---

[2] We should be wary, then, of the occasional journal article or website describing the value of science fiction in terms of its usefulness for literacy education (as in giving the children something fun to read so they won't even know they're reading). The real good of such a move will depend on what is meant by "reading." See Czerneda 1999 for one example of work encouraging the use of SF to develop scientific literacy in children.

Feyerabend echoes Jordan in his description of the fear-ridden producer of scientific knowledge: "Most scientists today are devoid of
ideas, full of fear, intent on producing some paltry result so that they can
add to the flood of inane papers that now constitutes 'scientific
progress' in many areas" (1998, 63). Unfortunately, this description can
easily be extended to every discipline in the university, where the tenure
system and the culture of peer review keeps so many of us in fear and
writing "just well enough to hold that job," publishing in order to keep
from perishing.

Lyotard, Jordan, and Feyerabend take childhood as a model for a
qualitatively different kind of rationality, and all three criticize contemporary educational systems on the grounds that they attempt to suppress
this kind of rationality. For all of them, the crisis of literacy—real literacy, in which the subject is constituted in relationship to language and
continuously transformed by listening to the other—is the crisis of the
democratic state. In other words, war has everything to do with childhood. The kind of society that prepares itself for war is the kind of society that cannot see, hear, or give voice to its children. In the throes of
endless conversations about diversity, we continue to fail to hear the particularity of children and learn from it politically.[3] We are too busy
obsessing about their cuteness and innocence—too busy *objectifying*
children—to address real, politically pressing issues, issues of human
rights, like the sexualities of children, compulsory education laws, gen-
ital reconstruction surgeries for intersex infants, adoption law, juvenile
detention law, and so forth. As long as children are only our imagined
objects, they cannot be speaking subjects on these issues, which concern
them so intimately.

> Who among us is competent to raise our children? Who among us is com-
> petent to have a love affair? Who among us is competent, who among us is
> strong enough and sure enough and safe enough and happy enough to truly
> love and protect those who are smaller and weaker than we are? . . . I am
> convinced that our children pose the question whereby we must justify our
> power over their lives, or give it up. It seems tragically evident that we have
> to give it up: our power, our coercion of new life into old stories. (Jordan
> 1995 [1981], 138)

Contemporary education gives us power over children. It is where we
force new lives into old stories, transforming children into servants of

---

[3] It is important to note that children are not the only marginalized group excluded
from current discourses around diversity and democratization.

the knowledge apparatus, so that they become "good" citizens and perform the tasks before them—not just the fighting of wars, but passive complicity with injustices and endless maintenance of the system. This kind of education has no room, no time, no budget for thinking.

> "So what do we do now?" asked Alai. "The bugger war's over and so's the war down there on Earth, and even the war here. What do we do now?" "We're kids," said Petra. "They'll probably make us go to school. It's a law. You have to go to school until you're seventeen." They all laughed at that. Laughed until tears streamed down their faces. (Card 1991, 304)

Thinking with Ender

It is when Ender finally leaves school—and Earth—that he begins thinking. Still very young, he leaves radically and irrevocably, traveling from planet to planet in search of a home—but not for himself. Ender Wiggin, Xenocide, becomes the Speaker for the Dead, the one who hears and bears witness to the destroyed queen's story, and spends his life searching for the right place to place the single surviving hive-queen (which the buggers managed to save and hide on a distant planet) so that she may bear offspring in peace. He never once questions that this is *his* obligation to fulfill.[4] This responsibility renders him a vagabond, homeless, forever displaced. He abandons all social life (except his bond with his sister, who accompanies him) and surrenders to his duty completely, at once the freest and most bound human being alive. What are we to learn from such an ending, from this intertwining of the motifs of listening, responsibility, and displacement?

When Ender asks one of his mentors, Graff, why the humans are fighting the buggers, Graff responds: "If the other fellow can't tell you

---

[4] Is it fair to say that Ender is responsible for the xenocidal destruction of the buggers? The text offers multiple indications to the contrary. Mazer reminds Ender that the human armies fought in a kind of self-defense, responding to two previous invasions by the buggers, which means that it was the bugger's own fault that they were wiped out of existence: "*They* decided that when they attacked us. It wasn't your fault. It's what had to happen" (297). Alternatively, the adults remind Ender that he was just their tool: "You had to be a weapon, Ender. Like a gun. . . . We aimed you. We're responsible. If there was something wrong, we did it" (298). Finally, of course, it matters that Ender is a child, and thus, in some sense, not a moral agent: "and then they would scream and shout and embrace him and congratulate him and show him the children they had named after him and tell him how he was so young it broke their hearts and *they* didn't blame him for any of his murders because it wasn't his fault he was just a *child*" (310). However, if Ender is not responsible for the xenocide, then the book's ending makes no sense.

his story, you can never be sure he isn't trying to kill you" (253). Ultimately, *Ender's Game* gracefully resolves into the story of "the other fellow's story"—of listening and witnessing. In order to fulfill the task of finding a new planet for the buggers, Ender must trust that they will not harm humans (in revenge, for instance) once they are born. Rather than leaving us with a portrait of a mature, fully-formed, stable Ender Wiggin safe at home or creating a new home for himself, complete with the trappings of adulthood (his own family, a career, perhaps a house or a farm on which he lives happily ever after?), this story of a mediated childhood ends with the portrait of pure, unmediated childhood itself, of a radical vulnerability to the other, of obligation, witnessing, and roaming infinite space in search of a new beginning. Our hero can look forward to the new beginning not because he has any certainty about the future—his faith in the buggers could always turn out to be misplaced—but only in the absence of any such certainty. It is precisely because "you can never be sure that he isn't trying to kill you" that you can be radically open to the difference that "the other fellow" embodies. In Jordan's words, only so can we hear the new stories.

"You cannot open yourself up to a question without leaving yourself open to it . . . without renewing ties with the season of childhood, the season of the mind's possibilities" (Lyotard 1993, 101). Contemporary education, *even the education we presently call "philosophical" and "liberal,"* does not allow the student to renew ties with the season of childhood. "The idea that we could put up with not making progress (in a calculable and visible way), that we could put up with always doing no more than making a start—this is contrary to the general values of prospection, development, targeting, performance, speed, contracts, execution, fulfillment," which are the values that govern contemporary education across the curriculum (102). We are not learning the patience required to put up with no more than making a start. This patience is the condition of the possibility of thinking. Just as Godzich urges us to read against literacy, Lyotard encourages us to think against education, even (or perhaps especially) in educational contexts. "Maybe there is more childhood available to thought at thirty-five than at eighteen, and more outside a degree course than in one. A new task for didactic thought: to search out its childhood anywhere and everywhere, even outside childhood" (107).

Childhood, then, turns out to be no small thing. Ender's search for a new beginning for the buggers is his search for a childhood of thought, well beyond his own chronological childhood. His vulnerability/responsibility and his corresponding hunger for justice have transformed him into a different kind of child playing a different kind of game. If it may be said that Ender Wiggin was a little boy who saved humanity from destruction, it is only from this point forward, only once he leaves behind Earth and its wars, the humans busy colonizing other planets (including the buggers' former outposts), and his own ascension to adulthood. Only from that moment, from the final chapters[5] of the story of Ender, do we (humanity and its others) stand something like a chance.

R E F E R E N C E S

Bradbury, Ray. 1976. "The Small Assassin." In *The Small Assassin*. Grafton Books.

Card, Orson Scott. 1991 [1977]. *Ender's Game*. New York: Tor.

Czerneda, Julie. 1999. *No Limit: Developing Scientific Literacy Using Science Fiction*. Toronto: Trifolium Books.

Feyerabend, Paul. 1993 [1975]. *Against Method*. London: Verso.

———. 1998. "How to Defend Society against Science." In *Introductory Readings in the Philosophy of Science*, edited by E. D. Klemke, Robert Hollinger, and David Wyss Rudge. Amherst: Prometheus Books.

Godzich, Wlad. 1993. "Reading against Literacy." In *The Postmodern Explained*, by Jean-François Lyotard, translated by Wlad Godzich. Minneapolis: University of Minnesota Press.

Jordan, June. 2003. "Problems of Language in a Democratic State." In *Some of Us Did Not Die: New and Selected Essays*. New York: Basic Books.

———. 1995 [1981]. "Old Stories, New Lives." In *Civil Wars*. New York: Touchstone.

Lyotard, Jean-François. 1991. *The Inhuman*, translated by Geoffrey Bennington and Rachel Bowlby. Stanford: Stanford University Press.

———. 1993. "The Subject of the Course of Philosophy." In *The Postmodern Explained*, translated by Wlad Godzich. Minneapolis: University of Minnesota Press.

---

[5] I am treating *Ender's Game* as a complete and finished entity and deliberately excluding all of the other books in Card's Ender cycle. The books which follow are good books in their own right, but present Ender as a new character with a new set of concerns that strike me as less philosophically significant.

Afterword

TERRY BISSON

*T*his SF, this kids' lit, this rude boy, this clever nosy girl, this literary *arriviste* that has illuminated or at least colored these pages, intervening if you will in scholarly interrogations of gender, history, racism, fashion, humor, class, and indeed popular culture itself: what exactly is it?

Is it a rocket ship, blasting us to other worlds, or a blimp, gaudy with ads, floating serenely over this one? Is it a telescope through which we spy on alien civilizations, or a magnifying glass through which we examine the crime scene of our own? Or a funhouse mirror, distorting our faces in comic and terrifying ways that we could never accomplish alone? Is it a hammer or a knife?

All of the above. SF is the original mixer of metaphors, the discount tonic diluting the Tanqueray of technology. It's everything but what it says it is.

Fiction? It's but fiction's poor cousin, never allowed a seat at the table; and the one thing it's never really been about, of course, is Science.

It is a privilege, and a satisfyingly rare one, to be positioned here as an SF author (and a male one at that) to close the book on this gathering of distinguished academics, many of them female scholars engaged in the constructing (or de-) of the ongoing *dissensus* that is modern feminism, and all of them using SF in the way that we in the biz use it ourselves (most of us anyway, cleverly disguising our essays as entertainments)—as a consciousness-raising device. Or to borrow a better term, an instrument for the "excavation of ignorance."

A shovel, dig? SF is not about predicting the future. It's about examining the present.

It wasn't always so. The origins of the genre are in travel tales: Gulliver and Crusoe, Halliburton and Frank Buck; spaceships carrying gangs of boys in literary steerage through Time and Space to exotic (if familiar) new planets.

And SF in its adolescence was nothing if not recognizable: garishly packaged pulp tales of exploration and discovery and their attendant perils.

It is no small coincidence that SF as a "literature" appeared on the scene precisely when the American frontier was closing. We could no longer look West for adventure so we looked Up. But we looked up with the same eyes and the same expectations that had brought us to the range of the buffalo.

The 500-year history of European discovery and exploration and expansion that shaped the modern world is the home terrain of SF, so is it any wonder that its first assumptions came out of this experience?

SF is described as a speculative literature by those who wish to elevate it, and its early *what ifs* were many, but not really so varied. Familiar riffs on familiar themes: What if our robots rebel? What if the aliens enslave us? What if our colonies forget us? What if we keep on getting smarter, going faster? Living longer?

Informing and framing all these was a grander *what if*, one that assumed the continuing rapid, indeed accelerating, development of technology: *what if* the inevitable expansion into space and encounter with the Other were to transform the Earth as decisively and irrevocably as the discovery of the New World transformed Europe?

What if it all were to happen again, on an even higher level?

Wouldn't that be fun?

This is a Eurocentric perspective, to be sure; but SF is a Eurocentric literature, viewing through European specs the experience of all humankind. And why not? The world transformed Europe, and through Europe, itself. It all happened in a tick of historical time, and now everyone is on the same clock.

If a stick is thrown into a fire, does it really matter which end starts to burn first?

SF was about Manifest Destiny—the expansion into space and the encounter with the Other. SF was propaganda for that journey, that encounter.

And it worked. Witness Apollo and SETI.

The story it told was a story we all knew well. It was our own story, our legendary *trek*, extrapolated into outer space.

But alas, it was not to be.

Space turned out to be nowhere. Robots turned out to be autistic children, good with numbers and not much else. And as for the Other—

The Moon is a cinder. The drifting sands of Mars fill in no ancient canals. The clouds of Venus hide no ruined cities. There are no wise or vicious aliens, no empires vast, no primitive versions of ourselves.

No Other.

The disappointment was palpable. It was as if Columbus had returned after landing on an uninhabited rock or two, and left his ships to rot in the harbors, just as the Saturn Vs are rusting in the parks of Huntsville.

Our Destiny is here on Earth, at least for now.

Get over it.

We got over it.

SF turned inward around the middle of the century. Outer space was replaced by cyberspace, galactic empire by virtual reality, invading aliens by disembodied AIs. The overarching theme was no longer change but "the ways in which science and technology do not change, but reinforce existing social roles." One might even say SF matured.

That women came on board at this time is not, I would argue, a fiat of gender, but an accident of history; the result of opportunity rather than inclination; but step aboard they did, and the women in the book, following in the footsteps of the Le Guins and Russes, were a significant part of SF's coming-of-age and maturing into the contours of its limitations.

SF was not about far planets but about this one; about ourselves and not about the Other (excepting of course that not inconsiderable slice of the readership for whom women were the Other).

Not that the boys gave up the game altogether. There is much talk in SF today, and by some of our leading practitioners and visionaries, of the Singularity.

This is that moment in the near future (twenty to thirty years away, at most) when machines will become smarter than the people who made them, computers will eat their own keyboards, and the world and indeed we ourselves will change quite suddenly into something wonderfully unrecognizable and strange.

We will become our own Other.

In a sense it's a variation on the new paradigm, and in another sense, an attempt to revive the old one: *what if* the demonstrably accelerating curve of technology that has carried us, like a tsunami, into the present were to continue accelerating, like a top-fuel Funny Car, faster and faster, straight off the charts?

Wouldn't that be fun?

But alas, it is not to be.

The Singularity is real enough, it's just that it has already happened. It was the twentieth century. The span of years from the telephone to the Web was only four score, as brief as a human life, but those years changed the world from a collection of villages and cities to an interlocked web of communications and connections, accessible at every point from every point, finishing the job Columbus and Magellan began.

My mother, your grandfather, and our Uncle Joe were born in one world and died in another—in a world that would have been unrecognizable to them *if they had not lived_through it*. Since then it has all been enhancements: the internet was in the radio; the Saturn V in the V-2; the 777 in the Ford Trimotor. You and I will die in the world in which we were born. The curve is already flattening.

The singularity has already happened, and it has not made us unrecognizable to ourselves; it had on the contrary made us more recognizable, and given us the tools to understand what we see.

Literature is about people. SF is about society. It amazes, whines, berates, and pleads. It's always *about* something other than its own characters, which is both its weakness and its strength.

The litcrits who deny us a place at their banquet are right. Our manners are terrible. We're more interested in the food than the company.

What we write is propaganda. Special pleading.

Looking through these pages I find scholarly writers who are engaged in exactly the same enterprise as the SFWA pros—using the tropes of SF, the gynoids, clones, aliens, and avatars, to examine the social roles in the world around us; to "excavate ignorance."

Oh, there are differences. We don't get tenure (well, some of us do) and they tell different sorts of stories—but their hands get just as dirty.

You dig?

About the Contributors

JEREMY BAILENSON is Assistant Professor in the Department of Communication and also director of Stanford's Virtual Human Interaction Lab. His main area of interest is the phenomenon of digital human representation, especially in the context of immersive virtual reality. He explores the manner in which people are able to represent themselves when the physical constraints of body and veridically rendered behaviors are removed. Bailenson's work has been published in several academic journals, including *Cognitive Psychology, Discourse Processes, Human Communication Research, Psychological Science,* and *PRESENCE: Teleoperators and Virtual Environments.* His research is funded by the National Science Foundation, Stanford University, and by various Silicon Valley and international corporations.

TERRY BISSON is the author of six novels: *Wyrldmaker* (Pocket, 1981); *Talking Man* (Arbor House, 1987), a World Fantasy Award nominee; *Fire on the Mountain* (Morrow, 1988); *Voyage to the Red Planet* (Morrow, 1990); *Pirates of the Universe* (Tor, 1996), the most-reviewed SF novel of 1996; *The Pickup Artist* (Tor, Spring 2001); and most recently, *Dear Abbey* (PS Publishing, 2003), a book-length novella published in England that has been nominated for the British Science Fiction Association (BSFA) award. He has authored three short-story collections. The title story from *Bears Discover Fire* (Tor, 1993), swept almost every honor in the SF field in 1990–91, including the *Asimov's* Readers' Award, both the Nebula and Hugo Awards and the Theodore Sturgeon short fiction award. *In the Upper Room* (Tor, 2000), includes the Locus- and Nebula-award-winning "macs," which also received France's Grand Prix de l'Imaginaire. His latest collection is *Greetings and Other Stories* (Tachyon, 2005). In 1998 he was awarded a Fellowship in Screenwriting and Playwriting by the New York

Foundation for the Arts. In addition to his many adaptations of films to novels and novels to comics, he has authored and coauthored many works of children's and young adult literature. He completed *Saint Leibowitz and the Wild Horse Woman* (Bantam, 1997), the long-awaited posthumous sequel to *A Canticle for Leibowitz*, for the estate of Walter M. Miller, Jr. Bisson's novels and stories have been published in France, Japan, Germany, Italy, Spain, Russia, Lithuania, and China. His nonfiction articles and reviews have appeared in *The Nation*, *Glamour*, *Automotive News*, *New York Newsday*, *Covert Action Information Bulletin*, the *Los Angeles Times*, the *Washington Post*, and the Park Slope Food Coop's *Linewaiter's Gazette*. He has also edited the writings of and written books about several American revolutionaries and political prisoners, including Nat Turner, Peter Coyote, and Mumia Abu-Jamal. Bisson hails from Owensboro, Kentucky, where he was inducted into the Hall of Fame in 1999.

HARVEY CORMIER is Associate Professor of Philosophy at Stony Brook University. He received his Ph.D. from Harvard University, where he wrote his dissertation with Hilary Putnam and Stanley Cavell. Among his writings are *The Truth Is What Works* (Rowman and Littlefield, 2000), a book on William James's theory of truth, and essays on diverse subjects including film and modernist art, civil rights and animal rights, Nietzsche's view of freedom, the relationship between the outlooks of William James and his brother Henry, and evolutionary psychology.

DENNIS DESROCHES is Assistant Professor of English at St. Thomas University, New Brunswick. He is the author of *Francis Bacon and the Limits of Scientific Knowledge* (Continuum, 2006). He has articles appearing in such journals as *Configurations*, *The Eighteenth Century: Theory and Interpretation*, and *The Midwest Quarterly*. His current research interests include the relationship between phenomenology and science studies, the politics of the archive and the scientific textbook, and the relationship between classical and nonclassical (quantum) experimental arrangements.

L. TIMMEL DUCHAMP is the author of *Love's Body, Dancing in Time*, a collection of short fiction; *The Grand Conversation: Essays; The Red Rose Rages (Bleeding)*, a short novel; and *Alanya to Alanya, Renegade*, and *Tsunami*, the first three novels of the five-volume Marq'ssan Cycle. She is also the editor of *Talking Back: Epistolary Fantasies* and *The WisCon Chronicles, Vol. 1*. She has been a finalist for the Nebula and

Sturgeon awards and short-listed several times for the Tiptree Award. Her stories have appeared in a variety of venues, including *Asimov's SF* and the *Full Spectrum, Leviathan, ParaSpheres,* and *Bending the Landscape* anthology series; and her critical essays have appeared in *The American Book Review*, *The New York Review of Science Fiction*, *Extrapolation, Foundation,* and *Lady Churchill's Rosebud Wristlet*. In 2004 she founded Aqueduct Press, which publishes feminist science fiction. A selection of her stories and essays can be found on her website: http://ltimmel.home.mindspring.com.

MARGRET GREBOWICZ is Assistant Professor of Philosophy at Goucher College, where she teaches classes in feminist theory, science studies, and contemporary European philosophy. Her research concerns the intersections of twentieth-century French thought and American feminism, with special attention to questions of knowledge production. She is the editor of *Gender after Lyotard* (SUNY Press, 2007) and coeditor of *Still Seeking an Attitude: Critical Reflections on the Work of June Jordan* (Lexington Books, 2004). Her articles have appeared in numerous journals and edited collections, including *Philosophy of Science*, *Studies in Practical Philosophy*, and *Addressing Levinas*, and are forthcoming in *Hypatia* and *Reading Negri*. Her translations of Polish poets Ewa Lipska and Jacek Podsiadło have appeared in a variety of literary journals, including *Field*, *Agni*, *World Literature Today*, *Poetry International*, and *Two Lines*. She is currently working on two new book-length projects: a volume of translations of Lipska's poetry and an authored book about Jean-François Lyotard's relationship to feminist theory. She is also a professional jazz vocalist in the Baltimore/ Washington DC area and coleader of the band Com Você.

NICOLA GRIFFITH is a native of Yorkshire, England, where she earned her beer money teaching women's self-defense, fronting a band, and arm-wrestling in bars, before discovering writing and moving to the U.S. Her immigration case was a fight and ended up making new law: the State Department declared it to be "in the National Interest" for her to live and work in this country. This didn't thrill the more conservative powerbrokers, and she ended up on the front page of the *Wall Street Journal*, where her case was used as an example of the country's declining moral standards. In 1993 a diagnosis of multiple sclerosis slowed her down a bit, and she concentrated on writing. Her novels are *Ammonite*, *Slow River*, *The Blue Place*, *Stay*, and *Always*. She is the coeditor of the "Bending the Landscape" series of original short fiction published by

Overlook. Her nonfiction has appeared in a variety of print and web journals, including *Out*, *Nature*, and *Paradoxa: The Journal of World Literary Genres*. Her awards include the James Tiptree, Jr. Memorial Award, the Nebula Award, the World Fantasy Award, and the Lambda Literary Award (five times). Her latest book, a memoir (of sorts) is *And Now We Are Going to Have a Party*. She lives in Seattle with her partner, writer Kelley Eskridge, and takes enormous delight in everything. Her homepage is www.nicolagriffith.com

ALICE KIM and JAIREH TECCARO received bachelor's degrees from Stanford University.

NANCY KRESS is the author of twenty-one books: thirteen novels of science fiction or fantasy, one young adult novel, two thrillers, three story collections, and two books on writing. Her most recent books are *Probability Space* (Tor, 2002; the conclusion of a trilogy that began with *Probability Moon* and *Probability Sun*), *Crossfire* (Tor, 2003), and *Nothing Human* (Golden Gryphon Press, 2003). The trilogy concerns quantum physics, a space war, and the nature of reality. *Crossfire*, set in a different universe, explores various ways we might coexist with aliens even though we never understand either them or ourselves very well. *Nothing Human* concerns a bleaker future, in which we have trashed Earth beyond the point of human habitability. So we genetically engineer our descendants—who may or may not be considered human. Kress's short fiction has appeared in all the usual places. She has won three Nebulas: in 1985 for "Out of All Them Bright Stars," in 1991 for the novella version of "Beggars in Spain," which also won a Hugo, and in 1998 for "The Flowers of Aulit Prison." Her work has been translated into Swedish, French, German, Italian, Spanish, Polish, Japanese, Croatian, Lithuanian, Romanian, Greek, Hebrew, and Russian. Kress is the monthly fiction columnist for *Writer's Digest Magazine*. She teaches regularly at the Clarion West writer's workshop.

E. THOMAS LAWSON, who works in the newly emerging field of the cognitive science of religion, is the editor of the *Journal of Cognition and Culture*. He has published *Religions of Africa: Traditions in Transformation* and with his colleague Robert N. McCauley, who is professor of philosophy at Emory University, has authored two books, *Rethinking Religion: Connecting Cognition and Culture* and *Bringing Ritual to Mind: Psychological Foundations of Cultural Forms*. He has also contributed articles about the cognitive science of religion to the

MIT Encyclopedia of Cognitive Sciences and the *Encyclopedia of Cognitive Science.* He is an avid reader of science fiction and is particularly interested in the creativity of the cognitive processes of imagining other worlds. He was originally an art major and finds pleasure in painting and playing the piano. He was born in Capetown, South Africa, but has spent most of his adult life in the United States of America.

MARINA LEVINA received a Ph.D. in communications from the Institute of Communications Research at the University of Illinois at Urbana-Champaign. Her research interests include cultural studies of science and medicine, monster theory, and critical media studies. She has published her work in *Journal of Applied Social Psychology, Psychology and Medicine,* and in the anthology *Vampires: Myths and Metaphors of Enduring Evil.* She is currently a lecturer in the Mass Communications Program at UC Berkeley.

NANCY MCHUGH is Associate Professor of Philosophy and Director of Women's Studies at Wittenberg University. She teaches courses in feminist theory, epistemology, and philosophy of the body. Her areas of publication and research are feminist epistemology, pragmatist feminism, and feminist critiques of science. Among her publications are *Feminist Philosophies A-Z* (2007) and "Telling Her Own Truth: June Jordan, Standard English and the Epistemology of Ignorance," in *Still Seeking an Attitude*: *Critical Reflections on the Work of June Jordan* edited by Valerie Kinloch and Margret Grebowicz. Nancy is also a founding member of FEMMSS (the Association for Feminist Epistemology, Metaphysics, Methodology and Science Studies).

HELEN MERRICK lectures in internet studies at Curtin University of Technology, Western Australia. She has published widely on the cultural history of feminist science fiction, including chapters in *The Cambridge Companion to Science Fiction* (2003), *Speaking Science Fiction* (2000), *Trash Aesthetics: Popular Culture and its Audience* (1997), and in the forthcoming *Queer Universe: Sexualities in Science Fiction* and *The Routledge Companion to Science Fiction.* With Tess Williams she coedited the collection *Women of Other Worlds: Excursions through Science Fiction and Feminism* (1999). Dr. Merrick is currently researching the intersections of feminist science fiction and science theory, and working on a book-length study of feminist cultural production in SF communities.

JUSSI PARIKKA teaches and writes about the cultural theory and history of new media. He studied cultural history at the University of Turku, Finland, and is currently Visiting Lecturer and Research Scholar in the Seminar for Media Studies, Humboldt University, Berlin. His *Digital Contagions: A Media Archaeology of Computer Viruses* is published in Peter Lang's Digital Formations series (2007). Parikka is currently working on a book on "insect media." In addition, two coedited books are forthcoming: *The Spam Book: On Viruses, Spam, and Other Anomalies from the Dark Side of Digital Culture* and *Media Archaeologies*. His homepage is http://users.utu.fi/juspar.

MARTIN PARKER is Professor of Culture and Organisation in the School of Management at Leicester University. He previously worked at Staffordshire and Keele Universities, but has never worked in space. His writing is usually concerned with organizational theory and the sociology of culture. His most relevant books for this piece are the edited collection *Science Fiction and Organisation* (Routledge, 2001), *The Age of Anxiety* (Blackwell, 2001), and *Utopia and Organisation* (Blackwell, 2002), as well as his resignation book *Against Management* (Polity, 2002).

ANDREW PAVELICH received his Ph.D. from Tulane University in 1999, with a dissertation on Descartes. His areas of research interest include the history of philosophy (particularly seventeenth-century metaphysics) and the relationship between science and religion. His work has appeared in *The Southern Journal of Philosophy*, *Hume Studies*, *Locke Studies*, and *Sophia*, and he is currently researching pet care ethics. He is Assistant Professor of Philosophy at the University of Houston–Downtown, where he teaches logic, ethics, and philosophy of religion. He likes to divide his spare time evenly between his juvenile interest in science fiction and his very mature interest in "extreme" origami.

EDRIE SOBSTYL started kindergarten the day the very first episode of Star Trek was broadcast, destining her to view intellectual work and science fiction as going hand in hand. She earned her Ph.D. in philosophy from the University of Alberta (Canada) in 1995, and has taught in Canada and the U.S. Her interest in feminist science fiction won her a Rockefeller Fellowship at University of Oregon in 2002, and she has published on feminist philosophy with and without science fiction in *Hypatia*, *Anarchist Studies*, and several anthologies. She teaches philosophy at Douglas College in New Westminster, British Columbia.

STEPHANIE S. TURNER is Assistant Professor of English in the Professional Writing program at the University of Houston-Downtown, where she teaches science writing, environmental writing, and medical writing. Her article "Jurassic Park Technology in the Bioinformatics Economy: How Cloning Negotiates the Telos of DNA," appears in *American Literature*, and "Open-Ended Stories: Extinction Narratives in GenomeTime" is forthcoming in *Literature and Medicine*.

TESS WILLIAMS is completing a Ph.D. at the University of Western Australia. Universities are her natural habitat. She went straight there from high school and never really left, but their relationship was a mixed package. She did sessional teaching for many years while supporting two human children and a variety of other species. In 1994 she returned to do an M.A. in creative writing. Over the next ten years she was to publish two novels, *Map of Power* (Sydney: Random House, 1996) and *Sea as Mirror* (Sydney: HarperCollins, 2000), and a number of short stories. In 1999, she coedited *Women of Other Worlds: Excursions Through Science Fiction and Feminism* (Perth: University of Western Australia Press, 1999) with Helen Merrick, and enrolled in a Ph.D. program. The title of the thesis is *Carnival in Time and Space: Shared Metaphors of Change in Post Neo-Darwinian Evolutionary Theory and Feminist Science Fiction.* Other things that have kept Tess busy are two fellowships which she held concurrently at SymbioticA, an art/science collective affiliated with the School of Anatomy and Human Biology at the University of Western Australia.

JANET VERTESI is a Ph.D. student in the Science and Technology Studies Department at Cornell University, where she is writing her dissertation on the visual technologies on the Mars Exploration Rover Mission. She holds degrees in the history and philosophy of science from Cambridge and the University of British Columbia. Janet's published projects span from critical studies of lunar mapping programs of the seventeenth century, to how subway diagrams like the London Underground Map affect representations of urban space. She is also a published scholar in Human-Computer Interaction studies and recently joined a Swarm Ethnography project on the Consumer Electronic Show in Las Vegas. She has been a Fellow of Cornell's Society for the Humanities, the Social Sciences and Humanities Research Council of Canada, and Action Canada, and is a former a Commonwealth Scholar. She feels especially cyborg while playing her plugged in electric concert harp with the Cornell Jazz Ensembles.

NICK YEE received his Ph.D. in Communication from Stanford University. His research focuses on virtual reality and online games. Currently, he works in Stanford's Human Interaction Lab, the Palo Alto Research Center, and Sony Entertainment designing and analyzing experimental studies exploring social interaction in virtual environments.

NAOMI ZACK is Professor of Philosophy at the University of Oregon. Her research interests center on race, mixed race, seventeenth-century philosophy, and feminism. She is the author of *Race and Mixed Race* (1993), *Bachelors of Science: Seventeenth Century Identity, Then and Now* (1996), *Philosophy of Science and Race* (2002), *Inclusive Feminism: A Third Wave Theory of Women's Commonality* (2005), and the short textbook, *Thinking about Race*. Zack has also authored numerous articles and edited the anthologies *Women of Color and Philosophy* (2000), *RACE/SEX* (1997), and *American Mixed Race* (1995). She is currently working on a book, *Moral Philosophy for Disaster*.

Index